Griffin, James, 1933-

Well-being : its meaning
measurement, and moral
importance

DATE DUE			

WELL-BEING

WELL-BEING

Its meaning, measurement, and moral importance

JAMES GRIFFIN

CLARENDON PRESS · OXFORD

Oxford University Press, Walton Street, Oxford OX2 6DP

Oxford New York Toronto
Delhi Bombay Calcutta Madras Karachi
Petaling Jaya Singapore Hong Kong Tokyo
Nairobi Dar es Salaam Cape Town
Melbourne Auckland

and associated companies in
Berlin Ibadan

Oxford is a trade mark of Oxford University Press

First published 1986
First issued in paperback 1988

British Library Cataloguing in Publication Data
Griffin, James
Well-being: its meaning, measurement and moral importance.
1. Health—Moral and ethical aspects
2. Quality of life—Moral and ethical aspects
I. Title
171   BJ1500.H4
ISBN 0–19–824903–9
ISBN 0–19–824843–1 (pbk.)

Typeset on a Lasercomp at
Oxford University Computing Service

Printed in Great Britain
at the University Printing House, Oxford
by David Stanford
Printer to the University

FOR CATHERINE

PREFACE

SOME years ago I gave a series of seminars with two colleagues, Jonathan Glover and Derek Parfit. For me those seminars were the occasion for first trying out the ideas that I present here. I learned a great deal from Glover and Parfit, much of it at so early a stage in the development of my ideas that sometimes I cannot now disentangle my thoughts from theirs. Recently I gave another series of seminars with Parfit, from which I also benefited greatly. But I have benefited most of all from Parfit's penetrating and stimulating criticisms of drafts of these chapters. He has been exceptionally generous.

We were lucky to have Richard Hare drop in occasionally on both series of seminars. My discussions with him then, and since, have helped me a lot; he has not always agreed with what I have to say but he has been an important stimulus to it. I owe him much.

Richard Brandt, John Broome, Amartya Sen, and Wayne Sumner read large parts of early drafts, and spent hours, for which I thank them deeply, writing or talking to me about them. I have also had much helpful advice from Kurt Baier, Timothy Besley, Roger Crisp, Ray Frey, Allan Gibbard, John Harsanyi, Brad Hooker, Joel Kupperman, Jeff McMahan, Joseph Raz, Donald Regan, Tim Scanlon, Larry Temkin, and Henry West.

Some of my chapters are revisions of material I have published already. I took a preliminary canter across the terrain in a survey article 'Modern Utilitarianism', *Revue Internationale de Philosophie* 141 (1982), and sentences from that article crop up here and there throughout this book. A very early version of chapter VII saw life as 'Intersubiektywne porównania użyteczności', in *Etyka* 19 (1981) and was resurrected, much changed, as 'Well-Being and Its Interpersonal Comparability' in a not yet titled collection of essays on R. M. Hare edited by N. Fotion and D. Seanor, forthcoming from the Clarendon Press; chapter VII is much the same in argument as the latter but rather different in focus. An earlier version of chapter X first appeared as 'Some Problems of Fairness' and 'Reply to Kurt Baier' in *Ethics* 96 (1985). And chapter XI appeared, in shorter form, as 'Towards a Substantive Theory of Rights' in R. G. Frey (ed.), *Utility and Rights*, Minneapolis: University of Minnesota Press, 1984. I thank the editors and publishers concerned for letting me use the material again here.

The bulk of this book was written during the two academic years 1982-4, while I held a Radcliffe Fellowship, a most welcome and well-conceived relief from teaching supported by the Radcliffe Trust. I thank them warmly for that support.

This book is printed from camera-ready copy. It took the kindness and skill of many persons to turn my scrawl into that final copy. Pauline Valentine typed successive drafts. Stephen and Alison Cope keyed the final one into the University computer. Michael Clarke of Bradley Computing devised Microset, the software for pagination. And, kindest of all, Catherine Griffin put aside hieroglyphs to program, and generally to oversee, the typesetting of this book in as humdrum a language as English.

J. P. G.

Keble College,
Oxford

CONTENTS

PART TWO · MEASUREMENT

PART THREE · MORAL IMPORTANCE

INTRODUCTION

In this book I offer answers to three questions. What is the best way to understand 'well-being'? Can it be measured? Where does it fit in moral and political thought? The third question is huge, and my answer is incomplete. I concentrate on issues that make up the subject of justice (a glance at the Table of Contents will show which I take them to be). Together they also make up much of moral and political philosophy, but not all of it. What I shall say about them has implications for the rest of moral and political philosophy, but to work out those implications, to add to them, and to generalize enough to answer my third question fully would take vastly more work than I have done here.

My three questions correspond to the three parts of the book. None of the questions has priority. We cannot just ask, What is the best account of well-being?, as if 'best' could mean 'most accurate'. Our job is not to describe an idea already in existence independently of our search. Before we can properly explain well-being, we have to know the context in which it is to appear and the work it needs to do there. It may be that different notions of well-being are needed in different theoretical contexts. Nor can we first fix on the best account of 'well-being' and independently ask about its measurement. One proper ground for choosing between conceptions of well-being would be that one lends itself to the deliberation that we must do and another does not.

I should say something about how I see argument in normative ethics proceeding. To justify my views on that subject would take another book, but I should at least explain them. The most common method in normative ethics is piecemeal appeal to intuition. 'It follows from what you say that it would be all right to do such and such, but that's counter-intuitive, so you're wrong.' Piecemeal appeal to intuition has been severely attacked, and the attacks seem to me fatal. Intuitions as a class have no probative force. Still, there are one or two intuitions that are solider than anything else that moral thought is likely to come up with—say, that battering babies is wrong. However, the few moral beliefs of this solidity do not get us far; they weed out only the wildest of moral theories. There is also the problem of distinguishing the solid from the only apparently solid. The role that intuitions can play in moral philosophy is the role that we are content to let them play in other departments of thought (it is only in moral philosophy that they have risen so far above their epistemological station). In mathematics, the natural sciences, and other branches of philosophy, finding a conclusion intuitively repugnant does not close an argument; it is a reason to start looking for a good argument.

I think that there are two tests for good argument in normative ethics. One is the test of completeness. We all wish to provide answers to roughly the same rather varied questions about what to do, and our answers will have to have a fair degree of complexity and we shall have to know how the various parts of what we say work together to produce the answers. In this minimal sense every moral philosopher has to develop a theory. It may be thought that introducing the word 'theory' already begins begging questions. It may look as if it suggests one particular, contentious conception of what it is that we need to test and also, within certain limits, what suitable tests for it will be: namely, that morality consists of a system of highly abstract principles and that it is rather like a natural science. But I am using the word 'theory' far more broadly than that—broadly enough to be acceptable to some, though perhaps not quite all, philosophers who think that morality does not constitute a 'theory', on some narrower understanding of the word. Having to produce a moral theory in my broad sense helps to guard against at least some errors. It forces an individual to find answers to moral questions that are both coherent and complete. For instance, contractualists, as I shall be arguing later, respond to the counter-intuitive permissiveness of utilitarianism by adopting principles that, seen against that permissiveness, look very attractive indeed, but then, when shifted on to different ground, begin to look counter-intuitively strict. Indeed, I suspect that, one way or another, quite a few moral theories that we now regard as plausible contenders will fail the test of completeness. It is a test of no small power.

Still, it is not powerful enough. All that coherence and completeness in the end require is that we come up with an answer to any moral question that presents itself and that we do not encounter conflicts of belief in the course of doing so. They do not require that the beliefs be appropriate or correct or reliable or true or whatever the standard is that one wants to appeal to in order to mark the difference—if it can be marked in the moral domain—between what is merely believed and what ought to be believed. What we need, if we are to get beyond completeness, is to find an exit from the circle of beliefs.

If we find one, it would supply the second and more important test of good argument, the test of correctness. There are various possible exits. We might think that a form of foundationalism is possible: we might, for instance, think that substantive moral beliefs could be derived from formal features of rationality or from the logic of key moral terms, although neither of these might be enough on its own to constitute an exit. We might become convinced by a form of naturalism: for example, we might decide to clarify the not entirely clear questions of prudence and morality by turning them into questions answerable solely by appeal to empirical facts and logic. We might accept constructivism: we might accept that some notion of what rational persons can be brought to agree upon constitutes what we mean, and all that we can mean, by 'correctness' in normative ethics. Or we might accept realism: we might decide that, when we speak about prudential and perhaps also moral values, we are speaking, without reduction to non-value terms, about something in the world.

The way to submit a moral theory to the test of completeness is to spread the theory as widely as possible, especially into areas where the chances are best of its running into trouble. The way to submit it to the test of correctness is harder to decide. We should have to decide which exit, if any, is to be taken. But even without settling that question—which is the question that needs a book to itself—we can do something. A good place to start on the search for standards of correctness in prudential and moral judgement is with developing as rich a substantive account of prudence and morality as one can. (I am using 'prudence' here in the philosopher's especially broad sense, in which it has to do not just with a due concern for one's future but with everything that bears on one's self-interest.) One cannot hope to find a possible route to standards of correctness until substantive prudential and moral theories take on far more detail than they have yet had. For instance, how can we decide on the role of reason and desire, how can we decide whether values are valuable because desired or desired because valuable, until we see in great detail what can be advanced in the way of argument for the existence of values? Some philosophers have in the past tried to derive substantive moral beliefs from the nature of rationality, or from the semantics of key moral terms, or from the need for moral restrictions to fit the human psyche. But if one believes, as I do, that none of this is quite enough to do the job, then one has to find another way to justify substantive moral beliefs. The most promising way, I believe, is to come to understand the nature of prudential and moral deliberation much more fully than we now do, and then to look in that fuller understanding, perhaps especially in an understanding of the relationship between prudence and morality, for the pieces out of which the standard of correctness, the exit from the circle of mere beliefs, is to be constructed. We ought not, I think, to treat meta-ethics as something that can be pursued for long independently of normative ethics. We cannot derive conclusions about the status of values from highly speculative and abstract metaphysical considerations that anyway need a decision about the nature of value to help prop up the abstract argument. What, to my mind, we need is a period in which philosophers build wide-ranging, detailed, substantive prudential and moral theories. That, I think, would help not only normative ethics but meta-ethics too.

PART ONE

MEANING

PART ONE

WINKLER

UTILITARIAN ACCOUNTS: STATE OF MIND OR STATE OF THE WORLD?

How are we to understand 'well-being'? As 'utility', say the utilitarians, aware that this technical term itself needs explaining.[1] What is 'utility'? 'Pleasure and the absence of pain', the classical utilitarians said,[2] not realizing how much the words 'pleasure' and 'pain', especially in the stretched sense they attached to them, needed explaining.

Two main traditions about 'utility' have grown up. One sees it as a state of mind, the other as a state of the world. Is 'utility' mental states (e.g. pleasure, pain) or states of the world which fulfil desires (e.g. economists' 'preference')? If mental states, is it only one sort, or many? If many, what links them? If fulfilment of desires, desires as they happen to be, or in some way improved? If improved, how? We can forget morality for the moment. Utilitarians use our rough, everyday notion of 'well-being', our notion of what it is for a single life to go well, in which morality may have a place but not the dominant one. This does not mean that our job is merely to describe the everyday use. It is too shadowy and incomplete for that; we still have to be ready for stipulation.

1. Mental state accounts

When some utilitarians have spoken of mental states such as pleasure and pain, they have meant these terms so widely that their accounts get very near desire accounts of 'utility'. So we cannot always take this verbal difference as marking any real difference.

Still, the difference is often real enough. Bentham and Mill are, with ample reason, taken to be offering a psychological account of 'utility'. Pleasure or happiness is presented as a 'state of feeling', and pain or unhappiness as a feeling on the same scale as, and the opposite of, pleasure or happiness. And the utilities of all our experiences are supposed to be determinable by measuring the amount of this homogeneous mental state that they contain.

The trouble with thinking of utility as *one* kind of mental state is that we cannot find any one state in all that we regard as having utility—eating, reading, working, creating, helping. What one mental state runs through them all in virtue of which we rank them as we do? Think of the following case. At the very end of his life, Freud, ill and in pain, refused drugs except aspirin. 'I prefer', he said, 'to think in torment than not to be able to think clearly'.[3] But can we find a single feeling or mental state present in both of Freud's options in virtue of which he ranked them as he did? The truth seems, rather, that often we just rank options, *period*. Some preferences—Freud's seems to be one—are basic. That is, preferences do not always rest upon other judgments about the quantity of some homogeneous mental state found in, or produced by, each option. When, in these cases, one speaks of one thing's yielding greater satisfaction than another, this seems best understood as saying that having the first is the fulfilment of a greater desire than having the second would be. One wants the first more than the second. But these desires are not ranked by independent quantities of satisfaction.

So, if the mental state account takes this simple form, the objections to it are insurmountable. And if we do not want to go over to a desire account, there are two ways we might now move. We might accept that utility is not one mental state but many, and then look for an explanation of how they are linked. Or we might, on the other hand, decide that utility is neither a matter of mental states nor of desire-fulfilment but of something, in a way, in between; we might say that it is a matter of finding enjoyment in various things, where 'enjoyment' is what we might call an attitude, or a conscious state, or a state of a person. I want to leave the second move until later; it is not easy to grasp, and it will be easier after we have looked at both the mental state and the desire accounts. So let us go back to the first move.

2. *Sidgwick's compromise*

Suppose we said that utility consisted of several different mental states. What then would make them into a set? The obvious candidate would be desire; we could say, following Henry Sidgwick in borrowing something from each of the competing accounts, that utility combines a psychological element and a preference element. 'Utility', we could say, is 'desirable consciousness', meaning by 'desirable' either consciousness that we actually desire or consciousness that we would desire if we knew what it would be like to have it.[4]

The trouble with this eclectic account is that we do seem to desire things other than states of mind, even independently of the states of mind they produce. This is the point that Robert Nozick has forcefully made with some science fiction.[5] Imagine an experience machine programmed to give you any experience you want; it will stimulate your brain so that you think you are living the most ideal life, while all the while you float in a tank with electrodes in your brain. Would you plug in? 'What else can matter to us', Nozick asks, 'other than how our lives feel from the inside?' And he replies, surely rightly, that we also want to *do* certain things, to *be* certain things, and to be receptive to what there is in life beyond what humans make. The point does not need science fiction; there are plenty of examples from ordinary life. I certainly want control over my own fate. Even if you convince me that, as my personal despot, you would produce more desirable consciousness for me than I do myself, I shall want to go on being my own master, at least so long as your record would not be much better than mine. I prefer, in important areas of my life, bitter truth to comfortable delusion. Even if I were surrounded by consummate actors able to give me sweet simulacra of love and affection, I should prefer the relatively bitter diet of their authentic reactions. And I should prefer it not because it would be morally better, or aesthetically better, or more noble, but because it would make for a better life for me to live. Perhaps some such preferences, looked at with a cold eye, will turn out to be of dubious rationality, but not all will. This fact presents a serious challenge to the eclectic account of utility. If not all desirable things are mental states, yet they matter to our well-being, the eclectic account is fissile. Which part of it should we retain: desire or mental states? It is hard to retain mental states, for if we did, we should then have, puzzlingly, to accept that when, with eyes wide open, I prefer something not a mental state to a mental state and so seem to value the former more than the latter, I get greater utility from what I value less.[6] Of the two, it is better to retain *desire*.[7]

Of course, 'mental state' is a vague expression. Perhaps Sidgwick and others use it broadly enough to include, say, knowledge. However, that does not seem to be Sidgwick's intention, and in any case it would still not be broad enough. I also want to *be* my own master, and it would take more broadening to include that. It seems more promising to abandon 'mental state' altogether and to try defining 'utility' solely in terms of desire: utility consists, we might try saying, in the fulfilment of desire.

3. *The actual-desire account*

The simplest form of desire account says that utility is the fulfilment of *actual* desires. It is an influential account. Economists have been drawn to it because actual desires are often revealed in choices and 'revealed preferences' are observable and hence a respectable subject for empirical science.[8] Also the same account of utility can then do service in both moral theory and theory of action; explanation of action has to appeal to what we in fact want rather than to such ideal notions as what we ought to want or would want if well-informed. And both philosophers and social scientists have been powerfully drawn to it because it leaves no room for paternalism; if actual desires determine distributions, con-sumers are sovereign and agents autonomous.

Yet, notoriously, we mistake our own interests. It is depressingly common that when even some of our strongest and most central desires are fulfilled, we are no better, even worse, off. Since the notion we are after is the ordinary notion of 'well-being', what must matter for utility will have to be, not persons' actual desires, but their desires in some way improved. The objection to the actual-desire account is overwhelming.

In any case, considerations of autonomy are, on reflection, no recommendation of it. Well-being and autonomy, no doubt, both matter morally. It is even likely that living autonomously would be part of any enlightened person's conception of a good life. But it just confuses two quite different ideas to adopt the actual-desire account of well-being just because it makes autonomy prominent. One consideration to keep in mind is that the question, 'What is the best account of "utility"?', should be kept distinct from the question, 'What is the account of "utility"—perhaps highly artificial and *ad hoc*—that yields a one principle, utility maximizing, moral theory that comes closest to adequacy?' It is wrong to try to build into the notion of 'utility' all the restrictions that morality needs, if they fit more naturally elsewhere in the theory.

4. *The informed-desire account*

At this point, an obvious move is to say that desires count towards utility only if 'rational' or 'informed'. 'Utility', we might try saying, is the fulfilment of desires that persons would have if they appreciated the true nature of their objects. But we shall have to tone this definition down a bit. Although 'utility' cannot be equated with actual desires, it will not do, either, simply to equate it with informed desires. It is doubtless true that if I fully appreciated the nature of all possible objects of desire, I should change much of what I wanted. But if I do not go through that daunting improvement, yet the objects of my potentially perfected desires are given to me, I might well not be glad to have them; the education, after all, may be necessary for my getting anything out of them. That is true, for instance, of acquired tastes; you would do me no favour by giving me caviar now, unless it is part of some well-conceived training for my palate. Utility must, it seems, be tied at least to desires that are actual when satisfied. (Even then we should have to stretch meanings here a bit: I might get something I find that I like but did not want before because I did not know about it, nor in a sense want now simply because I already have it; or I might, through being upset or confused, go on resisting something that, in some deep sense, I really want.) It is hard to get the balance between actual and informed desires quite right. But, to be at all plausible, the informed-desire account has to be taken to hold them in a balance something like the one I have just sketched.

The move to 'informed-desires' marks the first important break with the classical utilitarian tradition (we shall see several more in the course of the discussion). Bentham and Mill used 'utility' both to explain action and to set a moral standard; they used its empirical role in arguing for its moral role. But now 'utility' has taken on a shape to fit it for a normative role (it need not be only in moral theory; it could also be in an account of one person's well-being or an account of practical reason), and it is of doubtful relevance to a purely empirical account of motivation. So this account of 'utility' should no longer be seen to be attached, except historically, to certain theories of action. It is not committed to the view that action is the result purely of a vector of desire-forces. It is not committed to any Hume-like account of the role of reason and desire. We can no longer use historical connections as a guide to theoretical connections.

The informed-desire account starts with the recognition that actual desires can be faulty. What sorts of fault matter? Obviously, for one, lack of information. Some of our strongest desires rest on mistakes of fact. I make my fortune, say, only to discover I am no better off because I was after people's respect all along and mistakenly thought that making a fortune would command respect. Or I want an operation to restore me to health, not realizing that some pill will do just as well. What matters is the ultimate, not the immediate, object of my desire, and factual mistakes creep into matching the one to the other.[9] Or I develop one set of material desires not realizing that they are the sort that, once satisfied, are replaced by another set that are just as clamorous and I am no better off. The consumer-desires at the centre of the economists' stage can be like that.[10] Then another relevant fault is logical mistake. A lot of practical reasoning is about adapting means to ends and, like any reasoning, it can be confused, irrelevant, or question-begging. Then there are subtler faults.[11] Sometimes desires are defective because we have not got enough, or the right, concepts. Theories need building which will supply new or better concepts, including value concepts. For instance, it is easy to concentrate on desires to possess this or that object, at the cost of the more elusive, difficult-to-formulate, desires to live a certain sort of life. And it is almost impossible to strike the right balance between the two main components of happiness—on the one hand, the dis-content that leads to better and, on the other, contentment with one's lot.[12] One needs more than facts and logic to sort those problems out: one needs insight and subtle, perspicuous concepts. And with information, more is not always better. It might cripple me to know what someone thinks of me, and I might sensibly prefer to remain in ignorance.[13] What seems most important to the informed-desire account is that desires have a structure; they are not all on one level. We have local desires (say, for a drink) but also higher order desires (say, to distance oneself from consumers' material desires) and global desires (say, to live one's life autonomously). The structure of desires provides the criterion for 'informed' desire: *information* is what advances plans of life; information is *full* when more, even when there is more, will not advance them further. So there is only one way to avoid all the faults that matter to 'utility': namely, by understanding completely what makes life go well.[14]

This brings out another break with classical utilitarian tradition. Bentham, Mill, and Sidgwick all saw utility as having to enter our experience. But we desire things other than states of mind; I might sometimes prefer, say, bitter truth to comforting delusion. The informed-desire account has the advantage of being able to accommodate such desires. But the desire account does this by severing the link between 'fulfil-ment of desire' and the requirement that the person in some way experience its fulfilment, dropping what we might call the Experience Requirement.[15] If the delusion is complete, one believes that one has the truth; the mental states involved in believing something that really is true and believing a successful deception are the same. Or if a father wants his children to be happy, what he wants, what is valuable to him, is a state of the world, not a state of his mind; merely to delude him into thinking that his children flourish, therefore, does not give him what he values. That is the important point; the informed-desire account does not require that fulfilment of desire translates itself in every case into the experience of the person who has the desire, and that is what gives the account its breadth and attraction as a theory of what makes life valuable. This seems to me the way that the informed-desire account has to develop. The definition itself is short: 'utility' is the fulfilment of informed desires, the stronger the desires, the greater the utility. The way that the account develops, however, shows that all of those key terms are to a fairly large degree technical.

(a) *'Desire'*. In the present technical sense, desires clearly do not have to have felt intensities; they need not be linked exclusively with appetitive states (some are, but others are aims we adopt as a result of understanding and judgement); they need not have existed before fulfilment. Rather, desiring something is, in the right circumstances, going for it, or not avoiding or being indifferent to getting it.

(b) *'Informed'*. In its technical sense, 'informed'[16] is the absence of all the faults that I listed just a moment ago. There is a historically important account of practical reason that goes roughly like this: reason alone can never determine action. The end of action must be something fixed on, in its own reasonless way, by desire; we reason, but deliberation is only of means.[17] It is hard to see what is at issue between those who say, with Hume, that reason alone cannot supply a motive and those who say, with Kant, that it can. But those of the latter persuasion are right to this extent: in deciding how to act, we must try to understand what properties things and states of affairs have, and we must put our desires through a lot of criticism and refinement to reach this understanding.[18] In this sense, deliberation may be of ends, and important deliberation often is. So an 'informed' desire is one formed by appreciation of the nature of its object, and it includes anything necessary to achieve it.[19]

(c) *'Fulfilment'*. Being 'fulfilled' cannot be understood in a psychological way, or we should be back with mental state accounts. A desire is 'fulfilled' in the sense in which a clause in a contract is fulfilled: namely, what was agreed (desired) comes about.

(d) *'Strength'*. 'Strength of desire' has several senses,

appropriate to different theoretical settings. The 'strongest' desire can be the winner, or it can be the most intensely felt. But strength of desire, in its technical sense here, has to be understood in connection with the structure that informed desires have. One does not most satisfy someone's desires simply by satisfying as many as possible, or as large a proportion. One must assess their strength, not in the sense of felt intensity, but in a sense supplied by the natural structure of desire. The desires I feel most intensely could be satisfied by your constantly imperilling my life and saving me only at the last moment,[20] whereas I should clearly prefer peace to peril; anyway, felt intensity is too often a mark of such relatively superficial matters as convention or training to be a reliable sign of anything as deep as well-being. That I prefer peace to peril suggests that global desires provide, in large part, the relevant notion of strength of desire: I desire the one form of life more than the other. True, sometimes we form global desires only on the basis of having summed local desires (for example, the global desire for a way of life based on a reckoning that day-to-day pleasures will be maximized that way). But even then we must rank that way of life against others that it excludes, and our preference between them will, it seems, be basic—that is, a global judgment not based on any other quantitative judgments. This means that the relevant notion of aggregation cannot be simply that of summing up small utilities from local satisfactions; the structure of desires already incorporates, constitutes, aggregation. It means also that the relevant sense of 'strength' is not simply the desire that wins out in motivation. If my doctor tells me that I shall die if I do not lay off drink, I shall want to lay off it. But I may later crack and go on a binge, and at that point my desire to drink will, in a perfectly clear sense, be strongest. If strength were interpreted as motivational force, then 'utility' would lose its links with well-being; what would be good for me would then be fulfilment not of my informed desires but of what I 'ought to desire' or 'have reason to desire'. So to retain the links with well-being, the relevant sense of 'strength' has to be, not motivational force, but rank in a cool preference ordering, an ordering that reflects appreciation of the nature of the objects of desire.[21]

5. *Troubles with the informed-desire account*

There are strong objections to such an account. Is it even intelligible?[22] If our desires never changed with time, then each of us would have a single preference order, by reference to which what most fulfilled his desires over the course of his life could be calculated. However, life is not so simple; preferences change, and not always in a way that allows us totally to discount earlier ones. Suppose that for much of his life a person wanted his friends to keep him from vegetating when he retired but, now that he is retired, wants to be left to vegetate. Is there any intelligible programme for weighing desires that change with time and hence for maximizing fulfilment? If not, we may be driven back to a happiness or mental state account.

Yet all the problems that we have just seen with mental state accounts remain; defects in one account do not obligingly disappear with the appearance of defects in another. How do we determine how happy a person is? Is happiness a single mental state? If many, how are they linked? Mental state accounts are hardly a refuge from troubles. Moreover, there may be an acceptable programme for handling cases where preferences change with time. The notion of an informed desire needs still further development and may eventually be able to supply the weighting of desires that we need in these troublesome cases. Has our retired friend simply forgotten the satisfactions of a busy life? If so, his later desire has much less weight. Is it just a change in taste, on the model of no longer liking ice cream? If so, his earlier desire has much less weight. We shall have to come back to these problems when we discuss measurement, but for now I have to be content with suggesting that the prospects of making the informed-desire account work are certainly not less rosy than those of making a mental state account work.[23]

The other troubles are much more worrying. The breadth of the account, which is its attraction, is also its great flaw. The account drops the Experience Requirement, as we called it. It allows my utility to be determined not only by things that I am not aware of (that seems right: if you cheat me out of an inheritance that I never expected, I might not know but still be worse off for it), but also by things that do not affect my life in any way at all. The trouble is that one's desires spread themselves so widely over the world that their objects extend far outside the bound of what, with any plausibility, one could take as touching one's own well-being. The restriction to *informed* desire is no help here. I might meet a stranger on a train and, listening to his ambitions, form a strong, informed desire that he succeed, but never hear of him again. And any moderately decent person wants people living in the twenty-second century to be happy and prosperous. And we know that Leonardo had an informed desire that humans fly, which the Wright brothers fulfilled centuries later.[24] Indeed, without the Experience Requirement, why would utility not include the desires of the dead? And would that not mean the account had gone badly awry? And if we exclude these desires that extend beyond the bounds of what affects well-being, would we not, in order to avoid arbitrariness, have to reintroduce the Experience Requirement, thereby losing the breadth that makes the informed-desire account attractive? The difficulty goes deep in the theory. In fact, it goes deep, one way or other, in any account of well-being.

Another attraction of the account is that desires have to be shaped by appreciation of the nature of their objects. Without that restriction, the account is not even a starter. But with it, do desires even matter any longer? It may be somewhat too simple to say that things are desired because valuable, not valuable because desired. Yet the informed-desire account concedes much of the case for saying so. What makes us desire the things we desire, when informed, is something about them—*their* features or properties. But why bother then with informed desire, when we can go directly to what it is about objects that shape informed desires in the first place? If what really matter are certain sorts of reason for action, to be found outside desires in qualities of their objects, why not explain well-being directly in terms of them? It does not seem that it is fulfilled desire that is the basis of well-being, but certain of its objects. And that points us, depending on what we decide those objects are, either back towards mental states or beyond utility altogether.[25]

6. *Is there something between mental state and desire accounts?*

Mental state accounts are too narrow, desire accounts too broad. We ought to look in between.

I said a while ago that one way of correcting the flaws in the simple mental state account would be by making utility neither a mental state nor desire-fulfilment. I then postponed taking up that suggestion until after we had looked at desire accounts, and it is time to return to it now.

There is a cluster of terms which even in their everyday use seem to fall conveniently between mental states and fulfilment of desires: namely, enjoying or liking things, finding them pleasing or satisfying or fulfilling, being pleased or happy with them. Let us use the term *enjoyment* to cover them all. *Enjoyment*, in its ordinary use, is not anything so narrow as experiencing a single mental state or one of a range of states, but let us explicitly make it part of the present use of *enjoyment* that it is not. In similar spirit, let us specify that it is nothing so broad as merely having desires (even informed ones) fulfilled. Also, let us allow that people *enjoy* things other than states of mind; in fact, to treat the account sympathetically we should make the range of objects of *enjoyment* wide—wide enough to include, say, helping others or advancing knowledge. But let us put a limit to the range by requiring that all the objects of *enjoyment* fall within our experience. So we both push the boundaries out beyond its ordinary use and, at the same time, limit the expansion by reinstating the Experience Requirement.[26]

The enjoyment account will need a lot more work to make it clear. Is it just a desire account with the Experience Requirement tacked on? Does the notion of *enjoyment* do any work of its own? *Enjoying* and *liking*, in their ordinary uses, are closely connected with desire: the acid test for whether I enjoy or like something is whether, other things being equal, I go for it, or do not avoid it, or am not indifferent to getting it. *Enjoyment* in its technical sense is even more closely connected with desire. Many everyday uses of *like* and *enjoy* suggest a certain psychological tone, but that disappears in the technical sense. However, if *enjoying* is just having a favourable attitude, the revival of the Experience Requirement runs the risk of being *ad hoc*. I have favourable attitudes towards many things that do not enter my experience. Why do they not count too?

Still, the enjoyment account is clear enough for it to face one serious trouble. It is attractive because, with the revival of the Experience Requirement, it restrains over-wide desire accounts. The intention is right, but the particular restraint applied seems not. It seems in the end simply too drastic. It bans things that our ordinary notion of well-being cannot, without damage, do without. It is common that, as many persons' values mature, such things as accomplishment and close authentic personal relationships come more and more to fill the centre of their lives. If the Experience Requirement excludes these values from 'utility', then 'utility' will have less and less to do with what these persons see as making their own lives good. And those values do seem excluded. Suppose that someone is duped into thinking that those close to him are behaving authentically. What enters his experience is the same whether he has the real thing or a successful deceit. But it is only the real thing, he thinks, that makes his life better. According to the enjoyment account, what affects well-being can only be what enters experience, and the trouble is that some of the things that persons value greatly do not. My truly having close and authentic personal relations is not the kind of thing that can enter my experience; all that can enter is what is common to both my truly having such relations and my merely believing that I do. And this seems to distort the nature of these values. If I want to accomplish something with my life, it is not that I want to have a *sense* of accomplishment. That is also desirable, but it is different from, and less important than, the first desire. And if I want to accomplish something, it is not necessary that I want my accomplishment to enter my experience—say that I know about it. That too is desirable, but it is still not the first desire. If either I could accomplish something with my life but not know it, or believe that I had but not really have, I should prefer the first. That would be, for me, the more valuable life. 'Valuable life', of course, is full of ambiguity. It can mean a life that is valuable because of its value to other persons. It can mean a morally valuable life, or an aesthetically valuable one, or one valuable in terms of some code, such as a code of chivalry. But my ground for preferring the first sort of life would not be any of these; I should prefer it because it would be, considered on its own, considered simply as a life I must lead, a more fulfilling one. So it is a value that has to be found a place within the bounds of 'utility'.

The enjoyment account, too, has its serious troubles. To my mind, the best prospect for a utilitarian account of well-being is to hold on to the over-wide desire account and look for good reasons to rein it in.[27] It is harder to correct the over-narrow accounts. However, developing the desire account is a large job, which will be the subject of the next chapter.

II

UTILITARIAN ACCOUNTS: THE DESIRE ACCOUNT DEVELOPED

1. *How may we restrict the desire account?*

THE informed-desire account will have to be abandoned unless we can find a way to restrict the desires that count. But we cannot do it with the Experience Requirement. That is where the last chapter left us.

The trouble, you will recall, comes from examples like these: I want the sympathetic stranger I meet on the train to succeed; I want people in the twenty-second century to prosper; Leonardo wanted humans to fly. All of them informed desires, but (the trouble is) their fulfilment not part of well-being.

The notion we are after is not the notion of value in general, but the narrower notion of a life's being valuable solely to the person who lives it. And this must itself impose restrictions on which desires count. As these examples show, the desires that count have to enter our lives in a way beyond just being our desires. So what we need to do is to make clear the sense in which only certain informed desires enter our lives in this further way. Think of the difference between my desire that the stranger succeed and my desire that my children prosper. I want both, but they enter my life in different ways. The first desire does not become one of my aims. The second desire, on the other hand, is one of my central ends, on the achievement of which the success of my life will turn. It is not that, deep down, what I really want is my own achievement, and that I want my children's prosperity only as a means to it. What I want is *their* prosperity, and it distorts the value I attach to it to make it only a means to such a purely personal end as my own achievement. It is just that their prosperity also becomes part of my life's being successful in a way that the prosperity of the stranger on the train does not.

But that can be only part of the story. It is not that informed desires count only if they become the sort of aims or goals or aspirations on which the success of a life turns. Good things can just happen; manna from heaven counts too. So we should try saying, to introduce more breadth, that what count are what we aim at and what we would not avoid or be indifferent to getting. What counts for me, therefore, is what enters my life with no doing from me, what I bring into my life, and what I do with my life. The range of that list is not so great as to include things that I cannot (e.g. the prosperity of our twenty-second-century successors) or do not (e.g. the sympathetic stranger's success) take into my life as an aim or goal. And Leonardo's wanting humans to fly would not count either; to the extent it became an aim of his life it was unsuccessful, and to the extent it was merely a wish it does not count.[1]

In a way the account is now circular. I appeal to our rough notion of well-being in deciding which informed desires to exclude from this account of well-being. But that, I think, does not matter. If what we were doing were taking a totally empty term, 'well-being', and stipulating a sense for it, then we could not, in the middle of the job, appeal to 'well-being'. But our job is not that. The notion of 'well-being' we want to account for is not empty to start with; utilitarians use our everyday notion, and our job is to make it clearer. So we are free to move back and forth between our judgments about which cases fall inside the boundary and our descriptions of the boundary. Every account of this type will do the same. There is the same sort of undamaging circularity in mental state and enjoyment accounts, because they need to get beyond the ordinary senses of 'pleasure' and 'enjoyment', and they would have to go about fixing a new boundary in just the same way.

This narrowing of the desire account still does not get rid of the great embarrassment of the desires of the dead. Of course, a lot of the desires of the dead do count morally, but that is because they affect the living. There is a good case for honouring wishes expressed in wills. Inheritance satisfies the desires of the living to provide for their offspring and encourages saving that benefits society generally. There is a good case, too, for granting rights to the dead—say, to determine whether their bodies are used for medical purposes.[2] But that, again, does not require appeal beyond the well-being of the living. And, anyway, that a desire of a dead person counts *morally* does not show that it counts towards his well-being.

The real trouble is our counting the fulfilment of aims even if (as it seems we must) we do not require that the fulfilment enter experience. Some of our aims are not fulfilled until we are dead; some, indeed, being desires for then, could not be. But is this so embarrassing, after all?[3] You might have a desire—it could be an informed one, I think—to have your achievements recognized and acknowledged. An enemy of yours might go around slandering you behind your back, successfully persuading everyone that you stole all your ideas, and they, to avoid unpleasantness, pretend in your presence to believe you. If that could make your life less good, then why could it not be made less good by his slandering you with the extra distance behind your back that death brings? You might well be willing to exert yourself, at risk of your life, to prevent these slanders being disseminated after your death. You might, with eyes full open, prefer that course to longer life with a ruined reputation after it. There seems nothing irrational in attaching this value to posthumous reputation. And the value being attached to it does not seem to be moral or aesthetic or any kind other than the value to be attached to the life as a life to be lived.[4] Here is another example. It would not have been at all absurd for Bertrand Russell to have thought that if his work for nuclear disarmament had, after his death, actually reduced the risk of nuclear war, his last years would have been more worthwhile, and his life altogether more valuable, than if it all proved futile. True, if Russell had indeed succeeded, his life clearly would have been more valuable to others. But Russell could also have considered it more valuable from the point of view of his own self-interest. For instance, it would not have been absurd for Russell to think the same about devoting his last years to some purely intellectual project without effects on others' well-being, such as patching up the holes in the Theory of Descriptions. A lot of desires of the dead would be ruled out on the grounds we have already mentioned, but it seems right for some still to count.[5]

2. *Why we should resist restricting it more*

Excluding some desires raises the general question of whether the best account of 'utility' will not exclude desires of several further sorts. Should not other-regarding desires be excluded?[6] Those who not only want their own welfare but also, luckily for them, have others wanting it too count more heavily than those who do not; for instance, orphans count less than children with loving parents. But that yields Bentham out of Orwell: each to count for at least one but some for more than one. Should not irrational desires be excluded?[7] The principle of utility is a normative principle and ought perhaps, therefore, to grant weight only to what are, by its own standards, good reasons, such as benefit and freedom from harm, and to grant weight only to desires justifiable in terms of these reasons. Should not, for obvious reasons, immoral desires be excluded?[8] Indeed, should not desires of any sort of moral character be excluded?[9] If the concern of the principle of utility is with what ought to be done, then the desire for something because it is what ought to be done appears when the principle delivers its result and seems improper as a ground for the result. Do we not, in general, need a Theory of Types in utility theory to exclude certain desires from the argument place in utility functions?

I think not. First of all, it is impossible to separate self-regarding and other-regarding desires. Each of us wants certain pure states of himself (e.g. to be free from pain); but we also want our lives to have some point, and this desired state can be hard to separate from states of others. Also, if we accepted the restriction to self-regarding desires, we should sever the connection between utility and happiness (and happiness is a large part of utility even on the informed-desire account). A father's happiness can be at stake in his child's happiness—two persons' welfare riding on one person's fate. Allowing that is no violation of everybody's counting for one; it merely allows the father, like everyone else, also to count for one. We have to swallow a little harder when we shift from involvements such as love to involvements such as hate, envy, spite, prejudice, and intolerance. If these sorts of desires are going to count too, what awful distortions will creep into political decision? But if a lover's happiness counts, so does a hater's *schadenfreude*. It is an ugly sort of pleasure, and as pleasures go slight and troublesomely mixed, but still a pleasure. If it ought not to have weight in moral or political calculation, then we had better find a way to keep it out. But out of moral and political calculation, where it probably does not belong, not out of 'utility', where in some small way it probably does. Also letting other-regarding desires enter moral calculation seems to distort the notion of a moral reason. If one of my aims is to convince Britain that it ought to go over to comprehensive schools, why should you think that my desire constitutes yet another moral reason for going over to comprehensive schools? It would be absurd to introduce comprehensive education because it satisfied the desires of its advocates. What has overwhelming weight here, of course, is the good of the children and of society at large. But all that one really has to swallow is that the happiness of the advocates of comprehensives may in some small way turn on what happens, and that, at least, seems right.[10]

Simply to rule out irrational desires would also go too far. A compulsive hand-washer's desire is irrational, but its fulfilment affects his utility. So since irrational desires cannot be excluded wholesale, why not let them in, and if their fulfilment is sometimes morally intolerable, look to other moral matters besides utility to block it. True, the fulfilment of other sorts of irrational desires is more worrying. A misogynist might be put off his food by a woman's sitting next to him in the Senior Common Room. Consistency would seem to require that his desire not to have women around counts too. Well, why not? The suggestion earlier was that desires that are irrational on utilitarian grounds should not be given weight, because no utilitarian value is at stake. But if someone is upset or distressed, then there is a utilitarian value at stake. The theoretical oddity would come, not in giving weight to such desires, but in giving them none.

What if desires are not only irrational but downright immoral? Should we count, for instance, sadistic desires? This has seemed more of a challenge than it really is, simply because people still tend to think of 'utility' in rather narrow hedonistic terms. Anyone with much understanding would regard his own sadistic desires—even purely from the point of view of how good his life is for him to lead—as making virtually no claim upon being fulfilled. He would have formed second-order desires not to encourage or indulge them; he would know that, in his case at least, their gratification is mixed and brings no lasting or deep enjoyment; he would know that their opportunity cost is enormous. In fact, it is hard to think of any fairly normal sort who would not be better off, from his own point of view, frustrating his sadistic desires and trying for something better. Still, it would be a mistake simply to rule out sadistic desires. Not everyone is fairly normal. Perhaps there is someone for whom sadistic kicks are all he has, who is incapable of better. It might even be right, if he were also an inept sadist who aims to shock and upset but succeeds only in boring, to play along with him. The same holds for a desire to do something because it would be morally right. There are people for whom living morally is so much at the centre of their lives that their success there is a large part of their lives' being successful. The ideal development of human nature is for 'ethical push' (self-interest) and 'ethical pull' (obligation) to get progressively closer to each other.[11] That too complicates the notion of 'well-being', but desirably so.[12]

All these cases for further restrictions focus not on 'well-being' itself but on how it fits into moral theory. So this is another time when we have to remind ourselves that the question, 'What is the best account of "utility"?', is quite distinct from the question, 'What is the best account, as *ad hoc* as you like, that yields the most adequate one principle, utility maximizing, moral theory?'[13]

3. *How value and desire are related*

The danger is that desire accounts get plausible only by, in effect, ceasing to be desire accounts. We had to qualify *desire* with *informed*, and that gave prominence to the features or qualities of the objects of desire, and not to the mere existence of desire. Then, to prevent informed desires from spreading too widely, we had to give prominence to only a certain range of features or qualities. Does this not confirm the suspicion that desire is no longer playing any real part, and remains only as a token of piety to a utilitarian tradition that has now effectively been abandoned? The issue widens. Could desire be a *ground* of value, or is it at best only a *mark* of it? Are things valuable because desired, or desired because valuable? And widest of all, what place do reason (cognition, perception, judgment) and desire (will, appetite, conation) have in explaining value?[14]

In a way the order of explanation must be from *value* to *desire*.[15] We see that an object has certain features, such as that it is pleasant or healthy or that it gives security, or that it would be an accomplishment. And therefore we desire it. We have always to be able to cite some feature that makes the desirability of the object intelligible; otherwise the notion of 'value' loses hold. And that feature has to be generally intelligible as one that makes things desirable. No one can just make something valuable by adopting it as his own personal aim.[16] Of course, people can disagree in their values. I might find mountain-climbing exciting and value it highly; you may find it simply terrifying and not value it at all. But we do not disagree here in our values in any deep or interesting way. Virtually everyone values excitement and does not value pure terror, though people differ in what they find exciting and terrifying. We all have to be able to connect what we value to some generally intelligible desirability feature. What is more, we sometimes discover values. You may be happy-go-lucky and not even think about accomplishing anything with your life, but then come upon someone whose accomplishment makes his life seem to you exhilarating and fulfilled. And with time you may come to discover more and more what this desirable accomplishment really is; you see how to separate it from mere achievement and its value from merely gaining praise. When you see what accomplishment is, you form a desire. And there need not be any pre-existent background desire (except those of vacuous generality) of which your new desire is merely another instance.

But what is interesting is how little any of this shows. It still leaves a strong case for saying that the order of explanation is quite the reverse: from *desire* to *value*. True, objects are valuable because of *their* features. But how do we explain these various desirability features? How do we separate *desirability* features from the rest? Here we have to guard against taking one or two examples as paradigms, and missing the variety of cases. So consider the following ones.

Case 1: I have tasted both apples and pears. I like both but prefer pears. How do we explain my attaching more value to having a pear? The only relevant desirability feature is that they taste good. However, it is not a plausible explanation of *tasting better* that I perceive that pears possess this desirability feature to a greater degree than apples. We need to explain my liking pears more in terms of my wanting them more. That is true whether different persons' tastes coincide or not. But another important feature of tastes is that often they do not. We have no reason to expect, with many tastes, that differences in valuing shows that there is any lack of perception or understanding. My preference for pears is not open to criticism (though others of my tastes are—for lack of discrimination, experience, attention). There is a tradition, especially strong in the social sciences, that sees all preference on the model of the simplest tastes: a pre-existent motivation, not subject to criticism, unaffected by understanding; the explanation running from *desire* to *value*. But this is only one kind of case.

Case 2: A recluse may see what he is missing and come to prefer good company. Here perception plays a large part; it may even be a case of discovering a value. But why is good company itself seen as desirable? The explanation cannot be just in terms of perception; there is an important pre-existent motivation. The motivation is not a taste, which typically can vary from person to person; it is more a feature of human nature. We are social creatures; we want and, other things being equal, go for company.[17]

Case 3: Freud, in his last days, preferred thinking clearly to drugged comfort. Here there is a large element of perception but no obvious, at least simple, pre-existent motivation. We get no plausible explanation of this case unless we bring in both understanding what it is to think clearly and wanting it more. Explaining the state of *thinking clearly* as a desirability feature needs both perception and desire, without priority to either. To see this feature as desirable and to desire it on seeing it are the same. There is no plausible explanation of the one in terms of the other.[18]

Case 4: A person who in the past has frittered his life away comes to value accomplishing something with it. Here understanding plays an enormous role, and desire may seem to disappear altogether. Accomplishment, in the general sense I have in mind (making one's life valuable and not just frittering it away), is valuable for everyone; anyone who fails to recognize it as valuable lacks understanding. It is true that there will be odd types for whom, all things considered, it will be better not to try for it. Perhaps someone for whom any ambition sets up intense anxieties had better not. But that is a case of conflict of values, in which accomplishment is still a value. Does the priority now run the other way? Do we see a life of accomplishment as valuable and then, on the basis of that, form a desire for it? Clearly, this is not a case of first perceiving facts neutrally and then desire's entering and blindly fixing on one object and not another. The way in which we talk about the objects we value is far from neutral; we call it 'accomplishment' and explain it in terms of 'giving life weight and substance' or 'not wasting life'. The language we use in reporting our perceptions already organizes our experience and selects what we see as important; it is designed to show how we view certain things in a favourable light. Desire here does not blindly fix on an object; it is obviously pointed in certain directions by what we perceive favourably. But all of this, though true, explains too little. We also have to explain what goes on in our perceiving things favourably. And here desire comes back at a deeper level, as part of this explanation. Hume was wrong to see desire and understanding (appetite and cognition) as distinct existences. He was wrong to make desire blind. But it is a variety of the same mistake to think that one can explain our fixing on desirability features purely in terms of understanding. It is a mistake not only to keep understanding out of all desire but also to keep desire out of all understanding. Some understanding—the sort that involves fixing on certain features and seeing them in a favourable light—is also a kind of movement.[19] It requires a will to go for what has those features. There is no adequate explanation of their being *desirability* features without appeal

to this kind of movement. So we cannot, even in the case of a
desirability feature such as *accomplishment*, separate understanding and desire. Once we see something as 'accomplishment', as
'giving weight and substance to our lives', as 'avoiding wasting
our lives', there is no space left for desire to follow along in a
secondary, subordinate position. Desire is not blind. Understanding is not bloodless. Neither is the slave of the other.
There is no priority.

It may still seem that a value such as accomplishment has
to have some priority to desire. It may seem that such a value
cannot even depend upon what, if informed, persons would
desire. One thing that would show this is our deciding that
accomplishment is of absolute value. But few of us believe
that; it is much more plausible to think there could be the very
rare case in which trying to accomplish something was so
painful that it was not worth doing. Another thing that would
show it is our deciding that the value of accomplishment,
while not absolute, is not given by its place in informed desires
either, in other words that reflectively wanting accomplishment and recognizing its value to one can differ. But what
would the difference be? Where, for instance, would trade-offs
sanctioned by these different conceptions of the value of
accomplishment diverge?

So desire is more than merely a mark of value. It is a
ground, in the following sense: it is part of the full explanation
of prudential value. But this does not give desire priority. Nor
does the appearance of *desiring* in *valuing* mean that we are free
to make an existential choice of values. The desires that count
are not brute and unconstrained; they are informed. It is the
strength of the notion of 'informed desire' that it straddles
—that is, does not accept any sharp form of—the divide
between reason and desire.

The advantages of the informed desire account, therefore,
seem to me to be these. It provides the materials needed to
encompass the complexity of prudential value. It has the
advantages of scope and flexibility over explanations of
'well-being' in terms of desirability features. It has scope,
because all prudential values, from objects of simple varying
tastes to objects of universal informed agreement, register
somewhere in informed preferences. It has flexibility, because

not everyone's well-being is affected in the same way by a certain desirability feature, and we want a notion sensitive to these individual differences. We want to know not only that something is valuable, but how valuable it is, and how valuable to different persons.

4. *A formal account*

An old and potent objection to the utilitarian way of thinking is that it assumes that we value only one kind of thing, whereas we value many irreducibly different kinds of things. It seems to me undeniable that we do value irreducibly different kinds of things. But that point counts against certain mental state accounts, not against the informed-desire account. On the desire account one can allow that when I fully understand what is involved, I may end up valuing many things and valuing them for themselves. The desire account is compatible with a strong form of pluralism about values.

However, the desire account may purchase its pluralism at the price of emptiness.[20] If I advise you to maximize the fulfilment of your desires, I have not helped you much. I have not supplied you with the dominant end of human action by appeal to which you can resolve conflict between your subordinate ends. Nor have I given you a principle of choice of ends. It is no use to you to be told that you should decide what to go for by seeing what gives you most of what you decide to go for. Maximizing the fulfilment of one's desires does not yield, but presupposes, a hierarchy of goals. In contrast to this, the old notion of utility as a pleasurable mental state was both of these things—a dominant end and a principle of choice. And this contrast can easily give the impression that the desire account makes 'utility' almost empty.

But the charge that the new notion of 'utility' is empty is, I think, partly the charge that it does not do what the old notion would do, and that is certainly correct. 'Utility', on the old monistic interpretation, was the super, over-arching, substantive value. But now, 'utility', on the desire account, is not to be seen as the single over-arching value, in fact not as a substantive value at all, but instead as a formal analysis of what it is for something to be prudentially valuable to some person.[21] Therefore, utility will be related to substantive values such as pleasure or accomplishment or autonomy, not by being the dominant value that subsumes them, but by providing a way of understanding the notion '(prudentially) valuable' and hence the notions 'more valuable' and 'less valuable'.[22]

So when, for whatever purposes, we shift from everyday talk of pursuing various different ends to theoretical talk of maximizing a single quantity, 'utility', this quantity should not be understood as an end of the same kind, only grander.[23] There is simply no case for reducing these various ends to a single end in this sense. The most that can be said is that a person's ends are unified only in being his *ends*, things he *values*. When our various values conflict, we may attempt to resolve the conflict by trying to realize as much 'value' as possible, but the only substantive values present remain the various values that originally appear in our system of ends. We are still able to go for the most 'value', to step far enough back from all of our various particular ends and sacrifice the lesser for the greater, even in the absence of a single substantive end as mediator. We mediate, but without such a mediating value.[24]

Is this, then, a 'neutral' account of utility, in the sense in which accounts in recent economics and decision theory are? Yes and no. Yes, because this account, unlike hedonism or ideal utilitarianism, mentions no substantive values. But no, if the account is taken more widely to include the arguments for it, because then substantive values have to appear.

Is this account 'objective' or 'subjective'? By 'subjective', I mean an account that makes well-being depend upon an individual's own desires, and by 'objective' one that makes well-being independent of desires.[25] It may look as if an informed-desire account could not be anything but subjective, since it makes 'desire' part of the explanation of prudential value. But that entirely depends upon how we take the phrase 'an *individual's own* desires'. Values do not rest upon *one* person's desire. Values cannot be entirely personal, the result simply of someone's wanting the thing. That would not even be intelligible; persons generally have to be able to see a prudential value as something to go for if it is to be a prudential value at all. But the informed-desire account does make well-being depend upon variant, individual desires in this sense: it gives a place to both actual and ideal desires. *Lafite* may be worth much more than *Coke*, and might be to anyone at all if he appreciated all the flavours they contain, but is worth less to me with my untrained palate. And the account is certainly incompatible with some versions of an objective-list approach to well-being. An objective-list approach says that a person's well-being can be affected by the presence of certain values (which it lists) even if they are not what he wants. The informed-desire account can allow that the values on the list (enjoyment, accomplishment, autonomy, etc.) are values for everyone, but it also allows that there may be very special persons for whom any value on the list (say, accomplishment), though valuable for them as for everybody, conflicts enough with another value (say, freedom from anxiety) for it not, all things considered, to be valuable for them to have. If a certain objective-list approach denies this, then it is different from the informed-desire approach. If it does not deny it, and even plausibly includes enjoyment on its list, and furthermore accepts the complex view about the relation of value and desire that I set out in the last section, then it gets very hard to distinguish from the informed-desire approach.[26] Some philosophers treat the distinction between objective and subjective as if it marked a crucial distinction between accounts of well-being.[27] They do, because they attach great importance to whether or not well-being is made to depend upon an individual's desires, tastes, feelings, or attitudes. But, as we just saw in the last section, the dependence of prudential value on desire is much less simple, less a matter of all or nothing, than they assume. The best account of 'utility' makes it depend on some desires and not on others. So the distinction between objective and subjective, defined in the common way that I have defined it, does not mark an especially crucial distinction. It would be better if these terms (at least in this sense) were put into retirement.[28] But if they are not, if the question 'Subjective or objective?' is pressed, then the answer has to be 'Both'.

That answer shows how far what seems to me the best account of 'utility' has to move away from its classical beginnings. It has to move from mental state accounts to a desire account; it has to move from an actual-desire to an informed-desire account; and it has to set the standards for a desire's being 'informed' in a place not too distant from an objective-list account. This is a stiffer standard for 'informed' or 'rational' desire than other writers have wished to adopt,[29] so much so that it might seem that I should use a different label. But this label, it seems to me, has merits. It records the fact that this account is a development of one utilitarian tradition, that there is no plausible stopping point for the notion of 'utility' short of it, but that this point is still short of objective-list accounts. And it records the role both of understanding and of desire. But we need a fuller explanation of how prudential values are identified and what sort of argument about them is possible. I shall come back to that subject in chapter IV, section 3.

5. *Maximization and the unity of life*

Maximization, in some sense, is our prudential policy: we want to have the most valuable life we can. But is maximization, in this uncontroversial sense, a matter of aggregation?

To answer that, we have to be clear about the sort of unity life has. On desire accounts, aggregation is explained in terms of the structure of desires. If desires are fairly well informed, the structures are plans of life. This talk of plans of life does not mean that valuable lives must be highly planned.[30] One could have a life plan to take each day as it comes. Or one could have a minimal plan to live for short-term pleasures that, in aggregate, reach the greatest total. But for us to be able to evaluate any approach to life, even these, we have to see them in the fairly long term: as ways of living, which exclude other ways of living, all of which have—in those terms—to be ranked. We can never reach final assessment of ways of life by totting up lots of small, short-term utilities. We can do this totting up of short-term quantities, it is true, with certain prudential values in certain areas of life. We can say of pleasure, for instance, that this moment is pleasanter eating a pear than an apple, and the next moment will be pleasanter washing it down with *Lafite* than with *Coke*. But that cannot be the model for our final, authoritative calculation of utility. It has to take a global form: this way of living, all in all, is better than that.[31]

Let us return now to the question whether the (prudentially) most valuable life is the one with the greatest sum of utility. It is not, some persons think, because aggregation is insensitive to distribution, and distribution can matter in prudence as well as in morality.[32] I might prefer a life with a lower sum to one in which the bad periods got very bad—the sort of 'minimum acceptable level' requirement often imposed between lives now applied inside a life. But how could I know that it had a lower sum? That calculation seems to need the sort of totting up that I have just suggested could not, in the end, be utilitarian calculation. We might try various ways of introducing a metric—say, by comparing each of the items to some entirely different item about whose value we are clear. In this spirit, I might calculate: I should be willing to sit under the dentist's drill for a thousand hours to avoid the awful year, for two thousand hours to get the glorious year, and only four hundred hours for each of the two middling years; so there is more good in the good year than bad in the bad year, and more net good in that package than in the package of the two middling years. But then we have to go on to say: still I prefer, all things considered, the second package to the first. The difficulty is to know what is going on in the first set of estimates. The second, the final preference, ranks the packages as stretches of life to be lived. So that seems to be the only judgment on which talk of utilities can be based. The first set of estimates, if they can be given a sense, must be doing something else.[33]

The desire account, therefore, detaches aggregation from a totting-up conception. So, to understand aggregation, we have to understand how desires are given structure. Philosophy has not yet provided a fully satisfactory explanation of how we bring system to our various ends.[34] Pleasure, accomplishment, autonomy, loving relationships are all valuable. A life with only one or two of them, even in large quantities, would not be the best life. We cannot introduce system to our ends by calculating amounts of *this* value determined in isolation and amounts of *that* one, also determined in isolation. To some degree, estimating the values of these various ends is like determining the value of ingredients in cooking. We can measure the quantities of wine and beef and onions separately, but we can only measure their value to the dish by considering them in various combinations. With our different ends, too, the important estimate of how valuable they are is their contribution to a whole life. And although we can talk about the amount of some of our ends (e.g. pleasure) in isolation, with others it is more difficult (e.g. autonomy), and in any case once we talk about amount of *utility* we have to see these items as part of a life. So the amount of value cannot be decided by attaching a value to each separately and then adding. There is a notion of the amount they contribute to a life that is independent of anything we can say about each end on its own. On that overall judgment we are in a clearer position with cooking: there is a further value that we appeal to in assessing various combinations of ingredients—how good they taste. But when we assess various combinations of our ends, there is no further substantive value, no supreme or dominant end, to rank them. There is not even an inclusive end, some larger value of which they are a part—at least, if that value is thought of as substantive.[35] All that we can appeal to, in the last analysis, is our notion of 'a valuable life'. The form of the judgment is, *this* combination makes a more valuable life than *that*. And the notion 'a valuable life' used here does not serve to summarize further, more substantive notions; judgments about more or less 'valuable life', in those terms, are basic.

So if by 'aggregation' one understands addition on the totting-up model, then the desire account abandons aggregation. But I think that there is a strong sense in which it retains it. What are central to utilitarian calculation, on the desire account, are trade-offs. We make judgments of the form: this loss of value is less than that gain. And it is part of the desire account that the best prudential policy is going for net gains. We began this section wondering whether maximization, in the uncontentious sense, is different from aggregation, in the sense that the desire account attaches to it. It seems to me that it is not. The desire account may be too all-encompassing to be the account of 'well-being' that suits moral or political theory. But it seems unavoidable in prudential theory. In that sphere, I want next to suggest, it comes close to being what we mean both by 'good' and by 'value'.

6. *A (restricted) interest theory of value*

The desire account has all along been designed to keep 'utility' close to 'what is in a person's interest'. It is not that the expressions 'fulfilling one's informed desire' and 'being in one's interest' come out meaning the same. They certainly do not mean the same in the usual sense of 'desire'. Even in the technical sense of 'desire' that I adopt, they do not mean quite the same. For one thing, 'informed desire' is a formula devised with humans in mind, whereas 'interest' can be applied without strain to animals—even to plants for that matter. 'Interest', in that respect, is wider in application than 'informed desire', while in other respects it is narrower. For instance, I may desire turkish delight simply through having a weakness for it, but to say that it is in my 'interest' applies a heavy word to an entirely light subject. None the less, these are all pretty minor differences, and the application of the two expressions is very close.

The link between 'interests' and 'good', however, is one of meaning. The word 'good' has associated with it 'the condition of answering certain interests, which interests are in question being indicated either by the element modifying or the element modified by "good" or by certain features of the context of utterance'.[36] The use of 'good' that we are especially concerned with is 'good for such-and-such a person'. The relevant interests, therefore, are that person's interests, and for something to be good is for it to satisfy those interests of his. And since utility is linked to satisfying a person's interests, it must in the same way be linked to a person's good.

Now let us introduce value. A good starting point is the simple Interest Theory of Value, which says: for a thing to be of value is for it to be the object of, or the satisfaction of, desire or interest.[37] But that must be too simple. At best the Interest Theory fits the case of prudential value, and the word 'value' is used of far more than just prudential values. Morality itself may be said to be valuable, but on no plausible moral theory is its value exhausted by its status as an object of desire, even informed desire. So the only form of the Interest Theory that is plausible is one restricted to prudential value. There are two weighty doubts about it. It does not make value prior to desire, and there are cases where value seems to have that priority. And it does not allow the value we attach to our various ends ever to diverge from their place in the hierarchy of our informed desires, and there seem to be cases of such divergence. But these are doubts we have already tried to allay.[38]

So this restricted version seems to me right. There are, none the less, differences in tone between 'valued' and 'desired'. 'Valued' and 'valuable' are, like 'good' and 'interest', rather weighty words and do not sit altogether comfortably in cases where what one wants lacks importance. But these are minor troubles, the sort of linguistic strains that most theories involve. The links between utility, good, and value show how broad a notion utility, on the desire account, is and how strong its claims for the central place in prudential theory really are.

7. Is this account still utilitarian?

The desire account may seem to have few links left with the utilitarian tradition. But that is not quite right. The desire account is a natural development of classical utilitarianism.

Bentham often sounds like a thorough-going hedonist. But even in *The Principles*, once having made his declaration of allegiance to hedonism, in the next breath he talks of what is 'good' for people, or to their 'advantage' or 'benefit'.[39]

Mill, we know, felt forced to introduce his famous distinction between *quantity* and *quality* of pleasure. He explains quality in terms of informed desire: the pleasure of higher quality is the 'one to which all or almost all who have experience of both give a decided preference'.[40] Mill introduced 'quality' as a necessary supplement to talk about 'quantity', but the supplement then swallows up the rest of the theory. The criterion for differences in quality is the only one with the scope necessary for the theory, and the only intelligible talk of quantity is what can be defined on preference orderings. In fact, the desire account may be seen as a development of one side of Mill's theory to a point where the rest can be accommodated in subordinate places.[41]

Sidgwick knew well how much explanation the words 'pleasure' and 'happiness' needed in order to carry the theoretical burden utilitarians put on them. He adopts an informed-desire account (although one where 'consciousness' is a necessary part of our ultimate good). For instance, he explains a person's future *good* as 'what he would now desire and seek on the whole if all the consequences ... were accurately forseen and adequately realised in imagination ...'[42] The trouble with Sidgwick's account is that its two elements, consciousness and desire, come apart, and it seems best, for reason that we have seen, to follow where the desire element leads. Again, when Sidgwick's account is developed far enough, the notion of informed desire dominates, and consciousness assumes a subordinate place. It does because that arrangement yields the best account of 'well-being'.

Is it the best? That brings us to the most serious doubt of all about the desire account. If 'well-being' is defined to include fulfilment of desires that are trivial, abnormal, cheap, disgusting, and immoral, perhaps it is too wide. Doubtless it forms *one* notion of well-being, the broadest one, and one that we should sometimes want to use. Perhaps even it is the notion to use in prudential value theory. But do we not need a much narrower, more sharply focused, more discriminating notion for moral theory?

III

OBJECTIVE ACCOUNTS

1. *Two concepts of well-being*

ONCE we start using 'well-being' in moral theory, we come under strong pressures to make it much narrower than utilitarians do. Why should I accept that your mere desires make a claim on me? You may, when informed, want champagne, but if you do not need it, why should my obligations to you be at all engaged? On the face of it, the notion of 'need' suits morality far better than 'desire' does. Your informed desires are bound to range more widely than those interests of yours that the rest of us ought to weigh in deciding how to act. And consulting desires distorts moral calculation. If you are rich or bright, you will rationally form a conception of the good life adjusted to these resources and capacities of yours. But why should informed desires shaped, as they are, by resources that may have been unfairly distributed in the first place and genetic capacities that in any case have no moral standing then become the basis for determining what is just? It would be a crazy standard of justice. Clearly we have to get behind desires and expectations to the deeper considerations that show which desires and expectations have moral force. Fulfilling any informed desire may increase utility, but what morality seems to need is not the gross notion of utility, but a notion more finely focused on the vital interests, the basic needs, the central human concerns, that create obligations. We have two concepts of well-being, one broad and the other narrow. Both, no doubt, have their uses. But only the second, it seems, suits morality.[1]

The nature of our job, therefore, has now changed. Until now we have wanted to explain the rough, broad, everyday notion of well-being that is used outside moral theory. Our question was, What account describes and clarifies that notion best? Now we want to find the possibly much narrower notion that suits moral theory best. So instead of starting with a notion that we might later fit into morality, we start with morality and ask which notion fits it. In the end, the only conclusive way to answer the question is to wait and see what happens when we build an adequate moral theory. But quite a lot can be done in a preliminary way.

Of course, it is too simple to speak of just two notions of well-being. There is merit in a notion somewhere between the broad and narrow ones, or in an eclectic concept that borrows from each. One quite attractive position, for instance, is that 'well-being' includes both basic needs and mere desires, but that needs have priority over mere desires.[2] These are all possibilities that we should now consider.

2. *The need account*

Needs are not a sub-class of desires. They are not, say, strong or widespread or central desires. While 'desire' is, 'need' is not an intentional verb; I can only need a thing if I need anything identical with it. So, while 'desire' is, 'need' is not tied to a subject's perception of the object; if I need a thing because it will cure my headache, it really will cure it.[3] Desires have to do with how a subject of experience looks out on the world; needs have to do with whether one thing is in fact a necessary condition of another. Needs do not even have to be attached to subjects of experience. More than just living things have needs. An element needs a free electron to conduct electricity.[4] Statements of need are of the form: x needs a in order to ϕ.[5] And even judgments about human needs are made from the same detached standpoint and take the same form. Humans need vitamin C to avoid scurvy. Terrorists need cool nerves to plant bombs.

But let us focus just on human needs, in particular on the needs that persons have because of their aims or ends. And here there are two sorts. Some of them are instrumental: they are needs we have because of the ends we happen to choose. Some, however, are basic: they are needs we all have just by being human. We need food to survive; though we might in special circumstances choose not to survive, in general survival is part of what human existence aims at and is not in any

ordinary sense an object of choice for us.[6] We usually speak of
basic needs as if they were not only basic but also absolute:
humans need food and rest and health—not *for* anything; they
just do. But these claims are still of the form: x needs a in order
to ϕ. Humans need food to survive, rest to go on functioning,
health to do much of anything.[7] The question whether
statements of basic needs are elliptical should not be confused
with the question whether they, like hypothetical imperatives,
depend upon the adoption of some purpose. If they do not fill
the last place ('in order to ϕ') they are elliptical; but they do
not depend upon ends that we just happen to adopt. The ends
that fill that last place are the normal ends of human life. The
rough explanation of basic needs is clear: they are what we
need to survive, to be healthy, to avoid harm, to function
properly.

It is obvious that instrumental needs as such have no moral
weight; some have and some have not. But basic needs, on the
other hand, seem to have a quite special moral importance
simply in virtue of being basic. For one thing, the presence of
the notions of health, harm, and proper function make
statements of basic need normative—in the proper, strict sense
of the term that is not the contrary of 'descriptive'. They all
involve a norm falling below which brings malfunction, harm,
or ailment. And that explains why basic needs have an
especially strong link with obligation: my ailment makes a
claim on others that my whims, hankerings, pleasures, and
even happiness cannot. And these claims on others are of a
strong sort; they depend not upon this or that person's
particular wish or purpose, but upon something deeper and
objective—human nature.

These last thoughts lead naturally to the following proposal:
*Well-being, at least that conception of it to be used as the interpersonal
measure for moral judgment, is the level to which basic needs are met.*[8]

3. *Can we give a tolerably clear sense to 'basic need'?*

The key notions of 'ailment', 'harm', and 'malfunction' are too
indeterminate as they stand to do the work expected of them
by the need account. It is no good repeating the obvious
example of food: certainly without food we shall ail. But it is

not enough that a few needs fall clearly one side or the other of the boundary of 'basic needs' if most sit right on the line. Is interesting work a basic need? Well, without it, alienation, a kind of social pathology, results. Is education a basic need? Without it, one's intellect will atrophy. And how much education?

There are many ways of introducing more determinateness. We could try developing the idea of a minimum provision. We need a certain amount (not just of resources, but also of liberty and leisure and education) to be able to make something valuable of our lives; what we have beyond that minimum amount may make our lives pleasanter or easier, but it is not necessary to the basic task of living a worthwhile life. If one does not have that amount, then one's life is maimed. I do not want to gainsay any of this. This notion of the minimum ingredients of a worthwhile human life is indispensable to moral theory; for one thing, we could give no adequate account of 'natural' or 'human' rights without it. Since the notion is indispensable, it has to be made determinate. But it is certainly not determinate enough yet. How much education would the basic kit contain? Literacy? Enough to ponder the meaning of life? And what level of health? When life expectancy is thirty, or fifty, or seventy? One does not make a notion such as 'harm' determinate merely by linking it (correctly) to notions such as 'minimum provision' or 'human rights', both of which suffer from the same indeterminateness. We need a principled way to make all the members of this interconnected set more determinate. In any case, this way of making 'basic need' more determinate may be making it too basic, too ungenerous, for it to perform its function in moral theory. If we want a notion of well-being to introduce considerations beyond the sort of minimum provision guaranteed by human rights, we had better not link it too closely to human rights.

We might, instead, try saying that basic needs are needs for the all-purpose means to whatever ends different individuals may choose.[9] This would be to develop one part of our explanation of 'basic needs', namely, that they connect with ends that we do not choose but which are characteristic of human existence. Each of us chooses his own life plan; none of us chooses the sorts of things that are necessary for living out any life plan. But though this is of help with one sort of indeterminateness (namely, with the content of basic needs; they are, it says, all-purpose means), it is of no help with another. How much of these all-purpose means are *needed*? If we answer 'Any quantity', we have abandoned the conception of basic need that linked with obligation, because that conception has to retain some sort of reference to a minimum.

Of course, many supporters of a need account readily admit its indeterminacy. They admit that basic needs have a large 'conventional' element.[10] But they say that, although the line between basic and non-basic needs may change as society changes, there is still a rationale for fixing the line wherever we do. For instance, we can banish the indeterminateness by defining a standard on people's natural expectations in that society; expectations adjust to possibilities, and a standard of minimum acceptable level of life, admittedly very rough, will naturally emerge.[11] Although that is true, it is not clear why we should give this standard any moral weight. If we did, we should merely detach well-being from objective features of human nature and connect it instead to accidental social changes that have no obvious moral significance. A person's natural expectations are formed by much more than the real possibilities that face him; they are formed too by how good his education happens to be or by how much hope traditions or forms of government have left him. Since this approach is unpromising, we might instead try defining the minimum as what *most* persons have.[12] A few persons may be relatively well off, but what virtually everyone has can be taken as the lowest level society now finds acceptable. But this is not really any better. In a primitive country which has just struck oil, most persons may be at grim subsistence level and a few in utter luxury, but the mere largeness of the number at subsistence level does not make it morally acceptable.

It is not that there are no reasons, given the level of resources in a particular society, to fix a minimum at any particular place—and to revise it as resources change. There are, to my mind, perfectly good ones. The question is, rather, how much these reasons are supplied by the notion of basic needs. There is usually a large gap between the least and the most that a society can provide. And as the society gets richer and richer, how do we decide where the minimum stops? Does the amount of education that is a 'basic need' just increase in pace? The most sympathetic interpretation of the suggestion that basic needs have a large 'conventional' element is that the key terms—'health', 'harm', 'proper function'—have to be given fresh interpretations in each social setting. But it is not just a matter of applying them to new conditions; their own conceptual resources are not enough to enable us to apply them at all. We cannot just interpret; we have to stipulate. As things stand, the notion of a 'basic need' is playing very little role.[13]

4. *The link between need and obligation*

This indeterminacy loosens the link between need and obligation. If, over a wide area, what is harm, ailment, and malfunction is a matter of arbitrary or conventional stipulation, then over that area what constitutes an obligation is also arbitrary or conventional, which would be odd. Or if, in order to make 'basic need' determinate, we must largely forget the notions 'harm', 'ailment', and 'malfunction' and bring in others, then it is the others that do the important work, not 'basic need'.

Another consideration that loosens the link is this: whatever in the end goes on the list of basic needs, there are likely to be persons who want things off the list more than they want things on it. A group of scholars may, with full understanding, prefer an extension to their library to exercise equipment for their health. And part of what makes us think that basic needs, such as health, are more closely linked to obligation than are desires is that basic needs seem the 'bread' of life and desires mere 'jam'. But an extension to the scholars' library may not seem like 'jam' to them. On the contrary, if the scholars' preference is sufficiently informed then the library is of greater value to them. But then to maintain that needs create obligations where mere desires do not, or that they create stronger obligations, is to say that we have an obligation, or a stronger one, to the scholars to give them what they themselves value less, which would be odd. Much of the attraction of the need account comes from our deep intuition that mere desires are morally lightweight. But the need account, though intended to exploit just this feature of desires, does not really do so. It leaves in the class of mere desires many heavyweight values—as values go, far weightier in many cases than needs, and weightier in a way that morality cannot ignore. Just as we have to work our way behind desires to considerations with greater moral significance, it seems that we shall have in some way to get behind needs too.

There are plenty of reasons to resist this conclusion, but they all trade, I think, on a confusion. We ought to distinguish the question, What are the moral standards for distribution? from the question, What are the standards appropriate to distribution on a large social scale by a state? A social worker, confronted with a cripple who asks for a record player of equal value to the wheelchair that the state offers him, will turn him down. Similarly perhaps it is quite right for a state to go in for jogging tracks but not for manuscripts for the scholars' library. Still, what we are after, in the first instance, are basic moral principles—the principles of individual morality as much as of political morality. For many reasons, the principles of political and of individual morality are likely to be somewhat different. If the cripple is my son, and he says that he would much prefer an education in philosophy to lifts and wheelchairs, and I am satisfied that he knows what is involved, I should use my resources as he wants. His would certainly not be everybody's scale of values, but he himself might find ignorance more crippling than bad legs.[14] The conventional notion of handicap does not, from a moral point of view, go very deep. We are nowhere near tolerably firm moral bedrock.[15]

So the link between needs and obligation, at closer look, is more tenuous than it first seems. Some harms are trivial. This is not just again the point that the notion of 'harm' is indeterminate. Even if we take the notion at its tightest and least disputable—for instance, we are certainly harmed if our health is damaged, particularly if the span of our life is reduced—some harms are still minor, some reductions in span still insignificant, compared to other things, not harms according to need accounts, that can blight life. Why should harm to health matter morally and help to learning not? Health on its own is not valuable; it is necessary for life, out of which each of us in his own case can make something valuable. But then what moral status has a necessary condition of a good life, in a case where achieving it will not allow one, and may prevent one, from having a good life? It is an odd conception of well-being that gives moral weight to trivial effects on what is only a necessary condition and no, or less, weight to what can be central to the state for which it is necessary.[16]

Of course, needs generally trump desires. What is at stake with basic needs generally matters much more to our lives than what is at stake with mere desires, and governments should concern themselves with basic needs and not at all, or at least not much, with mere desires. But it is a great mistake to move from that truth to the conclusion that needs as such count morally and desires as such do not, or anyway count less. Not all basic needs are morally important; some mere desires are. What we need are deeper categories. We have to get behind talk about needs and desires to their deeper significance in our lives. This, then, becomes a serious threat to need accounts, for if prudential value turns out to be that deeper category we shall be back with the informed-desire account.

5. *Avoiding distortions to moral thought*

We do not, as a matter of fact, form our plans of life as if they were, in effect, choices from a Good Fairy's List—'whatever you want, just say the word'. Our desires are shaped by our expectations, which are shaped by our circumstances. Any injustice in the last infects the first. There is no denying that some accounts of well-being will, therefore, distort moral thought in this way. Actual-desire accounts will. A moral theory should not use as its base persons' actual expectations. It has to get behind them to what are in some sense legitimate expectations.

The informed-desire account and the need account agree on this. They both appeal not to persons' actual desires but to what really would increase or decrease the quality of their lives. It does not matter that some persons have modest expectations; their informed desires include what they would want if they raised their sights, and their needs are anyway independent of what they happen to desire. To that extent the two accounts agree. After that, though, they diverge. The case for the need account is that the class of 'legitimate' expectations is smaller than any desire account will make it. We spoke a moment ago about one reason—in the end not a very strong reason—for thinking so; some informed desires seem to create no moral obligations. However, another reason, which we should turn to now, is that 'legitimate' seems already to incorporate elements of fairness, and that unless we use this tighter sense moral thought still runs the risk of being distorted.

Of course, someone might develop expensive tastes just to skew allocation in his direction, but that cannot in the end be the important point.[17] What is important is that many persons, when informed, develop expensive desires for perfectly ordinary, even admirable, reasons—simply because they are necessary to what they see as living a good life. Someone dedicated to advancing knowledge, for instance, will come to want expensive libraries and laboratories. Why should these desires be excluded from 'legitimate' expectations? One answer is that we should otherwise give too much weight to chance, which has no moral standing.[18] It is true that if we do not exclude them, whether we maximize well-being or make it equal, then someone with expensive desires will get more of society's resources than someone without them. Certain abilities, such as great intelligence, are in part the result of the genetic lottery, and they lead naturally to certain aims in life, such as advancing knowledge, that happen to be expensive. But this case for excluding them runs into trouble over the indeterminateness of 'basic need'. Some of the ends of life adopted by an especially intelligent person are as much needs as desires. If giving more to him is unfair, the unfairness is likely to appear on the need account. And in any case, it is not true that these expensive desires are largely a matter of chance. Some persons have expensive desires because of ways of life that they have chosen after reflection. It is no good advising them to develop less expensive desires, although it is true that they could, because these desires are essential to what they see as making life valuable. Giving these desires weight is not, contrary to this argument, giving weight to chance. And treating these desires as matters of chance is seeing them too much as if they were tastes. Applied to simple tastes, the argument has some force; one can expect a person to look after the consequences of his expensive tastes. But applied to central prudential values—non-idiosyncratic, well-grounded, essential to human flourishing, not however basic needs—it has much less force.[19]

Is the point, rather, that unless we narrow 'legitimate' expectations, one person's vital interests can never be made secure from the swollen demands of others?[20] Is the narrowed sense of 'legitimate' the dike that morality must erect around a vital interest to protect it against inundation by aggregations of large demands of non-vital interests? If so, the need account is no answer; basic needs—health, for instance—can be less vital that non-needs. In any case, whether the protection is of each person's title to an equal share of all-purpose means or, more modestly, to a minimum acceptable level of life, it seems far too strong. Some societies do consciously satisfy the desires of minorities for libraries and universities, at the expense of, say, the level of road safety. Nearly everyone thinks it right to do so, even though it means that persons will lose their lives through no fault of their own who would not have done if non-needs had not been favoured over an all-purpose means or over a constituent of the minimum acceptable level. We cannot really assess this case until we determine exactly how strong morality should make this protection. That takes a well-worked-out, well-tested moral theory. The case often comes down to the claim that, to put it roughly, since an individual has to have strong protection, moral theory has to use the narrowed sense of 'legitimate' provided by the need account. But once we think for a moment, it is not at all obvious that the protection should be as strong as the one provided by the need account.

Or is the explanation this, that moral theory should concern itself with only all-purpose means in order to stay neutral between different persons' conceptions of the good life?[21] Equality of opportunity is often interpreted, especially in modern political life, in a way that makes it morally unattractive. It is thought of as being satisfied just by bringing to some starting-post persons who are unequal in education and influence and, unless their genes have been tampered with, also unequal in intelligence and health, and then letting competition largely settle who gets what. It is unattractive, because it totally ignores the demands of a deeper form of equality. We are all equal as moral persons; our fates matter equally; our fates should not be left to the mercy of *these* sorts of chances. Perhaps the same defence should be made of all-purpose means. Our fates matter equally; that you have a chance to make something valuable out of your life matters just as much as that I do. It does not matter that I think, perhaps rightly, that your conception of the good life is less defensible than mine; it does not matter that your life will in fact turn out less valuable than mine. In a deep sense, it is still just as important as mine. It is this deep sense of equality that the narrowed sense of 'legitimate' can be seen as designed to capture. If well-being is confined to basic needs or universal human concerns or all-purpose means, then morality will remain neutral between conceptions of the good.

However, this neutrality, though attractive at first glance, is pretty meagre. Can any moral theory get by with such a thin notion of well-being? Perhaps a government has good reason to remain largely neutral between conceptions of a good life. None the less, a father in distributing resources between his children, one of whom will simply waste them, ought to take this fact into account. And even a government cannot do its job if it ignores all values except basic needs. There comes a point when threat to some basic need, such as health, is so slight compared to what else is at stake, as not really to matter. But how can a government decide when it does not matter without deciding how valuable the competing value is? How can a government decide when to stop improving road safety and divert resources to art or education or libraries? It can make no sensible judgment about when that point is reached without making judgments about how valuable art, education, and libraries are. And it cannot make those judgments without implicitly making judgments about the relative value of at least some individual, non-neutral conceptions of the good.

Throughout these various explanations of a restriction to 'legitimate' expectations, questions of scale continually crop up. Some principles are especially plausible on the large social scale. It makes sense to concentrate on moral principles, especially principles of justice, that apply on the social scale, if, as many think, the features that stand out clearly on the large social scale turn out to be essential, though less obviously so, on the small interpersonal scale as well. For instance, governments lack knowledge of each citizen's conception of the good life; to get it would require intolerable intrusions on privacy; and in any case the information would usually be too unreliable and too little agreed upon to serve as a basis for interpersonal comparisons for social decisions that will command assent. All of this clearly points to governments' being in large measure neutral between different conceptions of the good. Then we may find different and deeper reasons—for instance, the deeper notion of equal treatment that we have just looked at—for neutrality in individual morality as well. But once these deeper reasons begin to look dubious, we should look again at the whole question of scale. Perhaps much of what is appropriate on the social level is not essential to a principle's being a moral principle and so will not appear on the small interpersonal scale. We are trying to establish *moral* principles, principles that are relevant—perhaps in different forms—on any scale. Certainly, what matters on the social scale (chance factors such as degree of knowledge and agreement) is often irrelevant on the small scale.[22] So we have to try to get behind these differences of scale as well.

6. *A more flexible need account*

Most need accounts make the mistake of being too rigid; they rank basic needs above mere desires, regardless of the levels or amounts of satisfaction of each that are in question, which is implausible. That was the moral of the story of the scholars' choice between a library extension and exercise equipment.

But this mistake can be corrected. We can introduce flexibility into need accounts by introducing a new notion: how important or vital or urgent a basic need is in a particular case.[23] A basic need, we can say, is generally less important the more it is already met, and at some level of satisfaction it will cease to be important at all. We can make how important it is also depend upon the level of satisfaction of other basic needs; if my needs for liberty and minimum material provision are not met, and are so unlikely ever to be met that life is not worth living, then health must matter less too. And if the amount to which a basic need will be met is only slightly affected by some change, we can regard the change as of little importance. We can then amend the need account of well-being: *well-being is the level to which basic needs are met so long as they retain importance.*

We have not yet got a general account of importance (we should, for instance, need to define an interpersonal use), but even as far as we have gone problems start to emerge. Important to what? The answer must in some form or other be: important to how good one's life is. But if we leave the explanation as wide as that, the need account is at risk of being absorbed by an account of prudential value. Yet it is hard to see how to make the explanation narrower and still have a notion of importance that does the work required of it. There must be a point, we all agree, at which the moral demands of health are fully met and beyond which we are not obliged to go. There must also be a point at which the demands of health, although not fully met, are so little affected that they matter less than some mere desire. But how do we decide where these points are? With eyes wide open, the scholars prefer a few more books to a few extra weeks' longevity. Is this basic need still important enough to trump this mere desire? It seems impossible to form any estimate of how important the need is without appeal to the same standard that gives us the value of the mere desire—namely, how each affects the overall quality of life. And there seems to be no criterion by which to decide whether the demands of health are fully met, no matter how minimal we think these demands are, without seeing what else, including mere desires, people value and how greatly they value them—in short, by seeing how all the competing options affect the overall quality of life. It is unlikely that the conception of *importance* can be, as the account requires it to be, independent of our general conception of prudential value.[24]

The introduction of flexibility into the need account really takes us behind the importance of need to deeper values, to the broader base of prudential values of which basic needs are just a part. All basic needs will have their place, and their importance marked, in the hierarchy of prudential values. The notion of a basic need is attractive because it goes deeper than the notion of desires. It goes behind the actual desires to the concerns that give them importance; needs connect more securely to the real stuff of well-being than actual desires do. But informed desires, as they figure in prudential values, go deeper than basic needs, as it is clear that we must.

7. *Neutrality, objectivity, and moral depth*

Suppose that we drop need accounts. There are other, and to my mind more plausible, objective accounts.

All need accounts rest on a distinction between, on the one hand, things that we aim at simply as normal human beings rather than as the particular human beings we are, things that are both necessary to and sufficient for a recognizably human existence, and, on the other hand, things that, as the individuals we are, we choose to go for. Keeping to the senses we used before,[25] 'subjective' standards are those that depend upon tastes, attitudes, or interests, while 'objective' standards are those that do not. So the argument for regarding the need account as objective is fairly easy and straightforward. Its standard rests on aims flowing from human nature and not on any flowing from a person's particular tastes, attitudes, or interests.[26] On this view, what is objective is also universal and neutral between differing conceptions of the good life.[27] But there is no good reason why what is objective has also to be either universal or neutral. Why not think that behind our varying commitments to particular ways of life lie objective standards by appeal to which we can, among other things, settle the value of these commitments?

Admittedly, the need account is not incompatible with this wider form of objectivism. But some of the appeal of the need account comes from the idea that these neutral, universal values are the only ones that could be objective. The root idea, I think, is this. Once we get outside the realm of basic needs, we are in the domain of mere desires: in this domain aims rest on the tastes, attitudes, and interests that we happen to have;

value is contingent upon our having certain desires.[28] But this thought gets its plausibility from treating variant, personal values as if they came from tastes or attitudes that we just happen to have, or from commitments that we blindly make. But most of our non-universal, non-neutral values are not at all like that. They are not capricious or accidental or arbitrary. Most of them are not a matter of taste. And it is odd to think even that we choose them; generally they choose us, by being the sorts of values that we have only to perceive clearly to adopt as goals.[29] A person might have as a central, animating goal of his life achieving some understanding of life itself. Certainly not everyone has this goal; it is a paradigm of a variant, personal goal. None the less, everyone may be worse off for not achieving this understanding. And it may be a goal that the rest of us should foster, even at some cost to health and survival. And the value does not depend upon desires in a way that makes it 'subjective': it, like many other values, owes is status as a value to its nature, the proper perception of which would lead anyone to adopt it as his goal.

So the most plausible form of objectivism allows that many values—many more than the ones linked to basic needs—are objective. The thought behind forming them into a standard of well-being would be this: when they appear in a person's life, then whatever his tastes, attitudes, or interests, his life is better.

However, if that standard is taken to mean that we can measure changes in a person's well-being just by the amount that he realizes objective values, it must be wrong. As we have seen,[30] there may be an unusual person for whom autonomy sets up such great anxieties for it not to be worth it to him. This is not to deny autonomy its objectivity; it is not to deny that it is a universal value; it still allows that autonomy would, other things being equal, make his life better. It is only that an objective-list account has to made more flexible, more sensitive to individual differences. It has also to be made more concrete; one objective value is enjoyment but what any particular person enjoys is very much a matter of the particular person he is. In just the way that we can make a fetish of goods—by using them, and not their effect on our lives, as our index of well-being—we can make a fetish of values: even objective universal values matter only by making individual lives better.

We have to find some mode of deliberation about values that sees them as they fit into particular lives. The manifestation of these objective values in particular lives is the deepest measure of value. And that again takes objective accounts very close to prudential value theory.

Objective accounts have obvious strengths. They get close to what really matters morally, certainly closer than the flux of actual desires gets us. But the need account is not rich enough. The simple objective-list account is not flexible or sensitive enough. Informed desires include both basic needs and the items on the objective list; they give them structure as prudential values. There remains, however, the persistent embarrassment of the desire account's over-extension; not all of one person's desires make claims on other persons. Another strength of objective accounts is their concern with the special demands on a *moral* notion of well-being. But we should not approach moral theory in too narrow a way. The structure of moral theory may, in the end, provide good grounds for counting some informed desires and discounting others. If so, then what moral theory anyway independently provides does not have also to be built into our notion of well-being.

IV

PERFECTIONISM AND THE
ENDS OF LIFE

1. *Prudential perfectionism*

WHEN we move on to perfectionist accounts of well-being, we change the nature of our exercise once again. Desire accounts aim at capturing everything that comes into human well-being. Objective accounts aim at explaining a narrower conception of well-being, one thought (wrongly, I have argued) to be needed by *moral* theory. Perfectionist accounts aim at explaining a notion not clearly moral in a modern sense, closer at points to prudential value theory, but more concerned with what a good life is for humanity in general. Desire accounts focus on a person in all his individuality; objective accounts focus on an index of goods that are good to everyone, regardless of the differences between them; perfectionist accounts focus on a species ideal.

At least, those are the differences that strike us at first sight. But just as the more adequate we make desire accounts and objective accounts the less clear the boundaries between them become, the more plausible perfectionist accounts get the less sharp are the differences.[1] This is because there are many different 'perfectionist' beliefs, some a lot more plausible than others. The historically most important one says nothing in the first instance about how we ought morally to act but tells us rather what makes an individual life good—a form of 'prudential perfectionism', in contrast to 'moral perfectionism'.[2] It says that there is an ideal form for human life to take, a form in which human nature flourishes and reaches perfection. And it offers an account of well-being strikingly different from either desire or need accounts: *the level of well-being for any person is in direct proportion to how near that person's life gets to this ideal.*

But is there a *single* ideal? Well, let us start by saying so. We can say that this single ideal may manifest itself in lives that outwardly look quite different (butcher, baker, philosopher, etc.); all that we have to insist on is that, to the extent that the ideal is really manifested in them, they will all be, on a higher level of generality, the same sort of life.

In the most famous version of this argument, Aristotle is confident that there is a single ideal because he believes that there is a single human nature. And it is hard to see what other reason one could have. Aristotle's own teleological conception of the single human nature, however, is a good deal less obvious. He believes that everything has its own natural function or task (*ergon*), the performance of which is its final end.[3] So he sets off on a search for the task or end of human beings. It is not simply life, he says, because plants have that too; nor is it sentience, because animals have that. It is, rather, rational activity.[4] But, as Aristotle is well aware, the expression 'rational activity' covers different things. It covers pure rationality, divorced from everyday life, the contemplation of truths; and it covers practical rationality, weighing the various demands of everyday life and striking a reasonable balance between them. These two forms of rationality leave Aristotle rather in two minds, so he ends up giving a two-part answer.[5] A human's supreme function, he says, is pure contemplation; that is the peak of human existence.[6] But the secondary human function, he adds, is living in conformity with practical reason. Not everybody, he allows, can attain the supreme end or, if they are able, sustain it for long; so the secondary end is more relevant to most persons' aspirations, a lower but more realistic peak of human existence.[7]

Neither of Aristotle's answers is persuasive. The first is clearly dubious. It pictures human flourishing as a God-like review of eternal truths as they march in orderly formation before the mind. This passive, narrow, austere, even rather boring activity would not go far towards making life valuable or giving it substance. There are many other activities that are also valuable in themselves: enjoying oneself, accomplishing things, deep personal relations. And it is not that one of *them* is the single peak either; no one of them on its own would do. Only a quite relentless, unsubtle application of a teleological conception of existence could yield such an unlikely result.

So we ought to shift to the far more plausible notion of rational activity not as pure contemplation, but as the practical weighing and balancing of the elements of a good life. Anyway, Aristotle's suggestion that this practical rationality is a matter of second-best does not carry conviction, because even if we accept the assumption that human life has a single supreme function to which all others are subordinate, it is as likely to be a blend of contemplation and action as contemplation alone. And 'rationality', in the practical sense in which we are now to understand it, is not the content of the ideal life (or else a version of the objection to the first conception of rationality would apply), but the capacity to determine what it should be. This shift to a formal conception of practical rationality, though more plausible as an account of the role of rationality in an ideal life, does not really help to advance an account of that life. The ideal life is one containing the right balance of virtues. Practical rationality is the procedure to decide what that is. But the ideal is not exercising our capacity to strike the right balance; the ideal *is* the balance. When we look for the ideal human life, we are looking for its content. Practical rationality—for example knowledge, autonomous choice—is part of its content, but only along with, for instance, enjoyment, accomplishment, and deep personal relations. So the shift to a formal conception of practical rationality is no improvement, because we do not want a formal account of the ideal. The first (material) Aristotelian answer is the right sort of account, but it is implausible. The second (formal) Aristotelian answer is plausible, but it is the wrong sort of account.

Nor is there a *single* right balance. The right balance is very likely to vary from person to person. Autonomy is valuable to everyone, but, as we saw,[8] a particular person might be made so anxious by being autonomous that it would be best for him not to be. That, admittedly, is an extreme case, but most of us, in some way or other, to some degree or other, fall short of the ideal. Certain of our capacities and skills are more limited than normal, and certain others more highly developed, and the ideal life for one of us would not be ideal for another. Even if we ignored the damage that the accidents of life can inflict on human capacities, even if we confined attention to the natural range of normal human capacities, there would still be no single ideal life. The natural and normal range would include an artist creating beauty, a researcher discovering truth, a politician realizing the good, a citizen tending his own garden. There is no one balance of prudential values in all of these lives, unless the description of the balance is so general ('the balance that realizes most value') as to be vacuous. And when we add the reality that most of us, as a result of the accidents of upbringing, have developed our native capacities to different degrees, then the perfectionist account of well-being seems not at all plausible. Your well-being and mine are not in direct proportion to how close our lives get to a single ideal life. There is no such ideal. And even if there were, it would be too insensitive to variations between persons to be the basis of a measure of each individual's well-being.

Are there, then, *several* ideals for human life? After all, one does not have to be a monist to be a perfectionist. One can accept a plurality of values, not just because for one person there are irreducibly many different values but also because for different persons there are irreducibly different ideal forms of life. Different forms of life (the artist, the researcher, the politician, the private citizen tending his garden), to the extent that they are good, might instantiate one or other of these ideals.

A pluralist form of perfectionism would have to say more than merely that there is an ideal life for each person, because there is nothing in that claim to make it especially 'perfection-ist'. Anyone with a conception of prudential value would say as much: the ideal life for each person is the one that is most prudentially valuable. To turn this sort of pluralism into a form of 'perfectionism' we should have to limit the ideal lives in some way, most plausibly by making them depend upon a certain number of kinds of human nature. But that is a tall order. People have different capacities and skills, which they possess in many different combinations and degrees. It would not be too tall an order to draw up a list of prudential values: accomplishment, enjoyment, deep personal relations, etc. We might even be able to complete the list. We can say that

persons with different combinations of capacities, or capacities
to different degrees, would be better off with different proportions of these prudential values. And we can perhaps go so far
as to give an account in the case of a particular person of what
balance of those values would give him the best life. But there
seems nothing in between the highly general list of prudential
values and the very particular judgment about an individual
life. For instance, there seems to be no place for an account of
a certain number of different ideal forms of human life, made
ideal by being the flourishing of a certain number of different
kinds of human nature. What we lack is a rationale for the
division of human nature into two or three (or fifteen or
twenty) different kinds.

2. *Moral perfectionism*

Perfectionism grows naturally from a prudential claim about
ideal human lives into a moral claim about what we ought to
do to promote them.

One form of moral perfectionism might be seen as a
development of Aristotle's first conception of human function,
namely rationality as pure contemplation. Aristotle's own
view seems to have been that very few persons can manage
pure contemplation, but that this sort of life of the mind is the
very peak of human existence. It is an easy step from
that—though not one Aristotle took—to saying that therefore
that sort of life ought to be enhanced above all others. It is the
Superman version of perfectionism: make the peaks as high as
possible, even if only one or two persons will reach them;
maximize height.[9] It has an obnoxiously élitist sound to
modern ears, but one does not have to go back at all far in
history to find it regarded as natural. Nietzsche's view that we
should all live for the good of 'the rarest and most valuable
specimens', like Socrates and Goethe, might be thought a
bizarre exception.[10] But the young Bertrand Russell could
write without a blush that an equitable distribution of wealth
'might, if things didn't improve extraordinarily, cut off all the
flowers of civilisation. The Shelleys and Darwins and so on ...
And surely one Darwin is more important than thirty million
working men and women.'[11]

We all find the Superman version unacceptable.[12] And that is not mere modern dogma. The Superman version is arid in spirit, immoral in recommendation, and, in the end, confused in formulation. Imagine an obsessional museum director who wants, say, only the one supreme Rembrandt and will pass up all the rest of the Rembrandts in the world to get it. For him, the single supreme Rembrandt would be better than any number of other Rembrandts, whatever their quality or variety of achievement, no matter how close many of them came to that single best, no matter even whether in aggregate they constituted something more important and more valuable. Even as an approach to art, it lacks any breadth. But writing off less than supreme works of art is a far cry from writing off less than supreme human lives. The museum director's policy would be merely narrow, but the comparable policy with human lives would be monstrous. There is agreement between moral theories that no theory is *moral* unless it grants some form of equal respect and unless it justifies trade-off of one person's good against another's by appeal to a certain range of human values. What is interesting about the Superman version is that it detaches the notion of perfection from prudential value, moral value, even aesthetic value. It makes the notion, in the end, unintelligible. Perfectionism urges us to go not for quantity of value, but for the height of its realization. But how are we to measure 'height'? We might have had a coherent account of it, if Aristotle's programme of finding the supreme function succeeded and if, in addition, he showed that 'supreme' in his sense was also a reason for action. But the programme certainly fails. For instance, if Aristotle's argument is that pure contemplation is our supreme function because it is the purest form of rationality, then it succeeds only if 'pure' is taken to mean something like 'most detached from effort to reach practical goals', in which case there is no reason to accept a move from 'purest' to any conclusion about how we ought to behave. What human achievement has greatest 'height'? The contemplation of truth? Why not the discovery of truth? Why not the creation of beauty? Why not a full, varied, and satisfying life? We can, of course, appeal to prudential value theory for answers to these questions, but that would be to admit, as I think we must, that 'height' is not a coherent independent notion.[13]

The Superman version ruins a good point by drastic overstatement. It is entirely plausible to think that there are values that represent human existence at its very best, and rationality and creativity are obvious candidates. So it is plausible also to think that we ought, either absolutely or relatively, to favour lives of learning and art in which they are embodied. Perhaps the good point is that we should go, not for the highest peak, but instead for either as many *lives* of this sort as possible or the highest aggregate *achievement* in art and learning. This is still élitism, but of a welcoming, proselytizing, non-exclusive sort. This is the Spread of Civilization version: work for a multitude of faithful rather than one or two saints.

It is certainly not obnoxious; there are even elements of truth to it. But it is not yet the good point buried in perfectionism. Its serious defect is that it picks out certain (few) features that make life good—for instance, knowledge and beauty—and elevates them above the others, and the collapse of prudential forms of perfectionism puts this whole procedure in question. Why are these few features to be preferred to the rest? They do not constitute ideal forms of life, because there are no such things. There are, it is true, features valuable to any life, but their value can be explained only within a theory of prudential value, where they are neither the only nor the supreme values. So to promote one part of what makes life valuable over the rest makes no sense as a moral policy. There is no form of prudential perfectionism that generates an acceptable standard of well-being. And once the link to well-being is cut, there is no longer any reason to move from prudential perfectionism to moral perfectionism.

Still, there is one more version of moral perfectionism—the most plausible of all, I think—and it escapes this criticism. It does so by not resting its case on a shaky substantive account of ideal forms of life. Aristotle wavered not only between pure contemplation and practical rationality as the supreme func-tion of human life, but also between material and formal accounts of practical rationality. It was his teleological metaphysics that pulled him towards the first option in each pair, but the most sympathetic interpretation would in each case choose the second. So we should regard practical rationality, and the virtues in which it displays itself, not as a substantive account of the ideal life, but as a formal account of the modes of approach that will fix on the best life. Moral perfectionism, thus, does not rest on the description of what the ideal life consists in; rather both are generated by the complex ways of functioning that make up human excellences —by display of wisdom, courage, temperance, industry, humility, hope, charity, justice, etc. Or, rather, it is not that practical rationality fixes separately the content both of prudential good and of moral obligation, but that it treats living a good life as a whole, not separating prudence and morality. Indeed, what many persons find attractive in this version is that it treats *good* as penetrated thoroughly by *right* and that it makes prudence part of a whole in which it is subordinated to morality. It sees acting rightly as acting in accordance with human excellences, the virtues; and acting that way, it says, is *also* the flourishing of human life. Another attraction for many persons is that it offers no formulas, no general principles, for moral decision; it sees moral decision not as the fitting of rules or laws onto experience but as the working out of human excellences as each particular case requires.

This Virtue version of moral perfectionism sees perfectionism as an account of the perfect way for a human to function—the spirit in which to approach life, meet its trials, decide on goals and action. But for all its plausibility, it is still not the good point buried in perfectionism. It tries to make an account of the virtues do more work than it can. It proposes an occasion-by-occasion approach, but we have never been given, and cannot easily find, an explanation of what this approach is that gets beyond the vaguely suggestive.[14] No account of the virtues seems rich enough to provide answers to all the questions that constitute the core of moral concern. For that we need a moral theory with more, and a different kind of, content. For instance, the virtues include justice, but justice is not merely approaching other persons in a certain spirit, respecting their interests. We have to know in what such respect consists. What restrictions, if any, are there on trade-offs of one person's interests against another's? What are our obligations to the Third World or to future generations? How partial to family and friends can one be and remain moral? When are abortion and euthanasia permitted? Is the policy of nuclear deterrence immoral? To fill out the account of virtues for it to answer these questions would be to abandon it purely as an account of practical rationality. Filling it out would require determining the sort of content for moral 'principles' that the formal account of 'perfect human functioning' was meant to do without. The virtues are 'corrective', serving us in such ways as bolstering our defences at likely points of temptation or increasing our spirit when it is likely to let us down.[15] Getting our motivation in good order is a large part of the moral battle. But it is only part. We also need answers to certain central questions.

3. *The ends of life*

The place to start putting content into our theories is with prudential values. Up till now, we have talked mostly of their formal features. But we certainly have also to know what substantive prudential values there are. For one thing, moral theory cannot get on without that knowledge. We cannot begin to work out a substantive theory of rights—what rights there actually are—without a substantive theory of goods. We need to know what is at the centre of a valuable human life and so requires special protection. And we cannot decide anything about the permissibility or extent of trade-offs between well-being and rights, or between one right and another, without knowing what makes them rights.

What sort of deliberation goes on in deciding the ends of life? How can claims about them be criticized and assessed?

From time to time, I have used accomplishment as an example of one of the ends of life, and let me take it now as my chief example. The rough, intuitive case for it is plain. We all want to do something with our lives, to act in a way that gives them some point and substance. That much is clear. But it is harder to see the sort of accomplishment that would have this status. It would have to be kept distinct from simply wanting one's life to be valuable. It cannot be part of what makes life valuable if it is identified with the whole. And the idea behind accomplishment is that *doing* something with one's life is part, but only part, of what makes it valuable. It would also have to be kept distinct from bare achievement. The compulsive achiever may reach the goals he sets himself, but that need not be the sort of accomplishment that we are after. The achiever may simply love competition and derive great joy from success in the contest, but that, though valuable as enjoyment, is not quite accomplishment. In any case, bare achievements, though difficult, can themselves lack point or substance; walking on one's hands from Oxford to London is a remarkable deed, of the Guinness Book of Records sort, but itself lacks the worth that is part of accomplishment. This shows too that the development and exercise of skills, though usually satisfying, is not accomplishment either. Nor can winning respect and admiration be taken as a sign of accomplishment. It is very easy to confuse what others, even what recognized authorities, admire with what is a real accomplishment, and then to confuse having accomplishment as one's goal with merely wanting respect and admiration. And it is terribly easy to confuse respect for one's accomplishment with respect and affection for one's person, and to want to accomplish something for the personal affection it is thought, usually wrongly, to win. Accomplishment, as a value, is valuable independently of its consequences, and it is not accomplishment that a person values if what he is after is one or other of what he supposes its consequences to be. Accomplishment need not be of something lasting. Developing a treatment for a major disease would be a great accomplishment, even if it were quickly succeeded by a better one. Nor does it have to be of something of wide or public importance. A person who lives a rich, rewarding personal life could make out of it, say, a private work of the art of life, and he could rightly regard it as no mean accomplishment.

This is one kind of reasoning that claims about ends are clearly subject to, the definitional. It whittles away what only looks like, or is confused with, the end itself. After whittling away, there might be nothing left; or there might be no new value, only an old one now separated from confusing appearances.

But why, once a candidate value is tolerably well defined, accept it as a value? Well, all that one can do to show that it is not a value is to keep whittling away—to show that what makes a candidate value look attractive is something else with which it is confused, or is something meretricious, which when isolated and seen plain is no longer attractive. But once all the whittling is done, one must just make up one's mind: is accomplishment, now that it is separated off and seen plain, worth going for? It is not that this is the end to all possible argument. It is just that, once the whittling is done, the argument has to become more radical. Accomplishment, like all prudential values, connects with many other values: what is accomplished has, by definition, to be worthwhile: it has to be the sort of thing that gives life point or substance. But then, to ask a radical question, does anything give life point? When we step far enough back from our everyday concerns, when we see life *sub specie aeternitatis*, is anything worthwhile? We do not even need the view *sub specie aeternitatis*; the view *de lecto mortis* is enough. But from death-beds a few things also look more important than ever. The arguments that nothing is worthwhile, though certainly important, seem all to rest on one confusion or other. Why is it all worthless? Because sooner or later we shall die and be forgotten, was Tolstoy's answer before returning to Christianity; therefore nothing can come of life, nothing is worth doing, there is no true accomplishment.[16] Because the constant increase of entropy ensures 'the vast death of the solar system', Russell added.[17] However, if merely my death makes my life meaningless, eternal life would restore its meaning. But if it would, then my life itself is not the problem. Why should more time allow something to come of life? If something can come with more time, it can come with less. Mere time cannot make the difference. And if it is not eternal life that answers but only eternal bliss, temporal bliss ought to answer a bit.[18] These steps back provide no new perspective. Radical argument about values is certainly possible,[19] but one can wonder whether all of the steps back that it might come up with are not also, like this sample of them, steps into confusion, steps off the edge of coherent talk about values.[20]

The final results of deliberation of these sorts—the proposals that emerge from the definitional sort, and the lack of effective challenge from the radical sort—are, I think, a list of prudential values something like this.

(a) *Accomplishment.*

(b) *The components of human existence.* Choosing one's own course through life, making something out of it according to one's own lights, is at the heart of what it is to lead a human existence. And we value what makes life human, over and above what makes it happy. What makes life 'human', in the distinctly normative sense the word has here, is not a simple thing. The systematic way to understand its complexities is to understand the complexities of 'agency'. One component of agency is deciding for oneself. Even if I constantly made a mess of my life, even if you could do better if you took charge, I would not let you do it. Autonomy has a value of its own. Another component is having the basic capabilities that enable one to act: limbs and senses that work, the minimum material goods to keep body and soul together, freedom from great pain and anxiety. Another component is liberty: the freedom to read, to listen to others; the absence of obstacles to action in those areas of our life that are the essential manifestations of our humanity—our speech, worship, and associations. To value our humanity is to value all of these components.

(c) *Understanding.* I have already argued that practical rationality is not one of the things that constitutes a good life, but that it is, rather, the capacity that allows us to identify what makes it good. Still, even putting practical rationality aside, there is something important left. Simply knowing about oneself and one's world is part of a good life. We value, not as an instrument but for itself, being in touch with reality, being free from muddle, ignorance, and mistake.

(d) *Enjoyment.* We value pleasures, the perception of beauty, absorption in and appreciation of nature—the enjoyment of the day-to-day textures of life.

(e) *Deep personal relations.* Personal relations can make life worse, or not affect its quality at all, but when they become deep, authentic, reciprocal relations of friendship and love, then they have a value apart from the pleasure and benefit they give. They fit Aristotle's model of the human *ergon* better even than his own candidate, rationality; they in themselves go a long way towards filling and completing life.[21]

This sort of deliberation about ultimate values, about ends, is consistent with any major moral theory. It is a misunderstanding to think, for instance, that utilitarianism limits deliberation to means-end. The conception of a self free from the inexorable working of appetite and taste, capable of assessing ends and choosing those that, by their nature, deserve to be chosen, is available to all major moral theories. Conceptions of the self do not serve to distinguish the good theories among them from the bad.[22]

4. *How morality fits into prudence*

Do ethical push and ethical pull eventually meet?

Generally, the more mature one's prudential values are, the more important among them is living morally. Perhaps the end towards which this maturation approaches (not asymptotically) is the intersection of ethical pull and ethical push. Perhaps the very finest life for a person to live, from his own personal point of view, however testing his circumstances, is a fully moral life. Certainly the most secure and stable condition for morality is when a person's conception of the right is rooted, not in inhibitions and self-denial, but in flourishing and self-fulfilment. And a sense of moral right belongs to any sensible person's good: peace with oneself and others, stability and richness in personal relations, fulfilment, even agreement with nature—certainly with human nature, possibly even with a moral reality.

But I doubt that ethical push and ethical pull will ever meet. Sometimes the idea that they do is just a confusion. Moral reasons do trump purely prudential reasons; morality does eventually take over. But that does not mean that push and pull meet or that moral reasons are generated out of prudential ones. It shows only that once our various reasons for action—prudence, morality, etiquette, and the rest—are brought together in a single hierarchy of reasons for action, moral reasons come out on top. But we want to know something different. When we organize the various things that make an individual life better into a hierarchy of prudential values, does morality then come out on top? Does it, in cases of conflict, trump, perhaps even extinguish all other prudential values?[23]

So the strong argument we need, which indeed many will make, runs something like this. There is no coherent concept of *good* in conflict with *right*; *right* is prior to *good*; *good* has sense only within limits laid down by *right*. Therefore, it would make no sense to say that morality required a sacrifice of good. Suppose I come upon several children trapped in a blazing building. Suppose, too, I ought to try and save them (for whatever reasons are strong enough to create an obligation: it is one life against many; I am risking fewer years than they have ahead of them; I am responsible for them). I might reason: I could well die in the attempt; my life—if I funk doing what I ought—would still be a lot better than no life at all; by funking it I would, of course, suffer terrible guilt and remorse, but I would eventually face up to them and go on living what altogether would be a good life. But this strong claim means that I cannot intelligibly reason like this. The moral failure would make it impossible for it to be a good life; it could not be a better life than one without the moral failure. It could not, no matter how small the moral failure, and how great the disaster to me.[24]

It is an extravagant claim, and one that again, I think, rests on a confusion. We need to split the notion of 'a good life' into two. There is a sense in which moral failure, being a failure to act for the best reasons, is a falling off from an ideal—and not just in the trivial, circular sense that it is not the most moral or most rational life. It is not the finest life: the life one would hope to lead. But there is another conception of a good life, a life one would hope to lead. It is the sense that appears in judgments such as that it is better to be moral *and* alive than to be moral and thereby lose one's life, or that it is sometimes better to fail morally and stay alive than not to fail and thereby lose one's life. And it is this second conception that should be the base for judgments of well-being in moral theory. This is not at all paradoxical. We want as the base for at least some moral judgment considerations of quality of life that are restricted to the prudential values on my list. And being moral enters that list only in a limited way: only by being part of what it is to be at peace with one's neighbour and with oneself. This sort of peace is a prudential value, and when morality enters consideration under that heading it takes on prudential weight. But as a purely moral consideration, not subsumable under one of these headings, it has no prudential weight. We do not want to lose this prudential notion of a good life by merging it altogether with morality. And we do not for reasons of moral theory; *it* needs the notion.

5. *What is the good point buried in perfectionism?*

The good, almost unavoidable, point in perfectionism is this. There are prudential values that are valuable in any life. There are not enough of them, nor is a specific balance between them prescribable universally enough, to constitute a *form of life*. They are the values on the list of the ends of life. As we have seen, our skills and capacities differ too much for all of us to want to realize them in quite the same balance. Indeed sometimes they should not be realized by a particular person at all (e.g. autonomy, when it sets up great anxieties in a particular person). Persons differ not so much in basic values as in their capacity to realize them. Some basic values (e.g. enjoyment) depend in part on persons' individual, varying tastes, but not many depend on taste. The values on the list of the ends of life provide us with an important standard for judging most (ordinary) human lives. They let us say, roughly, though only roughly, how good the life is and how it could be better. They do, because they rest on general features of human nature; for example, autonomy is central to living a *human* existence, and we all value our humanity.[25] Finally, these values are not restricted to all-purpose means to a good life. They include accomplishment, deep personal relations, and the enjoyment of beauty, none of which is a means to the realization of one's own particular conception of a good life, but is, or should be, a central part of that conception.

This is the unavoidable form of prudential perfectionism. It has a derivative moral perfectionism: if certain prudential values are valuable for anyone, why ever not promote them? We ought to go out and, in missionary spirit, lead persons to them. Certain values—understanding and enjoyment of beauty, say—enrich lives, and in promoting them a society would lead its members, if not in this generation then in later ones, to better lives.

Is this paternalism? That all depends on how far one's missionary zeal carries one. One can be non-neutral between different conceptions of the good life (e.g. putting forward the case for education and art, making access to them easy) without being paternalistic. Paternalism is not the central issue about neutrality. Anyway, this form of moral perfectionism has built-in checks on paternalism. A particularly stringent one is that one heavyweight prudential value is autonomy; any promotion of other prudential values must respect this (non-absolute but still important) one.

We are not in a position yet to carry the discussion of these issues much further. It would take a fairly fully developed moral theory to say precisely how far we can go with this form of moral perfectionism. But even the very modest degree that I am broaching now seems to offend the neutrality of a lot of modern 'liberal' political theory.[26] Society, that theory says, should stay neutral between values, except for a few, special, all-purpose means. That too raises issues that need the context of a moral theory to settle finally. But I suspect that sometimes neutrality looks attractive because of certain beliefs simply about the nature of values.

For instance, neutrality is suggested by the need account of well-being. But, as we have seen,[27] 'basic needs' do not go deep enough to yield a satisfactory account of well-being, and when we go deeper, we encounter values that no longer support neutrality. Neutrality is also suggested by a widespread belief about the difference between all-purpose means on the one hand and all the rest of the prudential values on the other. The belief is that once outside the realm of objective all-purpose means we are on the shifting grounds of *mere* preferences—tastes and subjective attitudes. Sometimes political theorists write as if the diversity of conceptions of the good life is ineliminable,[28] as if due to the diversity of tastes, which can itself be eliminated only in New Men, genetically engineered and regularly brain-washed in a Huxley 'Central London Hatchery and Conditioning Centre'. But this greatly misjudges the rest of the prudential values. They are not, in any simple sense, subjective. They are not a matter of taste. They too are, in an important way, objective goods.[29]

6. *The primacy of prudential value theory*

To get an account of well-being that would be of use in moral theory we have to move beyond forms of perfectionism (even my modest one) and on to what is valuable to the particular persons affected in each case we judge. For special reasons about Jessica, autonomy might not be the thing for her to go for. For Nicholas, totally absorbed in his work, with no taste for day-to-day pleasures, enjoyment may count for little and accomplishment for a lot. For Edward, risk stimulates; for Sarah, it is off-putting. We cannot make any useful judgments about how to act so as to promote well-being without having a notion of well-being that captures all of these variations.

We found with need accounts that, to give them the required flexibility, we had to go beyond the notion of a 'basic need' to the notion of its 'importance', which led us to a form of judgment that could take place only in a full prudential value theory. Now we find with perfectionism that it gives us no useful account of well-being unless it is incorporated in a full prudential value theory.

If we are interested, as we ultimately are, in the conception of well-being needed by moral theory, it seems that it must be the one supplied by the prudential value theory. Of course, the pressures of building a moral theory may put things in a different light. But the pressures would have to be very great to get us to abandon that conception. The end of the argument comes only when we have built an adequate moral theory with one conception or other of well-being. Short of that, all conclusions are tentative. But in this spirit we can draw a conclusion. Well-being is the same in prudence and morality.

In any case, the conception of well-being that has emerged in this Part of the book has important consequences both for measuring well-being and for the place it might occupy in moral thought, to which I now turn.

PART TWO

MEASUREMENT

V

ARE THERE INCOMMENSURABLE VALUES?

1. *On measuring well-being*

IN speaking of well-being, we all resort to quantitative language. We speak of 'more' and 'less'. At times we aim to 'maximize' well-being. It is what all of us try to do in our own lives.[1] And many of us, though by no means all, see it as one of the aims of morality. Yet how seriously does the quantitative talk have to be taken for this whole policy of maximizing to be feasible?

What we want to know is not just, Is well-being measurable? There are many different scales of measurement, and it would be astonishing if well-being were not measurable on at least one of the less demanding ones. Nor do we want to know just, Is well-being measurable on a scale with origin and unit?, as if the crux were whether that sort of cardinal measurement were possible, in principle, in any circumstances. Perhaps, in special circumstances, when things fall out conveniently, it is. But that would not get us very far. Is it possible often enough in the sorts of messy everyday situations in which we want to maximize? But then that is not the crux either. Suppose it could not be. Do we really need a scale like that in order to maximize? To the extent that we can get by on pair-wise comparisons or rough cardinality, we do not. Our powers of measurement may be limited. But our demand on measurement may also be limited. In the end, what we need to know is, rather, Do our powers match our demands?

There is one place they might not. If well-being were a simple state of mind that occurred in smoothly changing intensities, then we could at least hope to develop a powerful cardinal scale, and one that is without discontinuities or incommensurabilities. But well-being is nothing like that. It is the fulfilment of informed desire. So there may well turn out to be cases in which, when informed, I want, say, a *certain* amount of one thing more than *any* amount of another, and not because the second thing cloys, and so adding to it merely produces diminishing marginal values. I may want it even though the second thing does not, with addition, lose its value; it may be that I think that no increase in *that* kind of value, even if constant and positive, can overtake a certain amount of *this* kind of value. We can make no assumptions about what the structure of informed desires will turn out to be like. There may well be incommensurable values in this fairly weak (or, worse, in some stronger) sense. But again, the question is not just the stark one, Are there incommensurable values? Incommensurabilities of the relatively weak form of 'a *certain* amount of this is more valuable than *any* amount of that' are no threat to pair-wise comparisons, and it is clear that at least much maximizing deliberation uses only them. And if there are not many incommensurable values, or not many of a strong form, or not many at the centre of our maximizing deliberation, they may not be much of a worry.

When we shift from prudential to moral deliberation, the demand on measurement goes up. Again, the question is not just the stark one, Are interpersonal comparisons of well-being possible? That is not a very live issue; some comparisons on some conceptions of well-being obviously are. The live issues are, rather, Are comparisons possible on the best conception for prudential or moral reasoning? And furthermore, Can we make enough of them, and will they be reliable enough, for the policy of maximizing to be a practical proposition? How difficult that last question is will depend upon what the best conception turns out to be. If it is the narrow conception of all-purpose means to a good life, our problem is, of course, much eased. But, unfortunately, morality has to use the broad conception out of prudential value theory, so our problem is greater.

Still, in all of these cases, the important question comes down to, Will our measurement match our needs? That is the question for this Part of the book. I want to determine whether, and if so where, incommensurabilities appear and how they affect measurement; what sort of measurement is possible, and needed, in the one person case; and what interpersonal comparisons are like and how feasible they are in the practical setting in which our deliberation has to take place.

2. *Moral incommensurables and prudential incommensurables*

The word 'value' covers a lot of ground. It is sometimes used just of prudential values—what makes a person's own life valuable to him, the 'good' in contrast to the 'right', as philosophers sometimes use the terms. But it is also quite properly used to include moral values—the 'right' as well as the 'good'—and indeed to include anything 'normative' rather than merely 'descriptive'.

The word 'incommensurable', as we have just seen, covers a fair amount of ground too. In a strong sense it can mean that two items cannot be compared quantitatively at all; the one is neither greater than, nor less than, and not equal to the other. Some writers regard this strong sense as the only proper sense;[2] they use 'incommensurable' to mean 'cannot be fitted onto *any* scale of measurement', and one can see the point of the usage. But since there are many different scales, which can themselves be ranked from weak to strong,[3] it is useful to consider whether values commensurable on a relatively undemanding scale are incommensurable on a more demanding one. For one thing, although this sense can claim to be the strict sense of the term, we are interested in how incommensurability figures in the philosophical tradition, which has not always kept to the strict sense. Also, we have still to see how demanding a scale the policy of maximizing needs. So I shall use 'incommensurable' in a way that allows different senses. In a weaker sense, then, 'incommensurable' can mean, say, that no amount of one sort of item can equal, in respect of some quantity, a certain amount of another. And the term, as we shall shortly see, can mean several other things as well.

Are there incommensurable values?[4] Of course there are—if 'value' is taken broadly enough and on some sense or other of 'incommensurable'. For instance, the morally 'right' trumps the prudentially 'good'. At least, many moral theories, utilitarianism sometimes included, say so. If I could give my place in the lifeboat to two children whose prospects in life are every bit as good as mine, then utilitarianism would say that I should. I have the strongest possible prudential reason *against*, but I have a moral reason *for*, and no amount of purely prudential weight, a utilitarian can say, outweighs any amount of moral weight. So when we ask whether there are incommensurable values, we should keep in mind the domain of values and the kind of incommensurability that we are interested in. If the domain includes all practical reason, then it is highly likely that cross-category weightings (say, between moral and prudential reasons) will display, say, lexical ordering.

If, however, the domain is confined to *moral* reasons, then we need to have settled what the structure of moral theory is before we can begin to decide about commensurabilities. It certainly looks, on the face of it, as if there are many, irreconcilably different, kinds of moral reasons: rights, promotion of well-being, obligations of special relations (such as promisor, parent, etc.), commitments to particular persons and institutions, etc.[5] Two moral obligations can conflict, without, it seems, either's losing its standing as an obligation. In that event, it would help if we could find lexical orderings or relative moral weights. Perhaps we can even work out a scale of moral weight, formally analogous to the scale of prudential values.[6] But perhaps not; perhaps we shall find some conflicts that none of these devices are available to resolve. What we cannot do, however, is to decide, independently of a fairly well-developed substantive moral theory, what we shall indeed find. Otherwise, we should just be giving moral intuitions far more authority than they deserve. Are human rights 'trumps'?[7] It does not seem so; we think that a certain right can weigh heavily one time but not another, and that well-being can sometimes weigh more heavily on the same scale as rights. But we cannot really say, until we have a substantive theory of rights that tells us, for instance, what makes something a human right in the first place, and how the weight of rights is determined, and what governs trade-offs between one right and another and between rights and well-being.[8] And anyone who finds it obvious, without the aid of a fairly full substantive theory, that rights, whatever else they are, exhibit this or that sort of incommensurability has missed the difficulties, both of subject-matter and of method, in moral theory-building. The same stricture applies to other candidate moral reasons. Are all obligations of special relations *moral* obligations? It is, I believe, a conceptual truth that promises create obligations, but it is a matter for substantive moral theory to say which of the obligations generated by the internal workings of institutions such as promising, parenthood, and property are moral and so even contend for a place in a moral conflict.[9] And, yes, commitments to particular persons and institutions seem to set up moral claims on us. But even if they really do, we need to know at how deep a place in moral theory the claims appear.[10] And perhaps some moral conflicts—perhaps some of what are spoken of as 'tragic' moral dilemmas—arise from our having different moral points of view, different world views, none of which we are willing to drop, but not all of which we can reconcile within a single system of practical reason. Someone faced with the possibility of deliberately killing one innocent person to stop someone else from killing many more, might naturally, despairingly, think that there was simply no right thing to do.[11] Here the two options may not only fail to fit on any single scale of moral weight but also, more radically, even fail to fit on a single scale of rationality or of theory-acceptability.[12] This failure would raise questions not about the content of moral theory but about what a moral theory can, or should, be—what system or unity we can expect of it. I want for now to postpone the question, Are there incommensurable moral reasons? What I shall say later, in Part Three, will go a long way, as any substantive moral theory will, towards an answer.

For now I want to confine myself to the domain of prudential values. Are there incommensurabilities there? Can the ends of life be got onto a single scale? That is a big enough question to get on with.

3. *Forms of incommensurability: (a) Incomparability*

The very strongest sort of incommensurability arises if two values cannot even be ordered as regards value—that is, if, while *A* and *B* are both prudential values, *A* is neither more valuable than *B*, nor less, and not of equal value.

Are there values like that? In the moral domain, we might naturally first look for them among 'tragic' cases.[13] And, in the prudential domain, there are also some terrible choices. A talented but chronically depressed person may have to choose between suicide and accomplishment. And the two values, freedom from pain and accomplishment, are so far removed from one another that they are scarcely easy to compare. But, despite that, they come nowhere near strict incomparability. We can and do compare pain and accomplishment. If the pain is great enough and the accomplishment slight enough, we should not consider the accomplishment worth the pain. Of course, we might be pushed to know how to rank them if the pain got less or the accomplishment more. But true incomparability arises not when we cannot decide how to rank values but when we decide that they are unrankable. And this is not a case in which, since life forces choices upon us, we choose but do not prefer. On the contrary, what we think is, precisely, that it would not be worth it.[14]

We have to guard against exaggeration. We easily resort to hyperbole when we want to stress the difficulty of ranking certain values. For instance, we often despair of ranking artists of very diverse achievements: novelist A, say, is not better than, nor worse than, nor quite equal to, novelist B; they are good in such totally different ways that we cannot in any realistic way compare them. But though we find ourselves readily talking in these terms, they are overdrawn. A may be dry but full of insight, B unperceptive but hilarious. That they are good in such different ways of course makes it hard to compare them. But not impossible. If A were capable of only pretty minor insights, and B an absolute hoot, we could probably rank them. So, strictly speaking, their values to us—gaining insight, being amused—are not incomparable. Of course, when the values get close, we should probably have trouble with the ranking. We might wonder whether it is because it is hard to discriminate the differences in value that are really there or that there are no fine differences really there to discriminate. I think that it is not at all easy to determine which of those alternatives is true, but since the second one may well be, and is certainly the more awkward for prospects of measurement, let us simply assume that it is. Some values are only roughly equal, and the roughness is not in our understanding but ineradicably in the values themselves. Still, rough equality is a long way from incomparability.

Though rough equality does not create problems for commensurability, it does create problems, to which I shall return later, for finding any mathematical structure that will mirror the structure of prudential values. A feature of rough equality is that though novelist A is roughly equal to novelist B, C's being clearly better than B does not allow us to conclude that C is better than A; the most that we might be able to say is that C is roughly equal to A. And rough equality may not be a rare phenomenon; we may find, upon close examination, that a large number of rankings are of this kind. So rough equality raises the problem of what sort of ordering prudential values exhibit. *Strong* orderings, *partial* orderings, *weak* orderings are all well understood; but values seem to present a case of a *vague* ordering, which is a sort that is not understood.[15] Rough equality, therefore, leaves us with important problems about the sense in which well-being can be measured at all, which I shall come to in the next chapter.

Where else might we expect to encounter genuine incomparabilities? There is no denying that there are very sharp differences in kind between prudential values. Are they not sometimes sharp enough to constitute incomparability? For instance, Kant says that in the kingdom of ends things have either 'price' or 'dignity'—'price' being value in exchange (anything with an equivalent or a substitute therefore having a price) and 'dignity' being above all price.[16] It is a good distinction. Some values do indeed seem optional. I might go for a life of competition and achievement, or I might instead go for one of gentleness and contentment with my lot. We see these as alternative ways of living, one value to some degree excluding the other but also making up for it. If I am wise, I shall decide between them by deciding which will make my life better. But some values do not have alternatives; we do not think that we are similarly free to aim at them or not, as we choose. Some values constitute what we think of as the dignity of human existence, central among them being autonomy and liberty. If we surrender our human standing, we shall find no equivalent.[17] Still, this point, though true, is not strong enough. Non-equivalence is not incomparability. Nothing can take the place of human standing, but that is not to say that nothing can even be ranked with it as to value. In fact, in rare cases, other values can even outrank it. If for some unfortunate person autonomy brings extreme anxiety, it might be better to sacrifice some autonomy. The same is true of other examples. An individual human life has no equivalent. But that is not to say that nothing can be ranked with, let alone outrank, a human life. The French government knows that each year several drivers lose their lives because of the beautiful roadside avenues of trees, yet they do not cut them down. Even aesthetic pleasure is (rightly) allowed to outrank a certain number of human lives. It is easy here to move imperceptibly from Kant to cant. We want to express our sense of the enormous value of certain things—human standing, an individual human life—and once again we reach for strong expressions. But in real life, in concrete situations, we often do, and should, back down. We find that we did not mean literally what, in searching for strong expressions, we ended up saying.[18]

Perhaps, then, we have to look for genuine incomparabilities in more extreme clashes—the clash of different world views, of radically different metaphysics. In Part One of this book, I chose as examples of the ends of life such things as enjoyment, accomplishment, deep personal relationships, etc. They are all rather tamely secular. Someone else might see the ends of life as being self-denial, contemplation, solitude, etc.[19] But when metaphysical views clash, we must try to choose between them. We might, of course, run up against a radical sort of incommensurability if these competing views could not themselves be ranked as to rationality, or even as to plausibility, but that, besides being doubtful, is in danger of yielding altogether too strong a form of incomparability. We are interested in whether some of the values we use are incomparable, and if two sets of values are themselves incomparable as to plausibility and we must just opt between them, then, though the sets are incomparable, we use only one. And if we do in fact wish to use both sets of values, as doubtless sometimes we do, then we shall be forced to organize them. But this involves ranking. For instance, self-denial, contemplation, and solitude come out of a religious world-view, and they are not in the ordinary sense prudential values. They may be matters of vocation, and a calling from God introduces a change in category and so the live possibility of cross-category incommensurabilities of the sort that we saw earlier. World views may clash in a way that allows us to choose only one. Or they may clash in a way that allows us to choose both, but then they ought themselves to show something about the the relative status of the values they propose. They should show us how to rank all of them. Some values may indeed outrank others. But this is not incomparability any longer, but some weaker form of incommensurability.

Incomparability, I think, is too strong. We do not find values that are strictly incomparable. So we should look at weaker forms of incommensurability.

4. (b) Trumping

The next strongest form of incommensurability allows comparability, but with one value outranking the others as strongly as possible. It takes the form: *any* amount of A, no matter how small, is more valuable than *any* amount of B, no matter how large. In short A trumps B; A is lexically prior to B.[20] We just saw that the elements of what Kant calls 'dignity' were not, strictly speaking, incomparable with the elements of 'price'. Do they at least trump them? Even that, though, would be far too strong. How do we rank, say autonomy or liberty on the one hand, and prosperity or freedom from pain on the other? Nearly all of us would sacrifice some liberty to avert a catastrophe, or surrender some autonomy to avoid great pain. So people who would call certain values 'trumps' or give them 'lexical priority' probably do not mean these terms entirely seriously.[21] What they may have in mind is some weaker form of incommensurability.

5. (c) Weighting

It seems that we often find ourselves attaching greater weight, unit for unit, to one value than to another. For instance, we think that it takes a great deal of prosperity to outrank a pretty slight liberty or that it takes a lot of pleasure or happiness to outrank a fairly small amount of pain or misery.

These beliefs are entirely plausible. The second, for instance, is what gives 'negative utilitarianism' much of its appeal.[22] But the interpretation on which they are plausible is not the interpretation that yields any kind of incommensurability. What is plausible, for instance, is that it takes a relatively large amount of happiness, as happiness goes (that is, relative to other cases of happiness), to justify a relatively small amount of misery, as misery goes (that is, relative to other cases of misery). Thus, one is appealing, in a rough way, to two distinct scales. But neither scale is the ultimately important one, namely the single scale on which prudential values are ranked. And once we get on that scale, we shall find that the special weighting disappears. Since it is a scale of prudential value, a fairly small amount of misery will turn out to make life worse to a greater degree than a fairly large amount of happiness makes it better.

Admittedly, there is an interpretation that would preserve special weighting and so would yield a kind of incommensurability. To state it, however, we should need seriously to appeal to two scales. We should have to be able to say that n amount of misery is not equal in prudential weight to n amount of happiness, that only $n + m$ amount of happiness (where $m > 0$) has the same prudential weight as n amount of misery, and that only $n + m + 1$ amount of happiness justifies following a course of life involving n amount of misery. But is all that coherent? There is no scale on which we can fit all the various kinds of 'happiness' and 'misery', except the scale of prudential weight. Any scale that would have the scope necessary to let us talk about m or n amounts of 'happiness' and 'misery' would have to be built on a rich foundation of basic preference judgments—that is, judgments about relative prudential weight that themselves do not rest upon any other kinds of judgments about the amount of some quantity in the two options being ranked. This interpretation needs two scales, but there is only one coherent scale forthcoming, a scale of weight in choice. So this interpretation cannot even be stated.[23]

What I have called, 'weighting', therefore, is not a promising source of incommensurability, so we have to look elsewhere.

6. (d) Discontinuity

Incomparability is too strong; values can at least be ranked. Trumping is too strong; no value, no matter how little is at stake, outranks another, no matter how much is at stake. Weighting is a distraction. But that still leaves it possible that, so long as we have enough of B any amount of A outranks any further amount of B; or that enough of A outranks any amount of B. Both of these forms bring with them the suspension of addition; in both we have a positive value that, no matter how often a certain amount is added to itself, cannot become greater than another positive value, and cannot, not because with piling up we get diminishing value or even disvalue (though there are such cases), but because they are the sort of value that, even remaining constant, cannot add up to some other value. And here at last, it seems to me, we really do start encountering incommensurability.

Not, however, in the case of the two values, liberty and prosperity. When we see that liberty is not, in the strict sense, lexically prior to prosperity, it is natural to retreat to the view that, if prosperity is assured to some minimal level, then the priority holds. But that is very doubtful. Liberty, I believe and shall later argue,[24] may, from time to time, be at stake in only a small way. And on those occasions other values, such as the general prosperity of our lives, might well be at stake in a big way. So it might well then be better for me, all values properly considered, to surrender some small liberty to gain the conditions for bringing off some great achievement or to preserve deep, rewarding personal relations (for instance, staying in a country without certain political liberties because someone I love lives there). Liberty, as important as it is, is not such a heavyweight among prudential values that, even in the limited domain we have defined, it is bound to trump any other value capable of achieving fairly heavyweight status itself.[25] The mistake here seems to be to think that certain values—liberty, for instance—as *types* outrank other values

—prosperity, for instance—as *types*. Since values, as types, can vary greatly in weight from token to token, it would be surprising to find this kind of discontinuity at the type—or at least at a fairly abstract type—level.

It is much more promising to look at less abstract types, or at tokens. It is far more plausible that an *important* sort of liberty—for instance, the right to live out the very central parts of one's life plan—can trump any amount of a *trivial* kind of disvalue—say, one's neighbours' getting huffy.[26] Or, to take the purely prudential sort of case that we are concerned with now, it is more plausible that, say, fifty years of life at a very high level of well-being—say, the level which makes possible satisfying personal relations, some understanding of what makes life worth while, appreciation of great beauty, the chance to accomplish something with one's life—outranks any number of years at the level just barely worth living—say, the level at which none of the former values are possible and one is left with just enough surplus of simple pleasure over pain to go on with it.

Could this be right? Why, if prudential values do not show discontinuity of the first form I have just mentioned (with enough of B, any amount of A outranks any further amount of B) would they start showing them here (enough of A outranks any amount of B)? I have already tried to give part of the answer: before we had quite abstract types of values, each of which could vary greatly in amount; now we have much more specific values tied as to amount at the opposite extremes of the scale. But this is only part of the answer. We should not expect to find sharp discontinuities at either extreme of the scale. Fifty years at a very high level—say, with enjoyment of a few of the very best Rembrandts, Vermeers, and de Hoochs—might be outranked by fifty-five years at a slightly lower level—no Rembrandts, Vermeers, or de Hoochs, but the rest of the Dutch School. And then fifty-five years at that level might be outranked by sixty years at a slightly lower level—no Dutch School but a lot more of the nineteenth-century revival of the Dutch School. And so on, step by step, until, it seems, we must eventually reach the point where the original fifty years would be outranked by a *sufficiently* large number of years of life just barely worth living.

This step-by-step approach seems irresistible. Yet it presents us with two embarrassments: a Sorites Paradox and a slippery slope. If we take enough pebbles from a heap, it ceases being a heap. But then, since one pebble more or less could never make the difference between its being a heap or not, if we remove them singly it can never cease being a heap. Similarly, one might argue, with 'appreciation of beauty' or 'deep loving relationships'; with slow, step-by-step changes we can never lose the appreciation of beauty or deep loving relationships either.

But we obviously can—I want to put the Sorites problem to the side. We can indeed reach a point, with the series of subtractions that we just saw (first Rembrandt, Vermeer, and de Hooch, then the whole seventeenth-century Dutch School ...), at which we lost the appreciation of beauty. We may instead have the kicks of kitsch but they are different. Even with the loss of one important value, such as appreciation of beauty, it must be possible for enough more life with the substantial values that remain—deep loving relations, accomplishment, and the rest—still to be more valuable. That seems right, but then, by parity of reasoning, it would seem that, since kicks of kitsch are not nothing, enough of them must be more valuable than a certain amount of the appreciation of beauty, so we are on our way down the slippery slope. If we also lose deep relations, accomplishment, and all the rest of the substantial values of life, then, by parity of reasoning, since what is left is, though slight, not nothing, enough life with this residue must be more valuable.

But there is one impediment to this slide down the slope. We do seem, when informed, to rank a certain amount of life at a very high level above any amount of life at a very low level. And if we do, it is likely to be a basic preference; that is, it could not be based upon other judgments about the amount of value in the objects being ranked. Nor need there be any extreme perfectionism at work in this preference; those who held this preference could also be willing to sacrifice the best Rembrandt, Vermeer, or de Hooch, for all the various, though lesser, achievements of the Dutch School.

To call this preference 'basic' is simply to say that it is basic among quantitative judgments. It is not to say that it is ground-floor in every way. We can offer arguments—the sort of deliberation that I talked about at some length in Part One—for seeing the objects as valuable, which may also lead to seeing them as of varying value. Basic preferences can certainly be argued over. And we can dispel other doubts. The doubts about this kind of basic preference, I think, often come down in the end to an assumption of the totting-up conception of measuring well-being. They all focus on a series of small changes, as if the relation of one level of well-being to another had to be a matter of additions and subtractions of a small unit. But the assumption that there is a single additive measure of well-being continuously across its range is just what is in question. That additive scales of well-being are possible here and there in its range is a long way from one additive scale's being possible across its whole range. The assumption of changes in small units is plausible enough in some cases. When we move from portraits by Rembrandt to portraits by Hals, we lose something. We should be likely to attach less value to appreciating the beauty of one portrait by Hals than one portrait by Rembrandt. But if we have all of the rest of the Dutch school except Rembrandt then we might well attach more value to the number and variety of paintings that we should then have. This *looks* like a loss' being made up by the sum of a larger number of smaller values. However, when we get to the point where beauty totally disappears and only kitsch is left, it looks as if no totting-up could be done and only a basic preference is possible. We have simply to rank a life with beauty against a life with only lots of kitsch. And then, from this perspective, when we look back at the earlier cases where totting-up seemed to be going on, we can see that it was not what was going on after all. What goes on in comparing a few Rembrandts with all the rest of the Dutch School is not arithmetical addition of a larger number of slightly smaller values to get a greater overall sum. We have to decide how we value greater number and more variety against a few supreme, less varied examples. And that is itself a basic preference. Any additive scale that we might introduce in this domain will have to be defined on basic preferences such as this. Therefore, one cannot harbour doubts about the appearance of discontinuities in the addition of well-being by assuming the continuity of the addition.[27]

So there are, I wish to propose, incommensurabilities of the form: enough of A outranks any amount of B. That leaves us with the job of looking closely at each judgment of this form to separate the ones that are literally true from the exaggerations,[28] but some, I think, prove literally true.

7. (e) Pluralism

Pluralism says that there are irreducibly many prudential values. That seems to me right.[29] But how is pluralism connected with incommensurability? Is the form of reductionism that pluralism rightly denies a form that commensurability needs?

If the denial of reduction is just the denial that there is a single mental state running through all the things that we rank in terms of which we rank them (the denial of a crude mental state account, or of hedonism), then, it can be agreed by everyone, utilitarians included. In one sense, different kinds of pleasure, or pleasure on the one hand and pain on the other, are incomparable: namely, there is no deeper unitary mental state in terms of which they can be compared.[30] But the failure of crude mental state accounts, or crude hedonisms, does not mean that there is no single scale for ranking prudential values.[31]

If, on the other hand, the denial of reduction is the denial that there is a single substantive value running through all the things that we rank (the denial of substantive monism), then it seems to me entirely correct. There is no single substantive super-value.[32] But we do not need a super-value to have a scale.[33] It is enough to have the quantitative attribute 'value'.

If the denial of reduction is the denial of a single scale of origin and units continuous across the domain of prudential values (the denial of complete, strong cardinality), then again it seems to me right. Even if we abandon appeal to a super-value and use the concept of 'value' itself as our quantitative attribute, we do not get such a scale. But that does not show much. It does not show, for instance, that there is no single scale of well-being, nor that not everything can be ranked on it. And it certainly does not show that our powers of measurement are not up to the policy of maximizing.

So we might take the denial of reduction to be the denial of *complete* ranking. We might think that though some values are quantifiable others are not, or that though all are they are quantifiable only on different scales. The absence of a complete ranking would indeed upset the policy of maximizing (though upset and incompleteness come in degrees). Still, it is that strong form of incommensurability—namely, incomparability —that we found difficult to produce convincing examples of. The lure of the apparent examples is to be traced, I think, to a mistake about what the scale of well-being is. We can sometimes rank pleasures as to intensity, duration, and number. We can also measure degrees of one component of happiness (say, contentment with one's lot) and separately measure degrees of another, radically different component (say, achievement of one's ambitions). We seem therefore to have several partial scales—scales for certain dimensions of pleasure or happiness—but no super-scale. But it does not follow from there being no super-value that there is no super-scale. To think so would be to misunderstand how the notion of 'quantity' of well-being enters. It enters through ranking; quantitative differences are defined on qualitative ones. The quantity we are talking about is 'prudential value', defined on informed rankings. All that we need for the all-encompassing scale is the possibility of ranking items on the basis of their nature. And we can, in fact, rank them in that way. We can work out trade-offs between different dimensions of pleasure or happiness. And when we do, we rank in a strong sense: not just choose one rather than the other, but regard it as worth more. That is the ultimate scale here: worth to one's life.[34]

Commensurability does not require monism. At least on what seems to me the most common interpretation of the terms, the monism-pluralism issue is not especially central to the issue of incommensurability.[35] The quantity used to define the scale of measurement of prudential value is not itself a substantive prudential value. The real threat to prudential values is the threat that their diversity, their incompatibility, and, above all, the great value that each at times constitutes will be ignored. But that threat comes not from believing in commensurability, but from being arrogant and intolerant. It can come as easily from the pluralist who believes in incommensurability—from someone, say, who fervently believes that liberty is 'incommensurably higher' than prosperity, or even than life itself. If we assembled all the deplorable fanatics that history has ever seen and asked them to divide into two lobbies labelled 'monist' and 'pluralist', my money would be on the pluralists' winning hands down. It is hard to think that a happy, productive life counts for nothing but unfortunately it seems terribly easy to think that it counts for nothing up against what is seen as the 'incommensurably higher'.[36]

What needs defending is not the mere plurality of values but a certain important picture of how they are related—that they clash, that they all matter, that they all have their day, that there are no permanent orderings or rankings among them, that life depressingly often ties gain in one value to terrible loss in another, that persons may go in very different directions and still lead equally valuable lives—call this picture 'liberalism'. But one does not defend liberalism by attacking commensurability or computation. One does not defend it by denying the possibility of trade-offs between values, even of trade-offs between liberty itself and other values, or by denying that values can be ranked on a single scale. Trade-offs are possible; values can be ranked on a single scale. So if we want a defence of liberalism, it will have to take a different form. What is needed is to show just how valuable our being able autonomously to form and freely to carry out a life plan is, how central it is to our living a human existence, and just how greatly we value our humanity, even at the cost of our happiness. All of that has to be put as emphatically as we can. But it is easy to slide from emphasis to hyperbole. We reach for the powerful language of incomparability and trumping. But it does liberalism no service, it offers it in the end no real defence, to tie it to the indefensible. If liberty is to be defended, it has to be taken down from the shaky perch of 'incomparability' and placed in the same domain as other prudential values, where they will conflict, where none is above the fray, where some, however, are weighty enough usually to win a conflict, and where even, occasionally, a weighty value can assume in a particular case such weight that *no* amount of some lightweight value can overcome it. It is in those terms that liberalism has to be—and can be—defended.

VI

THE CASE OF ONE PERSON

1. Is well-being the sort of thing that can be measured at all?

THIS question, to which confident but contradictory answers are regularly given,[1] is itself far from clear. There are several forms of measurement. Are we asking, Is well-being measurable on *any* scale, no matter how weak? We tend to treat one scale, usually a fairly strong one such as a scale for measuring length, as the standard that we expect all measurement to live up to, which is a mistake. As a corrective, we might keep in mind S. S. Steven's well-known definition, 'Measurement [is] the assignment of numerals to objects or events according to rule—any rule'.[2] On that deliberately capacious definition, the following all count as scales of measurement. There are ordinal scales, where the rule assigns numbers in order to the objects or events we observe occurring in an order. For example, we can rank minerals by a scratch test for hardness and assign them numbers, either ascending or descending, in order of their hardness. Ordinal scales are unique up to a monotone transformation. Then there are more powerful interval scales, where the rule requires, more strictly, assigning numbers so that equal differences between them correspond to equal intervals in the attribute being measured. Here a unit of measurement and an origin appear, both arbitrary. Fahrenheit and Centigrade scales of temperature, for example, are interval scales. So interval scales are unique up to a linear transformation of the form $y = ax + b$. Then there are the still stricter ratio scales, in which the rule makes the further demand that the ratios of the numbers (doubles, trebles, etc.) be the same as the ratios of the amounts of the attribute to which they are assigned. Here the unit is still arbitrary but the origin no longer is. After the discovery of an absolute zero, temperature could be measured on a ratio scale, which, unlike the Fahrenheit and Centigrade scales, allows us to say that

20° is twice as hot as 10°. Therefore ratio scales are unique up to a similarity transformation of the form $y = ax$. I shall stop there, though that list is just a start. Since a rule of assignment defines a scale, and other rules are possible, other scales are possible. There is, in principle, a non-denumerable infinity of types of scale,[3] although in practice only a few are of empirical interest. None the less, more than I have listed have in fact proved of interest. For instance, the area between ordinal and interval is a rich one for the development of new scales, especially important in measuring psychological attributes.[4]

Another defect of the question with which I started is that it is not clear whether it is asking a theoretical or a practical question. The theoretical question is, What quantitative statements about well-being can we give sense to? Can we, for instance, give sense to ordinal talk about 'more' and 'less' and 'maximum' well-being? Can we go further and give sense to such cardinal talk as 'the gap between these values is greater than the gap between those' (interval scale) or even that 'this is twice as valuable as that' (a ratio scale)? But we might satisfactorily answer the theoretical question and it still be unclear whether, in the messy everyday situations in which our deliberation actually takes place, we can know enough for measurement, at least for reliable measurement, to succeed. It is not much help to practical deliberation if while certain forms of measurement of well-being can be given sense no form can really figure in our actual thought. Questions about measurability are often ambiguous as between the theoretical question and the practical question, and both are important.

And is the question asked of the one-person case, the many-person case, or both? It is easy to exaggerate or misconceive the difference between one-person and many-person cases. We are inclined to think that all one-person cases are relatively uncomplicated because we always have a single preference order to fall back on, while in many-person cases we clearly do not. But often we do not in one-person cases either. If I am faced with two very different courses of life, which will eventually bring changes to my tastes, attitudes, and concerns so that, whichever I choose, I shall end up happy that I chose as I did and not the other way, there is no single preference to fall back on either. Intertemporal intra-personal comparison can get very close to interpersonal. What I want to do, to isolate issues, is to concentrate in this chapter on the simplest case—one person with stable preferences—and take up the more complicated cases in the following chapter.

2. *An ordinal scale of well-being*

Let us start with the theoretical question. In general, we can prove measurability by showing that a system of empirical relations and operations is isomorphic with a certain system of numerical operations and relations, and by showing what in a numerical system is to be taken as having meaning when applied to the empirical system. This can be thought of as our having to prove two theorems: a *representation* theorem (that, by being isomorphic, certain aspects of the arithmetic of numbers represent certain aspects of the world) and a *uniqueness* theorem (that the scale of measurement that results has a certain sort of uniqueness; in short, that we can determine the sort of scale it is—ordinal or interval or ratio or ...).[5]

It is almost universally accepted by economists that in simple one-person cases well-being is measurable ordinally. Unfortunately, incommensurabilities create problems even for that relatively modest claim. 'Well-being' is certainly a quantitative attribute, in the sense that we can sometimes say that one thing makes us better off, or at least as well off, or exactly as well off, as another.[6] Let us concentrate on the relation 'at least as well off', in terms of which the others can be defined, and symbolise it '$\geq_w$'. Now we can show that well-being is measurable ordinally if we can show that '$\geq_w$' has the properties that constitute one or other logical ordering —for example, those of a *weak ordering*, namely:

reflexivity: $(\forall x)\ xRx$
transitivity: $(\forall x)\ (\forall y)\ (\forall z)\ (xRy\ \&\ yRz \rightarrow xRz)$
and completeness: $(\forall x)\ (\forall y)\ (xRy \lor yRx \lor x=y)$

(To put this into English, a relation is reflexive if each individual in a certain domain stands in that relation to itself; it is transitive if, for any trio of individuals, the fact that the first stands in the relation to the second and the second to the third implies that the first does to the third; it is complete if, for any pair, one stands in the relation to the other or the two are equal.) Does well-being behave like this? Over much of its range it does. But there are places where it seems distinctly not to. The trouble, therefore, comes with the requirement of completeness. As we have seen,[7] sometimes the best we can say is that one thing roughly equals another, where the roughness may not be in our understanding of what is before us but in the objects of understanding themselves. To say that $A \geqslant_w B$ is to say that either $A >_w B$ or $A =_w B$ is true. But rough equality does not behave like strict equality. If A roughly equals B, then we can add something to A (say, by improving it in some clear but slight way), getting $A+$, but it may still not be the case that $A+ >_w B$ nor of course that $A+ <_w B$ or that $A+ =_w B$. $A+$ may still be only roughly equal to B.

We could then retreat and ask whether '$\geqslant_w$' has the properties of a *partial ordering*, namely those of a weak ordering without completeness. But this raises the question of how extensive the phenomenon of rough equality is. If, as is likely, we find it here and there right across the domain of well-being, then the retreat to a partial ordering is not much help. The trouble with rough equality is that it makes the strict ranking statements that it infects neither definitely true nor definitely false. For instance, one might be able to decide that a life of great accomplishment even at the cost of day-to-day pleasure is better than a life of slight day-to-day pleasures. And one might be able to decide that a life rich in day-to-day pleasures is better than a life of only slight accomplishment. But when the balance between these two values gets more level, we enter the area of indistinctness. At a certain point in this borderland none of the claims—not $A >_w B$, $A =_w B$, nor $B >_w A$—is either definitely true or definitely false. We seem, therefore, to have not so much a partial ordering as something new and little understood, namely a *vague ordering*.[8]

What effect does this have on the measurability of well-being? There is no obvious mathematical model that mirrors the behaviour of '$\geqslant_w$' given its vagueness, so we may wonder whether we shall be able to prove a representation theorem. But I do not think that the vagueness has such devastating results. Rough equality (along with that other form of incommensurability, discontinuity) does certainly create problems for a cardinal scale with units that can be added across the domain of values. If A, $A+$, and $A++$ can all be roughly equal to B, small variations in value will get lost if we simply treat A and B as equal. But this will not matter if we can keep to ordinal judgements. And with ordinal judgements, it does not matter either that we have only a vague ordering. It is uncommon for rough equality to matter to prudential deliberation. Where we have rough equality, we treat the items, when it comes to choice, simply as equals. We are indifferent between them, even though our indifference in this case has an uneasiness to it absent in cases of strict equality. There can be, it is true, quite complex cases of rough equality, though they are fairly rare. For instance, we might have to rank not A and B, which are roughly equal to one another, but $A++$ and $B-$. But so long as we can rank $A++$ and $B-$ against one another, even if only by 'roughly equal to', we can proceed. It is a mistake to conclude from the fact that rough equality crops up fairly often that the difference between strict and rough equality matters fairly often.

But unfortunately we cannot just conclude that for purposes of deliberation we may treat '$\geqslant_w$' as a weak ordering. The indistinctness that gives rise to 'rough equality' also undermines the transitivity of '$\geqslant_w$' (which means that we cannot treat '$\geqslant_w$' for purposes of deliberation as a partial ordering either). '$\geqslant_w$' is transitive only if '$=_w$' is transitive, and 'rough equality' is only non-transitive. That is, if A is roughly equal to B and B to C and C to D, we might sometimes decide, in a pair-wise comparison, that A is roughly equal to D but also sometimes decide that it is not. Though we are assuming that the roughness of 'rough equality' is in the world rather than in our understanding of it, 'rough equality' will, as regards transitivity, behave like such epistemological relations as 'is indistinguishable from'. However, the breakdown in the transitivity of '$\geqslant_w$' would probably be very rare—far rarer, for instance, than the appearance of rough equality itself. And the transitivity of '$>_w$' and of '$<_w$' would remain undisturbed.

So '$\geqslant_w$' gives us what might be called a *partially transitive weak ordering*. The vagueness that sometimes disturbs the transitivity and completeness of the relation '$\geqslant_w$' is important and little understood, and I have only scratched the surface of the problems it creates. But it need not change our minds on the theoretical question now before us: well-being is ordinally measurable. The attribute *well-being* is itself quantitative in a sufficiently strong sense for the ordering it generates to constitute an ordinal scale.

There is one implication of the discussion of this section that is worth a comment. What is *not* at issue over the measurability of well-being is whether there is a single substantive super-value to serve as the common-denominator of all the other values. The dispute between monists and pluralists is irrelevant here. The measurement of values needs, not a super-value (fortunately, since there is none) but an attribute that is quantitative. And *well-being* and *prudential value* are themselves quantitative attributes.

3. *Pockets of cardinality*

Let us stay with the theoretical question for a little longer. We want to know in how strong a sense well-being is measurable, and we may be able to give sense to a much stronger scale of measurement for well-being than we find ourselves often able to use in practice.

Surely, well-being is *sometimes* measurable on a cardinal scale. But in now arguing that, we have to keep a firm grip on the quantity that we want to measure. It is very easy, in the course of arguing for the measurability of some quantity, to twist the quantity to fit the needs of the argument, so ending up with an impeccable proof of measurability but not of the quantity that we started with.[9] Our quantity is *the strength of informed desire*.

'Strength' and 'informed' have to be understood in the way that I explained earlier;[10] unfortunately neither is simply observable in action. The notion 'informed' introduces an ideal element: what one desires under certain conditions, which may or may not obtain. Let us, therefore, to improve conditions for measurement, restrict our attention to the not uncommon cases of desires which are in fact informed. And, as we have seen, the sense of 'strength' that is relevant here is not a felt intensity or a motivational force; it is, rather, a place in an informed preference order. So we cannot conclude from the fact that a reformed drunk's will cracks and he takes a drink, that his desire to take a drink was 'strongest' in the sense that we are out to measure. Nor can we conclude from the fact that a dedicated teetotaller never in his life takes a drink that he has never had a desire to do so. The link between *desire* and *action* is obviously nothing so simple. We have many desires, not all compatible; we have beliefs, which are themselves linked to desires, that certain desires ought not to be satisfied; we also have beliefs about which desires are within our capacity to fulfil, and these beliefs clearly affect action. But there is at least this link between *desire* and *action*: if a person believes that he can fulfil a certain desire, and he has no desire incompatible with it, then if he has the desire, he will act to fulfil it. This link is in part empirical and part what Wittgenstein calls criterial. We should have no understanding of what desire is unless desires had some connection with action. Our learning how to use the word 'want' involves learning what makes people act, so that if, when there are no obstacles to a person's doing what he sincerely says he wants to do, no competing desires or inhibiting beliefs, he does not do it, then we should (and he would too) give up the belief that he does actually want to do it. And the whole set of hypotheses that we operate with about the connection between beliefs, desires, and actions, has a large empirical element that must turn out to be descriptively adequate.

So let us now further restrict our attention to the simple, but by no means out-of-the-way, cases of desires that have no competing desires or inhibiting beliefs. An informed desire will now issue in action, and desires of different strengths will, in certain settings, issue in different action. Suppose, for example, that the County Council decides to change the layout of a road I use, threatening various things along the way that I find very beautiful. I decide that I am willing to give up five hours of my leisure time campaigning to save the chestnut tree, ten hours to save the stone wall, and twenty hours to save the copse. Of course, the marginal value to me of an hour of leisure can change as the amount that I have changes, but let us restrict attention to a range within which the marginal value does not change—say that I should not have to give up more than two hours of leisure in a week so that any one hour is the same sacrifice as any other. Then, too, the marginal value of beauty changes as the amount there is changes, but again let us just restrict attention to a range in which it has not yet begun to change—say that there is so little beauty along the road that the value of each of these beautiful things is the same whether or not the others exist. With all of these restrictions in place, our understanding of the relation of desire and action would lead us to treat these figures as representing how much I value each of the things at risk. We could say that I value the copse about twice as much as the stone wall, and the stone wall twice as much as the chestnut. And we could say that the combined value to me of the wall and the chestnut is still well short of the value of the copse. We might hesitate attaching much significance to the precise figures that I announce (but then we might also with my estimates of the length of the stone wall and the height of the chestnut).[11] Still, if we are satisfied that I have estimated carefully, we should be willing to treat them as accurate to within a tolerably small margin of error.

Have we got the makings of a cardinal scale here? The ingredients we now have are part of an economist's stock-in-trade. We have concentrated on the marginal rate of substitution between two goods. We can define a unit of well-being on a unit of leisure time. With it, we can measure the size of the gap between things we value. So we have at least an interval scale. Whether or not we have a strong form of ratio scale depends upon the nature of the zero point we use to construct the scale.[12] However, I want to leave aside difficult conceptual issues about 'zero' well-being; both scales are cardinal and allow addition in a fairly powerful sense. The important question is not which of these two cardinal scales we have got here, but what the scope of the scale that we have got is. An economist would stress—what is right—that this sort of approach will produce, at best, only cardinal measures of local significance, the locality of which (defined, for instance, in the case I have discussed by the range in which the marginal value of time and beauty is the same) may turn out to be very small. But one of the things that we want to know is to what statements about the measurability of well-being we can give sense. The existence even of pockets of cardinality shows that at least sometimes we can make sense of well-being as a cardinal notion.

These pockets of cardinality also show that, contrary to the claims of some advocates of a probabilistic notion of utility, we can make sense of well-being, and of its cardinal measurement, independently of probability. There are economists and decision theorists who take the tough line that it is only by *defining* utility in connection with probability that one gets a notion of utility worth bothering with. It is true that if utility numbers do nothing more than indicate place in an ordinal ranking they are not doing much. I prefer saving the copse to saving the stone wall, and saving the stone wall to saving the chestnut tree. If this ordinal information is all that we have, we can still attach numbers to each of the options: say, 1 to the least preferred, 2 to the next, 3 to the most preferred. We can even use these numbers to describe my behaviour; we can say that I behave so as to maximize the index number. But all that this talk in terms of utility numbers means is that I prefer saving the copse to saving the wall, and saving the wall to saving the chestnut. The numbers are unique only up to an increasing monotonic transformation; any three numbers in ascending order would do, say, -14, 206.3, and 3,000 (even three numbers in descending order would do if we were willing to give up the anyway not very informative talk about maximizing the index number). It is also true that, once probabilities are added to the picture in the following way, we need more than ordinal rankings to explain what is going on. I am sure, with some lobbying, to save the wall; or, by directing my lobbying efforts elsewhere, I have a two-thirds chance of saving the copse and one-third chance of saving the chestnut. An adequate explanation in this case requires giving weight not only to what probability I attach to the alternatives but also to how much I want each. As for the latter, it is not enough to know my ordinal ranking, because whether I should prefer the certainty of the wall to the gamble between the copse and the chestnut turns on where the middle item in the ranking comes in relation to the two extremes. We could then call how much I desire something its 'subjective value' or 'utility', and utility numbers now would have some explanatory role. So long as a person's choices satisfy certain axioms, say the von Neumann–Morgenstern axioms,[13] his behaviour can be seen as an attempt to maximize the mathematical expectation of these numbers. And these numbers will be unique up to a positive linear transformation; that is, they will constitute an interval scale.

But this is not really enough to justify the very tough line that the only interesting notion of utility must be *defined* in terms of probabilities, or that it is even 'mystical' to speak of utility apart from probability.[14] That tough line rests on the belief that the only way to cardinalize utility is in connection with probabilities. But it is not. And it would be surprising if it were. 'Utility' figures in a very complex theoretical setting; it connects with more than just probability, and these other connections, as we have seen, are rich enough to allow other forms of cardinalization. There is no denying that the pocket of cardinality in my example is not large. We have no theory that yields correlations of belief, desire, and action that permit scales as broad in application as do the theoretical correlations of temperature, pressure, and volume. And it is not just a matter of hoping eventually to find richer correlations between belief, desire, and action; once outside a fairly narrow domain, incommensurabilities start arising. But, despite all this, the correlations of belief, desire, and action that we are able to make are rich enough in themselves, without probability, to allow the introduction of a cardinal notion of well-being.

None of this is to deny that one of the advantages of taking well-being (even defined non-probabilistically) in conjunction with probability is that it allows us to expand the pockets of cardinality.[15] But that brings us to the practical question: how are we going to measure well-being in the messy everyday situations in which we have to apply the policy of maximizing? Can we devise a scale with sufficient scope and reliability for a prudential policy of maximizing well-being to be possible? I think that, even there, probabilities do not figure importantly. But let us turn now to these practical matters.

4. *What powers of measurement do we actually need?*

Suppose that I wonder, Should I go for a demanding life of accomplishment, or for a more tranquil life of day-to-day pleasures? It might look as if I could make my decision more rational by introducing measurement of, say, the amount of pleasure that would come my way in the life of day-to-day pleasures. But that would not help much. What I need is a scale, not of pleasures, but of prudential value, a scale on which I can fit both the lives that I have to compare. What seems most important is to get an imaginative grasp on each of these lives as wholes. When that is full enough, I can then just place each on the scale. It is not that I have first to measure the two options in respect of some quantity, 'prudential value', in order to be able then to rank them. The ranking is the decision about their value. Judgments of preference are often—as they are likely to be in this case—quantitatively basic: that is, they are judgments that do not depend upon other judgments about the amount of some quantity each option has. It is with basic preferences that the construction of a scale of measurement of well-being begins. The scale is generated out of these raw materials, so no scale of well-being could be used at this earlier stage to generate the materials. And although, as we have seen, in certain restricted domains, quite powerful scales can be generated, we do not need them in this case of prudential deliberation. It can get by on less—often on pair-wise comparisons.

The same seems true of many preferences which need not be basic. Suppose that I am facing an academic's dilemma, Should I take a job with fewer hours of teaching, but in a less beautiful town, and with more pay? Well, how much weight do I attach to hours of teaching, beauty of surroundings, and amount of pay? Perhaps here I could introduce an additive measure. But such an additive scale could be introduced only on a fairly rich base of information about my preferences on certain closely related matters. In most cases, therefore, it is as easy simply to form the preference between the options in front of me, as I would have to if they were basic, by grasping as fully as I can what the two options involve.

There may be a few cases—cases, say, in which there are too many *pros* and *cons* for me to be able to hold them all in my mind simultaneously—when deliberation in terms of cardinal measurement will seem necessary. Many economists have taken it for granted that only ordinal scales are needed in one person cases (strictly, in one person cases where preferences are stable). It is true that preference ordering is all that is needed, in theory, to find the maximum. But we are now concerned with what is needed in practice, and it may be that we cannot form any reliable non-basic preference between two many-sided options without resorting to some cardinal measurement. But it would be rare if rough cardinality would not do, and rough cardinality is much less restricted in application than the sort of full interval or ratio scale that appeared in the pockets of cardinality that we discussed earlier. Those scales met the most demanding requirements of isomorphism with arithmetical addition: cardinality with origin and unit. But we can still argue, though only impressionistically, for isomorphism between a system of combining rough estimates of the size of the gaps between items that are ordinally ranked and arithmetical addition. And it would be little upset to a prudential policy of maximizing that from time to time we met cases where our capacity for measurement was not up to producing a clear answer.

There is, though, the threat of incommensurabilities. But they too, if confined to rough equality and discontinuities, are not much of a worry for prudential deliberation. Prudential deliberation can get by largely on pair-wise comparisons, so it can tolerate those forms of incommensurabilities.

Additive scales have assumed great importance in the past because, whether we have been for or against utilitarianism, a rather crude mental state account of well-being has dominated our thinking. Even if we have dropped the mental state for the desire account, we have not always managed to drop its views about measurement. If the goodness of a life consists in a lot of short-term pleasures or experiences, then to rank two courses of life we should clearly need to do a lot of totting-up. Therefore we should need the equipment for totting-up, namely, additive scales. But such a crude mental state account is the wrong account. So prudential judgment does not depend upon totting-up. So the possibility of additive scales is not a central issue. What, for the most part, we need for measurement is knowledge not of a person's present, individual, perhaps idiosyncratic, tastes and preferences (they may not be for what is in his own best interests) but of what in general makes life good. And if the person deviates from the norm, then we shall still need general causal knowledge about how persons of this sort work. For the most part, what we need is the sort of knowledge of informed global preferences that is derivable from a general theory of prudential good and a causal theory of human nature. This general theory of prudential good and this causal theory are also, as we shall see in the next chapter, central to understanding the character of interpersonal comparisons. So far as prudential deliberation goes, the demand for additive scales is often a hangover from an account of well-being that we should anyway give up.

VII

THE CASE OF MANY PERSONS

1. *The link between conceptions of well-being and problems of comparability*

THE problem of interpersonal comparisons is itself problematic-ally protean. It changes shape with every change in conception of well-being. And we cannot simply decide on what is the best conception of well-being before broaching the subject of comparability, because the discussion of comparability is one of the things that helps us to decide on the best conception.

On a mental state conception, the problem about comparability is largely, though by no means entirely, a problem about knowledge of other minds. We saw earlier[1] some of the troubles that mental state accounts run into, the main one being lack of scope; they have a hard time accommodating all that it seems right to regard as part of well-being.

We might therefore use instead an actual-desire conception of well-being, say the conception of utility as the subjective value that a person attaches to a gamble. If we do, the problem about comparability is still largely one of knowledge of other minds, though with a different focus. One trouble with the actual-desire account, as we saw earlier,[2] is that, though it may suit empirical parts of decision theory and of economic theory, it is much less suitable for moral theory (and for welfare economics, and the normative parts of decision theory, and large parts of social choice theory).[3] A person may in fact want what will be bad for him, and the notion of well-being that we, as moral philosophers, are after must be centred on real, not subjectively perceived, benefit. So if we manage to give an adequate account of the comparability of utilities defined on actual preferences over gambles, it is not clear that we should yet have shown how well-being, in the sense that matters to normative theories, is to be made comparable.

Were we, therefore, to abandon conceptions of well-being out of the utilitarian tradition and use, say, an objective conception such as John Rawls' index of primary goods,[4] the problem of comparability would obviously be much eased. We should now compare persons in respect of such objective and relatively accessible things as their income and the social institutions in which they live. Still, as we have seen,[5] these narrow objective conceptions of well-being have their troubles too. They impose a cut-off on considerations available to moral theory that it may not be able to accept and still answer questions at the centre of its interest.

We ease problems about comparability almost as much, if we adopt what Derek Parfit has called an 'objective list' account of well-being.[6] How well off a person is would then turn on the extent to which he realizes the objective prudential values on the list—say, such things as autonomy, accomplishment, deep personal relationships, etc. But again, as we have seen,[7] objective-list accounts have their troubles. They are, at least on simple interpretations of them, too insensitive to variation between individuals to provide a plausible account of well-being, at least if 'well-being' is understood as an all-encompassing assessment of the quality of a particular person's life.

That brings us to informed-desire conceptions—say, the sort that I developed in Part One. Comparability would now, as it was on the actual-desire conception, partly be a matter of knowing how strongly a person wants something (when he is informed, or would want it if he were informed). But, since the informed-desire conception can be developed in ways that bring it at least in the vicinity of an objective-list conception,[8] many interpersonal comparisons might often be made simply in terms of the items on the list. Still, informed-desire accounts have their troubles, chief among them being whether, in the end, they really can explain comparability.[9] Can they even explain intrapersonal intertemporal comparisons, when the latter involve radical change in preferences? If not, the informed-desire account will not do even as a theory of prudence.

What these links between comparability and conceptions of well-being show is that we need three things to come together for us at the same time: first, we need the account of well-being that we adopt, whether it is of a broad utilitarian sort or a narrower objective sort, to be a plausible account of the domain of prudential value that it tries to cover; second, it must be what we want to use, for purposes of moral judgment, as the basis for comparison between different persons; and, third, it has to lend itself to the sorts of measurement that moral deliberation needs.

That these three things must all come together for us enlarges the problem of interpersonal comparisons. I think, however, that we ought not to let the problem get too large. Comparing different persons' well-being can be seen as, in effect, moving from the interests of several different persons, often in conflict, to some sort of common interest, and so, in effect, to the fair or moral decision. But then the choice of a particular method of making interpersonal comparisons becomes, for all practical purposes, the choice of a whole morality, or at least of the principles of fair distribution. But that is letting the issue get far too large; it is taking too many steps at once. We can decide about the comparability of well-being, on a certain conception, without begging questions about how this information is to be used in moral judgment. We can decide about it, leaving open which conception of well-being is the one that morality needs. And what we decide will be one, but only one, consideration in deciding which conception of well-being morality does indeed need. There is the question, prominent since Robbins' famous article,[10] of what value judgments one makes simply in making an interpersonal comparison of well-being, but that question has to be left until we have a much clearer view of the nature of these comparisons. So, for the time being, I want simply to ask, How do we make interpersonal comparisons of well-being, on the informed-desire conception of what well-being is?

2. *A natural proposal for comparability and a problem with it*

Let us, in order to get at what seem to me to be the most live and difficult issues about comparability, make some assumptions. Let us put complications about *informed* desires aside for the moment, by supposing that all the desires that we shall be talking about are in fact informed. And let us put the problem of knowledge of other minds aside, too, by making what most persons would accept as the safe enough assumption that we can to some extent know what experiences other persons are having, including the sorts of experiences relevant to their well-being. To make this second assumption may seem to be helping ourselves to far too much, in effect to most of what comparability needs. But it has a practical pay-off; it allows us to focus our attention on the remaining moves that comparability also needs. What exactly is the nature of an interpersonal comparison? Are comparisons possible on some conceptions of well-being but not others? Are they possible on the scale that moral and political thinking needs?

The first is the important question. And it is a difficult question even with the assumption of knowledge of other minds. Suppose I know a lot about your experiences. I can correctly, fully, even vividly, represent them to myself. But my being able to represent to myself the feel of your experience is, in a way, too much of a good thing. It leaves me with one perception of the feel of my own experience and a second perception of the feel of yours. There is still a gap. How do I get the *two* experiences on to *one* scale? Knowledge of other minds does not take us far enough.

It is natural, and nowadays common,[11] to answer along these lines. Preference bridges the gap. If I can represent two personal states to myself—say, in my shoes with my outlook on things and in your shoes with your outlook—I can rank my being in the one state against my being in the other. I can then take my indifference between the states as showing them to be equal, and my preference for one as showing it to be higher. This answer thus reduces interpersonal comparisons to intrapersonal comparisons by appeal to the judger's own preference as to possible states of himself.[12]

But there is a problem. Could the crucial judger's preference really be a preference of his at all? I am supposed to introduce interpersonal measurement for my own use by forming a preference between possible states of myself. I prefer, I decide, taking on a life like that quiet scholar's, with his risk-aversion and security and contentment, to taking on a life like that mountaineer's, with his taste for adventure and the perils and challenges he faces. Now, usually when I decide whether I should prefer one of these lives to the other, I appeal to my own values or tastes or attitudes. I might, for instance, prefer the scholar's life because I morally disapprove of risking one's life on mountains if one has, as that mountaineer has, children to support. But that would not be a preference that gets us at the well-being of the two lives. To get at that I must strip away my own moral views. But then, stripped of my moral views, I might still prefer living the scholar's life simply because I am, like him, risk-averse. But that would not get us at an interpersonal comparison of well-being, either; it merely shows what I, as I am now, enjoy. So I must strip away my own tastes and inclinations as well. Now, the problem is not whether one can ever learn enough about the scholar's and the mountaineer's lives to form a preference between them, or whether one can ever decide that one of them is better off than the other. It seems to me that one can. The problem is, rather, how I, stripped as I have to become in order not to distort the comparison, can form *any* preference of my own between what are supposed to be in some sense states of myself, *me-as-the-scholar* and *me-as-the-mountaineer*. By reference to what can I now form the preference? Disendowed as I have to be, I have only what anyone else has at his disposal, namely general knowledge of human nature and particular knowledge about that scholar and that mountaineer. I can appeal to the human sciences; I can appeal to information about the extent to which that scholar's and that mountaineer's interests are satisfied. But then the reference to *my preference*, to which states *I should choose* to enter, is superfluous. It is not, at least in the first instance, a matter of my personal choice or preference at all, but rather of judgment on grounds available to anyone about two lives. *I* enter only as making the judgment that the one person is better off than the other. My judgment in certain cases may be wrong; it may differ from yours. But these are possibilities with any sort of judgment. And if you and I disagree over the scholar and the mountaineer, our disagreement is not like a disagreement in our personal preferences, which typically arises from our differing tastes and attitudes.

The purified preference that this proposal for comparability needs, preference purged of any particular point of view, seems to leave too little; it looks like preference purged of what is needed to make sense of preference. Could there be preference in these circumstances? So could preference, after all, be what bridges the gap?

3. Can the problem be solved?

We could admit that my comparison of the scholar-life and the mountaineer-life is a factual judgment that I make based on causal generalities about human nature. But we could go on regarding it, nonetheless, as still a preference of mine in a special sense—the sort of preference that I have when I look at things in a certain detached way. This is a solution offered by John Harsanyi.[13]

If we lived in a simple world where everyone's preferences were the same, Harsanyi begins, then everyone would have the same utility function, and interpersonal comparisons could be made simply by reference to it and would, in this way, reduce to intrapersonal ones. Of course, in reality, people have different preferences. But one person's preferences, Harsanyi says, are formed by the same general causal variables that affect everyone else's. Thus, differences in preferences can be predicted, in principle, from differences in these variables. If two persons have the same biological inheritance and the same life history, then since they are subject to the same general psychological laws governing the formation of preferences, they will end up with the same preferences. Now, the form of an interpersonal comparison of utility is that the judger would prefer to be in m's objective position with m's outlook than to be in n's position with n's outlook. But since the utility that one judger assigns to this m state is based on general causal knowledge of what anyone with m's biological inheritance and life history prefers, the utility that all judgers assign will, if knowledge is full enough, be identical. If we call the utility that a judger would assign to his entering m's state or n's state his 'extended' utility, then everyone has the same extended utility function. Therefore although two persons' ordinary utility functions are likely to be different, their extended utility function will prove to be the same. This restores us to that favourable situation where interpersonal comparisons are reducible to intrapersonal ones. It is because interpersonal comparisons are a certain sort of factual proposition that they can also be expressions of personal preference.

Most of what Harsanyi says seems to me right. It is plausible that everyone's preferences are determined by the same general causal variables. And a loose way of putting this would be to say, as he does, that if I were like you in biological make-up and life history, then I should have the preferences you have. What strictly is meant, however, is a perfectly general causal regularity: *anyone* with a certain biological make-up and life history will have certain preferences. Therefore, with enough information about the scholar and the mountaineer and enough general causal knowledge, I can come to understand the preferences of each. But there is still the problem of the gap. How do I bring my understanding of their states together in an interpersonal comparison? Harsanyi says that I, the judger, supply the bridge. Yet, having banned *my* preferences, in the ordinary sense, by accepting that interpersonal comparisons are factual judgments, Harsanyi seeks to restore them by arguing that, since these factual judgments are the same for everyone, they justify the introduction of an extended utility function that is also the same for everyone. But all that the claim that there is an extended utility function in this case means is that preferences are subject to general causal regularity and that, for that reason, everyone is constrained to make the same causal judgments about preferences. The extended utility function is not *my* utility function. In ranking the utilities of the scholar's state and the mountaineer's state, I do not rank *my* utilities. It is not a question of which *I* prefer, *me-like-this* or *me-like-that*. Harsanyi moves from the causal explanation of preferences to the existence of a common extended utility function and, finally, to the reduction of interpersonal to intrapersonal comparisons. But what seems the best interpretation of the existence of a common extended utility function gives no adequate motivation for reintroducing preference.

We might, therefore, try solving the problem another way. Perhaps we ought to conceive of the differing utility functions of different persons as a rather superficial phenomenon. Our tastes and attitudes do indeed differ, but perhaps they represent merely different approaches to, in effect, the same substantial end. Perhaps, deep down we are all after the same thing—enjoyment in a broad sense would seem to be the most plausible candidate. This is the assumption that we all have the same deep utility function.[14] Therefore, when I think about the prospect of my entering a scholar-state or a mountaineer-state, I should put aside my personal tastes and attitudes, which constitute my superficial utility function, and work only with my deep utility function. Then the preference I should form would be the same as the preference anyone else would form from this ultimately authoritative, basic, perspective.

But this solution is even less promising. It falls back on the notion of a single, substantive super-value, and it is highly doubtful that there is one.[15] There are many different, substantive prudential values, and different persons may, and often do, differ over what they are. I may aim at realizing certain values in my life; you may aim at realizing others. Since there is no substantive super-value that our different aims may be seen as merely means to or parts of, there need not be any one thing that, over all, we are both in fact aiming at. So there is no deep utility function to ensure that our particularly basic preferences, on which interpersonal comparisons are to be defined, will coincide.[16]

Neither an extended nor a deep utility function solves the problem. Neither really manages to dispel the mystery of where, once his personal tastes, attitudes, and concerns are banned, the judger's preference will come from. It is hard to find any coherent explanation of comparability in terms of the judger's preference. This would be bad news for desire accounts if this were the only sort of explanation open to them. But I now want to suggest that it is not.

4. *Interpersonal comparisons of well-being*

There is another possibility. Interpersonal comparisons of well-being, we might say, are judgments of the following sort. I, informed as I am, want this thing very much. You, or virtually anyone, would want it, if informed, the same amount. It is, for most persons, roughly that desirable. He, on the other hand, wants it less; he lacks, let us say, certain normal capacities (for instance, he is depressed so wants nothing very much). The quantitative phrases 'very much', 'same amount', and 'less' that appear in these judgments come from the same scale. We can make judgments, based on causal knowledge about human nature and information about particular persons, of how much persons want things, and these judgments place the desires of different persons on the same scale. Perhaps the mistake made by accounts of comparability in terms of judger's preference is to misunderstand the forms that knowledge of other minds can take. If one thinks of it as limited, say, to representations of the texture of experiences, then of course there is a gap that needs bridging, and preference looks a likely bridge. But if we know that you want this only a little and I want that a lot, and these terms are not relative to others things that each of us, in his own case, wants but relative to each other, then there is no gap, so no need for a bridge. This seems to me the best solution to the comparison problem, and I want now to suggest a way of developing it.

We have a picture of normal human desires: virtually all persons, when informed, want to live autonomously, to have deep personal relations, to accomplish something with their lives, to enjoy themselves. With experience, we build up such a profile of the components of a valuable life, including their relative importance—a chart to the various peaks that human life can reach.[17] These values, if our profile is complete, cover the whole domain of prudential value. They are valuable in any life; individual differences matter not to what appears in this profile of general prudential values, but to how, or how much, a particular person can realize one or other particular value.[18] Then, we also build up understanding of how individuals deviate from the norm. For instance, one person may find autonomy anxiety-making, so his life is more complex than the normal one: he faces, as a normal person does not, a hard choice between competing values. Or you may enjoy things more than most persons, while he is depressed and enjoys nothing very much. Also, there will be differences in the form that a value takes in different lives: what you can accomplish, or enjoy, in your life may well be different from what I can in mine. But all this reasoning about individual differences takes place within the framework of a set of values that apply to everyone. And these three elements, a list of universal prudential values, general causal knowledge of human nature, and the information about particular persons relevant to these causal generalities, make up our grounds for judging how well off persons are.

Take this case. Smith's great ambition in life is to become a millionaire. He sees it as life's crowning achievement. Whether or not it is, that is how he sees things. Perhaps he lacks imagination; perhaps his horizons are limited; but he does not even entertain the possibility of another goal in life. In a way the very limits of his vision contribute to the intensity of his desire: being a millionaire gets invested with all the attraction of being what it is to have a valuable life. Jones, on the other hand, attaches no intrinsic value to money; his ends in life are to live autonomously, to love and be loved, to accomplish something important in his life, to enjoy himself. Suppose Smith and Jones both reach their goals. How do I compare their well-being? On the model of the judger's preference, my knowing Smith's situation and aims would allow me to form a desire of a certain strength about my landing in that situation with those aims—and similarly for Jones. But 'strength' in what sense? No doubt, with a million in the bank and seeing things Smith's way, I should want it a lot. And, with Jones's success seen through Jones's eyes, I should want that a lot too. But there is still a gap. How do I get these two strong desires on to one scale? We cannot be after 'strength' in the sense of felt intensity, because just how strongly we feel our desires is largely a matter of upbringing (Smith easily gets emotional; Jones has a stiff upper lip) and has no secure correlation with how well off we end up. Nor could it be 'strength' in the sense of motivational force; a person can succumb to desires that are not in his best interest. What we are after must be 'strength' in some such sense as 'place in an informed preference ordering'. The relevant desires here must be desires formed by at least some appreciation of the nature of the objects of the desire.[19] Maybe Smith is sufficiently cushioned by his lack of imagination that he is not at all disillusioned when he gets his million; maybe he simply enjoys the fact of his success. This is obviously important to how well off he is, and I should need information about him as an individual to know whether this is so. But perhaps also, if his horizons were not so limited, he would want some of the things Jones is after even more. Perhaps some things just do make life more valuable than others; some things may just be more desirable, when we are informed, than others. It seems very likely. But then judgments to that effect have little to do with the judger's own preference about entering one state or another. It is less a matter of what the judger in fact wants, even of his desires formed on the spot,[20] than of how desirable certain things are. The judger cannot form a preference between entering the total Smith-state or the total Jones-state until he knows the strength of Smith's and Jones' desires, in the relevant sense of 'strength'. The model of the judger's preference gives no clear answer to the question, What is the relevant sense of 'strength'? If the answer is, 'strength' in the sense of 'place in an informed preference ordering', then part of the ground for interpersonal comparisons, besides the things that are peculiar to Smith and Jones as individuals, are the things that are desirable for persons generally.

This case is reminiscent of Mill's interpersonal comparison of Socrates and the Fool. The Fool attaches no value to Socrates' life. Socrates attaches none to the Fool's life. How would each decide how relatively well off they are? This is a case where there is no obvious overlap in the values, tastes, and attitudes of the judger and his subject—at least, in the values, tastes, and attitudes relevant to the judgment that has to be made here. Socrates can, of course, decide: if I had the Fool's values, tastes, and attitudes, I should find the Fool's life valuable; I should actually want it a lot. But *finding* it valuable and *actually* wanting it in those circumstances cannot be what matter. In any case, would this decision of Socrates be a personal preference of his? And is this the sort of decision that leads to comparability? The answer in both cases seems to be, No. What Socrates needs to make is a judgment of a very different sort from what we ordinarily understand by a personal preference. He needs to know how much persons generally, when informed, would want each life, how desirable they are. This judgment *can* be expressed as a personal preference, but the nature of the judgment is very special: it is a judgment about prudential values that is independent of what any particular individual's desires or preferences happen to be. That is, Socrates should need to know, primarily, what made life valuable.[21] He should have to appeal to his understanding of what humans, or sometimes humans of a certain type, are capable of, and of the various peaks that human life can reach. Then he should have to decide how close he and the Fool came to some peak. What he should not particularly need to consult is the phenomenological 'feel' of their experience, nor their personal tastes and attitudes, nor his own preferences about landing in the one sort of life or the other.

It is true, of course, that Mill's own discussion of Socrates and the Fool gives preference considerable prominence, but I do not think that the prominence he gives it is at odds with what I am saying. It was not at all implausible of Mill to take as the authoritative comparison of Socrates' life and the Fool's the *preference* of persons who have experience of both. Still, there is an important sense in which the preferences that appear in this comparison are not personal ones; they are not expressions of each individual's tastes or attitudes or concerns. They are desires formed by the perception of the nature of the two lives. The preferences relevant to this comparison are not the ones formed by anything peculiar to the judger.[22] They are formed, in a way, both from scratch and from no particular point of view, simply from an understanding of the objects before us. So reference to the *judger's* personal preference between *himself-as-this* or *himself-as-that* drops away as irrelevant. And the judgements relevant to comparisons do not even need to take the form of pair-wise comparisons. Each object can be placed singly on the general profile of values: the values in a Socratic life matter a lot; the Fool's gratifications do not matter much.

Take one more case, a case in which individual differences matter much more. One prudential value is enjoyment, and it is the plainest of facts that different persons enjoy different things, or the same thing to very different degrees. So we cannot here make comparisons by appeal to the common profile. We have to appeal to the other grounds—general causal knowledge and information about particular persons.

When I go to decide whether you enjoy wine more than I do, I need to know what your powers of discrimination are and whether your capacities for enjoyment are more or less normal. If I decide that nothing has dulled your enjoyment, that your powers of discrimination are much greater than mine, and that for someone like you greater discrimination goes along with greater enjoyment, then I have my answer.

But even enjoyment is misunderstood if the large common element in it is overlooked. There are natural human enjoyments. When I consider ways in which my tastes and interests might develop, I look at general issues such as what normal human capacities are and how I am placed to develop them. For example, you like fine clarets; I like only plonk. My palate, no doubt, could be trained too. And faced with that possibility, I should reason something like this. Is it more enjoyable to have these powers of discrimination? Well, persons who have them do not, in general, lose their capacity to enjoy plonk, and most persons find that they have more to enjoy. So I, and most other persons, would be better off developing these powers of discrimination. And we decide this not by deciding how strong this or that particular person's desire is but by deciding how strong this kind of desire is compared to that kind. We enter them on the general profile of human desires. To decide how much someone enjoys life, one does not usually need to get inside his skin; one needs to know both what makes life enjoyable and how he, with his individual differences, is placed to exploit its possibilities.

So it is not that the general profile of prudential values is the whole ground of interpersonal comparisons. My point about the general profile is that the ground of interpersonal comparisons is not full without it, not that it is the full ground. Individual differences of the sort that I have just been discussing are obviously an important type of argument in any plausible utility function that aspires to completeness. The profile of prudential values gives the general framework for comparisons. It forms much of the ground of comparison when we choose between different ways of life. But often we are interested in how good various options are within a single way of life, and often with individual ways of reacting and responding. My stressing the role of the profile of prudential values may make my account sound too objectivist and so defective in just the way that I said at the start objectivist accounts tend to be. But one defect of objectivist accounts is that they have no place for individual differences, and the account of prudential values that I developed in Part One does. Another defect is that it is hard to see where an objectivist's values are coming from, but there is nothing to prevent our saying that all values in the general profile must find their place inside informed desires. If a solution to the problem of comparability is to be found anywhere, it has to be found in the context of a theory of prudential values—one that makes it clear both the extent to which values are not personal and the way in which individual differences affect values, one that gets the mix between the personal and the impersonal right.

Not surprisingly, using the wrong conception of well-being distorts the problem of interpersonal comparisons. If well-being consists in mental states, then interpersonal comparisons present the daunting task, first, of learning about the texture of individual experiences and, then, of finding a way of ranking them. If well-being is fulfilment of desires, but desires are seen largely as a product of tastes that are personal and varying, then interpersonal comparisons present the equally daunting task of learning each individual's desires and their intensity.[23] But tastes do not take up so much of the ground for comparisons. Basic prudential values provide us with an important standard for judging many (ordinary) human lives. They let us say, though only roughly, how good the life is, how it could be better, and how it compares to other lives. They considerably ease the burden of comparison. The deepest and most decisive issues about comparability are ones about the nature of well-being.

Does this mean that comparisons are value judgments? That is too vague a question to answer outright. What some writers mean in saying that interpersonal comparisons are, or involve, evaluations is often not clear, perhaps even to themselves. It is true that Robbins and many subsequent economists seem to have meant that there is no way to compare information about individual utilities without making what are, in effect, very strong assumptions about what would be fair for the group. For instance, the zero-one rule is the assumption that everybody's best state (give it the value 1) and worst state (give it the value 0) is the same. Our being able to measure each individual's own utility, even on a fairly powerful scale unique up to a linear transformation, is not enough for comparability. But the further assumption of the zero-one rule would give it to us. But the zero-one rule is just false. It is not the case that we all reach the same peaks and valleys. What is needed for comparability is something less than such strong assumptions about fairness but something more than simple matters of fact. Some comparisons are judgments about, say, the factual matter of whether you want to drink a certain glass of wine more than I do. But in focusing attention on informed desires in this way, we are already accepting one particular account of the nature of well-being. And on that account many comparisons involve appeal to a general profile of prudential values. So interpersonal comparisons are value judgments in this sense: they are part and parcel of a complex normative exercise.

5. *Intrapersonal intertemporal comparisons*

This account of interpersonal comparisons also helps with intrapersonal intertemporal comparisons. When I think at all ambitiously about what will enhance my own well-being, I do not consult my own present tastes and desires, as if which desires I have at any moment, and how they change, is something that just happens to me. In fact, when I am thinking radically, I do not consult any of my tastes and desires, seen as *mine*. Instead I consult the profile of prudential values. Would I be better off giving up my fool-like gratifications for a more demanding Socratic life? I should answer that question by deciding what sorts of life are valuable and what I am capable of. I should reason in much the same way even over rather trivial matters. Should I learn to like oysters? Well, if I am full of food fads, then I am missing a lot in life, and it would probably be worth changing. But if it is only oysters that I hate, and if I think that my dislike is pretty stubborn, then it would probably not be worth changing. I do not consult my own particular tastes, attitudes, and concerns;

I appeal to the same mix of the personal and the impersonal as before—what is valuable and how I am placed.

Part of the insight in the wish to reduce interpersonal to intrapersonal comparisons is that the reasoning in the two is virtually the same. Is Socrates dissatisfied better off than the Fool satisfied? Am I better off going down the Socratic path or the Fool's? I often need the same materials to answer either the interpersonal or the intrapersonal question. The problems thought to be connected with our forming desires about these two sorts of life are avoided if we realize that what we need is, not a personal preference of the judger (which, anyway, seems not to be available), but desires—yours, mine, and the other person's—shaped by our understanding of the two options (which is available). In first forming a preference between the options, I give expression to a value. I do not consult a value that is already built into me in the form of a utility function of one sort or other; on the contrary, I create and give shape to part of my utility function. Neither intrapersonal nor interpersonal comparisons are the more fundamental; both rely on the same sort of reasoning.

6. *Comparability on a social scale*

There are serious worries about comparability at the other end of the scale—on the large social scale. Could a government ever carry on its deliberation using a broad conception of well-being, such as one from the utilitarian tradition? Could it realistically expect to collect the enormous amount of information that it would then need? Could it hope to get its citizens to accept what would sometimes be bound to be deeply damaging results of interpersonal comparisons based on value judgments that they themselves might hotly dispute?[24]

This worry misunderstands desire accounts. To give a friend a present I should indeed want to know his tastes and interests. But governments are not in the business of giving presents. Their chief business is enhancing possibilities for co-operation. That involves setting up social institutions, defending and amending them, and remedying their unwanted consequences. It is not easy to say how much control and correction governments should go in for, but in general a government has to restrict its attention to the general framework of its citizens' lives. Any realistic government would accept the limitations imposed by the large scale of its operations: it would adjust to its own lack of knowledge of individual lives and to the intrusiveness needed to overcome it by keeping its hands off a lot of our business; it would meet the need for citizens to accept the outcome of its interpersonal comparisons by prudently steering clear of contentious issues as much as it can.

In any case, governments—just as you and I in our interpersonal comparisons—would use, for the most part, the list of prudential values, supplemented by their necessary conditions. So we should need to know not each person's individual desires with the intensities peculiar to his nature, but what is in general desirable in life. And we should need to know what the unavoidable means to those ends are: usually, the healthier, wealthier, freer, and more knowledgeable we are the better we can realize our life plans. So governments would in general compare different citizens' well-being by appeal to things that it is assumed they all value. They would do that in general, but not in every detail. There are items on the combined list of prudential values and their unavoidable means that not everyone aims at, but so long as governments do not become too contentious they can go beyond items that are universally agreed. As political experience shows, stability does not require total neutrality. Anyway, the basic list of prudential values and unavoidable means provides an 'objective' measure (in the sense that the measure does not depend upon persons' own individual desires),[25] which greatly eases the burden of interpersonal comparisons on the social scale.

In practice, governments face a wide variety of kinds of decision, and the basis of their interpersonal measurement should change from kind to kind. Any interpersonal measure meant for use on a social scale involves simplification, but the degree of simplification can, and no doubt should, vary. In any case, the difference between the way we operate at opposite ends of the scale of size—parents with their children, a government with its citizens—should not be exaggerated. Parents' judgments about their children are always made within the framework of their theoretical understanding of human nature. Think of how parents' views about the stress that their children feel have changed since Freud. And legislators appeal to the same sort of theoretical understanding of human nature. In simple cases, a legislator can just take an increase of something on the list of prudential values and unavoidable means as an increase in general well-being, as when the government can promote an increase in GNP that can be used to promote any of the items on the list. In more complex cases, a legislator has to decide between promoting one item on the list at the cost of another, for which purpose he will need a schedule of the trade-offs that virtually all of us are willing to make. For instance, most people rank health and freedom from anxiety high. Should a government promote polio vaccine though it will leave less money for the arts and education? It is not straining the normal trade-off profile that one would build up to say that, given the costs of a polio vaccination programme, the loss in promotion of the arts is less than the gain in freedom from disease and anxiety. Sometimes, however, our general theory of human nature will run out of answers. Would the residents of old people's homes prefer more privacy or more physical comfort? Perhaps a government ought to find out. Sometimes, of course, research or polls would be too costly or too unreliable to bother with. Sometimes, for lack of anything better, a legislator would just have to think himself imaginatively into the position of those affected by the legislation and guess the outcome. And, of course, one legislator's guess may differ from another's. When there is disagreement, we need a procedure, such as majority vote, to resolve it—not any longer to tell us what maximizes well-being but to do the different job of giving us a fair resolution. These disagreements do not, in fact, produce social instability. On the contrary, our legislators now reason far less satisfactorily than this, and if we can stomach what we get now, why should we be upset by better?

Some political philosophers argue that governments should restrict their attention to the all-purpose means to a good life, and stay neutral between differing substantive conceptions of what a good life is.[26] They argue this, not primarily because such neutrality would ease the burden of interpersonal comparisons (though it would), but because injustices would otherwise arise (some persons would, just because of the strength of their desires, come off better, even much better, in the distribution of society's resources than others, in violation of a deep requirement of equality). I find it doubtful that justice requires such strict neutrality.[27] But, in any case, a government would not survive if it restricted itself so severely. As we have seen,[28] if it did, it would not be able to make decisions that are central to its function. The appreciation of art is not part of everyone's conception of a good life; health, in contrast, is an all-purpose means. Yet there must be a point where the moral demands of promoting health are fully met, and also a point at which, though not fully met, they are so little affected that they matter less than some important but non-neutral value such as art. There seems to be no way to decide where these points are without deciding what else is valuable—say, art—and how valuable it is, and then ranking all of these competing claims on some scale of overall importance to the quality of life.

Governments need a standard of well-being that, like a dictionary, comes in many sizes. Usually they need consult only the 'pocket' standard; but sometimes they will need the 'desk' standard, and so on. The informed-desire conception allows this, while a neutral standard restricted to all-purpose means does not.

PART THREE

MORAL IMPORTANCE

VIII

FROM PRUDENCE TO MORALITY

1. *Morality as something alien*

SOME of us think that the question, Why should I be moral?, hard though it is to answer, raises no serious doubts. However, others of us, probably a majority, disagree. We feel morality as something to some extent alien, as something external to the workings of our own nature, as something imposed from outside. We have our own aims, commitments, attachments, bents, enthusiasms, often far from selfish or callous, and when they come into conflict with what presents itself, sometimes after rather abstract deliberation, as a moral requirement, we wonder what authority morality could possibly have.

There are various well-known, sometimes rather desperate, remedies for these feelings of alienation. They all involve reducing morality to something less external to human nature. One way is to reduce it to self-interest, the narrower the conception of self-interest the better. Another is to reduce it to some rich form of human flourishing. Another, more modestly, is to be content to find morality a place among many persons' own aims. Yet another, more ambitiously, is to make its requirements into requirements of rationality.

Moral scepticism certainly has dimensions not present in, say, scepticism about the external world. The problem it presents is not just one of getting one's beliefs well-founded. Morality ends up with decisions that guide action. Any acting-guiding principles must meet the Requirement of Psychological Realism: the source of morality can never stray far from the natural sources of action.[1] But what *are* the natural sources of human action? And more generally, what is the nature of the self? On this, we tend to divide, as much by inclination as by judgment, into two camps. One camp says: the deep sources of human action are sympathy, attachments, commitments—in short, sentiment or feeling. It is the answer of classical British Empiricism, most attractively stated by Hume and accepted by Bentham and Mill. The other camp finds that list of motives acceptable, as far as it goes, but simply too short. They say: there is a further source of human action, namely understanding or reason. This is where the dispute must focus. Morality cannot take its stand far from the sources of human action. But what are they? And can one see morality emerging from one of them? And can its restrictions fit into a social structure that persons of that nature can themselves fit into? The Requirement of Psychological Realism, in this form, clearly has got to be met. It gives us a natural starting place for our move from the discussion of prudence to the discussion of morality.

2. (a) Morality and self-interest

One way to make morality not at all alien is to reduce it to self-interest. Some persons are self-interested in a very cramped, crabbed, ungenerous way; nothing much matters to them but their own comfort and safety. If morality is to be reduced to self-interest in the sense of what about themselves persons actually care about, then it has to be reducible, in the case of a cramped, crabbed, ungenerous individual, to his own meagre range of concerns. But there are ampler, more enlightened forms of self-interest, and one might mean by the term one of these more idealized forms. For instance, one might see moral obligations as solutions to situations of partial conflict, the best bargain that any one person could strike, whether or not he actually knows it. Or one might mean by the term the flourishing of an individual life, on some rich conception of what human flourishing consists in. If we have the first, narrow sort of self-interest in mind, then the only hope of reducing morality to self-interest is with the help of sanctions. What authority has a judgment of moral obligation? One can answer: they are commands, backed up by sanctions. If the sanctions are severe and inescapable, then morality may well coincide with self-interest. But even most religious believers find it hard to accept that, since the sanctions in this world are not inescapable, life after death is tacked on as a sort of prison sentence. Anyway, religious believers do not often see self-interest as the source of morality. Life after death is, if nothing more, a human invention much of the purpose of which was to reduce morality to self-interest, but it is hard to see that it would also be God's purpose in his creation.[2] Bentham and Mill rightly stress the importance of social sanctions, but sanctions are important as the causes of the conformity that society needs. Since they are not always inescapable or sometimes even feasible, if the range of moral obligations is not to shrink much beyond our expectations, then social sanctions cannot be the source of obligations. Life cannot present the range of inescapable sanctions that the reduction needs; life after death could but does not.[3]

The reduction becomes more plausible when the accounts of self-interest become more idealized—not what we *think* is in our own interest but what actually *is*. If moral rules represent the best bargain each of us can hope to strike with the rest, and the bargain is better than no bargain at all, then they are reducible to an enlightened self-interest. This notion of moral rules as emerging from a bargain takes us into the territory of modern contractualism. One of the big attractions of contractualism is that it seems to manage many of the benefits of reducing morality to self-interest without its defects. But for now I want to look just at attempts to reduce morality to pure self-interest, and not to self-interest mitigated, as it is in contractualism, by some form of impartiality. It is true, and important, that many norms that are correctly regarded as moral rules are the best bargain that all parties can strike. Indeed, certain norms are so well grounded in that way that they never even need to be the subject of conscious or explicit bargaining. They emerged, and often quite complex social institutions embodying them also emerged, entirely naturally with the growth of social life.[4] I shall come back to this important fact later on.[5] However, the fact is important to understanding the limits to the forms that society and its norms can take and also the very considerable limits to the efficacy of moral judgment;[6] it is not important to understanding the authority of moral judgments. Again, unless we are willing to allow the range of moral judgment to shrink far behind our present expectations, morality cannot be reduced to this enlightened form of self-interest. There is more to

morality than resolution of partial conflict. There are, for
instance, moral obligations to those too weak to be in a
position to bargain effectively, such as the present losers in
some unfair but securely entrenched distribution of resources
or the members of some future generation who will suffer from
our high living.

The richer the notion of self-interest the more plausible the
reduction of morality to it and, up to a point, the more
plausible it will be as an account of self-interest. The most
plausible of all is the reduction to a rich conception of human
flourishing. There is, of course, the danger that one will make
the conception of human flourishing sufficiently rich by
packing it with ethical assumptions, so making it in effect
evaluative. For instance, one might contend that no one can
be 'truly' or 'deeply' happy unless he is to some fairly high
degree moral, where the effect of the qualifiers 'truly' or
'deeply' is to make 'happiness' a thoroughly evaluative
notion.[7] But that is not the real difficulty. We do not
need a reduction of morality to something entirely non-
evaluative. The question is, Can we make morality less alien?;
it is not, Can we make it less evaluative? We shall have solved
the alienation problem if we can reduce morality to some
normative notion that people see as less alien, that they more
easily identify with, than morality seemed at the start. All that
we have to do, for example, is convincingly argue that one
cannot be deeply happy (so long as the person we seek to
pursuade will accept that as a description of something that
comes within the compass of his happiness) without being to a
large degree moral. If certain moral categories, recognized as
moral, could be shown to be also prudential, without doing
violence to our original notion of the prudential, then we
should have gone a long way to solving the alienation
problem.

Still, there is another, altogether more familiar, obstacle to
reducing morality to human flourishing. A defensible conception of flourishing is bound to be too indeterminate to yield
interesting moral results.[8] Aristotle's conception, on some
interpretations, approached the degree of determinateness
needed to yield moral conclusions. But, as I argued in Part One,[9]
the most that we can hope for from an account of flourishing is

not a picture of the ideal form of life for all humans to adopt but a relatively short list of prudential values—the values that contribute to making a normal human life go well. Though these important values are valuable for everyone, and though the list of them does even constitute a kind of perfectionist picture of human existence, the conception of human flourishing they can be made to yield is far too indeterminate to serve in a reductionist programme. Even if one were willing to accept the list, even if one had no objections to its being so thoroughly evaluative itself, one would not have the materials to which morality could be reduced. The list, I think, includes all the following: enjoyment, deep personal relations, autonomy, accomplishment, understanding, and living a life of point and substance.[10] Perhaps the list should be a little longer. But these values can be realized in such different ways and combined in a life in such different proportions that there is no one form of life that emerges, let alone a form of life fully enough specified to provide materials for answering all the moral questions that life will present. They do not tell one, in any very definite way, what one ought to aim at in one's own individual life, and certainly do not tell one how one's own aims in life ought to be reconciled with the competing aims of others. They do not, for instance, provide even the rudiments of an account of justice.

That obstacle to the reduction is perfectly familiar. Another, and to my mind the greatest, obstacle to the reduction is less familiar. It is what might be called the penetration of the prudential by the moral. What I have in mind is this. One has not got a specification of the prudential at all without a pretty full account of what moral demands there are on us and how they are to be accommodated. Prudential value does not stop at the edges of an individual's own private life. Some persons may see their self-interest in a narrow, crabbed way. But anyone with a defensible idea of prudential values can see what he cares about not just as what as a matter of fact he *now* cares about, but as what he *ought* to care about or what he *will* care about after subjecting his concerns to full deliberation. He will find it hard, therefore, to keep moral and prudential values apart. One of the things he will want is a life of point and substance. What he will see as prudentially valuable, valuable to his own personal life, will to some extent coincide with what he will see as valuable morally. Our understanding of 'a good life' cannot be parcelled into 'good prudentially' and 'good morally'. The very phrase 'a good life' may seem ambiguous (good prudentially? good morally?), but at any deep level there are not two senses to be distinguished. Part of having a life of point and substance is having a life in which moral reasons take their place, along with other practical reasons, in motivation. This is a complicated matter, and I want to come back to look at it in greater detail shortly.[11] But for the moment let us accept that it is a marked and central part of some persons' experience that they cannot live a satisfactory life, seen simply in prudential terms, without some accommodation of morality —as marked and central a part of their experience as is their self-love.

That poses the following problem. To reduce morality to prudence is to reduce it to something that, without morality, has a gaping hole in it. One might think that this is not such a serious difficulty. Why not just say that if morality has been shown to be part of prudence then it has been shown to be reducible to prudence? But that will not do for a reduction, at least in the strong sense that we have so far had in mind. It does not find a place for determinate moral requirements in separate determinate prudential concerns. Instead, what we find is that both moral requirements and prudential concerns are indeterminate. Showing that morality is part of prudence might look like reducing morality to prudence only because the part of prudence to which morality will be reduced is already morality itself. But this is hardly, in any normal sense, a 'reduction'.

There is a parallel argument about motivation. One cannot treat prudential motives as basic and then establish a motive for morality by showing every moral act to be a necessary condition of reaching some prudential goal. A theory of motivation cannot itself be complete without an account of the force and place of moral reasons. An account of prudential motivation has to come at the same time as an account of moral motivation (and no doubt as accounts of other kinds of pracical reasons as well). There is, in that sense, no starting point in a theory of motivation. We have to deny the dualism of prudence and morality: they are not separable either as reasons for action or as motives. It is not that they are not different but that they overlap importantly.

I have just mentioned that, until now, we have been considering whether morality can be reduced to human flourishing in a pretty demanding sense of 'reduction': namely, that we can generate the content of morality out of the resources of the notion of flourishing. There is no reason why we cannot take a less demanding sense. What we want is to find morality a place inside the domain of prudence. We should still do that if the content of morality could in some way be generated independently of prudence, so that morality was already a set of satisfactorily determinate demands, and we merely showed that flourishing involved acting like *that*. Indeed, since part of flourishing, when it is properly understood, may turn out to be acting morally simply because it is morally, it may also turn out that, to use Robert Nozick's terms, ethical push (the push to our own action arising from our living a prudentially successful life) and ethical pull (the pull exerted on our action arising from the moral demands of others) eventually meet.[12] I do not think that they do, but I want to postpone that discussion until we come (very shortly, in Section 5) to how the push and pull of ethics do stand to one another.

Let us stop here with the relation between morality and self-interest. I realize that at points the case that I have set out has not been argued enough, but I shall come back to these matters too in Section 5.

3. (b) Morality and personal aims

To show that morality is not really alien, it is enough to find a place for it somewhere inside the self. And many persons have goals that are not self-interested, even goals that can plausibly be considered moral. They care about other persons, sometimes even more than they care about themselves. Sometimes they care about justice or about living a moral life. Admittedly, one cannot rely on some form of moral concern's being present in everyone, whereas everyone, or nearly everyone, can be relied upon to care about himself. But it is enough, for certain purposes, to find a place for morality inside *some* persons. If enough persons have enough moral concerns among their own personal aims, then morality will be an important social force.

It is undeniable that some persons aim at living moral lives. Now, there are many philosophers who argue that there are no reasons for action except for ones that link with some personal aim.[13] We all accept the Requirement of Psychological Realism. So if these philosophers were right, moral reasons would have to have the same sorts of links with personal aims. Bernard Williams, an advocate of this view, draws a useful distinction between 'internal' and 'external' reasons for action.[14] Internal reasons are ones that stand in a certain sort of relation, shortly to be explained, to some element of an agent's 'subjective motivational set'; an external reason is one that has no such relation.[15] Williams concludes that, once we see clearly what is involved in the existence of an external reason, we shall have to accept that there are none. The only reasons for action are internal. So if morality is to have any hope of meeting the Requirement of Psychological Realism, moral reasons will have to be reduced to internal reasons.

But there is this difficulty. Clearly not just any aim or desire or motive, just by happening to exist, will serve as backing for an internal reason. The difficulty here is very like the difficulty with desire accounts of well-being. A person's well-being cannot be explained in terms of just any desire that he happens to have. Persons sometimes actually want what will not enhance, and sometimes even harm, their well-being. The only remotely plausible desire-account of well-being has to be in terms not of a person's actual desires but of his informed desires—desires in some sense idealized.[16] Similarly, if a desire is based on false belief, then it provides no reason for action. As Williams, for instance, well knows,[17] internal reasons must also depend upon desires that are in some way idealized. But how ideal? Some candidate criticisms of desires appeal, in effect, to what look very much like external reasons. So the answer requires a full, detailed picture of how deliberation about values ought to go—a picture that those who advocate that all reasons are internal have never really given us.

We have just noted the obvious point that if a desire rests

on false belief it will not support an internal reason. What is more, a person might think that he has an internal reason when he does not (e.g. he thinks he wants such-and-such but does not really), or he might not know that he has an internal reason when he does (e.g. he is unaware that he does really want such-and-such). Also, a desire or an internal reason that one did not know one had can be uncovered in the course of deliberation. For instance, one wants x and comes to see, upon reflection, that y-ing is the most efficient way of getting it. Or one comes to see, upon reflection, that x and y, which seemed to clash with one another, can both be achieved. Or one wants x and comes to see, upon reflection, further or better ways of realizing it. These are all forms of criticism that Williams acknowledges.[18] There is nothing wrong with that list, I think, except that it stops too soon; it constitutes a rather meagre description of practical deliberation. If all reasons are internal reasons, then our 'subjective motivational set', though it does not have to be static, will change only in response to new facts or to some better entrenched member of the set. But we ask far more searching questions about our aims and resort to more radical forms of deliberation to answer them. Such searching questions arise, it is true, fairly rarely, but they are the especially fateful ones. We can change not only our desires by appeal to some deeply entrenched member of the subjective motivational set, we can also change the deeply entrenched members of the set. I went into such a case when I earlier discussed the relation of value and desire and, again later, when I discussed perfectionism.[19] Suppose that I have been quite content to fritter my life away with pleasant pastimes, until I meet someone who has accomplished something important with his life, and then, inspired by his example, I form a new desire to live a life like that. But upon further reflection, I see that not every achievement will serve to give life point and substance. A compulsive achiever may quickly mount the rungs of some conventional ladder of success but not get nearer to accomplishment in the sense I am trying to understand. And an achiever might get great joy from success in the contest, but this sort of joy is not to be confused with the sense of accomplishment that I am after. Nor is the mere exercise of skills or the winning of respect and admiration a sign of accomplishment. So one stage of the deliberation is to separate off what *is* to count as 'accomplishment' in the relevant sense. Another stage is to see whether, when all is said and done, what one has succeeded in isolating looks worthy of being an end in life.[20] And one decides this not by appeal to some still more deeply entrenched member of one's subjective motivational set. There is none to appeal to, except for the vacuous desire to have a valuable life, which would not in any case help because what we have to decide is whether accomplishment, defined as we now have managed to define it, is indeed valuable. What is important about this more radical form of deliberation is that subjective, varying, personal desires play very little part, while understanding plays a large part. What is central to the deliberation is seeing fully and independently what the sort of accomplishment in question is, and this is a sort of perception that introduces a new member into one's motivational set with much less aid from the old members than the picture of an internal reason permits.

This is not to say that things are desired because valuable, not valuable because desired.[21] For one thing, there are very many different sorts of case, my example of accomplishment being only one. In many other cases—simple tastes, for instance—the element of understanding is small and of desire large; rotting bananas are valuable to me because, odd though it may seem to most of you, that is the way I like them. Another thing is that, even in the cases where the element of understanding is large, as it is with accomplishment as a prudential value, desire also plays a role in its status as a value. There is no priority: desire does not precede value; value does not precede desire. In the case of accomplishment we desire it because we come to see what it is. But when we explain what it is we do not describe things neutrally. The language we use in reporting our perceptions selects what we see as important and shows how we view things in a favourable light. But this is where, in the middle of this explanation of what we perceive, desire re-enters at a deeper point. We have to explain what it is to see things favourably. We have to explain what makes certain features of objects *desirability* features. Some understanding—the sort that involves fixing on certain features and seeing them in a favourable light—is also a kind of movement. It requires a will to go for what has those features. There is no adequate explanation of their being desirability features without an appeal to this kind of movement. So we cannot, even in a case such as accomplishment, separate understanding and desire.

What this means is not so much that the advocates of internal reasons are wrong as that the distinction between internal and external reasons is unreal.[22] A prudential value such as accomplishment is valuable for everyone; anyone who fails to recognize it as valuable lacks understanding. It is true that there will be some special sorts of persons for whom accomplishment conflicts with other important values (it raises great anxieties, say) so that they had better pass it up; but these are cases of conflict of values in which accomplishment is still a value. It takes a quite complex story to make clear both the extent to which values are not personal and the way individual differences affect values, a story I told more fully earlier.[23] One outcome is that once we get the roles of desire and understanding straight, the distinction between 'subjective' and 'objective' also looks unreal. Are prudential values subjective or objective? I use 'subjective' here to mean 'dependent upon an agent's own desires'. Now, prudential values do not rest upon *one* person's desires. They would not even be intelligible if their status as values came simply from someone's wanting them; they have also to be something that persons generally can see as worth going for. But then it is also true that varying, personal desires matter to prudential values in several ways. Individuals differ in how, or even whether, they can realize some particular value. For instance, desires enter importantly in tastes. The distinction between 'subjective' and 'objective' has figured importantly in the history of moral philosophy in part because the distinction between the competing views *valuable because desired* and *desired because valuable* has been thought to mark a deep division in our options. But the dependence of prudential value on desire and understanding is much less simple, much less a matter of all or nothing, than these dualisms suggest. The distinction between objective and subjective, defined in this common way, does not mark an especially crucial distinction.

What this means is that the distinction between internal and external reasons is another untenable dualism. The doubts that some writers feel about external reasons is that it is hard to see how they could ever create a new motive.[24] An agent who acknowledges an external reason to x is supposed then to form, on the strength of understanding this reason, a motive to x, whatever motivations he originally had. What is thought problematic about this is that this new motive cannot stand to his old motives in the ways that the non-radical criticisms of desires allow, because they all depend, in the end, upon some member of the agent's personal subjective motivational set, thus making the reason internal, not external. Can one see any further way for a new motive to arise? Could it arise, in particular, simply from a change in understanding? But this scepticism about external reasons depends upon our keeping desire and understanding at a considerable distance from one another.[25] Any normal person who is frittering his life away has a reason to try to accomplish something with it. The sort of more radical deliberation I sketched a moment ago is the sort that he would have to go through to recognize this as a reason. It is not that it appeals to some pre-existent member of his subjective motivational set. But it is not free from desire either: the understanding that is needed is a grasp of certain desirability features, and they owe their status as such to normal human aims. It is on the nature of just this sort of deliberation that the important issues about external reasons turn. This deliberation is a matter of coming to see some new kind of thing as valuable, and the question is how it relies upon the present membership of one's motivational set. Certainly a lot is likely to be necessary for us to be able to come to see this new kind of thing as valuable. It is not just a matter of understanding features of the newly valued object that are expressible in value-neutral ways. One has to work one's way into the new vocabulary that gives expression to our fastening upon some features and not others as worth directing our attention to. This vocabulary expresses, so cannot be separated from, a sense of what is important for action. To work one's way into the vocabulary, to come to see things in fresh, subtle, complex ways, is unlikely to be easy. The point is not that one cannot come to see things in this way without also falling motivationally under the sway of the perceptions; on the contrary, it is possible, in the detached manner of a good anthropologist, to get inside highly subtle points of view without endorsing them. The point is, rather, that it will often not be at all easy. It may sometimes take guidance, training, and practice. But there is one sort of difficulty that it does not present. We are not faced with two outlooks—our old one and our new one—at a loss for a way of mediating between them. It may look as if this choice, being a choice between two evaluative outlooks, needs an equivalent outlook of the same sort but more basic than each of them. But that is not how such deliberation need go. We have to be able to decide that, say, a life with enjoyment and accomplishment is, other things being equal, better than a life without them. I can make that judgment from within the way of seeing things that sees enjoyment and accomplishment as valuable. What I need, in order to make that judgment without arbitrariness, is to be able to decide, also without arbitrariness though within that perspective, that enjoyment and accomplishment are indeed valuable. This kind of reasoning need neither appeal to a member of the present subjective motivational set nor proceed without touching motives. Understanding and motivation cannot here be very sharply separated. Practical rationality is not bloodless; it itself cannot even be understood independently of motivation. Motivation is not blind; it is shaped, though to different degrees in different cases, by our perception of the nature of its objects.

One of the things we have been trying to do in this discussion is to place morality sufficiently inside the self to meet the Requirement of Psychological Realism. But making morality internal is not the only job. We also have to show why morality should have any authority over our actions at all. Making it internal does not, in itself, make it authoritative. We have an alienation problem, but we also have an authority problem. We quite rightly ask, What authority over my actions do highly theoretical moral considerations have? But we should also ask, What authority over my actions do my present desires have? Why should I be moved by any present aim of mine, no matter how it came about, no matter how well founded? The authority of my present aims is hardly more obvious than the authority of my theoretical beliefs. Desires have histories. Some desires, no doubt, have the sort of motivational authority that we are after, but some do not. We need a way to determine which are which.[26]

So it is a mistake to think that the foundation of agency is the subjective motivational set. We ask, Should I want that? Agency has a role in determining the motivational set. It does not just start with motives; some motives have their origins in the search for the answer to the radical interpretation of the question, Should I want that? There is no starting point, no single foundation upon which all the rest of the building blocks sit, in either practical reason or in theories of motivation. The holism characteristic of theories in the natural sciences applies here too. The sorts of desires that have authority in motivation are shaped by understanding. Understanding gets its direction from the nature of human desires.

Reducing morality to present personal aims is puzzling in a way that reducing it to self-interest is not. Why should I accept some demanding moral requirement when it has a clear cost? It is implausible to answer, Because it is your *present* desire. It is implausible to answer even, Because it is your *desire*. What authority does any old present desire have? The concept of a reason is fairly strongly normative. One only gets at a practical reason if one can answer, Because it is *worth* desiring. Self-interest is a consideration that not only appears in desires but also deserves its place there. Its worth may be exaggerated and may indeed, upon close scrutiny, be much more limited than we tend to think,[27] but self-interest is not only internal to the self but also authoritative. On the other hand, the advantage of a reduction to personal aims over a reduction to self-interest is that many of us do care about things other than ourselves, and some of these other things are, unless we are all grossly deceived, well worth caring about. So the question that is important to each of us is, What do I most care about? Not 'do I happen to', as if I had to find out some fact about myself, but 'should I', given the sorts of radical and non-radical criticism of desire open to us. If I ask myself, Why should I be moral?, I cannot just answer, Because I now want to. The answer begs a very important question. Do desires, regardless of their content or their cause constitute a practical reason? Since they do not, I have to find a fuller answer. I have to satisfy myself that morality constitutes a good reason for action. What we can accept as worth desiring gives us a reason and also becomes, since it is part of a desire's being shaped, a motive. So we cannot first supply a theory of motivation and then show how it limits the nature of moral reasons. A theory of motivation cannot itself be complete without an account of moral reasons. If morality constitutes an object worth desiring, then it is part of what life aims at and one of the springs of action. A theory of motivation cannot, any more than a theory of self-interest could, limit morality, because it cannot itself be determined independently of determining moral reasons. It must all come at the same time. The Requirement of Psychological Realism imposes no independent restriction on moral reasons.

4. (c) Morality and rationality

Another important strategy in dealing with the alienation problem is to make morality a requirement of reason. Our reason is part of our nature, so morality can be seen not as imposed upon us from outside but as self-imposed. But, again, solving the alienation problem is only half the battle. There is also the authority problem. Would morality also then be something to care about? If my acting immorally is acting contrary to my rational nature—say, in the worst case, contradicting myself—why should I care? Self-contradiction seems an awfully small price to pay for what, in the moral stakes, can be very great gains.

When writers mention rationality, what they have in mind ranges from minimal conceptions that no matter how the notion of rationality might be filled out will have to feature in it (e.g. consistency) to quite rich accounts that embody stringent and contentious normative standards. There cannot be any even fairly rich account of practical reason without decision about how moral reasons fit into the set of good reasons. The only attempts at showing substantive moral principles to be a requirement of reason that have any hope of success are those that use a fairly rich account of rationality. The minimal account, an account that does not incorporate

among other things an account of moral reasons, delivers no
interesting moral conclusions. For example, at first glance,
Kant seems to use only the most minimal notion (indeed only
the notion of contradiction). The Categorical Imperative test
involves first universalizing one's maxim and then seeing
whether, when this new law of human operation is added to
the description of how the rest of the world operates,
contradiction results. But in cases of even blatantly immoral
maxims, it is very hard to uncover anything remotely approaching contradiction in the strict sense. But then Kant
explains that he has in mind either of two sorts of contradiction,
contradiction in formulation or contradiction in the will. And
his explanation of, in particular, contradictions in the will
draws upon a very rich account of rationality. There is
nothing wrong in this. But both his rich account of rationality
and his use of a much-enriched notion of contradiction as a
test of right and wrong carry a very heavy freight of
teleological views about human nature and, in the end, also
moral views. A rich theory of rationality and a substantive
moral theory have to be developed together.

   This means, I think, that it is best to postpone Kantian
derivations of morality from rationality until later, when we
have substantive moral reasons in front of us. There is no
sharp line between minimal and rich conceptions of rationality.
One feature of reasons is a kind of impersonality. In the case of
moral reasons, impersonality introduces some form of impartiality, a commitment to seeing everyone as due some sort of
equal standing—what, for short, one might call 'equal respect'
—and equal respect, when developed, brings us close to
standards of fairness. The movement of thought—rationality,
impersonality, impartiality, equal respect, fairness—passes
without obvious break from minimal to rich conceptions of
rationality. It is not so much that the later notions, once they
are given content, add yet more features to the earlier ones as
that the later ones make determinate earlier notions that are
otherwise largely featureless. It is some such movement of
thought that is the best prospect for grounding morality in
rationality. It is the really powerful argument of Kant, and
it is the argument of some modern contractualists.[28] But it
is not possible to assess it without assessing the related rich

conceptions of equal respect and fairness, which I shall come to in the next chapter. It might be possible to derive from a minimal conception of rationality, without intrusions into moral territory, a notion of impersonality determinate enough to enable us at least to answer the question, Why should I be moral? Perhaps, for instance, we can derive a requirement that reasons be impartial, where impartiality has enough content to show that moral reasons trump all other kinds of reasons, while not having so much content that we find ourselves committed to one or other contentious moral standard of fairness. I doubt that even this limited derivation succeeds, but it would be well short of the derivation of determinate moral requirements from rationality, which is our primary interest now. I think that the considerations I come to later go a long way towards suggesting that this more ambitious derivation does not succeed either, and that holism applies here too: the only way to decide whether to accept a certain rich account of rationality, with its considerable moral content, is also to have a way of deciding which moral reasons are good ones, with neither decision taking precedence.

It is true that moral language itself has implications for what a moral judgment can be like. To use certain key moral terms is to accept certain commitments, the best known being that a moral judgment must be universalizable, in the relatively weak sense of that term (the interpretations of which also range from the minimal to the rich) that we be able to purge the judgment of all references to particular persons, times, or places. But not only is this not a particularly demanding requirement, it is also an escapable one. It is a requirement at all only so long as one is willing to use those key moral terms as they are used now. The same is true if, to universalizability, one adds further features that one believes to be implied by moral language—for instance, as Professor Hare would propose, prescriptivity.[29] Prescriptivity is escapable in the same way. And prescriptivity is not, in any case, very powerful in its effects. Prescriptivity and universalizability can jointly turn into a test of moral right and wrong of the sort that the Categorical Imperative is only if they are filled out in the context of a fairly rich account of rationality, rich enough to embody judgments about what moral reasons are good

reasons. It is true that formal features, such as universalizability and prescriptivity, impose *some* limits on what can
count as a moral judgment. We cannot change the formal
features of moral terms too drastically before we find that we
have ended up with vocabulary with which we can no longer
make what we now understand by a 'moral' judgment. But
that is not much of a limitation. The questions that we ask
now may be slightly but importantly the wrong ones. And the
interesting moral features, such as universalizability, though
present now, are the sort that could easily be much modified
with further understanding. I doubt that they will be, but my
belief comes out of a set of views that includes a substantive
moral theory. In developing a moral theory all concepts are
up for revision. Holism encompasses the network of key
theoretical terms too. No firm conclusions about the content
of morality can be got out of moral language because the content
of morality is needed to help fix moral language.[30]

I shall come to attempts to make morality a rational
requirement later. Still, there is another important kind of
dependence of morality upon rationality, which I do want to
pursue now. We have a conception of what makes human life
in general good, which each of us adapts to his own case. And
maximization is the only plausible policy in the prudential
sphere: each of us wants, or at any rate should want, to make
his own life as good as possible. That is where Part One left us.
But there are many writers, especially in the utilitarian
tradition, who think that rationality will take us further. The
rational policy in the sphere of prudence, namely maximization, is, they believe, the rational policy in all practical
decision. This view crops up again and again in modern moral
and political thinking. What generates it, what causes and
seemingly justifies it, is well worth trying to pin down. It seems
to me to rest on a deep confusion—a mistake about how
prudence could possibly be related to morality.

In the domain of prudence, maximizing is irresistible.
Although we should reject a policy of maximizing one
particular value (say, pleasure) at the expense of others, it is
hard to resist a policy simply of making one's life as good as
one can. One does not aggregate, though, by totting up many
small values from various quarters of one's life; instead, one's

important global desires already incorporate the major magnitudes that determine one's choice. If one prefers living autonomously to the various comforts of a non-autonomous life, that very decision is a decision that an autonomous life is more valuable. Even when one does tot up, say, many small-scale pleasures to get an overall aggregate value, the value of the life containing these many local pleasures is fixed in comparison with competing forms of life, and so the finally effective magnitudes are fixed by global desires. I have argued the point earlier: desires form a hierarchy, and the whole idea of a hierarchy of desires brings the prudential policy of maximization along with it.[31]

This justification of maximization in the case of prudence really comes down to the observation that maximization is already built into a person's hierarchy of values. But is it built into it because of the nature of the *values* or because it is *one* person's life?[32] If it is because of the nature of the values, then behind the justification of the maximizing that we have been talking about there is another that would extend from the one-person into the many-person case. But if it is because it is one person's life, then if maximizing has a justification in the many-person case it must be a fresh one.

It seems to me that the especially clear justification for maximization that we have found in the one-person case is dependent upon its being a *one* person case. It is true that some prudential values, just as the values they are, ought to be maximized. They are such that, in general, the more the better. Pleasure ought, other things being equal, to be maximized; pain ought to be minimized. And this maximizing/minimizing policy would seem to have to do with the nature of the particular value at stake in this case, and not with its being part of one or many lives. But other values seem different in this respect. Having deep, loving attachments is, for many persons, one of the most valuable things in their lives. But do we think the more the better? Well, we do not seem always to aim at still deeper and more loving attachments. The words 'deep' and 'loving' describe a kind of relationship, and not values of which more is better. Nor do we want as many deep, loving attachments as possible. It is very implausible that this is the kind of value where nine or ten such relations are, if they

were possible, better than three or four. At least there is doubt
whether the point of maximizing comes from the nature of
these values. And there is little doubt that each of us aims at
making his own life as valuable as possible. So there seems to
be one strong justification for maximization that arises not
from the nature of the values but from their being found in a
context of one life.[33] So we have not yet found a way of
extending our maximizing policy from the one-person to the
many-person case.

One might think that decision theory has already shown the
way. The name 'decision theory' is used so widely that it
includes any theory, normative or descriptive, concerning the
choice, in uncertainty, of the optimal or rational action.[34] On
this capacious definition, morality and prudence are just two
departments of decision theory—along with, for instance,
empirical theories of action. What especially concerns us now
are the normative departments of decision theory. How might
normative decision theory manage to extend the policy of
maximization from the one-person case to the many-person?

Classical decision theory, in the Bayes or Ramsey tradition,
employs the framework of utility maximization: rational
choice is choice that maximizes expected utility. We can then
see reasoning as fitting means to ends.[35] We can assume the
existence of a dominant end, not necessarily hedonistic. Such
an end can then be seen as what makes rationality possible.
Conflict between goals is to be reconciled by calculating how
effective they are as means to the dominant end, or how likely
they are to lead to it. Conflicting aims can then always be
reconciled rationally—that is, by the computations just
mentioned—and need not be left to hunch or intuition or fiat,
and the operation of reason can be reduced to such computing.
These forms of decision theory, therefore, extend maximization
from the one-person to the many-person case in the name of
rationality.

But this way of extending it does not work either. In
contrast to this means-end conception of rationality, what we
ordinarily call rationality is much less restricted and sharp-
edged. It can also include deliberation about ends; it can
include the weighing and reconciling of conflicting aims that
are regarded as irreducibly plural. What we ordinarily call

'rational' merges with what we see as 'sensible' or 'justified'. Means-end rationality is not a superior, or the primary, sort of rationality. In fact, this particular sort of means-end rationality is not even possible. It needs a single substantive super-value, a dominant end in that sense, and there is none.[36] 'Well-being' or 'utility' is best understood as a formal analysis of the concept of prudential value. And prudential values are irreducibly plural.

So the use of maximization in this common form of decision theory and in a plausible prudential value theory is not the same. The defects in the first theory do not affect the second theory, because the defects arise from elements that do not reappear in the second. There is an important moral here. So many different theories have some claim to be called 'maximizing' or 'utilitarian' that they tend to get run together and faults in one seen as faults in another. It is easy to understand why many people are alarmed by this particular version of decision theory. If rationality itself demands a dominant end in prudential action theory, then it will demand it in moral theory too. Once that is allowed, the battle is over. All the competitors of utilitarianism would be proved wrong simply by appeal to rationality. No doubt some people are drawn to utilitarianism because it seems to them uniquely rational, but this appearance of unique rationality comes either from the dubious assumption of a dominant end or from their holding a view about rationality that does not even apply in prudential theory. On the other side, those critics who rightly object that utilitarianism has no claims to unique rationality[37] are not really attacking utilitarianism but only one form of decision theory that gets incorporated in some forms of utilitarianism.

The hope of an irresistible, uncontroversial extension of maximization from the one- to the many-person case does not die easily. We do, after all, generalize our notion of individual good into the notion of the common good. What is that if not a maximizing notion? In any case, there are standards for the good of many persons that are as obvious and inevitable as the standard for one person. There is this one, for instance: *if some in the group become better off and none become worse off, the state of the group is better.* It is hard to see how one could resist such a principle. Mill's defence of his proof of utility falls back on a similar principle, which is also hard to resist. He moves from the premises 'each person's happiness is a good to that person' to the conclusion that 'only the general happiness is a good to the aggregate of all persons'.[38] That looks like the plainest *non sequitur*: how can Mill's sort of ethical hedonism establish anything so specific and so strong as the moral requirement that each person act, at whatever sacrifice to himself, to maximize happiness generally? But Mill explained later in a letter that he did not have anything like so strong a conclusion in mind:[39]

'As to the sentence you quote from my *Utilitarianism*, when I said the general happiness is a good to the aggregate of all persons I did not mean that every human being's happiness is a good to every other human being, though I think in a good state of society and education it would be so. I merely meant in this particular sentence to argue that since A's happiness is a good, B's a good, C's a good, etc., the sum of all these goods must be a good.'

Perhaps by summing several persons' goods Mill meant no more than keeping them all in our mind together. But perhaps he also meant, a trifle more strongly, that any increase in the good of one of the members also makes the general good greater.

However, the type of addition in all these principles is different from the addition in the case of one person. With one person, the aggregation is to a large extent already incorporated in the individual's global desires, and there is nothing comparable to that framework in the many-person case. Also, in the one-person case we have addition in the sense of amalgamation of positive and negative values into an all-in sum; here we have addition only in the sense of the accession of further positive values. That is what makes these principles so hard to resist. But they pay a price in their scope. In most changes, some persons gain and some lose, and these principles can say nothing, therefore, about all of these cases. Mill talks about summing persons' goods as if it were bringing them together in a new, clear, and entirely uncontentious sense. But actually bringing persons together in a group puts them in relationships with one another in which one person's potential gain can be another person's potential loss. Certainly some changes involving both gains and losses will produce better states than others. So these principles, though irresistible, are inadequate. What they identify as better is better, but what is better will not always be identified by them, and they cannot identify the *best*. Also, they are highly conservative: if the *status quo* contains distributions that are, by any standard, unjust, these principles will not tell us to improve them.

There are various ways of trying to give more scope to these principles. With some groups, nations for example, there are goods that benefit everyone, what economists call 'public goods'—national security and roads are examples. They meet 'common interests' of a strict, uncontentious sort. But these interests are also of the gain-only sort. So not many interests are 'common interests' in this strict sense, and even those that are often benefit persons unevenly and so produce results that themselves need ranking. The scope, therefore, is still not great.

Another way of trying to extend the scope is the test of Pareto optimality with compensation. Indeed, the compensation test looks, at first sight, like a brilliant device for extending the justification of gain-only situations into gain-and-loss situations. The Pareto test is simply this: *the common good is to be considered greater if at least one person is better off and no one is worse off.* Changes, of course, seldom leave no one worse off, which is why it is usual to introduce compensation into the test, so that it goes: *the common good is greater if, after the gainers fully compensate the losers, at least one gainer is still better off.* But the compensation test seems as irresistible as the gain-only principles, merely because it is not in the end really different from them. If compensation does not actually take place, if the test is operated as welfare economists normally do and we ask only that compensation be *possible*, then the principle is clearly no longer irresistible. If compensation does take place, then all we have done is to bring more actual changes under the gain-only principle, while doing nothing to remove the damaging limitations of the principle. What it identifies as better is better, but it cannot identify everything that is better. And this makes it conservative: one question we want to ask, central to fairness, is whether or not it would be better *actually* to compensate, but this test gives no answer. Finally compensation is not always possible, a clear case being some changes that bring death.

Yet Mill, having advanced the modest, circumscribed gain-only principle, takes it at other points to be a principle of great scope. Perhaps his thought moved like this. The principle of utility, he says, incorporates the view 'that equal amounts of happiness are equally desirable, whether felt by the same or different persons'.[40] In 'happiness' he seems to include 'unhappiness' as well; his only assumption, he assures us, is 'that the truths of arithmetic are applicable to the valuation of happiness',[41] and addition now seems to be the gain-and-loss type. Finally, he takes the sum that results not only as a general assessment of states of affairs, including how fairly gains and losses are distributed, but also as a criterion of action. General happiness is, he says, 'the end of action' and 'the criterion of morality'.[42]

However, if this is indeed the movement of Mill's thought, it is blatantly unjustified. It moves from irresistible to altogether easily resisted principles. Once we move to situations of gain-and-loss, no one standard seems inevitable; minimal conceptions of rationality here force no principle upon us. Even within the theory of good, most people are somewhat attracted by the standard that the state of affairs is best which maximizes the sum of gains and losses; but many are *also* inclined to think that a state of affairs in which someone at a terribly low level of welfare is raised is better even if his own personal utility sum is somewhat less. And nothing that made any of the earlier purely maximizing principles seem irresistible supports a purely maximizing approach here. This is even more to the point when we move from prudence to morality. Perhaps there maximizing action should be subject to deontological checks. Perhaps the maximizing distribution is not the fair distribution. Nothing that made the earlier maximization principles irresistible helps pure maximization as a standard of moral action.

This shift from uncontentious maximizing principles to contentious ones, from prudential principles to gain-only principles, and then to gain-and-loss principles and finally to moral principles, is obviously eased by confusion. Different standards of maximizing are difficult to keep apart. Just as a successful attack on one is thought to be a successful attack on another, the obviousness of one is easily turned into the obviousness of another. But when we face up to gains and losses, and to how our actions should affect them, new problems, centring on distribution, arise. We cannot fall back on how apt maximization is in the simpler parts of prudential theory. Mill, in his proof, seems not to have realized this. Again and again in the utilitarian tradition problems about distribution are solved by working variations in rather simple conceptions of maximization, as if these relatively safe principles of maximization from the simpler parts of the theory have the resources within them to produce, just by some process of iteration, principles of fairness for the much more complicated parts of the theory.[43] A very neat illustration of this central confusion is the famous formula 'the greatest happiness of the greatest number', and the mistake on which it rests is instructive to lay bare.

This famous formulation had its heyday in the eighteenth century.[44] Bentham picked it up for a while, although he seems also later to have dropped it.[45] Mill, so far as I know, never used it.[46] Nowadays, it is often used to state the aim of utilitarianism, but typically by its enemies.[47] Its friends have good reason to steer clear of it: the formula requires double maximization of a kind that makes it incoherent.[48]

Consider this example. Suppose that, to stimulate production, a manager offers a prize to the worker who assembles 'the greatest number of radios in the shortest possible time'. One worker enters for the prize having assembled ten radios in one hour, a second enters having assembled forty in five hours, and a third with a hundred and thirty in twenty hours. The manager is in trouble; his formula does not pick a winner. He runs into trouble, as von Neumann and Morgenstern point out,[49] because his formula requires the simultaneous maximization of two non-independent functions.[50]

The formula 'the greatest happiness of the greatest number' runs into the same trouble. The number of persons happy and the amount of happiness are dependent functions, and we are instructed to maximize both at the same time. True, the amount of happiness and the number happy tend to be directly proportional: diminishing marginal utility means that the more persons happy the greater the quantity of happiness. So why does the formula present problems? The trouble comes simply from their being dependent variables. To increase the one merely *tends* to increase the other. But suppose that in certain circumstances it does not; maximizing happiness in these circumstances, say, is brought about by holding the number slightly under its maximum. And this is not an unrealistic assumption. The law of diminishing marginal utility applies in most but not all cases; some goods can only be acquired when assets reach a certain point, below which increases might be worth relatively little but just at which they might be worth a lot. But then what action is in accordance with the formula? The formula is, after all, offered as a principle by which the members of any set of choices may be ordered, while in the case I have just imagined the principle has no application. Of course, there are other formulae which do not always have an application that, nonetheless, are coherent. But the trouble with this formula is not that it sometimes fails to give an answer but the reason why it does. The simple formula 'the greatest good' might not give a result if a sort of incommensurability appeared: if, for instance, there were two kinds of goods where one was not better than the other, nor were they equal. But there a breakdown comes because the elements of the case cannot be brought under its concepts. With the formula 'the greatest happiness for the greatest number' the cases where it breaks down can be perfectly well brought under its concepts. It is the formula as a whole that fails; it points in different directions, which suggests that even when it points in one direction only one of the maxima is working as the standard.[51]

Why has this flawed formula beguiled so many intelligent persons for so long? I suspect that there are two explanations. One is the strong but confused faith that the obvious rationality of maximization in one-person cases must—it is only a matter of finding the right formula to explain it—be transformable into the rationality of maximization in many-person cases. This is von Neumann and Morgenstern's diagnosis in *A Theory of Games and Economic Behavior*. They contrast the economic problem for a solitary person (what they call the Robinson Crusoe case) with that of a person in a social setting.[52] Crusoe's aim is to maximize his own satisfaction which is a function of variables that either are subject to the calculus of probabilities or are within his control. But a person in the social exchange setting, though trying to maximize his satisfaction too, finds that the variables of which it is a function include the actions of other persons attempting to maximize their satisfaction. What it is for many persons to achieve maximum satisfaction is not simply the maximization of the number of persons each achieving maximum individual satisfaction. In many-person cases—for instance in Prisoner's Dilemma cases[53]—each party may individually seek to maximize his utility, while the others are doing the same, and end up with neither his best nor his second-best outcome. It is improper to assume that the rational procedure in the one-person case is transferable to the many-person case.

The other explantion is that the phrase 'for the greatest number' is a confused but reassuring gesture towards the moral demands of distribution in what seems still to manage to be a maximizing framework. In fact, some writers, aware that the two maxima in the formula point in different directions, suggest that the formula ought to be seen as an amalgamation of two independent principles: a principle of utility maximization and a principle of justice.[54] But a moment's reflection shows that it is a pretty feeble gesture towards justice. What does it mean to maximize the number of persons benefited? Well, if we take it to mean merely that benefiting more persons is to be preferred to benefiting fewer, that is still a long way from satisfying all plausible demands of fairness. If we take it, more subtly, to mean that a distribution benefits a greater number if it yields a net increase in welfare for a larger number, it still leaves us well short of a plausible principle of fairness.[55] Is there a still subtler interpretation? Why these two interpretations fail is that they permit very unequal treatment, and treating persons equally occupies a central place in our idea of fairness. Of course, we can go on searching for further interpretations of the phrase 'for the greatest number' until we find one that captures the requirement of equal treatment. But the interpretations already briefly canvassed suggest that the subtler interpretations necessarily will be *ad hoc* stipulations of sense for the phrase 'for the greatest number' that will make it near to, or the same as, some notion of equal treatment. And if some notion of equal treatment is what we want, it is better to introduce it undisguised, and not to suggest in this spurious way that it really is there all the time just beneath the surface of the formula 'for the greatest number'.

Why we are tempted by the illusion of an irresistible, uncontroversial extension of maximization into the many-person case is that each step along the way is so short and looks so innocent. We may move from one person's good to uncontentious forms of the common good to contentious forms and finally, with equity and fairness, to issues of morality. But issues of equity and fairness are not settled just with the resources of prudential good or uncontentious forms of the common good. They cannot be settled, either, by appeal only to rationality. To maximize in all many-person situations raises *the* central issue of morality—the kind of equal respect for all persons' interests that morality represents.

This expands somewhat John Rawls' unclear criticism that utilitarianism ignores the separateness of persons.[56] If the criticism is that it is a mistake for a moral theory to take maximization as appropriate in many-person cases *because* it is appropriate in one-person cases, then it cannot be denied. But one can hardly take the difference between the two cases as showing that the maximizing approach is inappropriate, or a non-maximizing approach appropriate, in the many-person case. It is possible to treat the move from one to many as less important than it is; it is also possible to treat it as more important. One should keep all the stages of the move from the one- to the many-person case in mind, because it is easy to mistake both the truth of one claim about maximization for the truth of another, and the falsity of one for the falsity of another. Mill makes the first mistake; Rawls, I shall shortly argue, makes the second.

When we come to views about contentious many-person cases, all the competitors need further justification: the mere fact of differences between one- and many-person cases shows nothing. All that we can conclude now is that there is no irresistible, uncontentious conception of rationality that will carry us from one-person to many-person deliberation. Part of fixing a rich conception of rationality, which might carry us that distance, is fixing our thoughts about what can, in the end, be regarded as good moral reasons.

5. *The nature of the self and the source of morality*

We have to find space for morality deep inside human motivation. We have also to find morality a position of authority, because there is a lot that is internal to human nature that we rightly choose to ignore. As we have just found, we are not going to make morality both internal and authoritative by making it part of self-interest, or of personal aims, or of some minimal notion of rationality. We have got to find some other way.

What I want to propose is that the reason-desire dualism has been as destructive of understanding in theory of action and morality as the mind-body dualism has, until recently, destroyed understanding in epistemology. We treat the word 'reason' (or 'cognition', 'understanding') and 'desire' (or 'conation', 'feeling', 'sentiment', 'passion') as marking two separate domains. Then we have to explain how they are related, and since the time of Plato we have reached for political metaphors. Those of us of a rational bent give 'reason' a commanding, God-like authority over human life. Others of us of an anti-theoretical, empirical bent, rightly suspicious of talk about the domination of reason, have made it the slave of the 'passions'. But these political metaphors hardly suit their subject. As we have seen, when it comes to practical deliberation, reason and desire are not independent enough for one to be master and the other slave. The lesson is that we have to scrap this model and all its related dualisms (objective/subjective, internal reasons/external reasons, desired because valuable/valuable because desired) and start an account of practical deliberation afresh.

A good place to start is with a fresh, more accurate picture of the self. We want things, but we do not regard a desire, just by its mere presence, as constituting a reason for action; it has also to be able to survive the sorts of criticisms that we have talked about. We acknowledge reasons, both to believe this or that and also to do this or that, but a practical

reason does not move us to action unless we care about what
the reason points to.

Each of us has a conception of what makes his life go well.
It is a highly complex conception. With experience and
reflection we arrive at some understanding of the ingredients
of a good life. A mature conception will include autonomy,
understanding of ourselves and our surroundings, enjoyment,
deep personal relations, accomplishment, and so on. Many of
these prudential values—say, deep personal relations—
incorporate major springs of human action. We are naturally
(to a large degree genetically) disposed to deep attachments to
certain persons, and the prudential value that I am calling
'deep personal relations' arises out of and supports these
natural attachments. The influence of desires and values
typically runs both ways: for instance, we naturally form
bonds to certain persons; these bonds are central to making life
good; so our judgments of value support these bonds. And our
judgments of value are capable of moderating our action; if
upon deliberation we decide that what we now in fact care
about is not worth caring about, we can stop caring and act
differently.

One of our aims is to live a life of substance or value or
weight. Another, not far removed, is to understand ourselves
and our surroundings. These aims are themselves quite
complex. We want to be in touch with a reality outside
ourselves. We do not want just to have convincing impressions
of having a life of value, of accomplishing something with our
lives. We also want to have clear perceptions of the reality
about us, including the reality of other persons. They too have
interests, which matter as much to them as ours do to us. And
since we want to live a life of value or weight, we have to
decide what a valuable life is. This is a point, among many
others, at which prudence and morality will not stay apart. A
valuable life, in the sense that we are now trying to understand,
cannot just be a life filled with prudential values conceived in
fairly narrow self-interested terms. A valuable life, in the sense
we are after, consists importantly in doing things with one's
life that are themselves of sufficiently substantial value to turn
back on the life itself and make it valuable. And we cannot see
what we do in those necessary terms if we have no regard for,

or if we damage, values generally, including the value of other persons' lives. This is not an argument for morality in the narrow sense. A person might be able to live a life of value and substance by single-mindedly painting his pictures, ignoring all his family responsibilities. But it is a life of value and substance only if his paintings are also of substantial value and, in the end, valuable to the rest of us. Prudence cannot be kept in narrow confines. What is prudentially valuable must, at various points, spread out into areas that do not look like a part of prudence at all. The boundary defining prudence cannot, along this frontier, really be fixed.

It cannot be fixed because one kind of value tends to spill over into another kind. Part of living a valuable life is living one with a sense of direction. It is a life open to value of any kind; it is one the direction of which is determined by what is really of value. I have explained prudential value as the fulfilment of informed desire. There are therefore two constituents to prudential values: *desire* that is formed by *appreciation of its object*. That it is my, or any one individual's, pain or accomplishment is not a constituent of my, or anyone's, conception of prudential value. How well a person's life goes matters—matters immediately to that person, of course, but also matters generally in this sense: depending upon what happens to him, his life will be more or less valuable. Valuable to *him*, of course; but I do not have to see things from his point of view or, alternatively, see them *sub specie aeternitatis* to recognize that. In any case, the subjective point of view and the view *sub specie aeternitatis* hardly between them exhaust the ways of looking at the world; most important deliberation about prudential value uses neither.

That value has the role in a life of point and direction that it does, and that the locus of value is not just oneself, brings one to a certain sort of impartiality. Should I, I wonder, sacrifice some trivial interest of mine (not to get my trousers wet) because an enormous interest of yours is at stake (not to drown)? But my interest, though tiny, is of importance to me, while your (great) interest is of importance of you. We need a move from importance relativized to an individual to a non-relativized notion of importance. And we have one: namely, the values at stake and the reasons for action that they constitute. My interest gives me a reason to do one thing; your interest gives me a reason to do another. In this extreme case the balance of reasons, even if I shall have reason to give more weight to my interests than to yours, is clearly on my wading out. We should lose all conception of strength of practical reason if we did not say so. And the conclusion about what the balance of reasons in this case is does not assume, or need, an independent *concern* on my part about your survival; one's concerns have to be responsive to how worthy of concern its possible objects are.

It underdescribes this case to say merely that, as a matter of fact, some persons care about morality, that they desire to act well. Some philosophers, in effect, stop there;[57] they find, at least in some of us, the sort of reason, namely an internal one, that they think necessary in order for us to have a reason to be moral. But it is not just that some of us care about morality in the abstract or about this or that substantive matter that makes it up, as if that fact about our sentiments were at the bedrock of the self. Rather, morality is one of the things worth caring about. That, of course, may be a conclusion that a person will arrive at reluctantly, because moral concerns can conflict with other, especially large and vivid personal concerns of his. One of our important prudential aims is understanding our place in the world, including understanding what are good reasons for action. But, apart from that, we also recognize the force of reasons, quite independently of the desires and concerns we happen to have. If we could not, then we would not recognize the independent authority of reasons in factual matters of truth and falsity. With reasons for belief too, our desires, though they can distort and obscure, do not undermine the independent force of the reasons. We subject both our belief and our action to impersonal demands, demands not associated with our personal desires. There are natural springs of action, including habits and desires. But in each case there are also independent reasons. No one thinks that subjecting our beliefs to those impersonal demands is, though often difficult, psychologically unrealistic. And it is not psychologically unrealistic, though it may usually be more difficult, to subject our actions to them either.

How do we resolve conflicts between reasons for action?

Reasons for action form themselves into a hierarchy. Some are stronger than others; some are global in scope while others are only local. Desires, as we discussed earlier,[58] also form a hierarchy. For all of us, our reasons for action shape our desires, though desires are shaped by reasons to different degrees and our hierarchy of desires is never wholly shaped by our hierarchy of reasons. Conflict can be between reasons for action, or it can be between a reason and a desire. If it is a conflict between reasons, we try to settle it by looking to their relative strength as reasons. That, in turn, means looking at the relative magnitudes of the values with which the practical reasons are linked, some of the complications of which we have seen in connection with the measurement of prudential value.[59] But only *some* of the complications, because earlier we were discussing only prudential values and now we are discussing values of all kinds, including moral ones. Since prudential values exhibited a complicated structure, with various kinds of incommensurabilities appearing, there is no reason to think that the relation between values generally is going to be simple. How are prudential reasons related to moral ones? Are moral reasons lexically prior? How are kinds of moral reasons related to one another? Are considerations of human rights lexically prior to considerations of general well-being? Certainly we are not always going to be able to determine the strength of practical reason by simple inspection. We say, 'No individual may be sacrificed indefinitely for the general good', and that seems to many of us as certain as any moral consideration is going to be. And so the notion of certain especially basic rights as trumps over the general good seems well established. But in this case, I believe and shall later argue,[60] appearances are deceptive. At any rate, *some* test is needed; in the face of, say, what seems to be a particularly crass, counter-intuitive consequence of utilitarianism we announce, with firm confidence in its correctness, this or that human right but then, up against some very different problem, find that we have overstated things and have now to back down. We must subject candidate moral reasons—and candidate practical reasons generally—to some test or other. In the Introduction I sketched the two main tests that I think we should try to apply: the test of completeness and the test of correctness.

So to resolve conflicts between practical reasons we have to decide just how much worth caring about certain things are. What seems unlikely to emerge from such discussion is what Sidgwick called the Dualism of Practical Reason.[61] At least, there is no problem just in the fact that there are prudential reasons and moral reasons and no super-reasons of some transcendent category in terms of which to resolve conflicts between them. We no more need super substantive practical reasons than we need super substantive prudential values. We resolve conflicts between prudential values by using the quantitative notion of value.[62] We can resolve conflict between prudential and moral reasons by using the notion of strength of reason. The same is true of 'oughts': we are not stuck with oughts (prudential) and oughts (moral), in need of a super, unsubscripted ought to mediate between them; what in the end concerns us are only oughts that connect with things (of any category) worth caring about. Furthermore, the penetration of prudence by morality, in particular that it penetrates it in a way that shifts serious deliberation on to the level of abstraction where the categories 'prudential' and 'moral' are left behind, makes dualism an unlikely model for their relation. This is not to say that ethical push and ethical pull eventually meet; so far as I can see it points to the opposite conclusion. It is hard to see how, even with a perfectly saintly person whose desires are in complete harmony with the hierarchy of practical reasons, what could be identified as prudential reasons would always support what moral reasons support. Though living a life of point and weight and of conformity to values generally may be seen as prudential values, it is hard to see how their value, purely prudentially, could be greater than a good life itself—if it came to the terribly hard choice between morality and survival. Moral reasons and practical reasons overall might outweigh prudential ones in such a case, but identifiably prudential ones still would be in conflict with them. It is not that death could never be better than dishonour, but rather that it is hard any longer to see the relevant notion of dishonour solely under the heading of prudence—it has to be something less hedged in than that. This does, however, call for some qualification. Since morality penetrates prudence, so making the prudence/ morality dualism hard to maintain, my talk about 'identifiably prudential reasons' is not entirely satisfactory; prudential reasons run, without boundary, into moral ones.

There is, though, another conflict that can look deceptively like a manifestation of the dualism of practical reason, namely conflict between the two hierarchies at work in action. Our hierarchy of desires can conflict with our hierarchy of practical reasons. What we recognize as worth caring about can conflict with what we actually care about. This is not a clash between two kinds of reason, but it is typically a clash between what we see should be cared about and the stubborn fact that we often actually care more about ourselves.

But the most important point to make about the putative dualism of practical reason is that deliberation of a sufficiently global scope is not conducted in terms of 'prudence', 'self-interest', or 'flourishing' on the one side and 'morality' on the other. It is conducted in terms of strength of practical reasons. This is not to say that reason in the end rules sentiment. That is the indefensible dualism again. It is to say that values, neither expressly prudential nor expressly moral but values taken at a higher level of abstraction, are what we appeal to: the notion of what, all things considered, is worth our concern. Just as when with prudential values we deliberate not by appeal to any one substantive prudential value but to the notion of prudential value itself, here too we step up another rung in the ladder of abstraction. There is nothing mysterious or suspect about this step; it is one more of the same sort that we have continually to take in deliberation.

How complete the resolution of conflict between practical reasons will be, and what complexities of structure the hierarchy of reasons will exhibit, we have to wait to see. The same was true with prudential values; we could settle the formal features of prudential values only when we also had a substantive account of what those values were. What resolution of conflict there is will start with one's representing practical reasons to oneself as completely and vividly as one can manage. Why should one be moral? One cannot answer: Because self-interest counsels it, or, Because it is among one's personal aims, or, Because it is a requirement of reason on some uncontroversially minimal conception of rationality. The only answer possible seems to be of the form that, when one represents the full range of practical reasons to oneself, moral reasons find a place in the hierarchy, and a place high in it. The strongest answer, of course, is that they occupy the highest place. But that depends upon the content of each moral reason. There is no dualism of prudence and morality to raise obstacles in principle to moral reasons' being strongest. But if acting justly might make the heavens fall, if that is the sort of requirement that justice turns out to be, then our collective self-interest might well outweigh it. If respecting rights could cause or fail to prevent catastrophe, then again self-interest probably outweighs it. Whether these would be cases of pure self-interest's outweighing morality or of self-interest's taking on moral weight would also depend upon the content of moral reasons. At this level of generality, with no well worked-out account of moral reasons to call upon, there is not much more that can be said in answer to the question, Why should I be moral? So what I have offered is not as decisive an answer as the rejected alternatives. It leaves hostages to fortune: we have to lay out moral reasons and see what place they take in the hierarchy. But until we do that, it is, I think, the best answer we are going to get.

EQUAL RESPECT

1. *Equal respect and psychological realism*

THERE are two topics from the last chapter that I want now to carry further. The first is what I called equal respect. I said that living in accord with practical reason brought along with it a commitment to a certain vague, not very rigorous form of impartiality—namely, that everyone is to be granted equal respect. By 'equal respect' I do not mean anything so demanding as what could be called 'equal concern'—for instance, giving as much weight, utilitarian fashion, to the welfare of a stranger as I do to the welfare of my children.[1] Yet even such moral theories as do allow some sort of partiality to family and friends also demand some form of equal respect; they accept, say, a weak form of universalizability that requires treating persons equally unless there are relevant differences between them. In more familiar terms, respecting persons equally is looking at them from the moral point of view. Now this vague, capacious concept of equal respect is too indeterminate as it stands to do much work. So philosophers develop it in various ways. Some develop it into the viewpoint of the Ideal Observer, and others into the viewpoint of the Ideal Contractor. One of the things I want eventually to argue[2] is that there is still scope for innovation here, that there are other, unfamiliar developments that are also promising.

The second topic is the Requirement of Psychological Realism. In one form or other the Requirement is undeniable. There is no point in announcing moral restrictions unless they fit the human psyche. Restrictions are meant to restrict, so if moral considerations are actually to shape action, they must be able to find a place inside human motivation and, what is more, a position of authority.

Now I want to bring these two topics together. How are we to flesh out the notion of equal respect so that it yields plausible moral restrictions but, at the same time, meets the Requirement of Psychological Realism?

The very importance of the Requirement makes it tempting to try to derive morality from ground that is not rich enough to yield it. The Requirement would easily be met, if morality could be grounded in self-interest. But self-interest seems pretty clearly not to be rich enough. The arguments for that we have already seen.[3] A shrewdly self-interested person is likely, simply for the sake of the quality of his own life, nearly always to respect the interests of others. But there are times when he will not—for instance, if he finds himself a member of an unjustly privileged class in a stable society. Furthermore, the best ways of reconciling morality and self-interest do not help meet the Requirement. There is much to say for the idea that no life can fully flourish, reach its highest peaks, unless it is a moral life. But this is plausible only because our conception of flourishing is so penetrated by morality that the reduction is no longer, in any interesting sense, a reduction of morality to flourishing.

We could broaden the ground, and still fairly easily meet the Requirement. We could ground morality in personal aims. Nearly all of us have aims which are not purely self-interested; we are also interested in the welfare of our children or our friends or institutions to which we are committed. Some of the ends of some of us are for the good of some other people. But these natural sympathies are still too limited to be a rich enough ground for morality. There is the same problem as before. The member of a secure privileged class may not feel much sympathy for the exploited. And even if these limited sympathies could be got to spread, the spread would be unlikely to be a purely involuntary movement. Sympathy tends to spread when we see reason for it to spread, and otherwise not. And even if the spread occurred without a reason, as just a brute fact about us, we should be unlikely to grant the restraints that such sympathy generates any authority if in reflection we had to referee between warring feelings of sympathy and self-love.[4]

The natural move at this point is to admit that the grounds are not yet rich enough and once again to make them richer, perhaps by bringing in more of the workings of society.

Morality, it is entirely plausible to suggest,[5] has an object, a point, a function—namely, to counteract what it is in the natural course of events that makes things go badly for us. And they are, primarily, limitations of one sort or another: limitations in resources, in our knowledge of facts, in our accord with logic, but especially in our sympathies.[6] Limited resources we often cannot do much about. But human limitations we can to some degree combat. Limited resources and limited sympathies together lead to competition, easily escalating into conflict, and we end up losing the benefits of co-operation.[7] That is the problem that morality is needed to solve. The object of morality is largely to counteract limited sympathy, and we might think that we can settle the content of morality simply by fixing how best to do it. For instance, when two persons find themselves in a situation that has the form of a Prisoner's Dilemma, or something close to it, they need to save the situation from deteriorating into the third best outcome for each. The best that could be achieved by any device that both parties would willingly go along with is one that leads to the best of the symmetrical results, so we need a device that would ensure the second-best outcome for each.[8] Thus, what we need to counteract limited sympathies are some or all of the following: we need more knowledge; we need organization, including legislative procedures; we need rules and coercion to back them up; and we need good dispositions.[9]

Most of that is true and important. But is it yet rich enough? Can we generate moral restrictions simply by deciding what is needed to make things go better? It seems not. Again, we cannot derive any recognizably moral instruction to the members of a stable but unjustly privileged class. We discover nothing about justice between generations, or about our obligations to the Third World. And good dispositions, especially disposition to benevolence, although an important part of the scheme, are not fertile enough to make up these deficiences. It is plausible that what would be needed to make things go better is a very wide benevolence, a sort that spreads far beyond family and friends, and it is furthermore plausible to think that once benevolence spreads that far it will naturally go on spreading quite on its own until it covers distant strangers and future generations too. This may seem to offer hope of generating obligations to the Third World and to future generations. But it is open to an objection similar to one made against rule utilitarianism: extended benevolence will be recognized, by the reflective among us, as being *generally* useful in making things go better but as having *no* use in the case of unpowerful distant strangers or totally powerless future generations. One would not have to be very bright to notice that a device of morality that has a point within certain confines has run on into areas where it entirely loses its point. So we should be right, to the extent we can, to fight the promptings of a very extended benevolence, and so we should have in the end no explanation of obligations to the Third World or future generations.

Our only resort, it seems, in trying to enrich this sort of ground, is to enrich the notion of making things go 'better'. Better for whom?, we might ask. If 'better' just means 'better for me', then it is no ground for morality. If 'better' means 'better for some and no one worse off', then it is no ground for morality because it fits so few situations. If 'better' means 'better for some some though worse for others but better *overall*', then it may be rich enough to yield morality, but only because we should have to have built most of it into the notion of 'better overall', which was meant to be the centrepiece in the device that would generate morality. This same shift from an interpretation too poor to yield morality to an interpretation rich enough but which no longer yields morality because it has had to presuppose it, appears in the report I gave a moment ago of the solution to the Prisoner's Dilemma. The best that could be achieved by any device that both parties to a dilemma would willingly go along with is, it was proposed, the best symmetrical result, namely the second-best outcome for each. Now if this argument amounts to saying that one cannot get a stable solution unless one settles for the outcome that everyone will freely accept, then no doubt it fits some situations. Sometimes, no doubt, that will be the only deal that can, as a matter of fact, be struck. But it does not fit all situations; sometimes one can have, for a while (perhaps even a century or two), a stable solution based on ignorance, indoctrination, apathy, or bullying, and then one has no reason not to opt for institutions that make one privileged.

The only way to give one a reason is to regard each person's *freely* accepting a solution as required, not by the facts of a situation, but by, say, the respect due to each person as an autonomous agent. But, again, what we are then doing is appealing to a conception of the moral person, which already carries much of the moral content that we were meant to generate.

So it seems to me that although the Requirement of Psychological Realism makes it tempting to ground morality in self-interest, or in personal aims, or in the social function of morality, none of these grounds is rich enough to give us what we think of as morality. We seem to need a notion of *moral* reasons for action that breaks away from self-interest or personal aims or universal social pay-offs. What I now want to argue is that familiar forms of utilitarianism break too sharply, and that familiar forms of contractualism do not break sharply enough. So the first have trouble meeting the Requirement of Psychological Realism, and the second have trouble generating moral requirements.

2. *The utilitarian view of equal respect*

I started by explaining that equal respect, the way I am speaking of it, constitutes the moral point of view. There are different ways of trying to capture it. One well-known way is the device of an Ideal Observer: the moral point of view, it is proposed, is a benevolent view from a position above the fray, granting everyone equal consideration. This can easily turn into the utilitarian conception of merging interests by maximizing utilities, counting everybody for one. John Rawls, of course, thinks that it merely turns into an undesirable impersonality and not the true impartiality of the moral point of view, which he sees as captured by a different device, the device of the Ideal Contractor:[10] the moral point of view, it is proposed, is the view of equal contractors from behind the Veil of Ignorance. There are still other accounts of the moral point of view, which I shall come on to later, but let me for the moment concentrate on these two.

The perspective of the Ideal Observer easily leads to utilitarianism, and that of the Ideal Contractor leads, Rawls thinks, to his two principles of justice. It is hard to see exactly how, in each case, the perspective stands to the substantive moral view derived from it. It is clear, at least, that they are not the same. Each perspective, though meant to make the moral point of view more determinate, is itself described so vaguely that it can be further specified in different ways. There is a strong argument that the *rationality* of the Ideal Contractor would lead him, not to Rawls' two principles, but to Average Utilitarianism.[11] And there are strong arguments that the *benevolence* of the Ideal Observer would not let him accept some of the sacrifices of one person to others that utilitarian aggregation permits.[12] Still, since notions like *rationality* and *benevolence* are very vague, one way to give these rather empty conceptions of equal respect more content is to fix what follows from them. So I want to take the view of the Ideal Observer as fixing on utilitarian aggregation, and that of the Ideal Contractor as fixing on Rawls' principles or something close to them.

Let me start with the utilitarian conception of equal respect. One element is the Benthamic formula 'Everybody to count for one, nobody for more than one', which is a principle of equal weight or lack of bias. It is not a separate principle over and above the principle of utility. Mill's account of its status, it seems to me, is right. It is, he says, simply part of what is involved in applying the principle of utility.[13] If one's aim is to maximize utility, whose utility it is is irrelevant. One is barred from being a respecter of persons by being a respecter of utilities alone.

I think that the second point to note about the utilitarian conception of equal respect is that merging persons' interests into a single moral judgment by maximizing them *is* a distributive principle. It is a view, right or wrong, about when sacrificing one person for another is justified. It is just a modern muddle to contrast sharply distributive and aggregative principles, as if an aggregative principle could not also be fully deliberately distributive.[14] It crops up commonly in regarding, as economists often do, an aggregative principle as a principle of 'efficiency' and other principles as ones of fairness. Similarly, no plausible principle of distribution—think, for instance, of Rawls' Difference Principle—could be purely distributive, without some maximizing tendency, as if reducing everyone to the same level of misery could satisfy it. Every plausible principle of equality is based on the thought that everyone matters and matters equally, and to stress only formal features of distribution is to recall the *equally* but to forget the *matters*. Even a principle of a minimum acceptable level of welfare has, if not a maximizing, at least a quantitative element. And the principle of utility, too, represents another conception of the distribution that equal respect for persons requires.

But that still leaves untouched what may seem to be the major fault in the utilitarian account of equal respect. Merging persons' interests is maximizing their utilities. The utilitarian conception of equal respect simply transfers the structure of intrapersonal trades to interpersonal ones. Does my justified willingness to suffer a cost now for a greater benefit for myself later also justify my having to suffer it for your greater benefit? And if it did, I might lose out not only in this trade to you but, for similar reasons, in another to him and in another to her. Should I accept the cumulative effect of those trades even if, were things to fall out awkwardly, they built up into something disastrous for me? The looseness of utilitarian restrictions on trade-offs creates problems with the Requirement of Psychological Realism. Would a person who believed that morality obliged him to go to the wall merely to increase the aggregate social utility be able to find a place for the obligation in his motivation? Would he if, in the name of morality, he had to sacrifice the persons he most cared about to benefit persons for whom he cared nothing?

It is at this point that many people also protest in the name of morality: 'One person may not be sacrificed, without limit, for the good of others', or 'The well-being of one person cannot simply be replaced by that of another', or 'This would not take seriously the distinction between persons'.[15] The first two protests announce what are clearly moral principles; the last seems to gesture towards some fact, and this appearance has led some writers to regard 'the separateness of persons' as a *reason* to drop the utilitarian conception of equal respect.[16] But since there is no fact of 'separateness' that anyone has overlooked, no delusion that a group of persons is one

super-person, the protest that utilitarians overlook separateness amounts to no more than the claim that one ought not to
transfer the model of intrapersonal trades to interpersonal
trades. It is an expression of one view about equal respect, and
so not a reason for choosing it. Still, for good reason or bad, it
is at this point that many persons turn to the contractualist
view of equal respect.

3. *The contractualist view of equal respect*

It is quite clear that Rawls regards the perspective of the
self-interested contractor behind the Veil of Ignorance as one,
though perhaps not the sole, moral point of view.[17] The
contractor's reasoning is an acceptable way of reaching many
different kinds of moral conclusions, not only conclusions
about justice. Roughly speaking, ignorance supplies impartiality, while self-interest supplies the moral significance of the
separateness of persons. As for justice, this productive tension
yields, Rawls thinks, two principles:[18]
1. Each person is to have an equal right to the most extensive
basic liberty compatible with a similar liberty for others.
2. Social and economic inequalities are to be arranged so that
they are both (a) to everyone's advantage and (b) open to all.

His two principles are certainly, at first sight, very
attractive. And they echo other most attractive-sounding
intuitive convictions such as one that Rawls employs, 'Each
person possesses an inviolability founded on justice that even
the welfare of society as a whole cannot override'.[19] But it is
strange that principles, a major motive for whose support
comes from the counter-intuitive consequences of the principle
of utility, should turn out to be every bit as counter-intuitive
themselves. Rawls remarks at one point that, no doubt, some
of these attractive intuitive convictions are overstated a bit,[20]
but the trouble goes far deeper than that. The perspective of
the Ideal Contractor yields a cut-off for all utilitarian trade-
offs: the worst-off group has to be as well off as possible. But
that restriction—at least our intuitions tell us—is far too strict.
Rich societies, where the worst off are well off, do, on the face
of it quite reasonably, allocate some resources—to art, for
instance—in a way that mainly benefits the better off. And all

societies allow some persons' life prospects to sink to disastrously low levels in order to protect the relatively minor benefits of the many. There are over twenty thousand avoidable deaths each year in England because of poor help or the victim's ignorance or hesitation, and to remedy the situation money could be, but is not, taken from art or education.[21] And the French Government knows that some people, through no fault of their own, die each year in automobile accidents because of the beautiful roadside avenues of trees, but it does not cut them down. So we do allow trade-offs between the common good and disastrous drops, even when the drop is as disastrous as death and the good merely more aesthetic pleasure. And even if the avenues of trees caused no deaths, the French maintain them at a huge cost that could be used to improve, say, the housing of the worst off.

How might Rawls reply? He might remind us that his two principles of justice are not meant to apply at every point in society; they are meant to apply to what he calls 'the basic structure', that is to say, to 'the way in which the major social institutions fit together into one system, and how they assign fundamental rights and duties and shape the division of advantages that arises through social cooperation'.[22] So they apply to the political constitution, to forms of property, to general economic organization, and suchlike. Once these general organizational features are in proper order, what happens thereafter, Rawls says, satisfies pure procedural justice; that is, it is the outcome of a fair procedure where there exists no other test for fairness of the outcome than that it is what in fact comes out.[23] Furthermore, the two principles are not meant to be applied to the worst-off individual, but to the worst-off 'representative' individual—that is, to a whole social group.[24]

But these exclusions clearly do not meet some, and probably do not meet any, of the examples. Since the contractors are self-interested, they see the society whose basic structure they are fixing as 'a cooperative venture for mutual advantage'.[25] They will not agree with one another at all, unless they secure as much advantage, and certainly as little disadvantage, as they can hope for. They will, Rawls thinks, adopt a maximin strategy, and this play-safe approach will

appear in each of the two principles of justice. It will appear in
the first one as a strong right to self-preservation,[26] so strong
that at one point Rawls gives saving life priority over even
avoidance of slavery.[27] It will appear in the second principle
as the requirement that the worst off be as well off as possible.
This Difference Principle, Rawls says, would require at least a
minimum acceptable level of welfare,[28] so it would, even
more, require protection of life. Both principles would have to
give an especially high priority to these protections, simply
because life is a necessary condition for the use of any liberty
or the enjoyment of any good. That the two principles apply
to the basic structure does not matter; they will also have to
apply, as Rawls openly acknowledges,[29] to 'life prospects'.
Just as principles that govern choice behind the Veil of
Ignorance (e.g. maximin) reappear in some form in the
principles of justice chosen there (e.g. the Difference Principle,
with its requirement of the best worst), so one would expect
the actual arrangements of society sanctioned by the two
principles to reflect certain of their most important features.
Rawls conceives of a sequence of stages: the original choice,
the constitutional convention, legislation, and finally judicial
decision.[30] The Veil of Ignorance does not totally lift as soon
as the first stage is through; it draws back slowly as we
progress through the sequence.[31] So play-safe will still have
some point at each stage, and the institutions, laws, and
priorities that appear further along in the sequence will
embody the important protections guaranteed by the principles further back.[32] Otherwise, Rawls' criticism of utilitarianism would entirely fail; he stresses the extreme demands of
utilitarianism ('the sacrifice of the agent's private interests,
when this is necessary for the greater happiness of all') and
argues against them that 'A rational person, in framing his
plan would hesitate to give precedence' to a principle that
allowed these sacrifices.[33] Whatever play is left in the basic
structure, it must not be play that can lead to such sacrifices.

So the same failing that appears in self-interest as a ground
of morality reappears in Rawls' contractualism, because
self-interest is not strongly enough checked there.[34] True,
Rawls places self-interest (as well as the demands of social
co-operation and narrow sorts of rationality) in an entirely

new setting, namely inside a conception of the moral point of view, where each is meant to be checked by the impartiality imposed by ignorance. But they are left too robust. Everyone has to benefit from the bargains struck by the contractors;[35] their decision has to be unanimous.[36] Everyone must think that he has struck the best deal he could.[37] Each must find the terms reasonable.[38] Now, the elements of self-interest, of best possible bargain, and of narrow rationality add, without doubt, to the attractiveness of Rawls' view of equal respect. They make it seem that contractualism manages at the same time to be a non-reductionist moral theory and yet comfortably to meet the Requirement of Psychological Realism. No heroic self-sacrifice is asked for; the burdens of moral commitment are kept well within human capacity.[39] Contractualism needs only, as Rawls puts it, 'the psychological law that persons tend to love, cherish, and support whatever affirms their own good',[40] whereas utilitarianism expects our sympathies to be widely extended. But morality seems uncomfortably more demanding on the human psyche; at least, it needs more than Rawls provides, and a large element of extended benevolence is an obvious candidate.

In recent papers, Rawls has, while not at all retreating from the ground of checked self-interest, made use of another ground. The principles of justice, he says, 'must issue from a conception of the person', the free and equal moral person.[41] But this does not really help. As Rawls well knows, the notion of a free and equal moral person is too empty, on its own, to generate many moral conclusions; it needs principles like the two principles of justice as its further specification. But only principles *like* them; it cannot be those two principles, because they are too strict. And the idea of the moral person does not show where else to go.

Of course, another place to go is to some other form of contractualism. Ignorance, as we have just seen, does not check self-interest toughly enough. Most recent forms of contractualism drop both self-interest as the contractor's motivation and the large element of ignorance that is consequently needed. Instead, they enhance the role of rationality and of social co-operation. For instance, we could take contractors to be motivated to find reasons for principles of conduct that others cannot rationally reject as a basis for informed, unforced general agreement.[42] Impartiality would then be represented largely by treating people as informed and unforced. Rationality would exclude any rejection of principles unreasonable *given* the aim of finding social agreement between informed and unforced people.[43] T. M. Scanlon argues that we should say 'No one could reasonably reject' rather than 'Everyone could reasonably accept', because the latter would not be strong enough.[44] Suppose there were a principle requiring quite severe sacrifices from a group, the members of which were, through the happy chance of their being public-spirited, willing to accept them. Their willingness might be reasonable; for example they might have some entirely worthy supererogatory reason. But, because of the great sacrifice, it would not be unreasonable for them to reject it. This version of contractualism is therefore just as strong as Rawls'. What is supposed to make it reasonable for them to reject the principle is that it is contrary to their self-interest. All this again gives too much scope to self-interest to be able to generate morality. The earlier examples that counted against Rawls count here too: for instance, a person who will die young unless a cure is found for his congenital disease has a reason to reject rules that allow diversion of funds, say, to the arts, which will satisfy what are clearly lesser interests of the rest of us. Moreover, its notion of rationality seems so narrow that it is doubtful that it can explain the authority of moral rules. It does not require us to be moved by more than the need for agreement and by a desire to justify our actions on grounds that no one can reasonably reject; beyond that our motives may remain intact. What all of us together can agree to is likely, therefore, to have large elements of compromise to it.[45] If someone sees an important interest of his threatened and is by nature not given to much self-denial—say he is an adult male who will have none of the 'women and children first' approach to life—then he has a reason to reject any set of rules with 'women and children first'. But then why should *I*, who am a little more altruistic and who believe that there is a lot to be said at least for a policy of 'children first', think that *my* obligations are determined by rules that emerge from a compromise with *him*? The trouble is that the device is meant to build only fairness into rules but it ends up building in more; it builds in self-interest of a form that raises doubt about their standing as moral rules.

The obvious change now would be to shift from 'No one could reasonably reject' to the looser 'Everyone could reasonably accept'. But we should need to make the notion of rationality compensatingly richer. Then, depending upon the degree of richness we add to it, either of two things is likely to happen. First, if we make rationality not very rich, we shall find that the ground of morality has not become rich enough yet either. Suppose, like David Gauthier, we see rationality on the model of rational bargaining.[46] The moral point of view, we could then say, is the view of an arbitrator trying to reach a fair compromise between persons with conflicting interests. He would not try simply to maximize the satisfaction of the interests, because that could sometimes require virtually sacrificing one of the parties; he would try to strike a bargain that is acceptable, always given the need to reach agreement, from the standpoint of every party.[47] But this would merely be the overly strong requirement yet again. But then, second, if we make rationality a very rich notion, we are likely to find that the ground is rich enough to generate morality, but only in the way we have already seen. We shall have already derived morality in some other way and planted it in the account of rationality. Suppose that, instead of making the moral point of view that of an arbitrator, we make it, as B. J. Diggs does, the view of a moral judge, who hears each party's advocate and then, in a spirit of reconciliation, renders a 'reasonable decision'.[48] But if the requirement that the decision be 'reasonable' is no stricter than that the judge cite good reasons, including moral reasons, then there is no doubt that the conception is rich enough to give satisfactory moral answers. But then what is reasonable is no longer worked out from the needs of mediating between conflicting interests, and the conception of a contract will be doing no work.

So the fault that appears in Rawls' contractualism reappears in these later versions, because their checks on self-interest, although different from Rawls', do not do the job any better.

Where can the contractualist go? It is hard to see how we ought to tinker with the contractualist machinery, because it is hard to see what else we want it to come out with. What cut-off to utilitarian trade-offs are we after? The thing to do, of course, is to look for a weaker restriction. A few years ago Amartya Sen looked for a much weaker one that would still have the form of an absolute cut-off for utilitarian trade-offs. If there were one, so weak as to be irresistible yet still eliminating utilitarianism, that would be a result of no small importance. He suggested the Weak Equity Axiom, which goes: if one person is a less good utility convertor than another, say, because he is handicapped, so that at any level of goods he is less well off, then he must be given *something* more than the other.[49] One might even make the requirement weaker still: the unfortunate one must not be given less, if he is below and the more fortunate one already above a minimum acceptable level of welfare. But these 'weak' requirements are still too strong. Surgeons, in choosing between patients for a kidney transplant, are often guided by a patient's prospects. If one patient, Adam, has been chronically ill, below the minimum acceptable level for most of his life, with poor prospects of surviving long after the operation, and another patient, Eve, never as ill, has good prospects, Eve may be the one to be operated on.[50]

That this very weak requirement turns out too strong is also a result of no small importance. It suggests that we ought to give up trying to make moral theory accommodate an absolute cut-off to utilitarian trade-offs. It suggests that instead the structure of moral theory should perhaps be a plurality of same-level principles. Instead of a cut-off to trade-offs, there would be a counterforce to them: say, a principle of welfare maximization sanctioning trade-offs and a principle of equal welfare restricting them, with sometimes the one and sometimes the other winning out in conflict. In the earlier case, the surgeon could help Eve, the better-off one, a lot and Adam, the worse-off, only negligibly, and it is obviously this great disparity that points towards helping the one who is better off. So let us change the story, now making the disparity less great. Adam, we shall say, is an otherwise healthy man of seventy who with a transplant will live about another ten years; Eve is a chronically ill woman of thirty-five who with a transplant would live about another five years.

Adam, we are strongly inclined to think, has had a fairly good go at life, and although his prognosis is better than Eve's, the pull towards levelling the balance is obvious. The benefit to Eve is less but not negligible, and she has had, and will at the end of her life still have had, so much less than Adam has had already.

But if intuitions are to guide us, we ought not to stop there. We ought to exercise our intuitions on more cases with just the features that in the last case seemed decisive against a purely utilitarian trade-off. Suppose Eve were a new-born baby with prospects of five years, and Adam six years old with prospects of ten. Now intuition strongly favours Adam. Or suppose Eve were six with prospects of five more years, and Adam twelve with prospects of ten. Intuition still favours Adam. What if Eve were fifteen with five more years, and Adam thirty with ten? Now intuition is probably just baffled. So, if intuitions are to guide us and, contrary to common practice, we consult a wide enough selection of them, they do not clearly support the model of same-level principles either.

Faced with a puzzling set of intuitions, what we should do is to probe more deeply and try to make sense of them. Why do our intuitions—not, of course, that they are unanimous—favour Eve, thirty-five years old, with prospects of five more years, over Adam, seventy, with prospects of ten? We tend to assume, in concocting examples like this, that the number of years may be taken as a measure of well-being. A prospect of ten more years, we seem to be assuming, is roughly twice as good as the prospect of five. But, on reflection, that is far from clear. Many central prudential values have to do with what gives a life point or substance. One's projects, what one accomplishes in life, are clearly central among them. Certainly not all years of one's life matter equally to the overall quality of one's life. Adam, at seventy, has probably largely made what he can of his life while Eve, at thirty-five, is probably just in the critical period. It is not that a seventy-year-old cannot still be in, or indeed just arriving at, this critical period, or that a thirty-five-year-old cannot but be in it. Individuals vary in this way, as in most others. But, as a general thing, years at the end of a normal span of life and, even more, years at the start, are not as crucial to the success of a life as years in the middle. And intuitions conform largely to the general thing. So in this case it is doubtful that Adam's ten years weigh as heavily, even in terms of prudential value, as Eve's five. This variation in the value of years of life also explains the other cases. If Eve is a new-born baby or a child of five and Adam is not only older but with twice the prospect of survival, then Eve's years, even though so much less than Adam has already had, do not (at least as a general thing) have the prudential weight that Adam's years have. If Eve is fifteen with five more years and Adam thirty with ten, the prudential calculations are far harder to do, and so it is not surprising that intuition is far more pushed to come up with a verdict.

I think that we are put off the mark in thinking about all of these cases by the incorrect totting-up conception of well-being. Under the sway of that conception, we think of overall well-being as a sum of several small values (in this case the number of years of life) each representing the same quantity of well-being. But this ignores how central global judgments are to the conception of well-being and to its measurement. The number of years in these examples do not represent amounts of well-being. Indeed, what we need to do is to take a case where they are more likely to do so. Suppose Eve were thirty with the prospect of five more years, and Adam thirty-five with the prospect of ten. Now perhaps intuition favours, as does almost universal medical practice, Adam. The result is scarcely conclusive, even within the severe limits of appeals to intuitions. But once the amounts of well-being at stake are identified accurately, their maximization seems to be playing a very large role.

It is easy—altogether too easy—to juggle numbers and produce examples that seem to support the model of same-level principles. What is far harder is to produce examples in which the numbers can be taken seriously as representations of well-being. Suppose we could bring about this outcome:

(1)	Adam	Eve
	50	50

To isolate issues, let us say that we, who can influence the outcomes, are not Adam's and Eve's parents, are not even known to them, and that neither of them is aware of what happens to the other. If we can juggle numbers ad lib, then we could get outcomes:

(2)

Adam	Eve
0	100

and:

(3)

Adam	Eve
0	101

On the maximizing model outcome (2) is not better than outcome (1), though (1) has the distinct merit of treating Adam and Eve equally. But then, if equality makes (1) better than (2), why should we ever accept the maximizing model? It is not at all clear what that model would say about the choice between (1) and (2); it might be interpreted as making them morally equivalent or merely as silent on the matter. If the latter, there might even be a case for adding to the maximizing model the tie-breaking rule that when the total is the same the (more) equal outcome is to be preferred. Perhaps we should give equality at least that much weight. This possible development of the notion of equal respect does not seem to me unimportant; indeed, it takes on, I think, great importance in another context, which I shall come to in the next chapter.[51] But it is not what we are interested in now. Our interest now is whether, if we give equality enough weight, as most of us would, so that we rank (1) over (2), we could give it *no* weight when the *tiniest* increase in the total appears on the scene, as in (3). Most persons find it deeply counter-intuitive to rank (3) over (1). And that seems to be as clear a demonstration as we need of the superiority of the model of same-level principles over the simple maximizing model.

But can the figures in (1) and (3) be taken seriously? They ignore at least two features of reality, one well-known and the other not. The well-known one is diminishing marginal utility. If the zeros in outcomes (2) and (3) represent a life of no value at all (and this suggestion gives the example a lot of its rhetorical force), then it is most unlikely that Adam and Eve, both capable of a good life in outcome (1), would, by a redistribution of the same resources, be capable of the outcomes in (2) and (3). The less well-known one is incommensurability. There are increases in well-being—clear, undeniable ones—that cannot be got on to the same scale with certain other values; no amount of one kind of positive value may equal a certain amount of another. That Eve might go from 100 in outcome (2) to 101 in outcome (3)—some tiny but undeniable improvement—does not mean that the increase belongs on the same scale of well-being as the measurement of the values of Adam's and Eve's whole lives.[52] The fact, say, that Eve finds a way in outcome (3) to get one more good meal out of the distribution than she could in outcome (2) gives her something of positive value. But one good meal, more or less, does not affect the quality of a life as a whole. There are losses in certain values (Adam's?) that cannot be made up by certain gains in other values (Eve's?). The judgments that most matter in all of these cases are global judgments about the value of whole lives.

That fact also provides one answer to the charge that the maximizing model ignores the separateness of persons. On the totting-up conception of well-being, overall judgments of value are reached by adding many small values. And so we think that there is no real difference between a case in which I endure a hard period of struggle and deprivation *now* to accomplish something *later* and a case in which *you* endure it so that *I* can accomplish it. But they clearly are morally different. In the first, intrapersonal, comparison my present loss is compensated by *my* gaining later; the compensation goes on within the boundaries of a single life. In the second, interpersonal, case, that sort of compensation is impossible. However, that is not the only morally acceptable sort of compensation; as we have seen, to think so is to accept the over-strict constraint of contractualism. Still, these two cases are not morally equivalent. We have to take your life and mine as wholes. The totting-up conception is not the right one. My life is better for enduring the hardship in order to bring off the accomplishment. That is a global assessment of one life. But that I can accomplish the same if you suffer the hardship tells us nothing about your life as a whole. We need another global assessment for that. And to make it we should have to look at what the deprivation does to your life, considering your life in all its other respects too. Just by knowing that a certain gain and loss would be justified in my life one does not know that the gain and loss divided between our two lives would also be justified. The notion of total well-being does not work like that, and a plausible prudential value theory would show why: to make the interpersonal judgment we should have to judge how good each life is, and we clearly lack the information for that. That is not to say that one person's deprivation could never be justified by another person's accomplishment. No one thinks that. It is just that justification has to be constructed out of materials that we have not yet got.

What we must do is to find cases in which the numbers can be taken seriously as indicators of well-being. Suppose that we could bring about either outcome (1) or:

(4)

Adam	Eve
45	56

It is possible to see how we might decide on such global values. We would use the measure at work in strategic prudential deliberation. We would estimate how much we should value Adam's or Eve's life in outcome (1). We would do the same for outcome (4). That is, we would rank the lives; we would decide that Eve's life in (4) was better than either life in (1), which in turn was better than Adam's life in (4). And we could, at least sometimes, introduce some cardinality; we could say that the gap between either in (1) and Eve in (4) was greater than the gap between Adam in (4) and either in (1). Since all of these judgments can coherently be made just by appeal to strategic prudential deliberation, the model of same-level principles can be coherently stated. It is the view that the moral turning-point is not the prudential turning-point. That is, it says that for a deviation from equality in (1) to be morally justified we should need more than just the simple excess of gain over loss that we have in (4). We should need much greater gain—say, the one in:

(5)

Adam	Eve
45	80

But where is the moral turning-point? The model of same-level principles cannot stop at saying only that we need 'a great excess'. It has to go on to say when the excess is great enough. If the moral turning-point is not the prudential turning-point, how do we find it? Suppose that this is the story. With our resources we could educate both Adam and Eve so that each would have an interesting, worthwhile career—outcome (1). Or we could, because Eve has exceptional musical talent, concentrate resources more on her; Adam would stop his education earlier and so be in the running for less interesting jobs, but Eve would be (let us make the excess really great) a new Mozart—outcome (5). I think that, if outcome (5) were a possibility, nearly all of us would opt for it—even just for Eve's sake, let alone for the benefit to mankind of having a new Mozart. But surely it does not take as great a bonus as a new Mozart to justify a deviation from equality. A new Brahms would do. Or a Richard Strauss. Or perhaps even a Franz Lehár. But then where does the turning-point come? It would be unreasonable to expect great precision in the answer, but still we need an answer. Even parents, who have many more reasons to keep to equal treatment of their children than we detached observers have with Adam and Eve, often think that it is justified to concentrate resources on a talented child if the child has prospects of ending up, say, as violin in a good quartet. No doubt, we should not think that it would be enough merely for Eve to get occasional fun from playing her violin later on in life. Occasional fun, like the occasional good meal, is probably not the right kind of value to change the global judgment about the prudential value of a whole life. To reach the moral turning-point, we should need something more. We should need, for instance, a change in the order of magnitude of what Eve could accomplish with her life. Becoming a member of a good string quartet seems the right kind of change. But this is also the kind of change we should need to reach the prudential turning-point, too.

The obscurity of both the prudential and moral turning-points makes conclusions difficult. But two conclusions seem to me plausible. First, the moral turning-point is at least not far from the prudential turning-point. Second, there are no obvious independent criteria for where the moral turning-point is. These two conclusions suggest that the model of same-level principles is also too strict. It puts forward the requirement of a 'great' margin of gain over loss, provides no clear criterion for 'great', and once we have a plausible conception of well-being we find it hard to distinguish the margin required from a simple margin of gain over loss.

4. *The two views compared*

Let me sum up what I have to say about utilitarian and contractualist conceptions of equal respect, turning now from particular versions of contractualism to contractualism in general.

In sharp contrast to the uninvolved, God-like gaze of the Ideal Observer, the Ideal Contractor is meant to be involved, but the constraints on him, in any version, strongly incline him to see the world through the eyes of the worst off. But this gives us the dictatorship of, or at least some strong dominance by, the worst off. Why think that *this* is the way to see things morally? It seems to suffer from distortion by not being uninvolved enough. It distorts moral judgment in areas outside justice, and it is too strict even as a criterion of justice.

It is because the principles that come out of contractualism give such strong protections that they so clearly meet the Requirement of Psychological Realism. But the attraction they get from this may not go deep. That every contractor has to be got to agree means that contractualism can advertise itself as 'a genuine reconciliation of interests'.[53] It would be a great comfort to know that the demands of morality will command universal assent, constrained only by ignorance or some fairly narrow conception of rationality. But the arguments so far suggest that it is unwarranted optimism to think that they will. Contractualism may look as if it has its roots in firm psychological ground, but no theory is well-grounded if, in the end, it fails to produce the goods.

The failing in Rawls' version of contractualism is not corrected in later versions and, what is more important, seems not correctable inside a contractualist framework at all. It is not easy to pin down the essence of contractualism, but I think it is this: an agreement on what are to be moral rules coupled with certain weak constraints on the parties to it. The constraints may vary from version to version but may not be too strong. They are meant to have minimal moral content, just enough to account for equal respect. So they must include such things as the parties' having to be motivated finally to reach agreement, or their being ignorant in certain ways, or their employing fairly narrow forms of rationality such as prudence or principles of bargaining. But they may not include specific moral constraints or a rich account of moral reasons for action, because this device is meant to generate them. But they must include enough to capture what we now mean by a *contractualist* account of equal respect: that is, they have to include something to bear the moral weight of the separateness of persons, because that has now become definitionally imbedded in the term 'contractualism'. Since 'separateness of persons' has no content except for the negative point that the utilitarian standard for trade-offs is wrong, contractualism cannot yield utilitarianism. Therefore, it cannot, even though this could be called 'contractualism' on some looser definition, require merely that the parties agree, ignoring their own eventual positions yet knowing enough to reckon reliably that they have an equal chance of being in each position,[54] because that yields average utilitarianism. So 'contractualism', as it is now used, needs self-interest in a form that prevents the sacrifices allowed by utilitarian trade-offs. And even if, to overcome the vagueness of this account of equal respect, we were not too strict about keeping the moral content to an absolute minimum but helped ourselves to some of the principles that supposedly 'follow' from it as fixing it further (so treating the account of impartiality and some of its main 'derivations' as a single package), we should still have to have this strong form of self-interest present; it is what gives moral weight to the separateness of persons. But then contractualism never adequately faces up to the threat to morality that self-interest poses; it never makes the decisive break with self-interest that morality seems, in the end, to be.

Meeting the Requirement of Psychological Realism is only a necessary condition. Still, it is necessary, and the utilitarian conception of equal respect seems to fail it. There is a distant but not unreasonable hope that if we build a fairly prosperous society, ordered by just laws, peopled by citizens with a secure sense of their own worth, then envy and rancour will disappear, and tendencies to opt out of or to cheat the system will wane.[55] But utilitarianism, since it demands great sacrifices, needs saints, and no happy growth of society is going to work that miracle. That is why John Mackie calls utilitarianism 'the ethics of fantasy'.[56] But I wonder whether that is not largely a misunderstanding. Of course, not many of us will behave like Captain Oates;[57] few people are going to agree to their own sacrifice. But this fixation on agreement is the contractualist's, not the utilitarian's, and it is just what produces the great distortion in the contractualist's outlook. What it is psychologically impossible for me to agree to do may still be morally justified for you to do to me. And the world does not generally *ask* for sacrifices; it exacts them. Surgeons decide who gets the transplant. Governments decide how much will go on health services or road safety. One might not cheerfully give to charities, yet still might fairly happily vote for political programmes that force one to do more or less the same through taxation. Anyway, if morality is demanding, it is demanding. The Requirement of Psychological Realism does not require that morality be comfortable, merely that we be willing to work at it.

So I do not think that the Requirement of Psychological Realism ranks the utilitarian and contractualist conceptions of equal respect. They both pass. What would rank them is the adequacy of their rules governing trade-offs. We have rather stark versions of the principle of utility generating restrictions on trade-offs that are too loose. We therefore devise rather stark anti-utilitarian restrictions, which are attractive at first sight (as indeed they should be, since they are largely shaped to look good up against utilitarian looseness), but then at second sight turn out to be too strict. That, I believe, is not too bad a summary of the present state of moral and political philosophy: there are two main competitors, one too loose, the other too strict. We have either to tighten the former or to loosen the latter.

5. *A view of equal respect that allows some partiality*

How much out of my own slant on things must I lift myself in order to rise to the moral point of view? Utilitarians say sternly that I must not look through the eyes of any interested party; contractualists let me look at things interestedly, while using constraints that mean that I must look through the eyes of the worst off. But each of us, in looking out at the world through his own eyes, finds natural and proper objects of regard, respect, and commitment; our attachments—not just to persons but also to causes, standards, and institutions—express much of what we value. Is this entirely to be left out of the moral point of view? And if it is, what mutilated rump of a moral agent is going to be left? Anyway, do we not deep down, despite the cant we all find it easy to fall into in theorizing, think that the partiality of some of these particular commitments is at the heart of the moral point of view? Do we not think that it is all right to care more for family than for just anybody, and not because some fully impersonal moral perspective finds itself able to grant us the dispensation but because the personal perspective is there, right at the base of morality, in the moral point of view itself? These are worries about any rigorously impartial form of equal respect, including both utilitarian and contractualist.

However, the rationale of this more personal view of equal respect cannot be that morality reduces to personal aims. As we have already seen, such a reduction would merely solve the alienation problem by ignoring the authority problem; personal aims are not always aimed at what is valuable. Any rationale will have to show both how to generate these more personal forms of obligation and how to link them to values.

A more attractive way is to say that there are not only personal and impersonal obligations but also, in parallel, personal and impersonal values.[58] An impersonal obligation is one that applies to all agents—such as certain duties of help and of avoiding harm, or the utilitarians' single super-duty of maximizing well-being. A personal obligation is one that arises out of an agent's standing in a special role relation to others—such as parent or friend or promisor or citizen. And one can see this distinction underpinned by a distinction between personal and impersonal values. From our personal point of view, we might think, we fix on many proper objects of attachment, which express much of what we value. Indeed, some values, we might say, can be seen only from a personal perspective. It is not that there are no impersonal values; on the contrary, some things are valuable regardless of personal perspective. For example, pleasure and relief from pain look valuable to any properly functioning human eyes. But other things are valuable only as seen from the point of view of individual tastes and aims and commitments—for instance, rock-climbing or playing the piano well. So, on the face of it, there are two kinds of value, personal and impersonal, and an account of the moral point of view cannot forget either one.

There is clearly some sort of useful distinction to be drawn between 'personal' and 'impersonal' values. The proposal a moment ago was that 'personal' values are tied to aims that vary from person to person. But it is not clear in what sense there are such things. For me to see something as a value, from any perspective at all, requires my being able to see it against a certain background. The background must include general human aims; my own individual aims are not enough. This is not at all to opt for an objective approach to values; it is to state what is required for any talk about values to make sense. Let me take prudential values as an example. Certainly some values can be called 'personal' with no problem. They are not widespread; they are tied to special, even rare, sorts of character. For instance, a few people find rock-climbing an achievement, and so they value it highly; more people find it terrifying and do not value it at all. But these two groups are not disagreeing in their values in any interesting way. Nearly all of us value challenge, excitement, and accomplishment, and none of us values simply being terrified. It is just that we differ in what we find challenging or terrifying. But we all have to be able to connect what we value to some characterization that makes it generally intelligible as life-enhancing. The mere fact that the object I aim at is aimed at by me is not enough. A child might aim at not stepping on any crack in the pavement, but that is not enough, either for us or for him, to decide that carrying it off is valuable to him. Of course, he might be unhappy if he does not carry it off; he might have fun bringing it off. But happiness and fun are impersonal values. We quickly start reaching for impersonal values in cases like this, because simply achieving the object aimed at does not make his life any better. Indeed, some aims, if brought off, make one's life worse. The relation between desire and prudential value is complicated, but, whatever the full story, nothing is made valuable just by being aimed at. And what more is needed—the characterization that makes it generally intelligible that the object aimed at makes life better—makes all prudential values in one way impersonal. *That it would make his life worse* is, like *that it would cause him pain*, an impersonal reason not to do it. What I see simply through my own eyes and cannot see through other eyes cannot count as a value. Nor, of course, can it be a reason for admitting partiality into the moral point of view.

What we very much need, therefore, is an account of the complex ways in which values are *not* personal (do not depend upon the varying desires of individuals) and the ways in which individual differences affect values. I said something about this earlier.[59] The analogy with secondary qualities does not seem to me really to help here. Where it fits best (but how well I shall leave open) is in an account of values generally: values depend in one way or other on the human way of seeing the world.[60] But what we are after now is an explanation of something else: a difference in kinds of value, personal and impersonal.[61] Personal values, in the way we are now using the term, do not arise out of the human way of seeing things. All values do that. Personal values arise out of varying individual ways of seeing things. The analogy is not with, say, colour perception but more with (but still very little with) the difference between normal and deviant colour perception.

None of this, though, helps explain the ways in which values are, and are not, personal. Enjoyment is a prudential value. It is valuable to anyone. But the particular ways in which persons do enjoy themselves, even can enjoy themselves, of course vary a lot. And it can be reasonable for a person to forgo enjoyments to devote himself to some all-absorbing project; there is no ideal balance of prudential values that means that enjoyment must figure to this or that degree, or to any degree, in a good life. Prudential values, as described at some fairly general level of classification, are valuable to anyone; individual differences matter, not to what will appear in a profile of general prudential values, but to how, or how much, or whether a particular person can realize one or other of these values. For instance, accomplishment is one general value. I may want to become an accomplished pianist, and that specific accomplishment may become very valuable to my life overall, while not being of the slightest interest to the rest of you. But this is a matter not of our having different ways of experiencing the same determinate object (on the model of variations in colour vision) but of our having different determinate forms of the determinable value of accomplishment. In addition, the general value of accomplishment goes on imposing criteria on candidate determinations. I cannot, just by having it as my aim, turn anything I do on the piano (say, setting a world record for the fastest playing of the black keys from top to bottom) into something valuable—a 'personal' value. Rapid playing of the black keys, like navigating around the cracks in the pavement, takes more than being aimed at to be a value.

In any case, we may not move from the existence of personal values, in the sense above, to the existence of personal moral obligations. It is true that deep personal relations are an important value, and that for different ones of us the value will be realized in relationships to different particular persons. But from the fact that it is those, and only those, particular relationships that each values, it does not follow that each has a moral obligation only to, or especially to, those persons. That may indeed be so, but not simply because the value is, in that sense, personal. The chain of reasoning, if there is one, will have to be longer than that.

There may, none the less, be one. And we can see the rough makings of at least a link or two of the chain. It is still plausible to think that moral obligations will rest, in a way that has not yet been spelt out, on what an agent does, or should, find valuable. Since we all admit that there are values that are in some sense personal, some moral obligations may be too. For instance, since the value of deep personal relations can be realized only in particular ones, if any obligation is to grow out of this value it may turn into an obligation not to persons generally but to certain particular persons. That there is no short-cut does not mean that there is no longer route to this conclusion. Obligations may then turn out to fit the human psyche more comfortably than they promised to do with, say, utilitarianism. And they hold out hopes of eventually, in aggregate, constituting a set of demands rather like the law: they may demand specific limited forms of positive action to identifiable and usually not too distant persons, and prohibit limited forms of negative behaviour, often to the whole of humanity. The whole set, one can reasonably hope, will turn out to be something that, like the law, we can live within. The familiar yield of this line of thought is, roughly speaking, common-sense morality. There will be such a thing as being morally quits, free to relax and go about one's own business. The moral point of view becomes in this way, the view of an individual agent, who forms intentions, acts, and can be held responsible for what he does. Then we might find, in the idea of an agent-centred point of view, scope for making an agent's intentional action the centre of moral assessment, thus demoting outcomes (even forseen outcomes) to which the action is causally connected to a peripheral place. And we might then also be able to give more weight to distinctions between acting and omitting, and between obligation and supererogation, than either utilitarians or contractualists can.[62]

If all of this can be carried off, it will deliver a deontological conception of equal respect. It would not be the only form the deontological view could take, but since it is so promising in coming to terms with the Requirement of Psychological Realism, it is an important one. But the number of missing links in this chain of reasoning is the great worry about it. By tailoring personal obligations to fit typical personal aims, it too solves the alienation problem without offering any clear solution to the authority problem. Where are these personal obligations coming from? Not from the Requirement of Psychological Realism, because that can be met in many ways. Nor from the mere existence of a distinction between personal and impersonal values either.[63] Impersonal values such as the well-being that both utilitarians and contractualists appeal to are clearly valuable, but the obligations connected to them seem to spread too widely and become too demanding. This sort of deontology generates obligations that do not spread too widely or become too demanding but are not founded in anything comparably obvious. By trimming obligations to fit personal aims one can get them inside human motivation. But it is likely that everyone will face moments when even this personal sort of deontology makes a moral demand on him that conflicts with his actual motivation. Then he will want to know what authority these obligations have, why they should move him. That is the trouble: since it is so hard to see where these personal obligations are coming from, it is very hard to accept that they constitute reasons for action, let alone reasons strong enough to outweigh one's actual present motivation.[64] The answer cannot be: These are reasons because they fit pretty well what anyway persons generally desire. It cannot even be: Because they coincide with what is prudentially valuable to you. Whatever the Requirement of Psychological Realism amounts to it cannot be anything as crude as that. That is not fatal to this sort of deontological view. It just shows that it too has to solve the authority problem. I shall be coming back to deontological views later.[65]

All of these views about equal respect—utilitarian, contractualist, and deontological—are views about how much one person's interests may be sacrificed to the interests of others. They are all views about fairness and justice. So what is needed is an account of equal respect that leads to satisfactory answers to that whole range of questions. There are no short cuts. General considerations about value do not supply one; moral psychology does not either. To think that they do is grossly to underestimate the scale of the problem. The only way to establish anything of interest is to produce a satisfactory substantive account of fairness and, in the end, of morality itself.

X

FAIRNESS

1. *Two problems: fairness and the breadth of the moral outlook*

EACH of us has desires that he can satisfy only along with other persons. I cannot rendezvous with you, unless we both go to the same place. We cannot free the car from the snow, unless we both push at the same time. This sort of case does not often raise problems. Since, typically, each party has the same aim, agreements or conventions arise easily, often spontaneously, to bring off the benefit of the co-ordination. But there are also cases where each of us has an aim that he can indeed bring off on his own, but where the results of his doing so are less good than if he brings it off together with the rest. I want to be prosperous, but I would prosper more by working with the rest of you. But what each puts in and each takes out can vary enormously, and agreements and conventions do not typically arise so easily. These cases raise some of the hardest problems about fairness—problems of *co-operation*.

The most famous example of a problem of co-operation is the Prisoner's Dilemma.[1] But there is another overlapping sort. Sometimes what matters are cumulative effects of action, effects which singly make only a small, often imperceptible difference, and occasionally no difference at all, but together make a great difference. If one person living in the centre of my town burns logs on his fire, the deposit that the smoke makes on the buildings will be imperceptible, and the rain will wash it away. But if enough people do, the buildings will be permanently damaged and everyone (even the ones who have enjoyed a fire) will, on balance, be worse off. This category only overlaps that of Prisoner's Dilemmas, because cases of this type can involve only one person. If I once cut across your lawn, no damage is done; if I do it often enough, I wear a path. The trouble in these cases, whether involving one or many persons, arises simply from the fact that each consequence on its own is slight or, with time, entirely reversed. Whatever other persons living in the centre of my town do, *my* burning a log fire will make no perceptible difference. Whatever I do at other times, my *now* cutting across your lawn will make no perceptible difference.

Co-operation raises many problems, including some of the most urgent political problems that we face. I want to talk about two central moral problems. Co-operation raises problems of *fairness*. What should the terms of co-operation be? If I voluntarily benefit from co-operation, should I not myself co-operate? And should I not even if nothing bad would happen if I did not? And co-operation raises problems of *moral outlook*. How wide does our perspective have to be to take in everything that matters morally? The problem of outlook is distinct from the problem of fairness, because although it arises in cases of fairness, it also crops up in cases where fairness does not. If a moral theory tells me to look only at the results of the act that I am contemplating and to compare them to the results of the alternatives open to me here and now, I shall miss the fact that acts can be parts of sets, of practices, of activities. What matters is the result not just of my now cutting across your lawn but of my making a habit of it.

These are difficult problems, one way or another, for all moral theories. In the case of utilitarianism, for instance, the problem of moral outlook arises like this. If no one in my town burns logs, then I do no harm by doing so myself and, what is more, I get the benefit of a log fire. If everyone does, the same is true. Whatever number between *all* and *none* burn logs, the same is true. So utility, it seems, will be maximized if I do.[2] And the problem of fairness arises like this. Suppose I know that virtually no one else will burn logs, although they would like to. Then it will produce no harm and some benefit if I do. But then I am just free-riding, exploiting other persons' restraint.

Recent reaction to these well-known difficulties for utilitarianism is itself curious. Contractualists complain, with some cause, about utilitarians' reducing all morality to benevolence. But then contractualists turn round and reduce all morality, with no more plausibility, to fairness. It is reasonable, in light of the trouble utilitarianism runs into over fairness, to think that a solution to problems of co-operation will have to occupy a central place in morality. Yet it distorts morality to make fairness the whole, or even the heart, of morality. For one thing, since contractualists concentrate on cases of co-operation, they naturally look for moral principles in an agreement between the parties who have to co-operate, but, as we have already seen, it distorts principles governing trade-offs to say that they have to emerge from agreement; it makes them much too strict. For another thing, fairness has trouble explaining benevolence. It is natural to look for the principles that should govern co-operation in what free and rational persons would agree to. We must expect to have to agree to some constraint, if we are to have a hope of benefiting from the constraint of others. But it is an unnecessarily roundabout explanation of why, say, cruelty to children or to animals is wrong. The constraint against cruelty has moral force not because it would emerge from an agreement; it should emerge from an agreement because it already has moral force.[3] What is more, fairness has trouble with sorts of obligations it ought to find easier. Should very long-term promises be binding, if entered into in good faith and if circumstances have not changed? Suppose a young bride promises her husband that, should he die first, she will never remarry.[4] Then suppose that, years later, with her husband dead, she deeply regrets that promise of her distant, youthful self, and wants to remarry. Is she obliged to keep her promise? How would it help to appeal to the rules that parties to co-operation would agree to? They could shape their institution of promising so that such very long-term promises, without legal standing, were binding or that they were not. But the benefits of co-operation would not be threatened by adopting either institution. So, to decide between them, they would have to look outside the contracting situation. They would have to appeal to some richer, wider conception of morality than merely rightness as fairness. Fairness, as important as it is, is neither the whole of morality, nor the device that generates the whole of morality.

Why have contractualists been tempted to make it the whole, or the heart, of morality? They seem to have confused —using the terms in the somewhat special sense I am attaching to them—equal respect with fairness, the rules governing all moral action with the rules governing co-operation. They seem to have regarded co-operation as an especially important case, as the place where the transition from the State of Nature to Society, from prudence to morality, takes place. But although there is a sense in which justice is the whole of morality and another sense in which it is only a part, it is equal respect that is plausibly thought the whole of morality; fairness is indeed just a part.

2. *The consequentialist's problem of finding a broad enough outlook*

A moment ago, I mentioned two problems that would be my subject, first a problem about the breadth of the moral outlook, and second the problem of free-riders.

The first is a problem for consequentialists. And most of us are consequentialists in the relevant sense; for most of us believe that *some* consequences matter morally in *some* way. But, then, how are we to take in all the consequences that matter?

One source of trouble is a plausible, and sometimes it seems even inescapable, notion of agency—the notion of each of us as an isolated agent, cut off from other agents whose actions we are driven to treat as part of what is given, cut off even from our own long-term, life-structuring aims. Morality has different branches; there is, most importantly, act-morality (assessment of the rightness and wrongness of acts), but there is also agent-morality (assessment of the goodness and badness of character and of responsibility for acts). But then what is the central concern of act-morality except evaluation of acts? And what are acts except what each of us can do here and now each time an opportunity to act arises? So an isolated agent, to the extent that consequences matter to him, reasons by listing his options occasion by occasion and calculating which provides the best outcome.

One example of an isolated agent is an act utilitarian, at least on a tight interpretation common now;[5] let me call him a 'strict act utilitarian'. Such a utilitarian reviews his options case by case and plumps for the one that has, impartially considered, the best outcome. But to reason in that way does not, in the end, produce the best outcome.[6] For most of us, one of the things that gives most value to our lives is deep attachments to particular persons. And these attachments are incompatible with strict act utilitarian reasoning; they do not leave one able, occasion by occasion, having reviewed all actions within human capacity, to choose the best. Of course, a strict act utilitarian can include among his options becoming a person of deep attachments. But that is not a mere action of the sort that the isolated agent passes in review. It changes the whole source of his action. We are naturally inclined to form deep attachments, and if we know what makes life valuable we will refine and reinforce this already strong inclination. But such an inclination forms part of the long-term life-structuring features of one's character; and it undercuts the strict act utilitarian's whole mode of deliberation.

The outlook adopted by the isolated agent could not be the right one, for *any* form of consequentialism. There seem to me to be three reasons for this.

For one thing, it ignores too much of our real situation of choice. Typically, we are short of time, facts, and fellow-feeling. Therefore, what guides our choice must take these shortcomings into account. And what guides choice are not just principles and beliefs, but also feelings, emotions, habits, dispositions, and policies. Modern moral philosophy has largely ignored the towering importance of moral education: we are set on a moral course early in life, changing which, except in small ways, is not often or easily done. It is always tempting to think oneself or one's situation an exception, so moral dispositions, to do their job, must go fairly deep. And dispositions have to be shaped to what usually happens, not to the exceptional case. So a moral person will be moved by inclinations that have to be, for good reason, to some degree insensitive to exceptions. Another important feature of our real situation of choice is our lack of agreement on matters on which, for the survival of our life together, we have to agree. Sometimes we need agreed practices. Sometimes a deal must be struck, even at the cost of one's own moral beliefs. I may think that *I* have the better moral principle to apply in a certain case; others may think that *they* have and we cannot here agree to differ;[7] so perhaps the best we can do is let the toss of a coin or a majority vote decide.

These thoughts prompt some distinctions. We ought to distinguish the criteria of right and wrong from a moral decision procedure.[8] The criteria are the features that make acts right or wrong, while a moral decision procedure is the thinking one should go through to decide what morally to do. Obviously we should want a person's moral thinking as much determined by consideration of right-making features as possible. But there are good reasons, some of which we have just seen, why moral thought cannot be so pure. Then it is worth distinguishing different sorts of moral decision procedures. There is a practical decision procedure: what should guide one in everyday life when one is short of time, facts, and fellow-feeling. Then there is a reflective decision procedure: what should guide one on the rare occasions when those shortcomings are absent. When they are absent, then, clearly, since the procedures designed for the typical case no longer fit, we should be dim not to look for new ones. I shall come back to this distinction in a moment, but it is clear that part of morality at least is a practical decision procedure. And as far as that part goes, the deliberation appropriate to it is nothing like the deliberation of the isolated agent.

There is a second reason why the isolated agent's outlook cannot be right. The value theory at the base of consequentialism rules it out. I discussed earlier[9] ways in which prudence is thought to, but does not, deliver important results for morality. Now I want to discuss one way it is not thought to, but does, deliver one. We naturally expect prudential value theory to be neutral as between different versions—say between act and rule utilitarianism—but I think that it is not so. This is because with the shift from a simple hedonistic account of prudential value to an informed-desire account, the focus of evaluation shifts from short to long periods of time, and in many cases to whole lives. For instance, a person may find that what would give his life value would be rich, loving relationships, or some measure of accomplishment, or living autonomously. Even valuable short-term pleasures have to be fitted into a fairly long-term context; a person would have to decide how much place to give to living for day-to-day pleasures compared to other ways of living. Therefore the isolated agent does not properly identify the primary object of evaluation; it is the quality of lives, not what we do occasion by occasion, which a hedonism of short-term experiences fits better. On a plausible theory of prudential values, the important values are what give life point, structure, or weight.

But then this must influence how moral thinking can be conducted. Anyone who centres his life on deep attachments to certain persons adopts a whole way of living. He makes commitments that themselves become a powerful source of action; they reduce psychological freedom. The same is true of a person who tries to lead a life that accomplishes something. He makes a commitment that changes his feelings and attitudes, that takes up his time and narrows his attention. These large-scale decisions are the ones that, for the most part, determine action, and they demote the sort of occasion-by-occasion decisions that the isolated agent goes in for to a modest corner of deliberation.

There is a third reason why the isolated agent's outlook could not be right for any sort of consequentialism. It fails to see the outcome of acting in concert with others. If the isolated agent is a utilitarian living in my town, he will, following the pattern of deliberation we have already traced, conclude that he ought to burn a log fire. And if this is the model for moral deliberation, then ideally everyone would think the same, and the buildings will be badly damaged and everyone will be worse off. This tunnel vision clearly misses too much. Before it missed the importance of *whole lives*; now it misses the importance of *whole groups*.

I have mentioned three reasons why a consequentialist would not adopt the isolated agent's outlook. Let me return for a moment to the distinction between a practical decision procedure and a reflective one. The first of the three reasons is that the isolated agent's outlook is not right for the practical decision procedure. That leaves it open whether it is right for the reflective procedure. However, the second and third arguments show that it is not right there either. When, very rarely, we are not short of time, facts, and fellow-feeling, we clearly should not use decision procedures made for normal times. Should we then use strict act utilitarian thinking? Well, 'act utilitarian' is a loose term, too loose to make an answer obvious, but there is at least some reason to answer, No.

With time, facts, and fellow-feeling, we can sit back and ask whether a certain rule of the practical decision procedure applies in a certain case, and if we decide that it does not, we can sometimes free ourselves from its grip. The rules of good citizenship, for instance, are like that; it does not take much effort to miss a vote, if one is convinced that it is all right to do so. One thing that makes it easy is that what many duties of citizenship require has value only as a means to other values, which sometimes are not at stake. Admittedly, the practices that form our practical decision procedure differ a lot in the strength of their grip on us. Still, some of the things we value are very different indeed from the rules of good citizenship. The central values of our lives always retain their value. Furthermore, they get a firm grip on our lives. For example, our deepest commitments to particular persons go so deep that we never recover our original freedom of action, if ever we had much. Some are genetically based; many that are learned still go deep. If the training starts early, we can to some degree overcome our nature. But if we see no reason to overcome it, if indeed we see every reason not to, then we allow it permanently to shape, and to limit, our action. We are no longer able to enter into, and exit from, the behaviour occasion by occasion.

Then there is another kind of central prudential value. If making some sort of contribution to knowledge is a large part of what gives weight to my life, this goal would then take a lot of my time. I might, if I had become a different sort of person, have been caught up, say, in politics. Indeed, as it is, I still might, even as I actually turned out, promote well-being more, all things considered, by taking time off now and then to serve some good political cause. But I should first have to find out how good the cause is, and spend even more time discovering how to be effective in helping it, and much more time in doing the job. It is not that I have not, strictly speaking, got the time. And, of course, I ought not to sit quietly at my desk, if I could help avert some political disaster. But there comes a point where I draw a line, even knowing that I shall be missing chances to do better. But once the line is drawn, my policy to get on with my work is not shaped by the normal shortcomings we have mentioned. The policy gets its point not because time is short to reach a decision, but because life is short.

These points about the reflective decision procedure raise again the question of exactly how ideal it is thought of as being. My points all rest on the assumption that it is not so ideal that it imagines human nature away; a decision procedure is, I assume, a procedure that people would sometimes use. This means that we may imagine people with ample time to reflect, in possession of the relevant facts, and finding their self-interest quiet; because all of this sometimes happens. But it also means that we cannot just imagine people emotionally tied to others at one moment and detached at the next, or the human life-span other than it is, or a person in society untouched by whether co-operation occurs. Any decision procedure ideal in such an extreme sense would lose interest for us.

So the practical decision procedure is this: I ignore case-by-case consequences and, in deciding what to do, consult the principles that express the habits, dispositions, and practices that have the best long-term consequences in the light of normal human shortcomings. The reflective procedure is this: when the shortcomings are absent, I assess the consequences occasion by occasion to determine whether a particular case is an exception to my general rules; I also assess consequences occasion by occasion at those early times when I choose the general features of my way of life; but then, having chosen them, I give up act-by-act deliberation in large parts of my life and settle what to do by appeal to my goals and commitments.

As any reader familiar with the recent work of R. M. Hare will have noticed, this contrast between the practical and the reflective decision procedure is in some respects like his contrast between two levels of moral thinking, the intuitive and the critical.[10] It is a mistake to regard these two procedures, or these two levels, as merely something to smarten up dowdy old utilitarianism. They are, as Hare claims, part of the structure of any moral thought. But my proposal is not identical to his. For one thing, I think that there are reasons for distinguishing more than two levels, as I shall explain shortly. Also, I should want to draw the lines between the levels somewhat differently. Indeed, there are many different forms that a multi-level structure can take. Clearly, much more must be said about, and in defence of, a multi-level structure; some of it I shall come to in this chapter, and some more of it in the next. One large difference between Hare's proposal and mine has to do with where act consequentialism fits into deliberation, and I should say something more in a general way about that.[11]

It seems that, although some thought that goes on in the reflective decision procedure is act consequentialist, some is not. Our commitments and life-structuring aims largely take away our freedom to deliberate occasion by occasion; this loss of freedom is not made appropriate by the normal shortcomings that shape the practical decision procedure, so it does not disappear when they do. I spoke earlier of *strict* act utilitarianism but it is hard to see how the reflective decision procedure could be thoroughly act utilitarian even in broader senses. Just as act-by-act deliberation is barred from the practical decision procedure, it is at times barred from the reflective procedure. If that is enough to say that the practical procedure is not act utilitarian, it is enough to say the same about parts of the reflective procedure. This conclusion does not mean that consequentialist deliberation is not, ultimately, at some particularly deep level, act by act. In a sense it has to be. One department of moral thought is act-morality. Its business is assessing behaviour, not exactly what people *do* but what they *choose* to do. What they *do* often comes not from choice but from habits, emotion, and so on. But we want to get at moments of choice, and in the case of emotions and habits the relevant choices lie back in such acts as those that formed the habits or did not curb the emotions.[12] Act consequentialism is true simply in virtue of the proper object of assessment in this department of moral thought. But the choices that matter are often not only in the background, but far in the background. *Ultimately* a consequentialist has to be an act consequentialist, but it is often very ultimate indeed. Where act consequentialism has its unqualified place is not in the decision procedures we have spoken about but among the criteria of right and wrong.

To the extent that consequences determine right and wrong, what makes an act right is there being no other possible act with better consequences. But even this role for act consequentialism has to be taken in a way compatible with prudential value theory. And there the primary object of evaluation is, as we have seen, lives looked at in a long-term way. So, to the extent that consequentialism has a hand in assessing what people do, it has to look at how what they do affects the quality of life. And what a person does can affect the quality of lives in very many different ways: by the dispositions he encourages or discourages, by the goals he sets himself, by co-operating with others, by adopting conventions, and so on. These are all things that we choose to do. We do not just look from an act outwards, towards its further and further consequences; the prudential value theory shows that we should also look from the whole of life inwards, to find the acts that give it its general contours. This means abandoning the narrow perspective that sees acts as making ripples, some of which admittedly last a long while, but also as having to be repeated again and again, with the deliberation appropriate initially appropriate repeatedly. Some of our most important acts are not like that; they are important because they alter the character of deliberation; they relegate act-by-act deliberation to a relatively small segment of life.

So, no consequentialist would want to adopt the local outlook of the isolated agent. It would certainly be wrong for his practical decision procedure; it would also be wrong for his reflective decision procedure. He would want to adopt a much more global outlook that took in not only the effects of individual acts but also ways of life, commitments, aims of life, and the cumulative effects of what groups do. This is still a consequentialist outlook, only not the isolated agent's.

My talk of local and global outlooks touches on many issues in Derek Parfit's discussion of whether certain theories are self-defeating.[13] But it seems to me that the framework of local and global outlooks is in some respects to be preferred to Parfit's own framework. It is not that it leads in the end to different conclusions from his but that it reaches them more directly. Parfit argues persuasively that someone adopting what he calls the Self-interest Theory, who thereby develops a disposition 'never to be self-denying', will often make things worse for himself simply in self-interested terms.[14] And he argues that a group adopting Consequentialism as a moral theory, the members of which thereby develop dispositions 'always to do good', would also make things worse even in their own consequentialist terms.[15] Both these theories are, he concludes, 'indirectly self-defeating'. They are because 'It would make the outcome worse if we were always disposed to make the outcome best'.[16] But what is it to be disposed to make the outcome best? It could be rather different things. It could be to be disposed always—on each occasion, taken occasion by occasion—to do what would make the outcome best. That is, it could be to apply one's standard of value, whatever it is, locally. Or it could be to be disposed always—consistently through one's life—to do what would make the outcome best, leaving it still to be decided whether one's standard is to be applied locally or globally. According to Parfit, *belief* in the Self-interest Theory or in Consequentialism will be likely to produce certain *dispositions* (never to be self-denying, always to do good), which in turn may produce bad effects. But all that belief in either theory will produce is a disposition of the second sort, while to get the result that the disposition would make the outcome worse, and so the result that the theories are self-defeating, we need the first sort.

More importantly, it would not be mere belief in these theories that produced bad effects in their own terms; it would be belief in them plus a decision to apply them locally.[17] Yet whether we should approach self-interested or consequentialist deliberation locally or globally depends upon the content of prudential value theory, and the best prudential value theory is not neutral between local and global outlooks. The Self-interest Theory does not lead us to be 'never self-denying', and Consequentialism does not lead us to be 'do-gooders'. Neither is capable of leading anywhere until it incorporates a value theory and so makes the closely connected choice between local and global outlooks. Once the theories thus become capable of motion, they will in fact lead us somewhere rather different. Parfit sees the Self-interest Theory and Consequentialism coming to advise their own abandonment; they become to some large extent 'self-effacing'.[18] But the best response to the real enough cases where applying the theories turns out to be self-defeating is not to stop believing the theory but to stop applying it tactically rather than strategically.

Can one apply them strategically without schizophrenia? Would desiring the best yet having to turn one's face, occasion after occasion, against doing the best require a divided self: one self rational grand strategist, the other unthinkingly obedient lower ranks? Is it better simply to suppress one's original beliefs? But this exaggerates the psychological tensions. I do indeed have to turn my face against occasion-by-occasion maximization. I have to live with knowing that my policy, centred on maximizing well-being, is not maximizing it in one way: I am passing up chances locally to maximize. But I have the consolation that, looking at things overall, and accepting the limitations that reality imposes upon me, I am doing the best. I know that I am psychologically incapable of entering and exiting, at will, from policies, commitments, and attachments. I have to live with that, and much similar, knowledge. But it does not take a divided self to be able to.[19]

Once a consequentialist shifts to a global outlook, Prisoner's Dilemmas look different. Merely by thinking strategically, even without thinking morally, he might sometimes agree to accept a political solution to a Prisoner's Dilemma. For example, we might all agree on an inescapable system of taxation, or one with swingeing penalties for cheaters. But, as is well known, such political solutions do not work in many real cases in which defection cannot be made impossible or sanctions effective. Then we need one or other psychological solution. And we have one: we are imagining an agent who is impartially benevolent. But acceptance of a principle of impartial benevolence, like most moral solutions, gets us only so far. It is true that if both parties are impartially benevolent, in one way we have a complete solution. Each party will co-operate whether the other party co-operates or defects; in either event co-operation would maximize benefit impartially. Still, that does not get us far enough. Anyone who is impartially benevolent will want to bring about mutual co-operation; that is the most beneficial outcome of all. And if he does not know that the other party is impartially benevolent, then he will want to look for a way to ensure that the other party will still co-operate. If the other party is indeed impartially benevolent, then he too will look for a way to ensure co-operation. But there are often different ways to do this. And then their problem becomes one of co-ordination.[20] In co-operation generally, even if everyone were impartially benevolent, and moreover thinking strategically, we should need both to co-ordinate action (for instance, if there were several equally plausible 'best' options) and to be assured both that enough others are going to co-operate for co-operation in fact to have the best results, and also that not so many will co-operate that it would be better if some struck out on beneficial action of their own.[21]

There are many important, sometimes life-and-death questions about the emergence of co-operation, not all of which is it reasonable to expect moral philosophy to be able to answer. For instance, there is the question, How can an individual with certain endowments (for instance, with a global outlook and a belief in impartial benevolence) find reassurance about the motives of other persons, or manage to co-ordinate his actions with theirs? That is a complex question about how co-operation in fact gets off the ground; it is not a question for moral philosophy. Then there is the question, Does a person with only these endowments have reason to be assured and to co-ordinate his actions with others? But that question is ill-conceived. There is much more to human nature than strategic outlooks and moral principles, and a good deal of it comes into play in making co-operation likely and so rational. There is genetically based behaviour; there is a wide range of emotions; there are natural dispositions—for instance, a willingness to gamble. It is most unlikely that a key social institution such as punishment, say, came into existence through an agreement that required trustworthy character and rational assurance of each other's trustworthiness. It is much more likely to have grown from feelings of guilt and anger, and from dispositions of self-protection and retaliation. And there is no sharp divide between 'political' and 'psychological' solutions to Prisoner's Dilemmas. Once key institutions have arisen, their rules, conventions, and sanctions produce practices and eventually habits and dispositions. Habits give more assurance about what others will do. The actual genesis of the social institutions and individual attitudes that promote co-operation is bound to be highly complex. Many institutions and attitudes existed well before humans rose to the level of self-consciousness that allows moral reflection. Moral philosophers, solely with rationality and moral principles as their resources, could not be the architects of our social environment; in any case, our social environment is already in place and moral philosophers are at best handymen capable of piecemeal alteration. Still, there are questions that a moral philosopher must face. It would be proper to ask whether, taking for granted all the various ways in which co-operation actually gets going, morality can give a reason to join in beneficial co-operation. And it would be proper to ask if, when beneficial co-operation is already under way, a particular morality will recommend undermining it or not doing one's bit.

To these questions, global consequentialism can often provide satisfactory answers. As we have seen, mere growth of altruism is sometimes not enough. But the global outlook would also tell us to do whatever is necessary—agreements, conventions, education, persuasion, punishments, forfeits—to hit on and sustain beneficial co-operation.[22] Or, rather, since this sounds too much like the implausible picture of the moral philosopher as architect, it would give us reason to sustain and refine those forms of co-operation that we find already in place.

A narrow consequentialist outlook gets one into troubles; shifting to a broader one gets one out of many. But how many? In particular, how much does it help with free-riders?

3. *The free-rider problem and a minimal solution*

Broadening the consequentialist outlook, on its own, is no help with free-riders. If enough people follow the rule not to burn log fires, the buildings in town escape harm, and I should increase welfare, impartially considered, by making myself an exception.

Perhaps, therefore, the fully moral outlook needs one more step back. Perhaps we should look at *hypothetical* as well as *actual* outcomes. 'What if everyone burnt a log fire?' The reply, 'Not everyone will', seems to miss the point. Of course, if they are decent sorts, they will not. But the point is that a few of us can indulge ourselves without damage only because the rest of you are denying yourselves. This line of argument obviously has some force.

However, the move to hypothetical outcomes seems to drain consequentialism of its intuitive plausibility. What matters morally are actual changes to people's lives. If the Town Council came to believe that not everyone's constraint was necessary to avoid the bad outcome and hatched a workable scheme to let us take turns burning log fires, there would be no moral objection to it. 'Not everyone will' seems not to miss the point. And this second line of argument has force too.

These two arguments seem to me to make up a deeper dilemma than the Prisoner's. The pull of each is a cause—not the only one, but nowadays an important one—of the deep split between Kantians and utilitarians.

What seems right in the first argument is that it is objectionable that my life can be made better with a log fire only because your life will be worse. I am being a parasite and so violating equal respect on some conception that we should not want to lose. And, in a way, what the rest of you actually do is morally irrelevant. It is beside the point that you will actually restrain yourselves. And that is because the point is my behaving like a parasite. But what is morally pertinent about my behaving like a parasite is not a hypothetical outcome either, what would happen if you all behaved differently from the way you will.[23] What seems right in the second argument is that the outcomes here are all real enough: I actually get the cream of life because the rest of you are actually making do with the skimmed-milk.

How much do we have to do to get fairness back into the picture? I cannot see how adopting a principle of maximizing well-being, even with a finely articulated multi-level structure that its global application could give, can get it back. And therefore I cannot see how utilitarianism, at least with the resources we normally associate with it, can get it back either. What I think we ought to do is to look for the very minimum resources needed to reintroduce fairness. A minimalist approach has not only elegance to recommend it, but also prudence. The greater the resources, the more likely they are to produce trouble elsewhere in the system.

One approach would be to take a hint from the fact that it is real, not hypothetical, outcomes that matter in free-rider cases and see how far we might get simply by developing or supplementing the principle of impartial maximization. It would be a relatively modest project. Our aim would be to find not answers to all moral questions, but merely a solution to the free-rider problem.

The place to start, I think, is with that vague but fateful notion of *equal respect*. Every moral theory has the notion of equal respect at its heart: regarding each person as, in some sense, on an equal footing with every other one. Different moral theories parlay this vague notion into different conceptions. Ideas such as the Ideal Observer or the Ideal Contractor specify the notion a little further, but then they too are very vague and allow quite different moral theories to be got out of them. And the moral theories are not simply derivations from these vague notions, because the notions are too vague to allow anything as tight as a derivation. Too vague, but not totally empty; although the moral theories that we end up with put content into all these notions, the notions themselves also do something towards shaping the theories. We move too quickly across this ground; there are positions that have not yet been properly explored.

So let us set off from this vague basic idea of equal respect, which impartial maximizers parlay into a principle of trade-offs: maximizing well-being, counting everybody for one and nobody for more than one.

What would such maximizers say, animated as they are by a certain conception of equal respect, about cases where maximization gives no result? Imagine a case where the welfare total stays the same and only chances of having it vary.[24] Suppose, for instance, that a government finds itself able to act in either of two ways. If it acts in one way, then, depending upon matters outside its control, either one group will be helped or another group will be equally helped. If it acts in the other way, then the first group is bound to be helped as before, but the second group will definitely get nothing. What should the government do? Whatever it does, the total help it gives will be the same; so the welfare sum provides no ground for choice. Yet there does seem to be an obvious ground: the first way of acting gives each group a chance.

What does an impartial maximizer say about this case? His principle of trade-offs (maximization) has no implications for it. The fault in that principle is not that it gives the wrong answer but that it gives none.

What answer, then, should he give? That question comes down to another question, What deep, animating conception of equal respect do we think his principle holds? We have to look behind the familiar principle of trade-offs (maximization), and its constituent principle of equal weight (everybody to count for one), to the conception of equal respect behind them both.

Suppose that you care equally about the welfare of your two children. You count each for one and neither for more than one; other things being equal you would have them at the same level of welfare; you would accept a loss of welfare for one of them as long as the gain to the other were greater. But then one day you find yourself confronted with a choice about which your view about trade-offs tells you nothing: the benefit will be the same whatever you do, the only choice being between directing it to only one of them or giving each a fifty per cent chance at it. From your moral views, as spelt out so far, it is unclear what you would do. There is no account of the principle of impartial maximization that provides reasons for doing either. You would have to think out your principles further. And here you might well reach different conclusions. You might conclude that your deep conception of equal respect can give no further guidance, that either some entirely new moral notion is needed or that the question is unanswerable. Or you might conclude that your deep conception, when developed further, gives the answer that the options are morally equal. Or you might conclude that your deep conception, when developed, points towards giving each child an equal chance.

The last seems to me a perfectly natural, perhaps the most natural, development. And there is this further explanation (I do not pretend that it is anything as conclusive as an argument). You as a parent would not be choosing between acts that determine the substantive well-being of your children. You would be choosing simply between acts that affect their chances. But chances may affect one's well-being. If one child's welfare matters just as much as the other's, then it seems in the same spirit to say that when it comes to chances of welfare, the one child's matter as much as the other's too. Where the notion of 'greatest sum' provides no criterion, it does not follow that an impartial maximizer has to be without one; there is no reason why his position cannot be taken to be rich enough to cover this case.

So if an impartial maximizer parlays equal respect in this way, he will have, first, a principle of maximization and next, when maximization does not rank options, a principle of equal well-being and finally, when equalization does not rank options, a principle of equal chances at well-being. It is, as principles of equality go, a modest addition to the principle of maximization. Still, no doubt some persons will want to deny that impartial maximization can be 'spelt out' to have even this modest egalitarian implication. What I want to say is that there is no good reason for their doing so. They might argue that if one adopts maximization as the principle governing trade-offs, then one accepts that, in a certain sense, individuals do not matter: the sum matters; which particular individuals get which part of it does not. But that individuals do not matter in this sense does not imply that they cannot matter in the sense that these further, tie-breaking egalitarian principles require. The sort of concern for individuals that is displayed in maximization is not inconsistent with the sort of concern displayed in this modest egalitarian addition. Indeed, the same deep consideration that generates impartial maximization can be seen as also generating these ways of filling its gaps.[25]

Yet if an impartial maximizer spells out his notion of equal respect in this way, what is it that he has added to his views? It might, of course, really be an entirely independent principle. The most powerful objection to impartial maximization is that it cannot account for fairness. So it is not surprising that its principle of trade-offs is silent on the sort of case that we have been looking at. But what I charitably call 'spelling out' the deep maximizing conception of equal respect may look to others suspiciously like recognizing its inadequacy and adding to it an independent principle of fairness that will turn around and start qualifying the maximizing principle itself in cases of other sorts. But I do not think that this is so. The addition is made within the constraint of the principle of trade-offs: loss is justified whenever gain is greater. And although the derivation is not especially tight, it is natural to think that each person's *chance* at welfare matters and matters equally, because of that deeper consideration that makes us think that each person's *welfare* matters and matters equally, and because of the causal connection between chance at welfare and welfare itself. The principle of impartial maximization plus the supplementary principle of equal chances constitute a combination of views that is no less natural, and no more or less puzzling, than any other important view about equality. It is little assurance, for instance, to be able to get such a view out of a contractualist framework, because there are many such frameworks, yielding principles on trade-offs that range from the quite strict to the quite permissive. Contractualists have to choose one particular framework, and that choice is itself the choice of a particular conception of equal respect. Nor is my suggesting that maximizers develop their own principle in this way any more puzzling or in need of justification than making equal chance an independent principle in some Ross-like pluralist kit. This sort of pluralism is incomplete; it has still to explain how we are to trade-off, say, a principle of impartial maximization against a separate principle of equality. To explain that would simply be to spell out this deep notion of equal respect. The spelling out that a pluralist has to do is the same sort of project as the spelling out that I have just done—neither one more natural or theoretically deeper than the other, and neither one different in kind from the spelling out that a contractualist has to do. All such spellings-out are conducted in much the same way and uncomfortably close to present theoretical bedrock.[26]

However, I hope that my disclaimers about the tightness of the derivation do not suggest that my argument is identical in form to certain arguments for indirect utilitarianism: namely, start with (usually conventional) results that you want the principle to yield and then tinker with the principle till it does yield them. On the contrary, my argument moves from the notion of equal weight in calculating trade-offs to a notion of equal chance; it tries to spell out in a natural way the deep notion of equal respect that underlies both.[27]

If the principle of impartial maximization can be spelt out in this way, then there is one implication to be faced. Utilitarianism, which is just the principle as the sole criterion of right and wrong, looks as if it might be similarly spelt out. But would we seriously contemplate giving the package of the principle of utility plus the two tie-breaking egalitarian sub-principles the name 'utilitarianism'? What I want to propose is that the answer does not much matter, that there is nothing deep at issue, that we might say what we like. We might prefer to say that a utilitarian is one whose sole criterion is utility maximization and that where it did not rank options there is nothing to choose between them. The principle of utility is silent on what to do about equal maxima. We tend to say that there is nothing to choose between them because usually there is not—on any version of utilitarianism, the spelt-out version included. But there are rare cases where the equal maxima differ because in one of them persons are benefited or get equal chance at the benefit whereas in the other they do not; and these cases pose a fresh problem. What should a utilitarian say about *them*? He might well indeed say that there is nothing to choose between them. Or he might say, I think, that he believes that the notion of equal respect comes back into play again here and gives us something to choose between them. Would the second position be 'utilitarianism'? If, as I think, there is no real case for saying that a principle of equal chances is contrary to the deep spirit of the principle of maximization, then it is hard to answer. It does now seem the sort of verbal question that needs legislation rather than argument.

This spelling-out may seem unimportant.[28] After all, it can help only where total welfare is the same whatever we do and it is merely chances that differ, and cases like this may seem of great rarity and little weight. But that is not really so. The spelling-out has implications for procedures. For instance, in all cases where benefit or burden is about the same for each member of a group but only some can or need to have it, it suggests that we ought to select randomly. Conscription is a good example. When the national, or other, interest points in no particular direction, then the chance of being selected should be made equal. And it should be made equal not because, say, any other procedure would cause resentment and unrest, although they matter too, but for a much more fundamental reason: each person's fate matters and matters equally and random selection is demanded simply by that. And a lot of cases of cumulative effects are also examples. If I were to burn a log fire, I would get about the same benefit as you would. So long as there is only one exception, whoever the exception is, the welfare sum will be the same; all that changes is the chance of having the benefit.

But does the spelling-out help with fairness? To return to our point of departure, free-riding: How do we get fairness back into the picture? If I burn a log fire because I need it and the rest of you do not, then my benefit does not rest objectionably upon your burden. That is because the introduction of needs also introduces equal respect: people's actual interests matter, and matter equally. But if I benefit because it is my turn, or because it is my name that came out of the hat, then my benefit also ceases to rest, in any objectionable sense, on your burden.[29] Chance at an actual benefit also matters. If I simply award myself the benefit, then not everyone has an equal chance at it. If, on the other hand, it is simply my turn, then everyone will in time have his chance. If my name came out of the hat, then everyone has had a chance. These modal matters—neither actual consequences nor hypothetical ones—also count.[30] I think that the principle of equal chances is also important in explaining what is objectionable in free-riding. To check free-riding, to get fairness back into the picture, we do not have to stop me from having the benefit while you suffer the burden. That still happens, but now unobjectionably because of the availability of one of a set of reasons for *my* getting the benefit: I needed it; I won the toss; it was my turn; etc. In other words, we need only show, by citing one of these reasons, that equal respect has not been violated. Equal weight in calculating different persons' interests would show it. Equal chance at a benefit would also show it. Do we need anything else? It seems not. We do not, for instance, need that extra step backwards to hypothetical consequences: 'What if everyone...?'

This has consequences for both those who frame and those who follow rules. To allow no one to burn log fires, when some could without harm and there are feasible ways of letting them, is senselessly stern. Those who frame laws could, as we have seen, give everyone an equal chance to have a fire; or they could amend the rules so that fires could be burnt in public buildings on special occasions. Sometimes they will have to play safe, because they do not know how often the rule will be broken or because what is at stake is so important. Sometimes they will have come to the point where finer calculation costs more than it is worth. But they should get as close to the edge as possible.

If they do, then those who follow the rule will not be left much room for manoeuvre. If the rule embodies the best estimate of compliance and of the importance of what is at stake, then generally I am in no position to conclude otherwise. That is why the *practical* decision procedure is so important in discussing fairness. Most of the rules, the breach of which is unfair, are rules of the practical decision procedure. They are framed for the usual context of choice.

But when, unusually, the context changes, those rules clearly suit less. There cannot be any easy move from the rules of a practical to those of a reflective decision procedure. Do I have a duty to vote? Well, suppose I ask as a citizen of a large marginal state in the United States, where the chance of my vote's making a difference is about one in one hundred million and where the population is two hundred million.[31] Suppose, also, that whether the better person wins matters; if he does, there will be some average net benefit to each citizen's life over a certain period. Then, I will have to reason roughly like this. There is only a very slight chance of my vote's making a difference. On the other hand, the expected benefit of my voting will be twice the average net benefit,[32] less the costs of my voting. So unless my case is most unusual, this sum will turn out positive. In general, in situations of that sort, I ought to vote. One does not have to look beyond outcomes to find a reason to vote, or to justify a rule about voting. But if I ask as a member of a much smaller body, say my college's Governing

Body, and it is a case where I know perfectly well how the others will vote and that my vote clearly will make no difference, then outcomes may give me no reason to vote. But there seems still to be a consideration of fairness: may *I* excuse myself from voting? May I, even if there are no other outcomes that matter? Why should *I* be the one to get the afternoon off? Perhaps I should toss a coin over lunch with you. It is easy to make what Derek Parfit calls mistakes in moral mathematics, such as ignoring small chances or small benefits.[33] But the free-rider problem is not solved just by avoiding these mistakes.[34]

This takes us to the reflective decision procedure, where deliberation gets complicated. There is the consideration of fairness, which can go beyond actual consequences: for instance, who should get the chance? On the other hand, only actual outcomes matter; maybe it is not worth the bother of tossing a coin with you, and since my vote will make no difference I need not go. We have also to keep in mind that although actually we have only partial compliance to our rule the ideal would be full compliance: burdens, let us say, would be fairest and outcomes best if we all faithfully voted, and my voting, joined with other persons', now and later, might be a break for higher moral ground. And we have to recognize that our attachments and commitments and life-structuring aims limit the freedom of our occasion-by-occasion deliberation. So deliberation on the reflective level has many sides.

I know that many persons will find this solution of the free-rider problem simply too weak.[35] They will think that it still allows too many exceptions, and they will insist that the free-rider problem shows that we need other, tougher principles. I want now to explain why the tougher principles seem to me to be too tough.

4. *The possibility of tougher, Kantian solutions*

Kant himself is not a consequentialist of the familiar modern variety. Consequences do enter his theory, but his test is not to determine first the consequences of everyone's doing such and such ('What if everyone ...?') and then their value ('It would be disastrous').[36] The test looks elsewhere: in one formulation, it asks each of us to see whether he can act on his proposed policy and simultaneously accept everyone's acting like that.[37] The question is not Would it be disastrous? but Would a contradiction appear? But, clearly, the appearance of the sorts of contradiction that Kant has in mind will turn largely on how we describe a person's policy. What I propose doing may be 'skipping votes', or it may be 'skipping a vote when there is one spare', etc. How specific can my description get?

If it cannot get as specific as we want (providing, of course, that it avoids any essential mention of particular persons, place, or times), and especially if it has to be kept at a fairly high level of generality, then perhaps one of the sorts of contradiction Kant has in mind will appear.[38] Even so, however, the test would not account for fairness. If it is kept at a fairly high level of generality, then the test would not allow me, or anyone else, to miss the vote, no matter how the lucky person was chosen. It would not allow me, or anyone else, to burn a log fire, even if the City Council drew names out of a hat. It is not only senselessly stern; it does not get to grips with what fairness is.

Perhaps, then, the account of a person's policy can be as specific as needed. It can mention anything morally relevant, and the fact that I do no harm by skipping the vote seems at least *that*.[39] You and I know perfectly well how the vote will go: the motion that we support will pass by two votes, when a one vote margin is just as good. But I am quicker off the mark in the car park. 'There is a vote spare, so I'm leaving', I say, and beetle off. You would not have minded a free afternoon either, but now you are stuck. My departure means that you cannot reason, If I skip the vote, no harm will be done. Yet, my behaviour, on a fully specific account of it, does not seem to lead to any contradiction. Still, what I do may be unfair. And not only does the test seem to allow the unfairness but also, worse, it does not locate its source. The intuitive thought behind this test is this: if it is morally all right for me to do it, then it is all right for everyone, similarly placed. Nearly all of us accept that; we disagree only over how to fix what it is to be 'similarly placed'. But your situation might be like mine in all relevant respects—your capacity to enjoy an afternoon off just the same; your need for extra time just as great; your absence no more harmful than mine. What is important to fairness need not lie in any feature of you and me, nor in any of our circumstances. It lies in the availability of one of a set of reasons for *one* of us getting the benefit. If you and I toss for the free afternoon, or if I do indeed need it more, etc., my missing the vote is fair. If not, it is not. Indeed, that is why the case Kantians sometimes put up for banning consequences from mention in one's policy (not allowing one to state it as, for instance, 'skipping a vote, *when no harm will be done*') is weak.[40] They rightly say that each of us would be able to argue that *his* skipping the vote would not be harmful and so each of us would be an exception. Nor does it help, they correctly add, that in fact not everyone will, because the rest may be decent sorts paying their moral fare while I ride free. However, the most that this shows is that the mere fact that I would do no harm in skipping the vote does not of itself justify me in skipping it. Justification needs more. What more, however, need not be, as they conclude, that my policy, formulated without mention of consequences, passes the universality test. It could instead be the availability of one of the reasons that I just began listing.

Suppose, then, we amend the test to accommodate this point. We now include how the benefit is distributed as part of the relevant circumstances. We might even find grounds in Kant's text for doing so. We could appeal to another and, according to Kant, equivalent formulation of the categorical imperative, the 'respect for persons' formulation: persons should always be treated as ends, and never merely as means.[41] And when I speed out of the car park, then whether or not I am conscious of using you as a means, I am none the less using your attendance in order to justify my freedom. I certainly give you no chance to exercise your rational will; I do not ask you, as a free and rational person, to consent. The 'respect for persons' formulation brings us very close to modern contractualism; the test is less immediately Would a contradiction appear? than Would free and rational persons agree?[42] And it seems at first sight as if this test is just what we need to generate the list of reasons that would justify exceptions. If you could do with a free afternoon just as much as I, then you are not likely to agree to my unilaterally awarding it to myself. What we both could agree to, however, would be some procedure, such as taking turns or tossing coins. We are likely also to agree, on maximin grounds, to give place to greater need. What more would we give a place to? The answer depends upon how rich a notion of rationality we are using. If we use the spare notion of self-interested rationality from modern contractualism, the answer is: nothing more than I have already proposed for the list. If we use Kant's potentially richer notion of a rational will governed by the objective ends of life, the answer is: it is hard to say. What makes my skipping the vote fair is my having the right sort of reason for being an exception, and it is hard to see how the Kantian test, made richer by his teleological account of life, identifies which reasons are of the right sort. It would be able to if its key terms 'categorical imperative', 'rational will', and 'respect for persons' had more content. It is true that it is a perfectly good thing to say of my giving you an equal chance, or of my weighing your needs impartially against mine, that I thereby show respect for your person. It is a good way to sum it all up. Still we have to know how to fix the content of this respect; we have to know which substantive reasons for my getting the benefit will make it fair and which will not. It is determining what constitutes fairness that puts content into the vague formula 'respect for persons', not the formula 'respect for persons' that discloses to us what constitutes fairness. The potentially richer, Kantian notion of rationality is so indeterminate that it does virtually no work.

These are, in outline, three ways of understanding Kant's test. If one of them is indeed correct, then in a sense it does not matter which it is: none of them helps enough with the problem of fairness. What seems most promising is taking the 'respect for persons' formulation in the direction that contractualists do. This might, depending upon whether the particular form of contractualism uses a narrower index of well-being, lead to slight differences from my proposal, but only slight ones. With something like health, say, it is hard to see how they could differ. For many diseases the optimum rate of inoculation is ninety per cent; inoculation beyond that brings no benefit to public health, and any inoculation imposes a real (small) risk on the child of serious illness. What rational agents

would be likely to agree to, either directly or through the
political structure, is inoculation to the safe threshold and fair
procedure for excepting people. The contractualists' way of
developing Kant's test produces a solution, but not the tough
one that we set out looking for. And, as we have seen,[43] it has
the disadvantage of being in other ways too strict.

5. *The solution of an agent-centred deontology*

The most interesting deontological solutions, I think, are
anyway not the tough ones. They are the ones that have about
the same practical results as my minimal solution but, many
would say, back them up with better theory. Indeed, my
minimal solution may seem not minimal enough. It uses a
rather wide-ranging principle, the principle of equal chances,
which applies to anyone whenever a tie between lexically prior
principles, which also apply to anyone, needs breaking. This
breadth creates trouble. Kurt Baier gives the following nice
counter-example.[44] Suppose I have two lottery tickets, each of
which would win me a million. I believe that two charities,
Oxfam and Care, would make equally good use of the million,
though of course the good they do would go to different
persons. Maximizing does not decide between them. But
would it be wrong for me to give both tickets to one charity
rather than one ticket to each? That is what an undiscriminat-
ing principle of equal chances seems to say, but it is most
implausible. What seems more plausible is that I am free
morally to keep or give away the tickets, or to give them both
to one charity, or to give one to each, just exactly as I see fit.
The examples that I used earlier—a parent taking a decision
affecting his children and a government taking one affecting
its citizens—were indeed intuitively plausible, but that may be
precisely because each is a case where an agent-centred
obligation is present, an obligation arising from special
role-relations (parent, government) involving responsibility,
including a responsibility to deal equally. My undiscriminat-
ing principle of equal chances, therefore, looks too broad, and
all that seems justifiable is one tied to a specific role.

This then suggests a rather different approach to free-rider
problems. Baier's own suggestion is this.[45] In free-rider

problems there is a network of special claims linking the
parties, a set of role rights to equal treatment. All of us in the
group benefit. So each of us, in return, is subject to a special
claim, arising from our role as willing participants, to help
produce the benefit. Not all of us are needed, so as many as
possible ought to be exempted. But no one has a special claim
to be exempted. So every one has an equal claim. The
reasoning all takes place within this network of claims.

The vocabulary of 'roles' and the 'claims' they give rise to
suffers from a lot of obscurity. Look at the decisive move from
a tough to a gentle solution—'When not all are needed, as
many as can ought to be exempted'. How are we meant to get
from 'No one has a special claim to be exempted' to 'Every
one has an equal claim'? The argument is supposed to work
within a network of moral claims but it starts, not with a
moral claim, but with the non-existence of any such claims.
How do we get from that to the existence of equal claims?
Well, some notion of equality is coming into play, perfectly
legitimately. But what notion? Is it not my general one?

No, one might think, it could not be such a general
principle; the Lottery Example shows at least that much. But
nothing is shown by one intuition on its own. We ought to
look at other cases of the same form (that is, cases without a
special obligation to treat persons equally, including granting
equal chances, of the sort that arises from role-relations).
Suppose we have a doctor treating victims of some disaster.
The victims have been sorted on reasonable criteria (for
instance, hopeless cases, non-urgent cases, etc.). In the savable-
and-urgent class you and I are left: each savable but time is
left to save only one. The benefit from saving each is
identical—and all the rest. Since you are injured in the legs
and I in the arms, I walk up to the doctor when he is free and
say, 'Here I am'. Would you not be inclined to shout, 'Not
fair—just because he can walk and I can't. Give me at least a
chance. Toss a coin.' Ought the one to be saved be chosen
randomly? Probably. But is this just another case of a
role-relation, where our equal claim is built into the role of
'doctor'? I doubt it. But, anyway, take next not a doctor but a
layman with first-aid skills that would save one of us. And
then take an ordinary person with food that will save one of us

from starvation. And then take a person not with food but with money with which one of us can buy food. And then take a person with a lottery ticket.[46] A fairly wide principle of equal chances does not seem to me to be ruled out by our intuitions.

To make his case, a role-deontologist has to be able to specify roles in a way that makes it clear that the related claims do indeed arise from them and not, say, from non-role-related principles hovering in the background. For instance, the role 'father' carries certain rights and is subject to certain claims, at least conventionally and often legally. But do these rights and claims also carry weight morally? The rights and claims that convention and law have granted to fathers have changed through history. There are two problems about reading claims off role-descriptions, which in the end reduce to one. If the claim is already built into the role-description, it is the result of historical contingencies and so has no obvious moral authority. If it is not, then we are choosing to build it in but have then morally to justify our choice. Of course, a claim's being the result of historical chance does not mean that it could not, after the moral assessment of the related institution, rise to moral status. It just means that it would have moral status only in virtue of the further judgement. In any case, the role-description in free-rider cases is something like 'co-operator' or 'co-producer', and it is very implausible that either description has built into it, as a piece of English or as a matter of convention, an equal claim on exemption from producing the benefit. So, since the moral claim is not already built into the description, we must be choosing to build it in ourselves. Our choice, of course, may be defensible. So the problem in these two alternatives comes down to the same. Either way we have to justify choosing to regard certain claims as part of certain roles. How are we to do it?

One answer is this. The role in question is 'co-producer of a benefit'. In general we each enter co-operation on a roughly equal footing. We agree, tacitly at least, to co-operate, and our initial equality transfers to equal claims to the benefit. Now, one benefit of the co-operation is ending up in the lucky position of being able to enjoy the benefit without having to put in the work, and the initial equality, it is reasonable to think, also gets transferred to an equal claim to this lucky position. Without such terms, free and rational persons would not agree to co-operate. But, as we have seen,[47] this contractualist argument seems weak at just the point we should have to rely upon it here. It can yield equal claims of too strong a sort, so it leaves us with the job of having to distinguish equal claims that have moral status from equal claims that do not, without supplying the equipment to do the job.

So let us translate the argument out of the contractualist mode, retaining most of the early moves: we co-producers enter the co-operation on roughly equal footing, so the benefits should be divided equally between us, including the chance at exemption, in virtue simply of our status as co-producers. But that cannot be the whole story. It is characteristic of role-deontology that it stops too early. What would it say of this familiar sort of case? Suppose two tribes, the Northerners and the Southerners, are driven by climatic changes to abandon their homes for the temperate middle region. They happen to settle on adjacent ground and start tilling and planting. Soon the Northerners find that their land is barren and that they cannot survive on it. They move in on the Southerners, whose early crops are just being harvested, and ask to share with them. They echo Locke: 'We did not get as much and as good.' Do the Southerners have equal claims on the benefits simply in virtue of being co-operators, that persons generally—the Northerners, for instance—do not? Most persons would say that Locke's proviso, or something like it, would have to come into play. The claim to any benefits, individual or co-operative, are limited by the claims of persons generally to an equal chance at a good life.

But a role-deontologist might now reply that, although a principle of equal chances strictly for co-operators has to be *sanctioned* by a broader principle of equal chances, nonetheless the narrower principle is *generated* simply out of the role-relations. It is because we co-operate in producing benefit that we *co-operators* have equal claims, in the absence of competing claims, on the benefit.

That does not matter. The crucial point is that to get the narrower principle in place as a moral principle appeal has to be made to the broader principle. So to solve the free-rider problem, we do seem to need the broader principle. In any case, it is by no means clear what the background for the co-operators' equal claim on the benefits of their cooperation is. It is initially attractive to propose that co-operators, as co-operators, ought to have special claims on the benefit simply because without their co-operation there would be no benefit. But the proposal is exaggerated. Sometimes they will co-operate without equal claim on the benefit, providing they have a reasonable hope of coming off better than they would without co-operating. Still, there is a point there. Sometimes, no doubt, we should co-operate only because we should have equal control over the benefit. The equal claim is sometimes an incentive to, indeed a necessary condition of, our producing it. In those cases it is odd to treat every one as having an equal claim; awarding them the claim ensures the non-existence of the necessary condition of what they have the claim to. But then a multi-level moral structure could accommodate the co-operators' equal claim on an upper storey, supported lower down by some more general principle of equality. What we all need to do, including the role-deontologist, is to find the best overall account of fairness. We also need to find a justification not only for claims arising from the role of 'co-producer' but also from the role of plain 'producer'; that is, we need a good overall account of property rights and how a person's labour comes into his claim to its products. And we need a much better general understanding of what it takes to turn the rights and obligations generated by social institutions into moral rights and obligations. These are the subjects of the next three chapters. I think that it is in these larger considerations that role-claims have a much harder time finding a place.

XI

RIGHTS

1. *The need for a substantive theory*

I want to take, as my point of departure, a dissatisfaction with the present state of philosophical discussion of rights that all of us, regardless of our views, feel. It is obviously unsatisfactory that the term 'rights', at least as it figures in the philosopher's lexicon, comes so close to being criterionless. It is still less satisfactory that the compound term 'human rights'— and it is on these rights that I want to concentrate in this chapter —comes even closer. As a result, philosophers often give the impression of plucking human rights out of the thin air. For instance, in the middle of a justly well-known discussion of abortion, we find the author settling most difficult problems by introducing a right to determine what happens in and to our bodies,[1] and if anyone should doubt, as many of us do, that there is exactly *that* right, we are unsure how to settle the matter. Also, we spend a lot of time these days arguing over the structural features of rights: whether they can be traded off against one another and against utility, whether they are, say, 'trumps'[2] or 'side constraints'.[3] Yet we all know that there is no real hope of settling these arguments until we can say what rights there are, what their extent is, and what makes them rights. We cannot, for instance, sketch out merely the rough outlines of a theory of rights—for example, rights as side constraints—and let the filling be added later. The filling is what settles whether one right can have different grounds on different occasions, and whether a right can differ in importance from one occasion to another, and whether a right with one kind of ground may be traded off against other rights or against utility, while a right with another kind of ground may not be. In short, structural features and substantive features have to arrive in a theory together. It would be perfectly safe to draw conclusions about the structure of rights in the

absence of a developed substantive account if the answers to
the substantive issues were obvious, but they are scarcely that.

But I think that virtually everyone agrees with these
complaints, including those who make claims about rights that
lack the foundations that the complaints desiderate. I doubt,
therefore, that I have really to argue the need for a substantive
theory of rights, but no doubt I should explain further what I
mean by such a theory. I think of a substantive theory in
contrast to a formal theory—that is, one primarily concerned
with the sort of structural features I have mentioned; and also
in contrast to a conceptual theory—one primarily concerned
to explore the relation of the concept of a 'right' to such
concepts as 'duty' or 'permission' or 'entitlement';[4] and also in
contrast to a taxonomic account—one concerned, as Hohfeld's
was, with cataloguing the different types of legal or moral
relations that rights consist in.[5] A substantive theory overlaps
these theories, but it is unlike them in being mainly concerned
with the content of the concept, with its criteria. And it does
not just tell us, as some philosophers have usefully done,[6] the
characteristics in virtue of which individuals are bearers of
rights. It would also tell us why those characteristics justify the
ascription of rights to them, and what else, if anything, does,
and how, if at all, our present criteria might be improved.

2. First ground: personhood

If there are such things as human rights, then they are rights
we have independently of actual laws, conventions, or special
moral relations. Therefore, it is likely that their substantive
theory will draw on, although also modify, elements from the
natural rights tradition,[7] and will go something like this.
Taking one's own course through life is what makes one's
existence human. We value our humanity, so we value what
makes life human, over and above what makes it happy. Now,
as we saw in Part One,[8] the freedom that makes life human has
many sides. The distinction between positive and negative
freedom is by now familiar to us, but perhaps the systematic
way to study all the complexities of freedom is to study the
complexities of 'agency'. One component of agency is deciding
for oneself. Even if I constantly made a mess of my life, even if

you could convince me that if you managed my utility
portfolio (on the usual understanding of 'utility') you would
do a much better job than I am doing, I would not let you do
it. Autonomy has a value of its own. But autonomy, on its
own, is not enough. It is not enough to be able to choose one's
path through life if one cannot move. One needs limbs and
senses that work, or something to take their place. But that is
not enough either; it is no good being able to choose and
having the capacity to act, if one is so racked by pain or by the
need to keep body and soul together that one cannot spare a
thought for anything else. We surely also need some minimum
health and leisure. Nor is this enough if others then stop us; we
need liberty.[9] We need other persons not to interfere in those
areas of our life which are the essential manifestations of our
humanity—namely, our speech and associations and worship.
Nor is this quite enough; it is not enough not to be fenced in, if
we are unable to form any conception of where to go. We also
need a mind capable of assessing things, which means that we
need some minimum education and access to persons worth
hearing or reading.

This personhood consideration, to give it a not unfamiliar
name, goes some way towards making the notion of a human
right more determinate. It generates most of the conventional
list of civil rights: a right to life, to bodily integrity, to some
voice in political decision, to free speech, to assembly, to a free
press, to worship. It also lends support to a form of positive
freedom, namely to a right to a minimum provision.[10] And it
says something about just how wide the concept of liberty is:
as far as the personhood ground goes, only a narrow concept
finds support; the right to liberty is not to do whatever fancy
prompts (so that *any* restriction on satisfaction of desires is *some*
restriction on liberty) but only, more narrowly, to do what is
essential to living a human life.[11] It also provides a right not
to be tortured, because torture aims at destroying one's
capacity to decide and to stick to the decision.

We say that personhood concerns what is needed for
human *status*, but it is tempting to be more generous and say
that it concerns what is needed for human *flourishing*. Yet
which should we say? What makes it so easy to shift between
the two notions, *human* life and *good* human life, is the difficulty

of knowing where to separate them. But it seems that the minimalist notion is the one that the philosophical tradition, with reason, supports. If we had rights to all that is necessary for the good life, rights would be too extensive. We should then have a right not just to minimum material provision, but to any unsubstitutable component of a better life. If this were the way that the tradition regarded rights, then we should obscure the distinction, with no obvious compensation, between, on the one hand, what enhances well-being and, on the other, what rights demand.

However, the personhood ground, despite its importance, may easily lead us to underplay the dynamic side of life. For instance, we know that a person can be oppressed, can even be shipped off to the Gulag Archipelago, and yet, because oppressors are not perfectly efficient, not only retain his autonomy and creativity but find them enhanced. But one who is oppressed can still ask of his oppressor, 'Who is *he* to have such control over me, whether it makes me or breaks me?' Rights, it would seem, must also secure the distribution of control over the central features of one's fate. Every responsible person must be granted control over certain matters affecting him. What is crucial is not just (human) status, but also control. The right to control the centre is a strong form of negative liberty. Liberty is the absence of barriers to living out one's life plan. In its weak form, one is at liberty if, for whatever reason, one can live by one's life plan, as someone still can who has a form of life imposed upon him which, by luck, he anyway wanted. But in its strong form, one is at liberty only if one could have lived by one's life plan, even if it had been different. The ground for the strong form of liberty is not obvious, but personhood must in any case be some of it. A person's values are not static; and fences that do not block now may block later. So personhood requires a strong enough form of liberty to guarantee the movement characteristic of human development. That still does not guarantee complete control of the centre; it is not so strong a form of liberty as to stop a paternalist from arguing that his short-term violation of someone's control of his own life will make him freer in the long run. But the plausibility of a paternalist's claim has to be assessed. Given human limitations, how likely is it that a paternalist will deliver the goods? But now the justification for strong liberty is beginning to shift from personhood to practicalities, which probably deserve to be regarded as a ground on their own.

3. *Second ground: practicalities*

The personhood consideration leaves a lot unsettled. For one thing, it says that there is a right to *some* political voice. Yet how much? And what, too, is the *minimum* material provision? Where life expectancy reaches 40? Or would it have to be 60? And what is *minimum* education? Literacy? Or would it have to be the ability to ponder the meaning of life? And we have, it says, *some* sort of right to bodily integrity, because without security of body we have no security of action. But, to raise Robert Nozick's question, does this right bar a state's forcibly taking one of my kidneys for transplant? Does it then bar a very accommodating state from demanding a pint of my rare blood which, it says, it will take in my own house while I sleep and leave me to wake in the morning as fit as ever?

Well, certainly it is no good expecting the personhood consideration to protect me against such an accommodating state, which threatens nothing essential to my human status. But there are practical considerations that are obviously relevant here. A line has to be drawn somewhere; the personhood consideration shows that much. And men and governments are not scrupulous and are prone to domination and self-serving. Moreover, the line has to be clear and, for safety's sake, at some remove from the vitals. I can, it is true, still lead a human existence if the state takes one of my kidneys, but one might well fear that the chances of doing so in such a pervasive and interventionist state would be slim. Whatever the result of this line of thought, there is no doubting the relevance of this *kind* of consideration. On any account of rights, I should think, practicalities play a large part in determining their final shape.

4. *Third ground: the private sphere*

Personhood supplies only the weightiest sort of reason for rights, the survival of one's human status. However, Mill thought that whether something, weighty or light, falls within one's private sphere also counts. How I dress or part my hair is hardly central to my living a human existence. Still, it is *my* business: even if what I wear upsets you, surely I am within my rights dressing as I please.

Is the private sphere, then, a further ground for human rights? Personhood yields a right not to a general liberty but only to certain specific liberties. Mill, however, proposed that liberty should extend to whatever we wish to do, so long as it does not harm others. His harm test allowed him to define a self-regarding, or private, class of actions. But there are problems with Mill's broad conception of liberty. First, it lacks any clear value supporting it. Our status as persons is clearly valuable to us, but control over what is merely private is far less obviously so. Second, the justifications of the broad conception of liberty that carry weight, Mill's own, for instance, seem really to be an elaboration of the old personhood ground rather than the provision of a new ground. Stopping me from wearing the clothes I want, as inessential as any particular set of clothes may be to my human standing, certainly touches my self-respect. The idea of a person that we have already made appeal to is of a self-determiner. But to deny me freedom to express my own tastes does indeed threaten my status as self-determiner. Exactly which clothes I choose may be trivial, but my status as an independent centre of taste and choice is not.

In the interest of keeping the concept of a right as sharp as possible, one might want to keep the personhood ground as narrow as possible—the absolutely minimum conditions for carrying out a life plan. If so, a right to dress as I please would not be supported by it. On the other hand, one might want to make it a bit more capacious—what is necessary for human dignity. One would lose some sharpness with the extension, but one ought to keep in mind that, in any case, the narrow notion would not itself be especially sharp anyway. It turns on what is *central* to human status and what is *necessary* for carrying out a life plan, and what is central or necessary is essentially moot, and can itself be seen narrowly or broadly. So, in any case, there will have to be a lot of not very sharp-edged debate about these moot matters, largely in terms of practicalities, in order to fix the boundaries of rights. The loss, therefore, from adopting the slightly more capacious conception is not great. And the gain is a notion of liberty which is more in accord with the philosophical tradition, yet which still has a ground of some substance. This ground, although not as circumscribed as it might be, is not so extensive as to give us, as Mill thought we had, a right to general liberty. Mill focused on the private domain when it seems better to focus on one's status as a self-determiner. And some things that are 'self-regarding' are also too remote from one's being self-determining to be protected by this slightly more capacious conception.

5. *Fourth ground: equal respect*

There is another consideration, equal respect, that seems different from any of the preceding ones. Utilitarian thought proceeds by the simple device of trading off goods and bads by their magnitude, paying no attention to whether the trade-off occurs within one life or between different lives. It is just this particular lack of attention that invites the rejoinders: one person may not be sacrificed, without limit, for the good of others; the well-being of one person cannot simply be replaced by that of another. Yet to say that it cannot *simply* be replaced implies that sometimes it can and sometimes it cannot. And to say that one person may not be sacrificed *without limit* implies that sacrifices are allowed but only up to a point. Each suggests a line but does not supply it. And it is not that we can expect rights to supply it, because this consideration is meant to be a more fundamental one from which rights are derived.

These lines represent what has been called the moral significance of the separateness of persons.[12] It takes a lot of work to see what this separateness consideration amounts to. It might be hoped that the separateness consideration could be made more determinate through the idea of contracting. If persons have first to agree with one another, then each can exercise a veto in his own interest, and a veto seems the ideal instrument for expressing the separateness of persons. But we must give the contracting situation concrete shape, for instance to decide upon what degree of ignorance to impose upon the contractors, in order to be sure that it will indeed express the separateness of persons. There are several different contracting situations. Which captures the right conception of separateness? It would help to have some rough independent idea of what that is. Besides, as we have seen,[13] contractualism gets the restrictions on trade-offs too strict.

I think that the way forward lies in this direction. One cannot sacrifice a person without limit because each of us has only one life, and each person's fate matters and matters equally. So we may take the separateness consideration as being, in effect, some form of a principle of equality, not a principle requiring equal treatment (say, meting out equal portions of resources) but that different and altogether deeper matter of treating persons as equals, of showing them equal respect. Thus, the limit on trade-offs that the separateness consideration desiderates will be the limit imposed by equal respect. But what is that? Equal respect is a little less indeterminate than the separateness of persons, but is still notoriously indeterminate itself. Does equal respect require (i) merely equal weight ('everybody to count for one, nobody for more than one' in the way that utilitarians mean), or (ii) a minimum level of well-being, above which obligations cease, or (iii) an equal start with equal prospects, after which inequalities resulting from just transactions are themselves to be regarded as just, or (iv) equal goods, except where inequalities work to the advantage of the worst off, i.e. Rawls' maximin, or (v) equal goods with equal prospects, or (vi) equal well-being, or (vii) equal opportunity? I know that many persons believe that the use of notions such as 'the separateness of persons' and 'treating persons as ends' is precisely to choose between those competing principles of equal respect. But this is to try to chose between these principles by appeal to notions so vague that they can be given content only by the choice between these principles. Nor can we remedy the vagueness by trying further to plumb the depths of our intuitions about either equality or separateness or respect for persons, because intuitions are superficial things. There will be no depths until we choose them and put them there. What we need is a well-worked-out theory of equality; such a theory would, at the same time, give content to all these notions.

We made a start on this theory in the last two chapters and shall not really finish it until we get to the final chapter.[14] Anyway, a theory of rights is an important part of it, so at this point we could only be in the middle of building it. Suppose, however, that what will eventually emerge will be certain rather demanding principles of equality—say, for the sake of argument, maximin or equal well-being or equal resources, all of which, I think, prove to have a place in a full substantive theory. If so, then equal respect constitutes a new ground for rights. Personhood requires, among other things, minimum provision. Practicalities may lead us to define the minimum fairly generously. But equal respect requires something stronger than either: some qualified form or other of equal share.

The only reason to doubt that equal respect is a new ground for rights is that it may turn out to be reducible to the personhood ground, or *vice versa*. There is a long philosophical tradition which has it that, a few difficult marginal cases aside, we are all possessors of human standing and hence of human worth. Clearly we differ in the degree that we possess the various features that constitute human standing—for example, in our capacity for autonomy, rationality, evaluation, and action. But, according to this tradition, the notions of personhood and moral worth do not admit of degrees; anyone inside the boundary, no matter how far inside, is equally inside. If, in the end, it is this equal possession of human standing that is the ground of all rights, then it is not clear whether equal respect reduces to personhood, or personhood to equal respect, or each is only part of another, deeper ground that combines both. But the notion of equal respect is still too obscure to allow us to settle the matter now. So, until we have a theory of equality that makes the notion more determinate, it is best for the time being to treat it as a separate ground.

6. *What rights does the substantive theory yield*

These then seem to me the three elements of a substantive theory of human rights: personhood, practicalities, and equal respect. (The privacy ground, the fourth possible ground I considered, is best thought of merely as a development of the notion of personhood.)

Do these three grounds yield the human rights that moral theory needs? I have suggested that, in some form or other, they yield rights to life, to bodily integrity, not to be tortured, to autonomy, to the central civil liberties, to minimum provision, to a strong form of liberty (that is, to sovereignty at the centre of one's life, so, for instance, I think that it could plausibly be argued, to sexual freedom and possibly, although less easily argued, to freedom to drink and take drugs), finally to some form of equal share (that is, share in what makes a good life possible: although whether the equality is to be, for instance, only at some starting-point or as far as possible continuously, and whether it is equality in resources or need-satisfaction or desire-satisfaction are all questions that the well-worked-out theory of equality will have to settle). And the equal share is not only a share in material goods but also in the powers and opportunities that matter just as much to a good life, and so it requires that advantages be open to all and that no advantages be denied without due process.

We have also seen, however, how much these three grounds leave indeterminate. Take, for example, the right to privacy. Is it a human right?[15] What are its boundaries? The personhood consideration would yield a right to whatever privacy is necessary to human standing: whatever privacy is needed for the thought and communication that go into forming one's life plan, whatever privacy is needed in developing the personal commitments central to one's life plan. But that, it must be admitted, is not a very extensive right. What, for instance, does it tell us about the invasions of privacy that worry us now: phone-tapping, electronic eavesdropping, access to one's medical or financial records? The only resources that the three grounds supply at this point are various tangled practical considerations. Why do governments want to tap phones? Which is now the greater danger—public intrusion in private life or private subversion of public life? What is at stake in debates about modern intrusions on privacy is a certain sort of power, and if nowadays the greater threat is from government power, and if the threat is great enough to undermine one's life plan, protection should go to individuals. But this sort of argument is not timelessly valid; it allows the possibility that at other times, in other circumstances, the powers should go elsewhere. In general, it would mean that, to the extent that practical considerations determine the boundaries of rights, they are subject to periodical redrawing. But I suspect that practical considerations are, at this point, all that we have to go on. And since practical considerations enter into the determination of virtually every human right, human rights have neither sharp nor fixed edges.[16]

Another important consequence of this account is that rights have more narrow boundaries than convention says. There is no general right to liberty, but only rights to specific liberties. There is no right to say or publish what one wants, not even a prima-facie right subject to limitation by conflict with other rights, but merely a right to express what matters to the centre of one's life. There is no broad right to determine what happens in and to one's body, only a limited right to the bodily integrity necessary to carry through one's central aims, where the boundary of the 'centre' is essentially moot.

7. *The need for a second level to the substantive theory*

Rights are linked to such values as autonomy, liberty, and equal respect. The substantive theory suggests that they are to be seen as protections of these values and so seen within a generally instrumental or teleological framework. That constitutes the first level in a substantive theory: showing in what rights are grounded. But, unfortunately, that does not yet get us very far towards understanding the structure of rights, for the teleological framework need not be utilitarian, nor even consequentialist. Autonomy and liberty are, on the face of it, not utilitarian values at all, and equal respect is less a consequence of respecting the corresponding right than a value the content of which is itself best expressed in terms of the right. And we need answers to many questions. Do rights conflict with one another? How can we settle conflicts? May rights be traded off against each other? Against well-being? Do rights differ in relative importance? How is importance estimated? Are any rights absolute? Should we aim at maximizing the observance of rights? Can rights be forfeited, or diminished, by wrongdoing?

These questions raise parallel questions about the values to which the rights are linked. Do these values conflict? Can they be reduced to one value, or to one metric? Are they all the sort of values that we should seek to maximize? All of these questions, whether about rights or values, are unavoidable and require a second and deeper level of explanation. The first level in a substantive theory is concerned with how rights are grounded in values. But the second has to establish the character of the values themselves.[17]

8. *A sampler of values that rights protect*

So I turn now to the second level of a substantive theory, the investigation of the nature and structure of the values that rights protect. I want to consider just three of them: autonomy, liberty, and equal respect. I consider just these three not because I believe that all rights can be derived from them alone; on the contrary, there is much more to the personhood ground than just autonomy and liberty, and I omit the practicalities ground altogether. I take these three simply as examples for closer study. But to them one must add well-being, with which I shall start.

Well-being is best explained, I argued in Part One, not in terms of states of mind, but in terms of fulfilment of desire, where 'fulfilment' is meant without psychological overtones and implies merely that what is desired comes about. The desires that are relevant on this account are not only persons' actual ones but also those they would have, if they understood the nature of possible objects of desire; a person's own conception of what is in his interest, therefore, is not definitive. This interpretation has an important consequence. 'Well-being' is not to be seen as the single overarching value, in fact not as a substantive value at all, but instead as a formal analysis of what it is for something to be prudentially valuable. Therefore, well-being will be related to substantive values, such as autonomy or liberty, not by being the dominant value that subsumes them, but by being an analysis of, and the related suggestion of a metric for, any prudential value. It should be seen as providing a way of understanding the notions '(prudentially) valuable' and hence 'more valuable' and 'less valuable'. Well-being, therefore, is not what it is about objects that makes them desirable. What makes us desire the things we desire is something about them—their features or qualities.

Now, on the face of it, the values that back rights—for example, the three values that I have singled out, autonomy, liberty, and equal respect—seem clearly to fall outside the ambit of well-being. However, sometimes that is because the notion of well-being in use is too narrow and would have seemed too narrow quite apart from this issue. Consider autonomy first. Would you, for greater serenity, surrender your autonomy? If you understand what is at stake, then unless the pain of autonomy is in your case very great, no doubt you will prefer autonomy. But that preference can, I think, be brought within the ambit of well-being. For what reasons might one have for thinking that the value of autonomy is not the sort of value that well-being encompasses? One reason would be that autonomy is of absolute value, value greater than any elements of well-being. But most of us think that, on the contrary, there could come a point, say with a psychiatric patient, where autonomy was so painful as to justify reducing it. Another reason would be that the value of autonomy, though not absolute, is not given by its place in informed desires either. One way to test that would be to see where trade-offs sanctioned by these different views of the value of autonomy—its values as its place in informed desires and its putative true value—diverged. It is hard to find examples, and that suggests that autonomy falls largely within the ambit of utility.

Liberty too, especially the strong sort of freedom to do not only what one in fact chooses but also what one might have chosen, seems clearly to fall outside the bounds of well-being. It concerns distribution of power, not distribution of well-being, even on its formal interpretation, because what is distributed here is not what constitutes the value or significance or quality of life. It goes beyond quality of life to considerations of control: every responsible person must be granted control over matters that crucially affect him. This is the point that John Mackie makes in arguing that, if we understand goals properly, we see that they are less theoretically deep than rights:[18]

A plausible goal, or good for man, would have to be something like Aristotle's *eudaimonia*: it would be in the category of activity. It could not be just an end, a possession, a termination of pursuit... But Aristotle went wrong in thinking that moral philosophy could determine that a particular sort of activity constitutes the good for man in general... People differ radically about the kinds of life that they choose to pursue. Even this way of putting it is misleading: in general people do not and cannot make an overall choice of a total plan of life... I suggest that if we set out to formulate a goal-based moral theory, but in identifying the goal try to take adequate account of these three factors, namely that the 'goal' must belong to the category of activity, that there is not one goal but indefinitely many diverse goals, and that they are the objects of progressive (not once for all or conclusive) choices, then our theory will change insensibly into a right-based one. We shall have to take as central the right of persons progressively to choose how they shall live.

All that Mackie says here about goals seems to me true, but no stopping point. It is not likely that control would be valued for itself; it is valuable because of the value of what can be controlled. If others were to intrude but only at the very periphery of one's life, the power to repel the intrusions would not matter much. If the intrusion were at the centre but were motivated, for instance, as with some surgical intrusions, by an uncontentious and beneficial aim and carried out by sure techniques, again the power would not matter much. However, in the real world, intentions of intruders rarely are honourable, or values agreed, or techniques sure. So, in the real world, power at the centre of one's life matters immensely. But its value derives from the value of the whole way of life at stake.

Mackie's argument is that since what is valuable in life is a kind of activity, a way of life, and since conceptions of the good life are diverse and developing, liberty must be 'central'. But liberty's being 'central' in this sense is compatible with its being derivative. Mackie's argument is meant also to establish that liberty is not part of a more fundamental teleological structure, but that is what it does not do. Certainly the fact that what is valuable in life falls under the category of activity would establish this, only if an activity could never be a goal. But it can. It can even, on a proper conception, be a component of well-being. 'Socrates dissatisfied' describes not a state at the end of an activity, but a way of life. The fact that a person's conception of a valuable life changes and matures does not suggest that a right to liberty is in some important way more basic than goals. It suggests only that no *one* goal may be permanent or authoritative. But it is that we have goals, that we have the chance of making our life valuable, which gives value to the right to liberty. So, contrary to what Mackie suggests, it is not the right to liberty that is basic but the valuable life, *on some conception or other*. And the valuable life is basic in just the sense that Mackie tells us he has in mind: it captures what it is that gives point to the rest of the moral structure.

There is another reason that might lead one to think that liberty falls outside the bounds of well-being. Utilitarians, Mill for example, have claimed that we ought to respect liberty because, if we are at all wise to the ways of the world, we shall realize that paternalism is largely counter-productive and that in the long run general welfare is best served by strict non-interference.[19] All that is true, but many find it, with reason, a lame defence of liberty. Liberty, they would plausibly insist, is itself valuable, valuable apart from this link with well-being. But when one spells this out sufficiently, one merely discovers a new link with well-being. We value our status as persons and want to live recognizably human lives, and liberty is a central component of that. But then liberty, like autonomy, can be fitted into the scheme of our preferences, and its value explained by its place there. So there is more than one kind of link with well-being. It is a mistake to move from liberty's being valuable in itself to the conclusion that well-being does not encompass it. Using the formal notion of well-being does not commit one to monism in values. One can value many different things, and value them not for any state of mind that they result in, but for themselves. And since well-being encompasses two central features of personhood, autonomy and liberty, that common disjunction between either grounding rights in well-being or grounding them in personhood is unreal.[20]

Liberty seems, then, best understood as belonging to a teleological structure. Whether the ends of that structure, the valued ways of life, can be brought within the ambit of well-being is contentious. But the contention is between conceptions of prudential value. Nothing that has so far entered the story about rights rules it out.

So let us move on to the last and hardest case. Equality is a very different kind of value from the others. Unlike autonomy and liberty, which focus in a way on the value of one life, equality focuses on the comparison of lives. It is not a prudential value at all; it is a moral value, in a way *the* moral value. So equality presents the best case for saying that rights are grounded in more than just prudential values.

Yet when we survey principles of equality, we are faced with an *embarras de choix*. I mentioned earlier seven perfectly familiar principles, and there are still more. So our first job is to make the notion of equal respect more determinate. Now, when one reflects on these various principles of equality, one sees that some belong on different levels; they are not, after all, competitors but principles about different things. For instance, there is the most fundamental level where equality is to be seen as an interpretation of impartiality—that sort of impartiality that constitutes the moral point of view. We all agree that to look at things morally is to look at them, in some sense or other, impartially, granting every person some sort of equal status. Of course, we should have to make this notion of equal status more determinate—say through one interpretation or other of the Ideal Observer or Ideal Contractor. In any case, principles of equality can be principles of impartiality in this sense: they can express the spirit with which one will, if one is moral, consider the facts of the matter.

Then there is a second level, the level of moral principles resulting from applying first level principles to facts. For instance, Rawls derives, from his Original Position, his two principles of justice.[21] And on this second level there are different kinds of principles generated which can reasonably claim to be principles of equality. There are, for instance, theories of rights which see people as possessors of equal basic protections and entitlements. There are also theories of distribution of resources which might, for instance, say that resources themselves should be equal, or that their pay-off in well-being should be equal. Then there is a further wrinkle: I made a case in the last chapter for distinguishing a reflective from a practical decision procedure, so one might see this level itself splitting in two. But we can leave that aside for now.

Then there is a third level of principles simplified for action on the large social scale, where knowledge is short and justice rough. For example, a utilitarian might adopt a principle of equal resources, because on the level of social policy one cannot consult individual utility functions or hope effectively to control utility levels by manipulating shares of resources.

Hence, equality is a multi-level and, within a level, multi-dimensional notion. This is not surprising: equality is merely a formal notion (sameness of some feature), and sameness of different features matters morally. Our moral notion of equality fragments. There is not one principle of equality, but many.

Now how do principles on these different levels support rights? Third level principles, being rough rules of thumb, would support rights which were themselves only rough rules of thumb and so rights of a kind less strong then we are interested in now. First level principles, on the other hand, principles which in effect express the moral point of view, would support perhaps too strong a kind of right. John Mackie and others think that they provide the one absolute human right, namely, a right to equal respect in the procedures that determine the compromises and adjustments between all the other, non-absolute rights.[22] But the doubt here is whether this is too much the whole of morality to be anything as specific as a right. It is absolute because it is moral standing itself, and morality can never recommend suspending the moral point of view. But whether or not it is best to regard this as a right, it is the principles on the second level that are the promising candidates for what we normally regard as human rights, and it is on them that I want to concentrate.

The competing principles on the second level provide rival ways of fixing the moral point of view. Some, as we have seen, seek to express the moral significance of the separateness of persons. Others give expression to the demands of everybody's counting for one in utility calculations. What they are all concerned with is what is permitted in the way of trade-offs between prudential values. They are all views about rights and distribution. What is common to all conceptions of equal respect is the belief that *some* sacrifices of one person for another are permissible, but that a limit is imposed by everyone's equal status as moral persons. Well, what limit? To explain that is to explain our conception of moral status. And to explain it demands going beyond such edifying but empty formulas as 'no person may be sacrificed without limit' or 'respect for persons', which leave so much undetermined that nothing can be got out of them until more is put into them. And the most promising way to do this is to use second level principles as their further determination.

The way to fix the second level is to fix the principles restricting trade-offs.[23] We have already looked at various models for the restriction, and the argument was roughly this.[24] One model is that of a line beyond which trade-offs are not allowed, a line which defines one's unbargainable person-hood. Suppose one proposed the generous line supplied by maximin: the worst off to be as well off as possible. But this is not a line we should long defend. Maximin, intuition tells us, has exceptions; rich societies where the worst off are well off do, on the face of it quite reasonably, allocate resources—to art, for instance—in a way that further benefits the well off. Suppose then, to accommodate this, one redrew the line so that it prevented *sacrifices* of one person for the already better off, disastrous drops in welfare or, at least, drops to dismally low levels. But recall the example of the beautiful roadside avenues of trees in France. We do allow trade-offs between the common good and disastrous drops, even when the drop is as disastrous as death and the good is merely more aesthetic pleasure. Suppose, therefore, that one accepted that neither of these lines would do and that one looked for something weaker, something like Amartya Sen's Weak Equity Axiom, which goes: if one person is a less good utility producer than another, say because he is handicapped, so that at any level of goods he is less well off, then he must be given *something* more than the other. But this 'weak' requirement is still too strong. Surgeons, in choosing between two patients for a kidney transplant, often rightly give it to the one with better prospects of survival, even if the other has been chronically ill and has always been less well off in the past. Intuitions, therefore, go against the model of an uncrossable line. A natural move at this point is to fall back on the familiar model of same-level principles: to abandon the idea of a cut-off for utilitarian trade-offs and opt instead for a counterforce. There are certainly examples that seem to support this model, especially against the model of maximizing well-being. But if we look at enough examples, we can also find plenty that go the other way. We can generate both sorts of examples just by juggling the figures in the transplant case for the age of the patient and the years of survival. So on the testimony of our intuitions none of these models is satisfactory: not the model of an uncrossable line, nor that of same-level principles, nor that of maximizing well-being. It is easy to announce attractive-sounding principles. But if one collected the trade-offs that fairly widespread intuitions support, and if one took the task seriously enough to collect a large number of them over a wide range of cases, this 'undisputed set of trade-offs', so to speak, would undermine every proposal that moral philosophy has yet produced of principles governing trade-offs. This is not fatal to them, but it certainly shows how far we are from having any satisfactory arguments on the subject.

In a situation like this, one has to get behind the intuitions to see how they work. I tried to do this earlier.[25] What emerges, I suggested then, is that the model of maximizing well-being has a role to play in certain fundamental deliberations about trade-offs. It is not that my earlier argument was decisive in favour of any single model. There are many other tests that a model of equal respect has to pass, one important one being the plausibility and explanatory power of the substantive theory of rights that it is part of.

9. *The second level*

The second level of a substantive theory has to explain the structure of rights—how we can settle conflict between rights themselves and between rights and well-being, whether rights differ in importance not only among themselves but also a single right from occasion to occasion, how such importance is estimated, and so on. The first level stated the existence conditions for rights, the second level must state the rules for their operation.

The trouble with bringing values such as autonomy and liberty within the ambit of well-being and, in addition, accepting a maximizing model of equal respect is that the restrictions on trade-offs that look likely to emerge are unpromisingly weak. We should look for stronger restrictions on the maximizing model—not arbitrary ones tacked on to turn it into what we should like it to be but ones that it itself implies. There are, I think, at least two.

First, there are restrictions in prudential value theory that, because of underdevelopment of the theory, have not begun to be properly appreciated. We have still to understand, and to work out, how radical the consequences are of the shift to a formal conception of well-being. Since well-being is not itself a substantive prudential value, it is the nature of those values that are that determines the structure of informed desires. Thus, there is nothing in the formal conception of well-being that rules out one value's being incommensurable with another. We have to look at the substantive values to see. And what we find, I argued earlier,[26] is that they do exhibit one form of incommensurability—discontinuity. We find values such that no amount of one can outweigh a certain amount of the other. So there are certain inflexibilities in prudential value theory that therefore get transferred to a metric of well-being. If I had a friend prodigiously shrewd and overflowing with *savoir faire* who could save me a dozen minor false turns if he took over the management of my life, I should still value my autonomy so highly that I would not contemplate surrendering it. But what if he could save me, not a dozen, but a hundred minor false turns? But the trouble is this: minor false turns do not seem to be weighty enough, even in large aggregates, at least the aggregates that life presents us with, to balance the value of living life autonomously. Some things might indeed be weighty enough—great pain or anxiety, for instance—but minor false turns are not. Not even a thousand —someone might press—or ten thousand? But now the problem is to get one's mind around the question. If one's life contained a huge number of false turns, one right after the other, they would scarcely leave space for anything to go right; they would be a pretty good indication that something else, far more serious, was wrong. Or consider another case, liberty. Can the value of a person's being free to live what he regards as the only life of substance and significance open to him be equalled by the upset or distress that his doing so might cause others? Well, Mill has plausibly argued that upset and distress are simply not in the same league as a person's making something out of his life. The stakes are so different, given the world as we know it, that not even large aggregates of persons upset and distressed, hundreds of them or thousands, come into the same league. If it were a matter of some minor liberty, say one's liberty to bathe nude, one would expect upset and distress, if there were enough of it, to match the value of the liberty. But if it is one's most major liberty at stake—to live out one's life plan—why believe that life presents us with aggregates of upset and distress that will, judged simply on the values accounted for in a prudential value theory, match it?

This suggests a certain structure for the second level of the substantive theory. We need rights to be strong protections of the individual, but not too strong. That remark is a bromide, of course, but it does also state the greatest problem facing any substantive theory. There are no absolute rights except for the dubious 'right' to moral standing itself, which it is probably less confusing not to regard as a right at all. Otherwise, the existence conditions for rights give no reason to think that rights cannot be traded off against one another or against well-being. And rights differ in importance: both one right with another and (as we have just seen in this last mention of liberty) one right on different occasions. So we need a theory that not only allows trade-offs but also explains how they work. They work because behind rights is the deeper notion of the differing importance of rights. So the theory must supply the criteria of importance and a metric derived from them. This is the chief job of the second level of a substantive theory.

Our notion of importance must come from the weight of the values to which rights are linked. It is hard to see what else it could possibly come from. This would provide a basis both for trade-offs between rights and between a right and well-being. We can see this in the case of liberty: two liberties will differ in importance depending upon how close they get to the centre of one's life plan (say, freedom of worship for a religious person compared with the freedom to dress as he pleases), and a minor liberty (say, the freedom to go on wearing imported clothes) can be less important than a substantial economic improvement (say, by import controls). And the theory could also explain why rights have some kind of priority over well-being. Rights are grounded for the most part in the values of personhood, and though these values come within the ambit of well-being there is a tradition in political theory that contrasts them with 'well-being' on a narrower but not uncommon understanding of the term. To bring out this contrast, we might distinguish personhood from prosperity, where 'personhood' means what I have been using it to mean and 'prosperity' means all the rest of the values that make up well-being. (So 'prosperity' has still to be understood quite broadly; it would include, for instance, certain forms of intellectual and artistic as well as purely economic flourishing.) Then, using this narrower conception of well-being, we could say that rights characteristically outrank well-being, that often rights should be respected even at the cost of maximum well-being, meaning that the values that make up personhood characteristically outweigh those that make up prosperity and that protecting them is often more important than maximizing prosperity. And we can say that certain key rights, such as the liberty to live out the centre of one's life plan, trump certain increases in prosperity, because here we start encountering incommensurabilities: for example, no amount of upset and distress can match the value of such a major liberty. But all of these judgments take place within a framework that also shows when trade-offs are allowed and how they work. So rights have priority over well-being but not a strict priority. The full account of this priority is a large part of the job for the second level of the substantive theory, and talk about rights' being lexically prior to, or trumping, well-being does not do justice to the complexity of what goes on.

That is the first restriction, which comes out of the prudential value theory. A second restriction comes from the notion of equal respect. Equal respect, whatever else it might lead to, leads to maximizing well-being and so to a threat of over-weak restrictions on trade-offs. But, as we have seen,[27] the home of the maximizing model is in the most general characterization of the criterion of right and wrong; maximization has a smaller role in the reflective decision procedure, still smaller in the practical decision procedure, and smaller still when we get away from individual decision procedures to a political one. So there is another restriction on maximization; it comes into play only occasionally. There are, as what is already a large literature on indirect applications of maximization makes clear, several different forms that this restriction may take.[28] I began describing a multi-level structure in the last chapter, and should say what more I can about it now.

We are led to some form of multi-level structure, I believe, by reflection on the differences in kind between moral considerations. One example is this. It is clear that some moral principles are indeterminate; they have exceptions that need stating, and they need constant interpretation to adapt their key terms to fresh circumstances. Often, though perhaps not always, behind those principles there are other, more fundamental ones, that help shape these determinations and interpretations.[29] Another example is this. A principle that fits one setting (say, small-scale interpersonal dealings) does not fit another (say, large-scale social arrangements), for which we need either a new principle or a new version of the original principle. At various earlier points,[30] we came upon reasons to think that the principles of beneficence needed on the large social scale would be different from the ones needed on the small interpersonal scale. So we end up with rather different principles, but close cousins of one another, and we need to understand more clearly what the relation between them is. A multi-level structure seems to me the best explanation of these, and many similar, matters. But I do not want to overstate its powers of explanation. The multi-level structure that I want to describe may not exhaust morality. But it is, at any rate, the structure of that large part of morality that has to do with our concern for well-being. Also, it seems to me somewhat arbitrary exactly how many levels of moral thought one distinguishes and precisely where one draws the lines. The types of moral considerations that I have in mind shade into one another; there are no sharp divisions between them. Still, I want to suggest that it is useful to distinguish four levels. I mentioned earlier three levels, one of which might be seen as splitting in two, and that is the idea I want now to develop.

On the deepest level of a moral theory, in what earlier I called the general characterization of the criterion of right and wrong, on a level where one defines how one person's fate weighs against another's, the maximizing principle applies.[31] It may not be the only principle that applies there, but that anyway is where it applies. It is a principle that applies to single acts. That is so simply in virtue of the department of morality of which it is a general characterization, namely act morality. It is the job of act morality to provide principles of intentional action. But the maximizing principle is indeterminate. It gives us the aim or object of moral action. But when we add to it the most plausible prudential value theory and when, further, we acknowledge the need for co-operative action among moral agents on fair terms, then the focus of moral principles moves away from the single acts of an isolated agent to life-structuring commitments, attachments, agreements, and institutions.

This brings us to the next two levels, what earlier I called the reflective and the practical decision procedures.[32] One important influence on the shape of principles is our actual situation of choice. We are characteristically short of time, facts, and fellow-feeling, and we need standards for these circumstances. These standards constitute the practical level. But we also need criteria for going behind those practical, everyday standards in order to decide on their exceptions, to amend them, and in general to deliberate when we find ourselves free of the restrictions characteristic of normal life. The considerations we then use constitute the reflective level. For example, since it is rare for us to know reliably how much different persons get out of some good, we need a policy for usual cases, and so on the practical level the principle of equality that we shall apply to them is: treat persons equally. But on the reflective level, when our knowledge is not restricted in that way, the principle of equality will take the form of equal respect, which allows trade-offs—as in, for instance, the medical cases that we discussed at some length earlier.[33] Still, we have already seen too that many principles change little between these two levels. Any decision procedure, including the reflective one, has both to deploy a prudential value theory and to accept the importance of group action. Our commitments, attachments, aims, and co-operative enterprises incorporate central and important values. The principles on the practical level governing those parts of our lives are not replaced by other, radically different principles on the reflective level. The only difference between the two levels in this respect is the presence of those further considerations on the reflective level that come into play when we amend or interpret our principles.[34]

These two decision procedures are for an individual; they answer the question, How should I decide what to do? But we also need an answer to the question, How should we as a group, especially as a large society, decide what to do? This shift to a political decision procedure brings with it systematic changes in the principles we use. A change in scale imposes further limitations in knowledge; now we typically lack knowledge about not just how much different individuals get out of some good, but also, since most of them are total strangers to us, what their conception of the good is. It also brings with it limitations in trust; we cannot depend upon an office-holder or an ordinary citizen in a large impersonal setting always to be perfectly scrupulous, so we must take the wide and long view and find rules that can cope with these variations in moral reliability. Beside limitations, change in scale also brings changes in function; our government has as its job promoting not your and my happiness but the setting in which we can pursue it. So the social principle of equality should take the form: equalize all-purpose means. For one thing, it does not matter how admirable one individual's conception of the good life may be; what is to be protected is our living a human existence, and that means protecting one person's capacity to live out his life plan as much as another's. And a society needs procedural principles. Each of us has a right to be a self-determiner. But the right, formulated no more fully than that, is indeterminate; it needs spelling out both for the individual decision procedure and especially, and rather differently, for the political decision procedure. Each of us should have a voice in political decision. But precisely what sort? Each of us also wants good social decisions, and so we want complicated questions to be answered by knowledgeable persons. The determinate form of the principle is likely, therefore, to embody some compromise between values—say, a right to a vote in elections in a representative democracy.

That is a proposal of one way—to my mind a useful way—to divide up the levels. But is the effect of the division to *restrict* maximization? Does it not, instead, just usher maximization from the moral scene altogether? My proposal that maximization should be thought of as part of the general characterization of the criterion of right and wrong looks rather like the proposal that Geoffrey Warnock and John Mackie both make that, though concern for well-being does indeed enter morality, it enters as its general aim or object and not as part of the content of its principles or rules.[35] And Warnock and Mackie see their proposal as the abandonment of the maximizing test, at least in any recognisably utilitarian form. But I think that they want the levels more insulated from one another than they can be. If making life go well is the aim of the rules, it cannot be kept totally out of their content. It would be extremely odd if it were not allowed to play at least some role in making the rules determinate, in interpreting and amending them, or in reconciling their conflicts. For instance, as we have just seen, we have to get behind rights to the values they protect, and when these values conflict we have to know how to weigh them against one another, and the maximizing test enters there. It plays a role on the reflective level and also, though to a lesser extent, on the practical and political levels.

But the greatest worry about a multi-level structure comes from moral psychology. Can the various psychological states that it posits all co-exist? The worry arises at many points, but let us consider just one. Bernard Williams poses the question, Where, either in society or in the human psyche, are we going to find a place for a division between a practical and a reflective decision procedure?[36] In a society we might just manage to locate it in a division between social classes—a moral élite, say, who will manipulate the beliefs and dispositions of a moral proletariat, who, for their own or the common good, will be denied much access to the workings of the reflective decision procedure. But where can we possibly locate

it in the human psyche? We might try locating it in a division
between more and less reflective or reliable parts of human
nature, with the first manipulating the dispositions, perhaps
even the beliefs, of the second. But both suggestions are
suspect. The behaviour of the élite class looks very much like
plain deceit, which, though it may in the end have a
justification, certainly calls for one. But the sort of manipulation required inside an individual life looks simply psychologically impossible. No one individual, at least no tolerably
healthy, integrated individual of the sort that we should want
both to be ourselves and also to have around us, could
maintain on the practical level full-blooded commitments to
co-operation, to individual persons, to his own life-structuring
aims and, at the same time, on the reflective level regard all of
these values as merely instrumental.

But these worries largely rest on a misconception. It is
wrong to assume, as Williams does, that a multi-level structure
with the maximization of well-being at its base has to treat
well-being as a substantive super-value, all other values being
merely instrumental. For instance, a person might value
commitments to certain individuals. It might be central to
what makes his life valuable, and its value would partly
depend upon his sense of the value of the fate of the other
person. Of the values that come into this story, none is
instrumental. In general, any prudential value, and its related
principle of action, will be intrinsic, not instrumental. The
case of the principles of fair co-operation is more complicated,
but they too in an important sense are of intrinsic value. They
have an instrumental side to them: they define necessary
conditions for our reaping the benefits of co-operation. But
they also in part spell out the consequences that our notion of
equal respect has for co-operation; for instance, the principle
of equal chances states a requirement that does not have
merely instrumental force. There are, it is true, some rules and
attitudes on the practical level (for instance, respect for
promises) that will have only instrumental force. But virtually
everyone accepts that some rules and attitudes are merely
good policy, their justification coming from outside themselves.
That fact, of itself, hardly raises problems of moral psychology.
So whether there are problems depends upon precisely which

rules and attitudes are regarded as instrumental. Since thought about well-being will, as we have seen,[37] focus on the shape of whole lives and on the importance of the action of whole groups, we need not in general worry that our important commitments at the practical level will be unnerved by thought on the reflective level; most of them reappear there. And the ones that do not are, I think, psychologically manageable without intrinsic status. It is a mistake to regard the practical and reflective levels as consisting of entirely distinct kinds of deliberation. Many of the principles of the reflective level reappear on the practical level. There is no level, including the reflective, on which one can reason in the occasion-by-occasion manner of the isolated agent.

There remains the considerable problem of telling when to shift from one level to another, and the related danger that we should always want to, or perhaps think that we ought to, shift to the one most authoritative level and stay there. But there is, I think, no one 'most authoritative' level. The idea that there were would get some support if there were a single substantive super-value and one level of deliberation to which it was confined. But the general characterization of the criterion of right and wrong, for instance, has no more authority than the personal decision procedures. The reflective and practical decision procedures do not deal with what has only derivative value; on the contrary, it is only on those levels that we get proper representation of substantive prudential values and the importance of groups, both of which make it impossible for us to assess acts occasion by occasion. And it is only on the political level—with, say, the right of each citizen to a vote—that we can accommodate certain values—say, autonomy—given the need for a decision procedure for that large scale, with all the constraints that it brings. Our choice is not between thinking about political matters on a more or less authoritative level; with certain issues our choice is between thinking about them on a political level or not at all. As to when to shift levels, any fairly full account of the multi-level structure, in defining the levels, will give some guidance. I doubt that any multi-level theory, no matter how fully developed, will make it entirely clear when the shift should come. That will always to some extent present problems. But many problems about when to shift level seem to me to be an ineradicable feature of moral life, and though a good account of the multi-level structure should ease them, it will not entirely remove them.

To return now to rights. Where do they fit into this multi-level structure? Clearly rights will appear on the reflective and practical levels and also on the political level, and any particular right is likely to need somewhat different formulations for its different appearances. There is unlikely to be one fully determinate set of rights appropriate to all levels. But generally the most important appearance of rights will be on the political level: they will define how society ought to be arranged to protect certain central values. Even when the threat comes not from the government but from other individuals, social arrangements are usually the most effective protection. On the social level it is likely that we should want much tougher principles than we should want for an intelligent, scrupulous individual in his private life. And since political principles have to deal with what is generally the case, the restrictions arising from prudential value theory—that personhood is characteristically more important than prosperity —have even more effect. Consider, for example, the right to minimum material provision. Both a government's knowledge and its aims are limited. The first, rough definition of the right is to 'minimum material provision', provision needed to live 'a recognizably human existence'. But this definition leaves the right highly indeterminate. Each particular society has to make it determinate in the light of its own circumstances. How high can a particular society afford to set its minimum? Practicalities will have to enter. At this stage the maximization of well-being doubtless will have to play some role. As a society gets richer, at any rate if it is not already very rich, we should want to fix the minimum at a higher point, not because it strictly follows from the concept of the 'minimum' that we should, or from the notion of what humans 'need' in contrast to what they merely 'desire'. As we have seen,[38] those notions are too indeterminate to have such logical powers. But by an appeal to practicalities a minimum is finally fixed. A public policy is adopted. What one can then claim as a right is determined by the policy, and not by considerations of well-being. It would not matter that in a particular case well-being, on the broad conception, might be increased by holding some individual under the minimum material provision. The social structures have been fixed where they have for good reason, and this fact does not constitute a reason to change them. And denying someone minimum provision is wrong in itself, and not because it produces, say, pain or unhappiness.

I started out by suggesting that the first level of a substantive theory will ground human rights in personhood, practicalities, and equal respect. Still, a substantive theory cannot stop there; it has to answer questions about the structure of rights, in order to do which it is forced on to a second level of theory about how these values and well-being are related to each other. I finished by suggesting a framework for their trade-offs and two sources of restrictions on them. To object to this substantive theory, contrary asseveration is not enough—for instance, to insist that it is of the essence of rights that they are 'side constraints' or that they are more potent 'trumps' than this theory makes them.[39] Nor is it enough to back up the asseverations with an intuition or two. Those who object will have to come up with a better substantive theory, if they can.

XII

DESERT

1. *The moral interest*

IF we gathered persons equal in strength, intelligence, wealth, and political power and gave them an equal start in some job, inequalities would soon appear. Some would do more or better than others. Our responses to persons are dictated not only by their sameness—by the equal respect we owe them—but also by their differences—by their desert.

However, the word 'desert' is not used quite as narrowly as I have just suggested. Some uses are of no interest to moral theory. Others are of interest but have already entered the theory under another heading (e.g. 'equal respect'). So what moral theory needs is not so much 'analysis' of the word 'desert' as isolation of the uses that matter to it.[1] Let me quickly explain the uses that I think do not matter.

A woman certainly deserves the same wage as a man for doing the same work. But this is not the desert we are interested in. That is because it appeals to equal respect: everyone is to be treated equally unless there are relevant differences between them, and sex is irrelevant to pay. So this case matters to moral theory but is already catered for under a different heading from 'desert'. Someone in a dangerous or hard job deserves extra pay. But this is not the desert we are interested in either. The extra pay is not reward but compensation; we want to make the person suffering risk or extra burden in some way equal to the rest of us who do not. The same is true of an injured person's deserving compensation; compensation is an attempt to equal things out.

Also, not all differences between persons matter. In deciding that Miss Grenada deserves to win the Miss World Contest, I may show each contestant equal respect, but in this case the relevant differences have nothing to do with moral merit. Miss Grenada deserves to win but does not deserve any credit for having been born beautiful. You may deserve more pay than I because you pick more grapes, but if you pick more simply because you have more strength and stamina, then what you do is the natural result of these endowments, and they, like Miss Grenada's endowments, are not enough to earn you moral credit.

And the sort of desert that matters to us should not be confused with entitlement either.[2] If I am silly enough to offer £1 to any child in a nursery group who says the alphabet standing on one foot and ten children up and do it, then all ten deserve £1. Since they met my conditions, they are entitled to it. Some cases of desert mix entitlement and genetic endowment and so are doubly not the sort of desert that matters. If Jessica writes a good examination paper, she deserves a good mark. She is entitled to it even if she is effortlessly bright and has not done a stroke of work. But an effortlessly good mind is like a pretty face, no moral credit to its owner.

What then is the sort of desert that matters? It obviously does not come just from success—from picking more grapes or writing a good examination paper. That might tempt us to think that it comes from effort—from being able to say 'I try harder'. But it cannot be simply that either. Effort can be aimed at the wrong things, or it can be bungled. Also a person who manages self-control from the start of his life, bit by bit, may in the end be both more creditable and spend less effort overall than a person who did not manage it from the start and now always struggles greatly but in vain.

The sort of desert that matters is, I think, part of a simple, even rather crude, and by no means unchallengeable conceptual framework. At its centre is a notion of *par*: what people of a certain type—with certain physical and psychological assets —would find it natural to do. I speak of a type of person, but the assets that matter morally are often so widely distributed that the type then becomes any normal human. Where there is a par, people can do better or worse. When a person meets an obstacle that is not the sort that he naturally scales, he has to try to overcome it. And if he comes to a pit that is not the sort that he inevitably falls into, he just has to take care that he does not. He becomes deserving, of praise or blame, by scaling the obstacle or falling into the pit. In the case of deserving praise, for instance, a person must do something (an element of success) better than type (an element of effort) and do better than type when he need not have (an element of autonomy).

That is the not entirely trouble-free conceptual framework into which the notion of desert that I want to examine fits. It is not easy to make precise what persons with certain physical and psychological assets find it 'natural' to do. What is 'par' for someone cannot be defined in terms of his own past performance, because then anyone who already does well could earn credit only by doing better and better. Effort, it seems, has to have some place. Anyone who regularly does well earns credit if he could easily not do well. And anyone whose doing well has become habit earns credit now for his having made himself into this sort of person, which is no easy job. And what is 'natural' is not to be taken to exclude what is 'learned'. It is natural to be tempted; it is all too natural to succumb. Only stiff training changes that. But this training should probably be thought of as among the psychological assets of some types of persons, making a new, more self-controlled kind of behaviour natural.

This account of desert sounds commonsensical, but it is also, by the standards of contemporary political thought, revisionary. A highly responsible job, society thinks, deserves more pay. But why? It cannot be on grounds of compensation, because greater responsibility generally makes jobs better, not worse. Nor can it be on grounds of earned credit, because the attractions of a responsible job are so great that what is hard is to resist them. And, according to this account, other common political sources of desert—brains, brawn, value or contribution to the community—fail to qualify for moral desert too.

Is anything left? My scaling the obstacle and your not may just show that we were not equal to start with anyway. It may all be the result either of the genetic lottery or of the environmental lottery. This is the determinist attack on the conceptual framework, the strongest attack of them all. I believe, and shall just assume, that the framework survives the determinist attack, that people can deserve the fairly full-blooded moral praise and blame that I shall go on shortly to talk about.

There is another, though less serious, attack on the framework. With time, people change, and sometimes in ways that make us wonder whether praise or blame is still appropriate. Is it right to blame the seventy-year-old for his misdemeanour when he was ten? Is it right to go on blaming the criminal who repents and changes? These worries are connected with, but not exhausted by, worries about personal identity. Perhaps the only conception of personal identity that would make praise and blame appropriate is itself indefensible. Again, I believe, but shall just have to assume, that the most plausible view about personal identity leaves intact all of the problems about desert that I shall now turn to.[3]

2. Is desert a moral reason for action?

Let me, to focus our minds, start with something obvious. It is our nature to respond to what other persons do. We characteristically have certain feelings about what they do, and the feelings lead naturally to action. Each responsive feeling has its own appropriate object and leads on to its own appropriate action. At the sight of courage we feel admiration, which naturally leads to praise. If we are helped, we feel grateful and offer thanks or return the favour. If we are harmed, we resent it and retaliate. Sometimes our feelings are inappropriate: only envy, and no admiration, at another's achievement. Or they are the wrong degree: small grudging admiration for a large achievement. And we know that some objects are entirely inappropriate to certain responses. Indeed, the introduction of an inappropriate object has a devastating effect on the response; it destroys it. I can admire what a person achieves. But if I am told to admire him because that will make him happy, I just cannot. His happiness, whatever it might be a reason for me to do, could not possibly be a reason for me to admire him. And if, solely to make him happy, I gabble words of praise, the last thing I am doing is praising him. The introduction of his happiness into the situation is like finding a painting beautiful and being told by its owner, who wants to help one's response along, how much it cost.

But now, granted that certain responses are appropriate to their object, why think that it is a *moral* matter whether or not I have them? Granted that they often give me a reason for action, why regard it as a *moral* reason? Another person's desert surely enters into my moral assessment of his character. But why think it enters the assessment of how I ought morally to act towards him? When someone harms me, it is natural to retaliate but ought I to turn the other cheek?

What is striking about most standards of right and wrong is that they leave no place for desert. Of course, a pluralist's standard, such as W. D. Ross', does,[4] but that is because it can accommodate anything that intuition prompts one to add. But other tests, tests which look to a unified standard based on goodness perhaps, or on a fount of morality such as rational autonomy, have no place for desert. This is true even of Kant's Categorical Imperative test. Though Kant has the strongest possible views about the obligation to punish wrongdoers,[5] it is hard to see how he gets them, or indeed any view that makes it an obligation to respond in certain ways to desert, out of the Categorical Imperative. I shall come back to this shortly. And modern contractualists, whose test is close to Kant's, have no place for desert either.[6] Contractualists look at the world through the self-interested eyes of the worst-off representative person, and our obligations derive, though sometimes only indirectly, from what is in *his* interest. So when it comes to rewards and punishments, a contractualist will look to incentive, deterrents, and protection, perhaps checked by rights to liberty. But these are all inappropriate to desert; they are the sorts of extraneous considerations that destroy response to desert as desert. Of course, the same is true of the utilitarian test, according to which incentive, deterrents, and protection matter but desert does not.

Either these tests are all too narrow or desert does not belong in a test of right and wrong. That is what I want now to try to decide.

3. *Is merit?*

Suppose someone achieves something quite out of the ordinary; I admire it and praise it. Suppose it benefits mankind; I am grateful and would happily join with the rest of you in honouring and rewarding him. It is the most natural thing in the world for these private responses to grow into public institutions, giving voice to responses that, if left private, might never find adequate expression. Persons are morally equal but are not equal in the way we regard, honour, or reward them. All of this is natural, reasonable, and not to be inhibited. A good society will, for many reasons, be rich in these diversities. There need not be anything misdirected, out of proportion, confused, or irrational in any of it.

Indeed, what would be wrong is not to respond. But what sort of wrong would it be? Sometimes it would be unjust; we might honour a minor benefactor while ignoring a much greater one. But that answer does not go far enough; we might ignore all benefactors equally, which would be wrong simply because they deserve our thanks. Desert is itself a justification, not needing to be bolstered up by another. It is right to thank benefactors simply because that is the response that is fitting. It is wrong to ignore them because that response does not fit their acts. Talk about 'fittingness' is, I know, sometimes dismissed as obscurantist. Reasons for actions, some say, have to be on the order of utilitarian reasons. But this is just fiat. Desert is a reason on its own, governed by criteria that are far from obscure. What would be entirely wrong would be to try to introduce utilitarian reasons into desert.[7] As we have seen, it destroys a response to inject extraneous considerations into it, and utilitarian reasons are extraneous. Authenticity is not merely the best or the purest form of responses such as admiration, gratitude, or appreciation; it is the only form. A person who utters words, or does acts, of admiration, gratitude, or appreciation only on utilitarian grounds becomes a person without admiration, gratitude, or appreciation. If utilitarianism has no place for desert, desert has no place for utilitarianism either.

However, that these responses to merit are natural, even fitting, does not yet mean that merit is a moral reason for action. Is it? Ross thought it clear that gratitude was sometimes a moral duty. When I read my colleagues' manuscripts for them, I hope they are grateful. But if, when I send mine to them, they read them only because they now see themselves as obliged to, they may be helping me, but it is far from clear that they can also be expressing their gratitude. Perhaps, when it comes to desert, even moral duty is extraneous matter the injection of which destroys the response. Certainly, if you, as depressingly many people do, turn the help I give you into a debt which I can collect, then you destroy gratitude. You transform it into exchange. You destroy my act as a favour, and you destroy your response as thanks. Repayment is certainly not gratitude. And duty does not look much like it either.[8]

Perhaps gratitude is not quite the thing for us to be focusing on. Gratitude is a feeling, a motive, a source of action, while actions, not feelings, are the primary subject of moral duties. Still, if 'gratitude' is not quite the word for Ross to have used, it is clear that he had an act in mind—the act of returning good for good. It may destroy your motive as one of gratitude to inject considerations of duty into it, but none the less perhaps you morally ought, considering that I read your manuscript, to read mine. But if we now shift our focus to acts, there are several easy confusions that we need to avoid. It is easy, in the way I mentioned a moment ago, to transmute, without being quite aware what one is doing, a good turn into a process of exchange and so a grateful act into paying a debt. But the fact that a great many persons make returning good for good into a duty gives the rest of us no reason to think that it really is. It is also easy to confuse the moral assessment of agents with the moral assessment of acts—agent-morality with act-morality. We are now interested in the second, and in the first only to the extent that it bears on the second. And it is easy to slip unawares between deontic categories—for instance, what is morally admirable but not a matter of right and wrong (say, an act of heroism), what one ought to do but is not strictly an obligation (say, a simple act of charity), and what one must do (say, keeping a solemn promise). Unfortunately moral philosophy has not yet come up with any clear definitions of deontic categories, nor indeed any satisfactory argument that we need a distinction between, for instance, what we merely ought to do and what we strictly must do. But for our present purposes we should concentrate on a fairly weak deontic category: ought one morally to return good for good? Does the fact that I read your manuscript enter into the set of considerations that determines what would now be morally right or wrong for you to do?

It is hard to enlist intuition on either side of this question. Suppose that you feel genuinely grateful to me and yet, at the same time, follow a policy of reading only the manuscripts on which, in the time you have, you can help most and that I do not qualify. Would you be doing wrong? You would not, it is true, be ruled by feelings of gratitude; you might also be inhibiting the action towards which these feelings naturally prompt you. But that hardly settles the matter. Even in cases in which good turns pile up mountainously, as they often do in parents' help to a child, it might not be wrong for a child to ignore them in deciding what to do. If the child's policy is to help where he can help most so he leaves home for field-work with Oxfam, does he do wrong? Certainly if you did not *want* to do me a good turn for reading your manuscript, something would be wrong with you. And if a child were not deeply moved by the needs of parents who have been good to him, something would be much more seriously wrong with him. And there is a good case for thinking that the wrong in each case would be moral. But some of the morality that enters here looks very much like agent-morality. Since feelings connect with emotions, what feelings we have can, of course, be of great moral importance. To be deficient in certain feelings is to be insensitive to, in certain ways unsympathetic towards, other persons. How one relates to persons emotionally is part and parcel of having the dispositions that enable one to act morally towards them. And failing in feelings of gratitude, while not dead centre of this set of moral emotions, is still a member of it. But this is not the sort of link with morality that we are after. That there is a link between one's feelings and generally desirable behaviour does not show that one's having received a good turn is to be placed among the criteria of what it would be morally right or wrong for one now to do. That morality needs certain emotions does not mean that it would be morally wrong ever not to follow them. Admittedly, any child whose feelings are in proper order will have deep emotional ties to parents who have done him great good. Such ties grow naturally, and they, along with other deep personal relations, constitute one of the central prudential values of life. A child would need a strong reason to free himself from the ties and the actions to which they lead. It would take something like the chance of saving others' lives in a famine, and not just a chance of conferring some marginally greater benefit, to justify a child's going against the prompting of these deep ties to his parents. They are too large a part of what makes the lives of all of them valuable to be put aside lightly. The wrongness of ignoring those ties does probably qualify as a moral matter, even as a matter of act-morality. But the reason for this has nothing to do with a duty to return good for good; this link with morality is still not the kind we are looking for. Indeed, it is because feelings of gratitude are so important that a duty to return good for good is suspect. It would make for a dreary life to have the duty replace the feelings, and following the duty would have the effect, in the way we saw, of undermining the feelings. It is probably better to live a life in which the feelings, and not this duty, are at work.

Justice, I think, is a better case to press than gratitude. I said before that desert is a reason on its own, not needing to be bolstered by other reasons such as justice. But the cases of desert that most have an aura of moral right and wrong seem also to be instances of justice. We have to remember that sometimes desert rests on the obligation of equal respect, and then, of course, desert is a case both of justice and of moral right and wrong, but that is not the sort of desert that we are interested in. We are interested in merit. Is merit a matter of justice?

Having an Order of Merit does not make Britain juster than the United States. Awards are not a moral matter (though giving them unfairly is). Rewards, however, look more like one. Is it not unjust not to give more—say more pay—to one who meritoriously contributes more? Are not American universities juster than Oxford, because their salaries recognize meritorious production while Oxford's recognize only the passage of time? Some people display determination, dedication, or industry, while others around them, who are like them, do not. A person expects, at the end of the day, even if he worked freely and unselfishly, to be treated with some regard for what he did. He wants to be acknowledged for what he is, and what he does is much of what he is.[9] But what should we conclude from this? No one would deny that there are powerful arguments for differences in pay: incentive, compensation, efficient distribution of labour. But merit lacks their obvious power. Oxford salaries are not obviously less just than American. Where merit has overwhelming power is in an argument for differences in response, even in reward. But rewards need not be money. At the end of the day, a person does indeed want to be acknowledged for what he is and what he does. And we, his partners in the enterprise, would be wrong not to admire his achievement and to be grateful for the benefit it confers on us. But the wrong need not be a moral wrong. All meritorious benefactors—good workers, social reformers, poets, musicians—deserve these forms of recognition. But admiration and gratitude have, in the end, to be in people's minds. What societies may choose to do can only be tokens. Nor can admiration or gratitude be commanded, even on moral grounds, without injecting destructively extraneous matter. And they lead naturally to actions, to forms of respect and recognition. Now some societies are content to leave it at that. Other societies believe that it is better to give these spontaneous workings an institutional form. But few people who prefer institutional expression think that leaving it to spontaneous expression is morally wrong. Admittedly, if we leave it to spontaneous expression, and if we are all brought up extremely undemonstrative, some meritorious benefactor might go all the way through life not knowing how much he is appreciated. That would be the greatest of pities; it would show a great fault in us. We ought, in some way, to have made him understand. But it seems best, all things considered, to say that we ought because only that is fitting and its omission unfitting, and let it go at that, and not make it into a moral wrong.[10]

Sometimes, however, the case for institutionalizing a response is irresistible, and the arrival of an institution brings along with it a new set of moral issues.[11] The appropriate response to a student who does well is admiration and praise, and to a student who does better it is greater admiration and praise. By institutionalizing these responses in a system of marks, we do more than just praise. Marks become statements:

they inform whomever it may concern that Sally is a little better than Paul, who is a lot better than Ann. The core of the institution, however, remains a response to achievement. What is extraneous to the response remains extraneous to, and potentially destructive of, the institution. Utilitarianism is still destructively extraneous. And for any institution of great value it matters greatly that we separate clearly what is essential to it from what is extraneous. Of course, nearly all of us accept that an extraneous consideration may come along weighty enough to outweigh the demands of the institution, but it will still remain extraneous. Yet, once there is an institution, giving a student a mark that he does not deserve is a plain injustice: it deceives and it can injure. And the institution consists in criteria of success that contain a promise: if you do this, you get that; so entitlement also enters. Clearly, then, moral obligation enters with the institution. But it does so, because honesty, injury, and entitlement enter, and none of these is the sort of desert that concerns us now.

Is merit then a moral reason for action? It seems not. Even allowing that people are responsible for what they do, even giving them all credit for what they do, it is hard to find a case for turning that credit into a criterion of moral right and wrong. This might look puzzling: what sort of reason for action could it possibly be, if not moral? It is not a prudential or aesthetic reason; it is not a reason arising from personal aims. Still, there are, I think, other sorts of reasons. Another person's merit is a reason for me to respond in a certain way simply in virtue of its being the appropriate response: it is not just that my feelings would be functioning badly if they did not prompt me in this way, but also, beyond that, that my response, my action, would not otherwise fit the situation. The element of appropriateness itself constitutes a reason.

4. *Is my own demerit?*

How do I respond to my own wrongdoing? I find that I am a pretty willing retributivist in my own case. Only occasionally do I see myself as a suitable subject for manipulation. I do, I suppose, when the trouble is a relatively simple bad habit that hypnosis or aversion-therapy would break. Still, some wrongdoing, even if it could be stopped that way too, is more complex. I do not fully understand its origin, which is a lot of the trouble. It comes from my not seeing things straight: from coarseness of perception, lack of imagination, atrophy of feeling, bad values, self-deception, insecurity. In those cases I do not know how I should want the manipulation to work: will it cure one fault and make others worse? There is no alternative but to see things straighter. To manipulate myself, or to get others to do it, with sufficient fineness of control would require that I already have so grown morally as to make the manipulation largely unnecessary. Anyway, only with such growth would I stay autonomous; I am not prepared to turn my moral fate over to someone else's idea of how I ought to be functioning.

I do not suppose that I am at all unusual in this. For most of us, therefore, there is no alternative to moral growth. That is what makes certain responses to wrongdoing not only natural but fitting. I feel guilty: I know that what I did was wrong, that it matters that it was, that I am responsible; and I therefore feel 'depleted of energy, unable to stand upright and partake of life'.[12] And if I see that I have acted not only wrongly but shabbily, I also feel shame. Sometimes I might be able to decide that I was so frightened or threatened or provoked that I could not have done otherwise. But sometimes I can find no excuses. Is there anything inappropriate in my then feeling guilty? If what I did was wrong and matters and is inexcusable, it is proper that I should sense its wrongness, fatefulness, and its source in me. What would be inappropriate is *not* to react like this; a person without these responses would fail in perception and understanding. And the fact that the perception is charged with feeling does not make it any less a matter of understanding. The understanding would fail on its own terms if it were not highly charged.

But is it right that I should also be unable to stand upright and partake of life? Well, it is hard for my understanding to be adequate without these effects following naturally. And the period of suffering and detachment has value. I cannot easily take part in life when I am absorbed in coming to terms with what I have done. The human frame supplies only so much psychic energy. The sense of crisis, of the impossibility of carrying on without first coming to terms with what one did, are important in bringing about deep change.

None of this is to dismiss these natural responses as merely serving some practical purpose, as utilitarians sometimes do. What they often have in mind is that guilt has no value in itself but can be a useful handle for steering behaviour. However, guilt is not just an instrument of manipulation; it is a response the appropriateness of which must be come to terms with.

Yet any case for the appropriateness of guilt will also show that it is often inappropriate. It is notorious that feeling guilty and being guilty often disastrously part company.[13] But this ought not to raise any general mistrust of guilt feelings. For instance, it would be a superficial psychological theory that claimed that all guilt feelings are pathological. Sometimes I see my wrongdoing all too plainly, and I hold myself responsible, and guilt feelings follow. If my beliefs change in these cases, my feelings change accordingly; there is nothing pathological. If one wants to argue that *all* guilt feelings are pathological, one has to attack at a very deep level. One has to argue that our using the concepts 'right', 'wrong', and 'responsible' to organize our understanding of ourselves is itself mistaken, a symptom of the same pathology.

However, for our present purposes the greatest flaw in guilt is this. The most appropriate outcome of the perception of guilt is moral growth. But what if further growth is not possible? Suppose that I see that my wrongdoing was genuinely just a slip that I shall be able to guard against in future. Or suppose that I have gone through the painful moral growth and am really now changed. It would seem in each case that then I should shake off the guilt and go back to my normal life. That is what we might call the Repentance View, according to which the appropriate pattern is: perception of wrongdoing, guilt, and finally repentance and correction. According to it, once I have gone through that process, I do not have to do more; that—neither more nor less—is the appropriate response.

Yet if I go through the process quickly, though I have repented, have I yet atoned? When I confess to a priest, he may accept that I am already a changed person, but he still gives me a penance. Atonement is the purest form of the wages of sin; the wages do not depend on moral growth and, if one believes that Jesus atoned for our sins, they can even be paid by someone else. On what we might call the Atonement View, the appropriate pattern has one last stage: perception of wrongdoing, guilt, repentance, and (the last stage) payment of the moral debt.

Let us think for a moment about the relative merits of the Repentance and Atonement Views. Dostoevsky, the most powerful advocate of the belief that criminals themselves feel the need for punishment,[14] might be enlisted on the side of the Atonement View. But he is really, I think, in the opposing camp. There is a strong widespread feeling, a feeling which moves Raskolnikov in *Crime and Punishment* to turn himself in, that one must suffer to atone for wrongdoing—not suffer to grow, but suffer simply to atone. But that is not where Dostoevsky leaves things. Raskolnikov goes to prison ready to atone but not prepared to repent. On the contrary, at first in prison he sees his crime merely as a blunder; he simply lacked the psychological strength to carry off his vision of a masterful Napoleonic life. But eventually, through the example of Sonia, who follows him to Siberia and devotedly attends him, he begins to see the hollowness of the vision. He sees how empty his life would have been even if he had managed to rise to truly Napoleonic force. The displays of power he valued were not the opposite, but the obverse, of his weakness. His problem was not impotence but emptiness, and the murder he committed was an exercise of power that left him even emptier —'agonizing, everlasting solitude'. And he finally finds in the possibility of his feeling toward Sonia as she does towards him a way in which his life might take on the substance that it has lacked. It is only then that Raskolnikov, not having before seen any point in his punishment's coming to an end, looks forward eagerly to release. It is spring, just after Easter; Sonia had recently read him the story of Lazarus. Raskolnikov, Dostoevsky says, 'had risen again and knew it'.

So what Dostoevsky has to say about guilt and punishment is, as one should expect, far subtler than the Atonement View. He says, with Nietzsche,[15] that guilt can be an illness like pregnancy—its outcome a new life. He says that the criminal's need for punishment, if it takes the form of a desire for atonement, can be superficial, incomplete, and self-interested.[16] He sees that it can be completed by becoming repentance, and that without some such completion a criminal's need for punishment will be propelled by the same destructive forces inside him, only now turned against himself, that led originally to his crime. Once Raskolnikov has changed, atonement is of no interest to him; it is merely the social penalty to be got through.[17]

One way to test the Atonement View is to consider the question, If Raskolnikov had been condemned to die, would he, after his moral change, have been able to see his execution as a further appropriate, required, event? Of course, in some moods, especially with certain examples at the front of our minds, we are ready to say *yes*. If all the Nazis on trial at Nuremberg had in the end truly repented, not all their judges would have been willing to let them off. Still, despite the power of such examples, the Atonement View threatens our whole grasp on the concept of the appropriateness of responses to wrongdoing. The Atonement View focuses on wrongdoing. The most appropriate object for our response, however, is something more complex: what a person did—both wrongdoer and wrongdoing. But then, when I repent and change, I create a problem. Now that I and my act have in a way come apart, to which should one respond? According to the Atonement View, the appropriate object is still the act (or, perhaps, the evil of the act). But this sets up a strain. It divorces the appropriate object from the enduring moral person with whom one now can deal. I would not want such a divorce in my own case. I should want people to respond to my wrongdoing by regarding me as accountable and as able to come to terms with my own wrongdoing. I should want that respect, and also concern and help. But if I change, I should want them to respond now to the person I am now.

What leads people to the Atonement View is, I suspect, an attempt to match up my response to my own wrongdoing with other persons' response to it. The two responses would certainly not be identical. My response would be: guilt, repentance, and (according to the Atonement View) paying the penalty. Your response would be: resentment, anger, sometimes also fear, avoidance, self-defence, retaliation. Both of these chains of responses can be appropriate. At a certain point they converge: your retaliation can be my penalty. If both responses are appropriate, then it seems necessary for me to pay a penalty; otherwise your appropriate response, retaliation, would be left without the partner it needs in my appropriate response. But when I do repent and change, a lot in your response loses appropriateness. Certainly fear and self-defence do. So, I think, would anger and retaliation. Your anger is aimed primarily at the complex of my person and my act. But now I have changed. Why not now accept, as the aphorism puts it, that 'He that repents is angry with himself; I need not be angry with him'?[18] The slippery moral notion of what is 'fitting' gives no help here. To be used correctly it has to be tied to our notion of an appropriate response. Admittedly, someone might insist that only Raskolnikov's death would fit the intensity of people's reactions to the murders he committed. But the intensity of people's reactions has no independent moral status. It has itself to be appropriate, and will be appropriate only if it fits Raskolnikov's wrongdoing. That has to be the primary judgement of 'fittingness'. Nor will the elusive, near-empty notion of 'respect for persons' help much. Kant relies on this notion to justify his allegiance to the Atonement View. But it does not do it. The alternative to the Atonement View is not to deny a person the dignity of being morally accountable. To think so is to succumb to the false dichotomy that bedevils this subject. There is nothing mechanistic, manipulative, degrading, or lacking in respect in the Repentance View. The Atonement View is not the only way to show respect for persons. And once the Atonement View is separated from the notion of 'respect for persons' and stands on its own, it looks both inappropriate and empty. On its own, there is nothing characteristic to it but insistence on the collection of moral debts. If anything, it is the Repentance View, in which a person is given more weight than an act, that shows respect for persons.

Well, then, is my demerit a moral reason for action? In the case of merit, there is no move from a response's being appropriate to its being a moral reason. But demerit is

different. Though both reward and punishment are responses
with standards of appropriateness, punishment is a response to
something moral and gets its moral status from that. You
respond to my wrongdoing with self-defence and retaliation.
You do it to protect rights that I infringe. It is morally wrong
of me to infringe them, and this gives you a moral reason to
stop me. And I respond to my own wrongdoing with
repentance. If I ought not to have done it, I ought to do what
is necessary not to do it again. So there is a moral reason to
punish. But is it based on my demerit? The analogue of the
claim that one must reward for the good done is the claim that
one must punish for the wrong done. But the ground of the
moral reason to punish turns out to be something different
from pure desert. It is protection of other persons' rights and
my repentance and change. The effect of choosing the
Repentance View over the Atonement View is both to give
desert a large role, but, so far as it is to have moral force, to
restrict it to its workings in repentance and change. So if the
claim that one must punish because of the wrong done is taken
to mean that we must take the further step represented by the
Atonement View, then there is no reason to agree. My demerit
is a moral reason only within the limits imposed by the
Repentance View.

5. Is the demerit of others?

Whatever is right for me is also right for anyone like me in the
relevant ways. If, say, you punch me on the nose, it is all right
for me to punch you back—with certain provisos. So long as
you are in fact like me—capable of repentance and reform
—then my response has to be appropriate to you as a possessor
of these capacities; it may not go beyond what is appropriate
to your exercising them (e.g. no pure atonement); and it must
be in proportion to your wrongdoing. Turning the other cheek
would be right only if it spoke to, challenged, helped
transform, the wrong in the wrongdoer; otherwise it would be
not noble but narcissistic.[19]

Whether I may punish others all depends, therefore, on
what the wrongdoer is like. If the wrongdoer is an exceptional
moral agent who spontaneously repents and reforms, there is

virtually no place for punishment. If instead he is a normal sort, whose response is confused, ambivalent, and weak, punishment may provide him with the urgency to find the clarity, the unity of purpose, and the strength. If he is an adult who still needs to learn but resists the lesson, then maybe punishment would teach the seriousness of wrongdoing where words alone would fail. If he is someone who cannot learn no matter what the lesson, then punishment has no place as a response to the person that we are dealing with.

The hardest claim to accept, I think, is the last—the response to someone who cannot come to terms with his own wrongdoing. Punishment takes the form of a dramatic acting out of a spiritual movement that ought to be taking place in the wrongdoer: a wrongdoer naturally suffers guilt and cannot partake of life. Punishment gets moral force from being an external form of, a symbol for, this internal process.[20] But then confusion is almost irresistible: symbol gets mistaken for symbolized. We start to think that to be punished is actually to go through what one ought to go through. But if the wrongdoer is incapable of going through the internal process, then, putting the interests of other persons aside for the moment, we have no reason to put him through the external. Why use symbols when there is no one to communicate with? The symbolic status of punishment no doubt also partly explains our intuition that, besides deterrents, protection, and reform, a further justification of punishment is its being *fitting* or *appropriate*. We think it fitting not only that a wrongdoer be unhappy but that everyone recognize what he did as wrong, and the strongest form of recognizing this is by making him suffer. But this is pure confusion. It *is* fitting that he suffer and that what he did be recognized as wrong. But making him suffer does not always, and often will not, make him suffer in the way he should. It is an entirely different form of suffering, which needs an entirely new justification. One does not transform a monster by imposing upon him for a while the outward trappings of the inner life of a beautiful soul.

All of that concerned our response to the person of the wrongdoer. Part of our response to any wrongdoer, however, looks to ourselves. Of course, it is all right for me to protect myself and others. That needs no arguing. So for now I shall just acknowledge it and say more about it later.

Before moving on to the large social scale, let me sum up what lessons I think we should carry over into it from small scale interpersonal dealings. Punishment has a rich life of its own, quite independent of social institutions. It starts with the appropriateness of a person's response to his own wrongdoing. This, since it is purely a one-person affair, is not yet what can be regarded literally as 'punishment'. But it influences the appropriateness of interpersonal responses to wrongdoing, which certainly can be called 'punishment'. The appropriate response to wrongdoing is: perception of wrongdoing, guilt, and repentance. That is true in the one-person case; it is also true in the interpersonal case. My response to your wrongdoing is appropriate only when, and to the extent that, it contributes to your going through the same process: perception, guilt, and repentance. Considering only the person of the wrongdoer, punishment has no place at the two extremes: with a good person who spontaneously reforms or with a bad person not capable of reforming. It has a place only with the majority of us, who fall between the extremes, but then only as part of our coming to terms with our own wrongdoing, which severely limits it. But considering the victims as well, we may all defend ourselves. This means that demerit on its own—pure payment of moral debt—has no moral force; it gets it only through its connection with values such as good or right. It connects with good through protection of would-be victims. It connects with right through reform of wrongdoers; reform gets its importance not from making the quality of a wrongdoer's life higher but from making his acts better. Prudential values are not the only ones with a place here; there is also the moral value of doing right and doing what is necessary to do right.

6. *The social response*

As soon as punishment becomes a social institution, it becomes in an important sense less pure. It is used not just to respond to wrongdoing but also to solve a lot of social problems. Let me just tick off a few of the extra jobs that punishment takes on.

First, punishment is put to the rather different job of

teaching, a job that it does well. It is an emphatic denunciation of crime; it is a symbol of society's reprobation.[21] However, its message is not always or primarily directed to the individual actually being punished, but to society at large, and these two interests may well diverge. Second, punishment is put to the job of deterrence. Having the rule, 'Anyone who does *this* gets *that* as punishment', deters only because it is meant seriously, which requires punishing offenders. Third, punishment is pressed into the service of reform, because it is a good way of putting new pressure on the psychic mechanism and because it will serve as an occasion for autonomous moral growth. But reform, especially if it is moral growth, is a reasonable aim only in some cases. Fourth, punishment is put to the job of public relations. People have not only to be taught and deterred and reformed, but also to be reconciled to living in peace with one another. Justice has to be *seen* to be done. Since most persons do not notice fine details of particular criminal cases, and since judgements about the amount of fault are subtle and contentious, there is strong pressure to punish kinds of acts rather than particular ones.

But all of these additional jobs assigned to punishment make it less and less pure. That is to say, they do not sit at all comfortably with punishment seen merely as an appropriate response to wrongdoing. The large-scale social perspective is hard to reconcile and harmonize with the small-scale interpersonal perspective. Punishment, from the small-scale perspective, can accommodate the job of reform, at least the sort in which the wrongdoer comes to terms with his own wrongdoing by repenting and changing. But further jobs such as protection, deterrence, and education, if they become too central to the institution, will destroy it as punishment. Yet protection, education, and especially deterrence, are important—some would say *the* important, even the justifying—functions of a social institution of punishment. Once punishment becomes a social institution we seem to have a conflict on our hands between the small-scale perspective in which guilt appears at the centre of the picture, and the social perspective, in which solving co-operation problems is central.

It would certainly be a mistake to make what dominates the small-scale perspective—wrongdoing, guilt, repentance

—dominant in a social institution of punishment. Parking on a double yellow line brings a fine, but unless it is also dangerous guilt and repentance are inappropriate. And society has as one of its chief functions fostering and protecting beneficial co-operation, and that requires sanctions for welshing on agreements or for not doing one's bit. The most successful strategy for an individual in iterated, few-person Prisoner's Dilemma games is what game theorists call Tit for Tat: to co-operate initially, to be quickly provoked into punishing the other player's defection by defecting oneself next time, and then to repay co-operation with co-operation and defection with defection.[22] Co-operation on a social scale would be even more efficiently promoted if society as a whole were provocable by deviations from its rules. Though rules do not get their whole justification from providing solutions to co-operation problems, they get much of it there. The social institution of punishment has a rationale independent of guilt and repentance. It comes from the causal chain: certain great social *benefits* require *conformity*; *conformity* requires *sanctions*; *sanctions* require *punishment*.

This clash between large-scale and small-scale perspectives is connected with a clash between retributive and utilitarian justifications of punishment. The widespread belief that any entirely satisfactory justification will have to combine elements of both retributivism and utilitarianism could then be rephrased: it will have to manage to see its subject from both of these perspectives. And this is not going to be easy. What is dominant in one perspective destroys what is dominant in the other. The social institution of punishment serves very many interests, which are not easily made compatible. The various elements of the structure can, it seems, be kept in balance, but it is an extremely precarious balance.

The social institution of punishment, it seems to me, has some such structure as this. At its core is one person's response to another's wrongdoing: the deliberate imposition of an unwelcome state in return for wrongdoing, where the notion of a 'return' carries with it a rough notion of proportionality. Next, outside the core but still close to it, is the job of bringing a wrongdoer to his senses. Next, shifting attention from the wrongdoer to his future action, comes the job of protecting potential victims. Next is the job of deterrence, first of the wrongdoer himself and then, at one further remove from the centre, of others. Next, at some distance from the centre, comes the job of education, teaching others or raising the general moral tone.

The core and what surrounds it are in unstable relation. If what surrounds it displaces the core, the institution collapses. Even something as close to the core as self-defence, if it becomes too much the centre of society's activity, will destroy the activity as punishment. If I sit on someone to stop him from attacking me, and if I go on sitting on him because each time I go to get up he starts again, I am not punishing him. It is a perfectly appropriate response, but since the core is missing, it is not punishment. And a social institution centred on self-defence would be concerned with anticipating, preventing, warding off wrongdoing so that it never becomes actual, not with responding to it once it does. The same is true of every other surrounding function of punishment: reform, deterrence, teaching, public relations; if any of them gets too close to the centre, it destroys the whole institution.

However, these surrounding functions can hardly be dispensed with. They are what justifies punishment. Desert, which appears in the core in the notion of a 'return', is not a justification. It played no role in the justification worked out earlier, so can play none here; the introduction of a social institution opens up no new place for it. So if there were no surrounding functions, there would be destruction of another kind. Justified punishment needs both core and surrounding functions. If no core, then no punishment; if no surrounding functions, then no justification. Once we give up the Atonement View, as many Kantians and all utilitarians do, then we face a problem. All of the justifications of punishment appeal to features that are not only inessential to but also, if they loom too large, destructive of its status as punishment. This has been recognized as a problem for utilitarians, but it is far more general. The misimpression that it is particularly utilitarians who are in trouble may be helped along by the fact that the important modern Kantians, the contractualists, generally avoid the whole messy subject of punishment.[23]

How far can one go? How far can one increase the

importance of the surrounding functions, which are after all what justify the whole business, without destroying the core? We should not have gone too far if, say, we were to do the following. If we had a wrongdoer who could be brought to his moral senses whom we punished with that hope, then we should be acting in return for his wrongdoing and *also* in hopes of his changing. The core survives alongside its extra function. But exemplary punishments usually go too far. To survive as punishment they have to stay within the bounds of an appropriate response to the wrongdoing. There is a rough proportionality built into the essence of punishment—very rough indeed, hard to make precise, but undeniably there.[24] A state could hang shoplifters. The authorities could even call it 'punishment', but the rest of us would not go along with it for long. It is no longer an institution whose purpose is to make return for the shoplifting but becomes one whose aim is controlling behaviour by fear. The same applies (although it is a good deal harder to argue) to capital punishment. It is certainly never an appropriate response to the person of the wrongdoer—not if he can repent and certainly not if he has already repented. Its justification has to be the general deterrent effect of the rule, 'if you do this, you will be executed.' For the most part, attention focuses on whether such a rule does really deter, but it should also focus on whether what would successfully deter would also succeed in falling within the range of responses appropriate to the particular act. For if it does not, then the desert at the core is missing.

Still, desert, I want to say, is only the core and not a justification. But then all the worst fears seem to rise; all sorts of abuses seem to be allowed. Punishments need no longer fit the crime. Worse, we may punish the innocent. But these fears, which probably account for a lot of allegiance to desert, are caused by misunderstanding the different roles desert can play—as core and as justification.

Does the punishment no longer need to fit the crime? May we impose a penalty of whatever size proves to have best effects? No, as we have just seen; and no, because of desert.[25] Punishment, in its core, is a return for wrongdoing; a rough proportionality is part of it. It destroys the institution to let the degree be fixed by anything extra. That is what the institution is; that is the institution we are interested in. Considerations of utility maximization have no more place here than they do in marking a student's answer (though, as before, this is not to say that they have no moral place at all; nearly all of us accept that they can override the internal considerations).

May we punish the innocent? Suppose a government took to trumping up charges of currency irregularities against political dissidents. Well, even if it did, it would not be a case where what justified punishment was also justifying punishment of the innocent. For reasons we have already seen, it would no longer be punishment. This is not a semantic point. A prison guard can well say to the dissident he locks up, 'I am punishing you for something you didn't do'. For the word 'punishment' to be used correctly, it is enough that there be some *deemed* wrongdoing. There is enough of the normal semantic background there for the guard not to have made a linguistic error, though also enough missing for him to feel a bit uneasy about going on talking in that way. And if this case is not isolated, if the state regularly uses the trappings of punishment for political suppression, people are likely eventually to stop calling it 'punishment' or to shift to a new or obviously ironic way of using the word. Desert is necessary, in general, for the institution to be punishment and to be regarded as such. Political suppression is plainly not punishment.

This argument is like one that, some years ago, Anthony Quinton used. He proposed that certain forms of retributivism be seen as a claim about the meaning of 'punishment', and Herbert Hart later dismissed this as the ploy of putting a 'definitional stop' to serious objections to utilitarianism.[26] But my point is not quite Quinton's. He wanted to rest the weight of the argument upon the semantics of the word 'punishment', and it would not carry the burden. I rest it on the character of the institution of punishment, the rich connections it has in our life, with its accommodation of our natural and proper responses to our own and other persons' wrongdoing. The important point is about the institution the justification of which is in question. We need not follow what a prison guard or a man in the street would say. Our purpose is rather different. We are building a moral theory, one of the aims of which is precision and the avoidance of confusion. Other institutions—e.g. institutions of political suppression—are not punishment. To talk about them is not to talk about punishment. What justifies punishment may not (often does not) justify them. And if it is replied that political suppression is justified by considerations out of the same stable as the ones now being used to justify punishment, what would this show? All that it would show is that, although we may have a good justification of punishment, we had better also have resources to prevent those considerations' going on to justify those other institutions—when, that is, they are not justified.

But what if the abuse was not on a large social scale, but was a lone individual twisting the institution, unobserved, to some good end? Cases would, no doubt, be very rare, but life might sometimes take on the flavour of an Agatha Christie story. We can imagine a detective, in what looks like an open-and-shut case, getting the hunch that not all is as it seems. Green, let us say, had a flaming row with his partner Grey, who was heard to threaten him, and an hour later Mrs Green found Grey, smoking revolver in hand, standing over her husband's dead body. Everyone is satisfied of Grey's guilt, except our detective, who begins to find a trail leading to Mrs Green. But she has five young children who need her; Grey is a bachelor; it was probably a crime of passion. No one will know if the lone detective probes no further, and even if the truth eventually comes out, no one will lose faith in the police for not being as clever as Hercule Poirot.

Still, strictly speaking, what will happen to Grey will not be punishment. It will not be the workings of an institution whose justification we are trying to determine. This may not seem to matter much; we could just call it pseudo-punishment instead. But it matters because, as calling it pseudo-punishment shows, it brings a change in subject. The real complaint is not that the Repentance View would justify punishing the innocent, but that it does not prevent pseudo-punishment. Why is that a complaint? Why should its job be to do that? It is only one part of moral theory and should not be expected to have *all* the answers. All that can be reasonably asked of it is that it is able to fit into a larger moral theory that does supply the rest of the answers.

There is a better way to resist the Repentance View. It is to take up a position somewhere between the Repentance and Atonement Views. Desert, one would say, *allows* punishing a wrongdoer (it does not require it; the permission may be subject to the restrictions in the Repentance View), but lack of desert *prohibits* punishing or pseudo-punishing an innocent person (it prohibits it more strongly than the Repentance View does, in which the prohibition comes from what is necessary for the institution's survival, while now it comes from lack of desert). We can call this the 'Accountability View'.[27]

There is an ambiguity in the Accountability View that needs clearing up right at the start. Should we interpret its prohibition as being absolute? The moral prohibition, *Do not intentionally kill the innocent*, has great moral weight, but there is the rare exception. It was right for the sailors to eat the cabin boy since otherwise most of them, including the cabin boy, would have died.[28] Similarly, the prohibition, *Do not execute the innocent*, must have exceptions, and if it does, the vastly more general prohibition, *Do not pseudo-punish the innocent*, which covers actions ranging all the way from execution down to a £1 fine, is likely to have many more. The tendency in modern discussions of punishment is to set the demands far too high: a justification of punishment is often regarded as ruled out if it *ever* allows pseudo-punishing the innocent. But few of us are absolutists in general moral theory, and it is hard to see why we should be in this department of it.

But if the prohibition is not absolute, the divisions become altogether more difficult to locate. It is easy to *say* how the Accountability and the Repentance Views differ. The basic idea of a non-absolute version of the Accountability View is that desert has moral weight and that it is wrong, other things being equal, to punish the undeserving. The Repentance View contains nothing comparable to this prohibition. So, according to the Accountability View, we need extra counterweight to balance the moral weight of desert, and therefore more weight to justify pseudo-punishing the innocent than the Repentance View requires.

That is the theory. But when we get down to particular cases, it is not at all clear that we do require this extra counterweight. Of course, there are examples that spark our intuitions. But is it *desert* that has weight in those cases?

The Accountability View consists of two claims, a permission and a prohibition: one may punish the guilty because they deserve it; one may not punish the innocent because they do not. But if, as seems desirable, the permission is interpreted in a way compatible with the Repentance View, the only point of difference between them will be the prohibition. But a theory of punishment is not the whole of moral theory. So although the Repentance View restricts pseudo-punishment of the innocent only so far as the institution's survival is at stake, the whole moral theory of which it is a part is likely to provide other restrictions. An obvious one is rights. I spoke of the status and moral weight of basic rights in the last chapter. Liberty is such an important right that it takes a very great moral counterweight to override it; and it protects an innocent person threatened with pseudo-punishment. Does the Accountability View give any greater protection? If not, then the Repentance and Accountability Views merely offer different explanations of the same degree of protection, and we should not need 'desert' to explain that degree.

Think again of Mrs Green and Mr Grey. And suppose it was Mrs Green, after all, who did it. Then we have Mrs Green on one side, a woman who had something in her that led her to murder, who will be or should be torn by remorse and unable to carry on with life until she has come to terms with her own guilt, who needs punishment and whose punishment should end when she no longer needs it. Then, on the other side, there is Grey, who has no guilt to come to terms with but has a life to make as much of as he can. It is hard to see how, even without giving desert a moral weight, it could be right to let Grey be convicted.

Of course, the case need not be so straightforward. Perhaps the legal system is corrupt; perhaps Mrs Green would get a much longer sentence than she deserved. That would then make the moral reasoning much more difficult; now it becomes, among other things, a choice between injustices. But the complication that interests us is different. To test the two views properly, we should need to take a series of cases, in which we added bit-by-bit to what rides on Mrs Green's escaping punishment until we reach the point where they outweigh Grey's right to liberty, and then we need to see whether they are not yet enough to balance Grey's desert. Give Mrs Green not five children but ten. Add a child with a fragile psyche who would kill himself for the shame of it all. Have we got there yet? And does desert need still more?

Since rights have instrumental value (protections of the greatest prudential values), we have some rough notion of how to weigh them. Desert is quite different. It is not just that our intuitions about its weight will differ greatly. That would be all right if, with thought, we could bring them into some order. But that is what is so hard to see how to do. And that is the result of its being so hard to attach a sense to the notion of 'desert'. When it is what persons deserve in return for the good and ill that they do, we understand the rough proportionality involved. But negative desert, a person's not deserving punishment, when the prohibition is not absolute, introduces a different sort of proportionality. And, to fit into the structure of the Accountability View, the protection conferred by negative desert has to be different from the protection conferred by basic rights. That is the notion that is so difficult to attach a sense to.

Let me sum up what I have to say about the social institution of punishment. It is a natural growth that owes little to conscious human decision. It has grown from two very different grounds. It grew up as a solution to certain co-operation problems. It grew up simultaneously as one of a large set of natural responses to the behaviour of others, each with its own criteria of appropriateness. We tend now to see conscious human decision as more influential than it is. An institution like punishment has not been, and could not be, created by a rule utilitarian or a contractualist decision about which laws and institutions to install in a society. One does not choose one's deep responses to other persons, and without them one would have only a pale imitation of the institution of punishment. What is more, although we might, we seldom do consciously choose a solution to a co-operation problem. The size and complication of the set of co-operation problems that a large society presents have meant that our solutions to them have come from many different sources, conscious decision being only a minor one. It also means that one has to be cautious about grand-scale social engineering. It is not that we should not try to introduce much more conscious choice into our social institutions than is there already. It is, rather, that we are not the architects of our social institutions. We inhabit them rather as we would some natural shelter, and both our freedom of movement and our understanding of the structure are limited enough so that we can, at best, only alter them a bit here and there.

These limitations cast more light on the nature of the multi-level structure of moral thinking. We are tempted to think that the practical, everyday level (what I earlier called the practical decision procedure) contains rules and institutions that we choose on the more detached, critical level (what I called the reflective decision procedure). But there is a sense in which institutions cannot be chosen. As we have just seen, an appropriate response to wrongdoing, which is part of the institution of punishment, is not the sort of thing that one chooses. One could, it is true, choose not to have an institution of punishment at all, but that is the kind of decision that means knocking down props of that natural structure the architecture of which we scarcely fully understand.

7. *Retributivism and utilitarianism*

There is a lot to be said for avoiding talk of 'retributivism' and 'utilitarianism' for as long as we can. Each term covers a confusion of views, many of which have attractions; and neither term adds much to our conceptual kit for exploring the middle ground.

Utilitarians, rightly it seems to me, stress that punishment is justified only by being something more than a return for wrongdoing. But they tend then to concentrate on general prudential values (in some versions, simply happiness) and to ignore other values that are especially important to punishment —namely, moral values. If what I have done is wrong, then it is right for me to do what is necessary to avoid doing it again, even apart from the effects on the quality of my life. True, 'reform' is one of their justifications, but they tend to see it as change caused by social pressure, rather than as an agent's autonomously coming to terms with his own wrongdoing. And they generally underestimate the role that desert plays in punishment. By doing that, they turn punishment into a social institution without depths, as if it were entirely the creation of social planners without life before they came on the scene, whereas it is its rich prior life that largely determines what they can do with it.

Retributivists are right, it seems to me, to stress that desert has a central place. Still, it is not the large place assigned it in the Atonement View, nor even the smaller one in the Accountability View. Retributivists misplace desert. It belongs in the core. It is what makes sense of guilt, remorse, and repentance, without which punishment becomes a bloodless imitation of the real thing. One of the strongest arguments for retributivism has always been that it dignifies the person as someone capable of accepting responsibility, whereas utilitarianism demeans the person as one suitable for manipulation. But this argument is no longer available. There are alternatives to retributivism that do not deny moral responsibility. The trouble is that famous classical utilitarians have *sounded* rather toughly determinist,[29] but this is only another example of the baleful legacy of psychological hedonism with its simplistic language of the push-pull of pleasure and pain pay-offs. However, one does not have to give desert moral status to make room for responsibility. One does that just by giving desert its place in the core. And that role for desert is compatible with utilitarianism. On its central claim about desert, indeed, retributivism is wrong. Desert does not require, permit, or prohibit punishment. More generally, although desert is often a perfectly good reason for action, it is never a good moral reason. Moral reasons have a special kind of urgency, which desert has not got.

XIII

DISTRIBUTION

1. *'Distributive' justice*

WE punish, reward, exempt, promote, and elect some persons and not others. But that is not what we usually regard as 'distributive' justice. A transfusion can shift blood from someone who can spare it to someone who needs it. But that is not it either. What we usually have in mind, instead, is distributing material goods and services: food, clothing, shelter, tools, land, raw materials, education, medical treatment, labour. And in a mature industrial society in which land, factories, raw materials—tangible goods generally—become less important in generating wealth and government-granted licences, franchises, and benefits become more important, we also have in mind certain legal powers, titles and claims. And we have in mind, of course, the general wherewithal, money. What about happiness or pleasure? Happiness and pleasure partly turn on how one responds to goods, services, and powers, and one's responses, though affected by what is distributed, cannot themselves be distributed.

All of this is a bit arbitrary. There is no best way to divide off the potential objects of distribution; the division will be in some measure stipulative. I prefer to keep the class fairly narrow: what is up for 'distribution' are holdings: material things, services, certain legal powers, money. One reason for concentrating on holdings is that they specially lend themselves to distribution. They can be easily parted from their holders; they can be amassed in excess of their holder's need; they are easy to shift from person to person. Holdings are, therefore, tempting to redistribute. Another reason for focusing on them is that someone usually claims them as soon as they come on the scene; they often owe their existence, after all, to some person's work. Though holdings, because of their transferability, attract redistribution, they also, because of ownership, especially repel it.

No setting for distribution seems really paradigmatic; settings vary along dimensions all of which seem to matter to what we say about distribution. So each position on one of these dimensions can be seen as a value of a possible variable in the ultimately authoritative distribution function that we must now try to find.

First of all, the nature of the group of persons varies. The group might be a family, or a commune, or a city-state, or nation-state, or the entire population of the world at a given time, or the world population over several generations.[1] Will the moral principles governing distribution not vary as the group varies?

Second, the nature of the holdings varies. Some, such as natural resources, are in effect manna from heaven. Others exist only because certain individuals have put a lot of work into making them. Can principles of distribution apply regardless of how holdings appeared on the scene?

Third, the nature of the economy varies. There are autarkic economies, where people are able, perhaps even forced, to make things for themselves. There are exchange economies with specialization of labour and complex forms of co-operation. It is easy to identify the producer in the first setting but not the second. Will an individual claim to holdings not also depend upon what the methods of production are? Is even the notion of 'property' stable across kinds of economy?

Then the affluence of groups varies. With superabundance, Hume remarks, questions of distributive justice do not even arise.[2] We might find that each of us may take what resources he wishes, leaving as much and as good for the rest. Or we might find that we would leave enough but not as much. Or perhaps, whatever we do, not everyone can survive. Hume also thought that when we get to the other extreme, when persons have to fight for survival, distributive justice is 'suspended'.[3] But the two extremes—superabundance and struggle for survival—are not symmetrical. Plausible principles of distribution just do not apply to superabundance; they do, however, *apply* to desperate scarcity—it is only our psychological capacity to live up to them that characteristically runs out.[4] So once below the level of superabundance will not persons' claims to holdings depend upon how much there is to go around? And are there any principles of distribution that apply to all levels of wealth, from comfortable abundance to desperate scarcity?

The intersection of two or more of these dimensions defines a possible setting for distribution. One setting would be a modestly well-off family. It is tempting to treat the family as a paradigm for all distribution. What should we strive for if not the brotherhood of man? Why not then use in society a principle of distribution close to the one at the heart of the family: from each according to his ability, to each according to his need? Then the bulk of society's assets could be regarded as forming a common stock, and the notion of 'private property' would have only a peripheral part to play. The principle of distribution that mattered would then be what has been called 'patterned' or 'end state', not 'unpatterned' or 'historical'.[5] But at the same time it is most odd to take the family as a general paradigm. There is the obvious problem: why take the brotherhood of man as a political ideal if it is a psychological impossibility?

Another setting for distribution, one that fascinated seventeenth- and eighteenth-century philosophers, is settlers landed on a new continent each of whom can take what resources he can use and leave as much and as good for the rest. In this setting a new principle appears: property. It is not that it is totally missing from families but here for the first time it becomes central. If I take and till a plot of land when the rest of you have perfectly good ones yourselves, most of us would be willing to say that I develop claims that the rest of you do not. While it is easy to see why a family would be taken as the paradigm for distribution, it is harder to see why an autarkic collection of New World settlers would be. Labour seems central to our conception of ownership, and autarkic gatherings provide relatively pure cases of one person's labour, which help to fix our thoughts about ownership. There is that much justification. But it has often been pointed out that there is nothing like seventeenth-century abundance any more. There is very little in the way of autarky either; what is produced now is usually the result of such complex interaction that it is hard to isolate one person's contribution. And what does it help to be clear about just acquisition, when most important original appropriations happened so long ago that we cannot now begin to recover all the information about them that we should need to decide about their justice?[6]

Autarky, because of its inefficiencies, will, where possible, give way to an exchange economy, which presents a new setting for distribution. Exchange usually brings with it the institution of money, which allows storing value and concentrating power in a few hands. All the principles that apply to autarky apply in an exchange economy too. But there are, in addition, the principles that govern agreements. And there are also the standards of fair exchange. Equal respect would require that the parties to the bargain start from equal bargaining positions, and large concentrations of power threaten that. And once there is fair exchange, procedural justice enters.[7] Any group with fair exchange will be prepared to accept that, up to a point, there are fair outcomes that cannot be described in advance—unpatterned ones, ones that are fair merely through being the outcome of a fair procedure. So although 'end-state' principles still apply, 'historical' ones seem to apply now too. Whatever case there is for making the abundant autarkic economy our paradigm applies even more to an exchange economy; the introduction of exchange is a small move towards present reality. But since the move is so small, the case against applies just as strongly too.

The inefficiencies of solitary production are likely to lead to a co-operative economy. Now, let us say, you organize, I prepare the raw material, and he assembles it. As products become more complex, techniques become more important and are borrowed freely from others. Life is better; population gets larger. Soon abundance of resources disappears. What I have inherited gives me a holding, but you arrive on the scene to find nothing left for you to appropriate, let alone as much and as good. What principles apply now? One important addition is fairness in participation. If I voluntarily benefit from co-operation, it would seem that I should not free-ride. But what is striking is the principles that no longer apply at all comfortably. The deepest requirements of equal respect, the

ones that seem to justify ownership, are now unmet: you do
not find as much and as good for you. That hardly reflects
badly on my distant ancestors, who probably satisfied the
Lockean Proviso. Nor does it reflect badly on my nearer
ancestors, who may also have satisfied it. The problem is ours
and in the present: what may well be at fault is my now going
on holding the resources. And products are no longer just *my*
doing, or even yours, mine, his, and hers in identifiable
proportions.[8] Society now makes its own important contribution; so does tradition. Not even the products of thought retain
much purity. A medical researcher might make a discovery of
great commercial value. He might have worked terribly hard
to bring it off. But even so, who trained him? Who moved the
subject to the point where the discovery became possible? Who
built the lab in which he worked? Who runs it? Who pays for
it? Who is responsible for the enduring social institutions that
present the commercial opportunities? One who cleverly
exploits the social framework has both his cleverness and the
framework to thank. In short, life has got not only better but
also so much more complicated that justifications for property,
imported from simpler times, fit awkwardly. Anyway, the
concentrations of wealth and power that a co-operative
economy generates are likely to lead to central government's
exercising, in the name of liberty, more and more control. And
in a mature industrial society services begin to take on as
much importance as manufacture. Land, machines, and raw
materials become rivalled by government-granted licences (for
example, to a doctor to practise), franchises (for example, to
run a television network) and benefits (for example, to the
support of the welfare state) as means of livelihood.[9] Then our
concept of property, developed in the days of the supreme
importance of tangible goods, fits even more tenuously. Why
should we have property rights defending our tangible goods
against invasion and have no comparable rights defending
what are for many of us even more important to our lives? It
cannot be because governments granted the licences, franchises, and benefits; so did they in many cases originally grant
the lands. There is an obvious reason for our taking a
co-operative economy as our paradigm: it is where we are
now. But that is no reason for us to treat it as paradigmatic in

other settings in which distribution also takes place: our families, to take the very small scale, or the world divided between rich and poor nations, to take the very large.

I shall stop there with my sampler of paradigms. A lot of confusion arises from our not appreciating how many and how heterogeneous the paradigms are. Some persons see most goods as ultimately part of society's common stock and so they look for moral principles to use in distributing them fairly.[10] Others see goods as by and large coming into existence with name tags already on them and so they deny that society has any moral right to distribute them at all.[11] Both attitudes are appropriate, but in different settings. And the setting that we are most interested in—a modern, fairly affluent industrialized nation-state—is just the setting in which it is hardest to tell how far either set of attitudes fits. So let us now concentrate just on that setting and ask, Which principles really apply to it? and, Are they moral principles?

2. Role-based principles

There must be *something* that a person can do to earn himself some moral claim on holdings. If so, his claim will rest on what he did; it will be tied to a status that he has and that persons generally do not. But we need, as always, to find what precisely the status is that has these powerful effects.

It cannot be merely 'appropriator'.[12] Even appropriation that satisfies the Lockean Proviso is not enough. Suppose I appropriate a bit of land, leaving as much and as good for the rest of you,[13] but that, because of my constitution, I consume practically nothing. Everyone's equal share, let us say, even when worked, still gives a pretty meagre life, and if the rest of you could use my plot productively you would be an important bit better off. It was reasonable of Locke to add to his Proviso about as much and as good a second Proviso against waste.[14] The two Provisos together, however, reduce the bare act of appropriation to insignificance. What is at work in generating the claim is some such general view as that everyone's well-being matters and matters equally. The act of appropriation on its own seems to be playing no role—not less than a full role but no role at all. Appropriation leaving as much and as good seems more an application of a general rule of assigment of holdings—namely, everyone should have equal holdings for productive use—than an act that generates its own moral claims on them.

Is the relevant status then 'producer'? There is a long tradition in political theory that sees the act of mixing one's labour with resources as the key claim-generating fact. Now, there are ways of interpreting this view that make it quite ridiculous (for example, the one that Nozick guys: 'If I own a can of tomato juice and spill it in the sea . . . do I thereby come to own the sea, or have I foolishly dissipated my tomato juice?').[15] But there are much more sympathetic interpretations. If I collect seed that would otherwise rot and plant it in earth that would otherwise go unused, and do not thereby deplete the soil, then the crop is almost entirely my doing. And it is hard to resist the thought that the more purely a product comes to being all my own work the stronger my claim to it is. What I have a claim to, then, is not the land I have used but the crop, the value that would not have existed but for what I did. It is true that some contributors to the happy outcome —the seed and the use of the land during the growing season—were not my doing, but it would be the meanest dog-in-the-manger attitude to deny me the use of what no one else wanted in the production of what I definitely needed. My labour is in the crop, so in a way I am in it too. We move easily along the path of thought: 'It's my doing; I am in a way in it; it's mine.' This sentiment is natural and deep and worthy of respect. It is a sentiment that, as has been pointed out,[16] has even become well embedded in many languages in an etymological link between the words for 'proper' and 'property'. The sentiment is very likely also to have some evolutionary source; some form of property may be a human correlate of animal territoriality.[17] The labour theory of property can be seen as what much good philosophy is: an attempt to put before us in an accessible, articulate form parts of common sense that are themselves shaped by powerful, natural sentiments.

The weakness of the labour theory is not its ancestry but its scope. It does not get us at all far. If my claim is limited to what does not involve appropriation, I have claim to very little indeed. Even my using land for one growing season constitutes short-term appropriation. No product is purely my own work, devoid of trace of resources that others might have used. What comes closest is the product of thought, say a new technique that I think up on my own, but even then I use food and shelter while I do the thinking. Clearly, I ought to have *some* security of claim on what I need to labour on, but the labour test is largely silent on what my claims would be. If I till and plant land, may I claim the crop or the land? If the land, for how long? Does my power extend to transferring it to someone else? Anyway, we are talking about the modern world and, as we have seen, it is often dauntingly difficult to identify what a final product—even a lone scientist's discovery in his lab—owes to one person all on his own. The pure labour test is too indeterminate in any distributive setting and too tenuously connected with our actual setting. It is not that it has *no* weight: it gives a producer *some* claim on *some* objects in *some* circumstances. It is just that the labour test scarcely advances us beyond the vague intuition from which it starts.

Perhaps there is something behind the labour test that is more determinate. Does the labour test really have a desert test at the back of it? Is it not the mere producing that matters but the desert it creates? The heart of the pure labour theory is the movement of thought, 'It's my doing, so it's mine.' But I doubt that it could be desert at work here,[18] at least in the strict sense of desert centred on actions sufficiently out of the ordinary to attract praise or blame. We should not want claims to holdings to rest on that, or else only the specially meritorious would have them. New World settlers, each harmlessly tilling his plot, may show no special merit to speak of, but they ought to have some claims on holdings. And, in any case, as we saw earlier, merit does not itself have moral force so it cannot confer it.[19] I think that it is only another, broader use of desert that comes into play here. We use 'desert' not only when we think there is special merit, but also when we think merely that something ought to happen. The movement of thought, 'It's my doing, so it's mine', can be construed, 'I did it, so I deserve to have it' (i.e. 'I ought to have it'). This, I think, is the way to understand the argument at the heart of the pure labour theory. It rests not on merit but on pure doing. Desert-*qua*-merit can be the ground of a claim about desert-*qua*-ought. But a claim about desert-*qua*-ought is just the assertion of what ought to be done, not a reason why it ought. Desert-*qua*-merit is not the right kind of backing for the labour test. Desert-*qua*-ought is not backing of any kind.

Since each of these two tests, appropriation and labour, is inadequate on its own, the obvious thing to do is to merge them. Locke, for instance, used not a pure labour test, but one incorporating large elements of appropriation. However, this mixture, though better than either ingredient on its own, does little to cure either the indeterminateness of the pure labour theory or its tenuous relevance to the present. We are still left with the problem of getting beyond the truism that productive users have some claim on some holdings in some circumstances. How do we make these claims more determinate? What is going to make them relevant to the modern world? Role-based considerations are at best the shortest of first steps towards distributive principles. They leave us to take all the rest of the steps in some other way.

3. *Rights-based principles*

We all have a right to minimum material provision—the right to what is necessary to carry out any life plan.[20] What that comes down to, however, is a claim on secure use of goods, not a claim that approaches ownership of them. It could be met without property at all—say, by a sugar-daddy who attaches no strings to his gifts. Also, as we have seen,[21] the notion of *minimum* provision suffers from no small indeterminateness itself, and the resources of a theory of human rights on its own cannot remedy it. Still, minimum provision is clearly a claim on the distribution of holdings.

Does the right to liberty also generate distributive claims? Say that you and I want to strike a bargain with each other. When the bargain benefits us both, it seems gross interference for others to stop us, unless we are harming them.[22] So if we have a claim to secure use of goods, then we have some power over their transfer, and we are on our way to the usual rights of ownership. But whether that is so all turns on the extent of liberty. I argued earlier[23] that our human right is not to a general liberty, so long as no harm is done to others, but only to certain specific liberties, namely to the freedoms necessary to live out one's central life plan. In any case, my freedom to act is not cancelled just by my act's causing harm.[24] For example, the fact that my deciding not to marry Sadie will distress Sadie, even blight her life, does not threaten my right to marry whom I wish. Sadie's liberty does not include the freedom to violate my equally important liberty. But once the necessary conditions for everyone's living out his life plan are met, we move out of the realm of major harms into the realm of relatively minor harms. Now what I do will not affect that crucial matter of whether or not you can make something valuable of your life; that, we are supposing, is already guaranteed. It can only determine just where in the positively valuable range it will fall. Suppose that you want to buy and build on some land, and that you, the seller, and the builder all happily reach agreement. The building, however, will be an intrusion into an area of great natural beauty. Zoning regulations and planning permission do constitute an interference in your deal, but not the sort that infringes your liberty. Once in the realm of relatively minor harms, we have to balance gains and losses. The public loss of amenity may well outweigh further enhancement of your personal resources for living a good life. So, rights give us claims on property no stronger than what can be shown to be essential to living out our central life plan. This takes us back to the minimum material provision. But that requirement seems satisfiable without property rights of *any* strength. If property gets moral backing, it cannot be at as deep a level as human rights. Human rights have to do with the necessary conditions of living a recognizably human existence, and property, whatever importance it may have, does not have *that* kind of importance.[25]

Why not then be content with claims to minimum provision and not look for anything stronger? The Lockean Proviso of as much and as good imports further distributive claims set up by equality. But why not think that, once everyone is up to some minimum acceptable level of well-being, we have satisfied all patterned demands on distribution and where holdings go thereafter may be determined by the

unpatterned demands of fair transaction? But then if I were to
chance upon some minerals on my vast estates that would
greatly improve the quality of life, and in amounts far more
than I and my heirs could ever use, and the rest of you are just
at the minimum acceptable level, then I would do nothing
wrong in hoarding them. And if there were no demands on
distribution except minimum provision, then if, by chance, I
were the first settler to scuttle off the boat, I could do a few
quick calculations and claim vast tracts of land leaving just
enough for the rest of you to toil your way up to the minimum
level. There must, at least in some settings, be distributive
claims arising from equality.

4. *Equality-based principles*

In those rare cases in which social life starts from scratch
—take again a boatload of New World settlers—equal respect
requires equal distribution. In start-from-scratch cases, a
principle of equal distribution might be subject to qualification,
but nonetheless it would dominate the scene. At least, so
virtually all philosophers say. However, many of them go on
quickly to add some such point as this. Other considerations
do indeed soon appear on the scene. The settlers mix their
labour with the land, and this creates special claims. Some
work harder than others, and this creates personal desert. One
freely exchanges with another, and liberty protects the inequalities that inevitably emerge. And labour, desert, and liberty all
push equal distribution well into the background. No doubt,
equality carries over into this more complicated setting in at
least some attenuated form (say, in the idea of a minimum
provision), but other principles now dominate the scene.

However, we have seen that the other principles meant to
push equal distribution into the background do not themselves
have the muscle to do so. Mixing one's labour yields only the
slightest and most indeterminate of claims.[26] Desert has no
moral weight on its own, and if it figures in moral and political
thought it does not do so at any very deep level. And liberty
supports a claim to no more holdings than are necessary for
carrying out a life plan.[27] So equal distribution remains an
important principle even in our actual, complex setting.

What form does this egalitarianism take? I must now draw together what I have said about equality here and there earlier in the book.

There is no *one* moral or political 'principle of equality'. Equality of different things matters at different points in moral and political theory, and we have to keep them straight.[28] At the deepest level, there is the requirement of equal respect—to see things morally is to grant everyone some sort of equal standing. But the notion of equal respect is extremely vague and needs to be made more determinate, for instance through the device of the Ideal Observer or the Ideal Contractor. What is common to all conceptions of equal respect is the belief that some sacrifices of one person for another are allowed but only up to a limit. Different determinations of equal respect place the limit at different points. This gives us a new level of moral theory, the level of determinations of the root notion of equal respect—for example, a contractualist's principles of justice or a utilitarian's principle of maximizing. Also on this second level there are likely to be different kinds of principles that can reasonably be claimed to be principles of equality. There is a principle of equal rights: that everyone possesses equal basic protections and entitlements. There is some sort of principle of equal distribution: for example, that everyone should have equal holdings, unless inequalities would have desirable incentive effects. Then, there would be another level, on which principles are adjusted to the needs of decision on a social scale, where knowledge is short and a government's role is limited by the workings of whatever other social institutions there happen to be. For instance, a society would want to define both rights that go beyond strictly human rights and also principles of distribution responsive to the conditions of the particular society. And it is likely that disagreement about principles at lower levels will give way to a greater measure of agreement at the social level.[29] In short, equality is a multi-level, and within a level a multi-dimensional, notion.

So principles of equality are prone to level-ambiguity. They are also prone to object-ambiguity. We are now interested in principles of equal distribution, but very different views are possible as to what a distribution ought to make equal.

Equality of exactly what? It might be equality of holdings, or of the well-being that the holdings produce, or of only a certain part of well-being such as meeting basic needs, or of only (or perhaps especially) a certain part of basic needs such as needs for basic capabilities of limbs and senses that work, and so on. As we have seen,[30] we have to get behind talk about basic needs and basic capabilities to the importance they have in our lives; it is prudential values that constitute the ultimate consideration. It is true that needs look as if they connect more securely with obligation than mere desires do; basic needs look like the 'bread' of life and mere desires like the 'jam'. But, as we have seen,[31] this appearance is deceptive. No matter what appears on the list of basic needs, there are likely to be persons who want things off the list more than they want things on it. For instance, a group of scholars might well want books for study more than they want exercise equipment for health, and if they see clearly what they are about, the books will not seem like mere 'jam' to them. Once one sees how substantial the values may be that connect with mere desires, it is odd to insist that needs create obligations where desires do not (or create greater ones). That would be to insist that we have an obligation (or a stronger one) to give the scholars what might be of considerably less value to them. If we want to claim that needs have more importance than desires, it is unlikely to be that they have more *moral* importance. It must be a different claim—for example, that needs have more *political* importance. A government might decide to provide wheelchairs and ramps for cripples but not allow any individual cripple to substitute what he might care for more—books, say—to the same value. But a father might well accede to his crippled son's request for books in place of ramps, if he were satisfied that, all things considered, that would make his son's life considerably more valuable. Health is always and mobility is usually a necessary condition of living a good life. But what moral weight has a necessary condition to a good life when achieving it might prevent one from having a good life? It is an indefensible position that gives moral weight to trivial effects on what is only a necessary condition, and no, or less, weight to what can be central to the state for which it is necessary.[32] Disagreement with this conclusion usually rests on a confusion of levels. The standards of distribution for a parent are not likely to be identical to the standards for a government. Needs *generally* trump desires; what is at stake with basic needs generally matters much more than what is at stake with mere desires. Governments will therefore naturally concern themselves with basic needs, which is a demanding enough job on its own, and with mere desires less or not at all.[33]

This assignment to different levels may look a bit too easy. There is a case, of no little strength, for saying that moral judgement—at any level—ought to deal only with the neutral all-purpose means to a good life, with basic needs in that sense. The case for saying so rests, indeed, upon equality. We think that equality of opportunity is not nearly strong enough to satisfy moral demands; in the world as it is, with persons of different genetic and social endowments, it merely lets competition decide who gets what and some persons go to the wall. Equality of opportunity offends our deep sense of equal respect. The fear is that so does equality of well-being.[34] It seems to let in too much—for example, the expensive demands of those dedicated to learning and the arts. You with your modest aims in life should not be pushed aside by me with my resource-hungry aims, as worthy as my aims may be. Our deep sense of equal respect seems to require our staying neutral between conceptions of the good and our equalizing all-purpose means rather than well-being. But, in the end, morality cannot stay neutral. No moral theory could get by entirely on a thin, neutral conception of the good.[35] Perhaps a government could, and should, often stay neutral. But a father, in distributing resources to his children, ought sometimes to take account of the fact that one of them will just squander them. And even a government cannot do its job without taking a view on the relative merits of at least some competing conceptions of the good. It could not decide when its obligations to health care were sufficiently met, unless it made up its mind how valuable other claims on its resources were—for instance, the cultural values of society, its learning and art. This again suggests that we must avoid level-confusion. Some principles fit one level far better than another. We can avoid object-ambiguity partly by avoiding level-ambiguity. Equality of what? It depends on the level.

It is no good arguing over principles of equality unless we are clear what level we are talking about, sometimes even what place within the level. Equality is merely a formal notion: sameness in some respect. Sameness is relevant at many different points in moral theory. There is, in a way, no philosophical topic of 'equality',[36] and the move from egalitarianism or anti-egalitarianism in one level or setting to the same in another is always dubious and often illicit. The debate between egalitarians and anti-egalitarians, everyone would agree, has tended to take place too much at the level of asseveration. Egalitarians have the upper hand, because equality, in the form of a deep principle of equal respect, is clearly central to all morality, and it is easy to slip from that relatively uncontroversial basic-level egalitarianism to more contentious forms of egalitarianism at higher levels. In contrast, anti-egalitarians often argue as if all that they need to do is to define their non-egalitarianism, as if egalitarianism wins the day only for lack of alternative. But the most intuitively plausible position on this matter is egalitarianism in some levels and settings, and inegalitarianism elsewhere. But to know where to be egalitarian, and where not, requires a well-worked-out account of equality, starting with the deepest notion of equal respect.

What then does equal respect require? As we have seen,[37] it does not require an uncrossable line, a line protecting one's unbargainable personhood. It does not require, as contractualists think it does, maximin. It does not even require that, if possible, everyone be brought up to, or not be pushed below, some minimum acceptable level. These restrictions are all too strong. The natural thing to do, in response to their excessive strength, is to look for some weaker restriction which is still an absolute cut-off to maximizing trade-offs—this one, for instance: in distributions between two persons one of whom is worse off than the other at all levels of goods the worse off should get at least not less. Weak as this is, it is still too strong. Surgeons deciding who will get the transplant often rightly ignore it. There is no absolute cut-off on maximizing trade-offs. In view of that it is natural to change tack and to suggest that equality of distribution is one among several same-level principles, a principle of maximizing well-being perhaps being another. Equality then imposes not a cut-off on maximizing trade-offs but a counterweight to them. But this model fails too.[38] In small scale interpersonal dealings—say, a surgeon deciding whom to save—the trade-offs that are morally allowable are largely, perhaps entirely, determined by maximum well-being.

All of that is just drawing together what I have argued earlier. Our current question is, Are there equality-based principles of distribution? We have to avoid level-ambiguity. We are now interested in distribution on the social scale, in a modern, fairly affluent industrial economy. And that, I think, is the level that most of us have in mind when we talk about 'distribution'. The state is now the big force in distribution; the important disputes these days are about what governments should do.

If, as nearly everyone agrees, the principle of equal distribution applies in start-from-scratch settings, then it applies in our present-day setting. None of the moral considerations meant to supplant it—mixing labour, desert, liberty —manage to do so. One obvious feature of the large social scale is plurality of agencies of distribution, so in a society with a tradition of family responsibility, churches, and private charities, the government will tend to operate on the large scale. Another obvious feature is the government's lack of knowledge of individual utility functions, and for that reason governments will often have to treat persons as if they all had about the same needs and capacities. Yet another feature, if the society is unregimented, is that persons will have very different aims in life. In these necessarily rough deliberations, nearly all of us would be willing to use the same principle: that we should equalize holdings. And it would be a particular sort of holdings, namely all-purpose means, that we should distribute, not out of moral respect for neutrality between differing conceptions of the good life but out of ignorance of individual differences and a belief that there will be plenty of them. Even a utilitarian would accept the principle; if everyone has about the same needs and capacities and it is all-purpose means that we distribute and Diminishing Marginal Utility applies, then to maximize is to equalize. We would start off, then, with a principle of equal distribution of all-purpose means.

Next we would start qualifying. There would be an incentive qualification. Every plausible principle of equality grows out of the root thought that everyone matters and matters equally. So to stress only the formal features of distribution is to recall the *equally* but to forget the *matters*. It would obviously not do to reduce everyone to the same level of misery. There is a quantitative concern in the deep notion of equal respect, which both tells us how to take 'equal distribution' and prompts us to qualify it. If an inequality would work as an incentive to make the worst off better off, it should be allowed. Then there would be a non-envy qualification. If an inequality would make the better off still better off without depriving the worse off it too should be allowed. There would be a perfectionist qualification. Governments should not be entirely neutral between conceptions of the good; some goods constitute the central cultural values of society. Although subsidies to art and learning benefit some persons, often the already better off, more than others, they should be allowed. And finally there would have to be some sort of limited utilitarian qualification. The package of equal holdings is unlikely to give the crippled and ill as good a life as it gives the average citizen. Certain kinds of person should get bonus holdings. And even normal persons could sometimes come under this qualification. In those special circumstances in which a government does know something about individual utility functions, then it would be a waste to deny extra to those who have worthy but expensive aspirations when others can achieve their aspirations with less.

No doubt these qualifications would then attract qualifications. All of them would attract what could be called, after a prominent member of a certain set of values, the fraternity qualification. Equality of holdings measures outcomes in terms of material goods and services. But some prudential values are little affected by our holdings—for instance, the quality of our personal relations. If inequalities in wealth are of any size, they will, by dividing society into the powerful and the weak, destroy its sense of fraternity. What one means here by 'fraternity' is not easy to pin down. It is sometimes used of the relation of granting another person equal respect. This is *the* moral relation between persons and is already taken accout of in the moral point of view. But 'fraternity' is also used of a kind of free, easy, naturally concerned relation between persons. It is a relation that not only makes moral relations more natural but also makes life better. It is yet another but also an important prudential value, and as such needs to be balanced against those prudential values that are enhanced by holdings.[39] What is worrying about a society guided by a principle of equal holdings along with an incentive qualification is that it seems to regard holdings and the values they promote as all the values there are, or at least all that a state need be concerned with. But they are not. And who better than the state to concern itself with such large scale values as fraternity?

These are, then, the equality-based principles of distribution that apply to our present-day setting—the principle of equal holdings of all-purpose means with its nimbus of qualifications.

5. *One setting and its principles*

How should we apply these principles—role-based, rights-based, and equality-based—to a modern, fairly affluent industrial society? Role-based principles are particularly elusive. When one tries to pin them down, they slip away into considerations of either rights or equality. What precisely is the obligation-generating role? Is it 'mixer of labour' or 'productive user' or something not yet described? In a way, the precise description does not matter. When resources are plentiful, we need a way to parcel them out. And when persons are more or less alike, an obvious way is to give control to whoever can productively use the resources, leaving roughly the same for others. Mixing labour with them is generally both a sign of productive use and a strong emotional link which makes their assignment obvious and natural. But this is largely an appeal to equal distribution; mixing labour and productive use are doing little work at any deep level of justification. And the idea of mixing one's labour owes much of its power to our feeling that, through our labour, we become in some sense part of what we make, and that therefore the inviolability of persons gets transferred in some measure to things. It does not matter that I am part of what I make in only a metaphorical, perhaps even quite strained, sense. The inviolability of myself is connected with my right to make something out of my life, and in virtue of that right I should be granted some degree of control over resources. This line of argument gives a basis for control of resources and a limit to it. It explains the need for a Locke-like Proviso that I must leave what the rights of others demand for them. And it explains why some of the things I mix an enormous amount of labour with, say my children, I can never own. I cannot control, in the name of the inviolability of my self, what would violate another's self. But here an appeal to 'mixing labour' turns into an appeal to rights.

This reduces the list to two: rights-based and equality-based principles. It is not that a philosopher treats this as a list of the material out of which he then constructs distributive rules for his society. That would again be the mistake of seeing the philosopher as the architect of social institutions and the institutions themselves as constructed out of purely philosophical materials.[40] The distributive rules of any actual society are made from far more varied materials. One important material is deep human sentiment. We are people of limited altruism; we will work for ourselves and for those close to us but not for just anybody. We are people who naturally enough see ourselves in what we make. Even though the moral significance of mixing one's labour is obscure, its emotional force is clear, and that is enough to make certain possible distributive rules salient. And the sentiment is entirely appropriate; in some sense, obscure though it may be, I am in what I make, and to ignore that is to ignore me. Mixing one's labour matters more in the genesis of distributive rules than in their justification. Another important kind of material is the social and economic relations that we find ourselves in. We are not a tribe; we are not linked hierarchically by personal ties. In the early industrial period there was no powerful central government and few of the political institutions that would make a welfare state even a possibility. Another material is the solutions that we come up with to Prisoner's Dilemmas and related cases. We desperately need institutions that encourage co-operation. Another material is what we think will prove productive of well-being. And to some extent, though probably relatively small, our moral beliefs no doubt also go to shape our actual distributive rules.

It is not that solutions to Prisoner's Dilemmas and other cases get us, just by themselves, to a determinate set of distributive rules. Many different sets would do equally well as solutions. Nor for the same reason, do human sentiments move us much along the way towards determinate rules. What take us to a determinate outcome are probably the influence of economic and social relations, considerations of efficiency, and no doubt also historical contingencies that I have not even listed. The full causal story does not matter to us now. Some such forces have shaped the distributive rules that we in modern Western industrial societies have: our mix of government economic regulation, taxation, welfare state, and a large measure of private property. Our social institutions have already been built, largely out of non-philosophical material. A philosopher arrives late on the scene. His job is to assess what has arisen perfectly well without him.

When we turn to that job, two facts strike us. Economic relations have become so complicated and resources so unplentiful that considerations of mixing one's labour scarcely any longer fit. And governments now have the power and the institutions to minister to needs that previously, for lack of alternative, could only be met privately; we could now, if we wished, adopt a principle for social distribution from the family paradigm, perhaps such as 'From each according to his ability, to each according to his needs.' What generated many of our present distributive rules can no longer justify them. Many of them are glaringly obsolete.

Our rights-principle will do some of the job of assessment. Institutions must ensure the minimum material provision. But that gives us only a moral floor and leaves unassessed everything above it. For that further job of assessment we have the principle of equal holdings with its array of qualifications. However, those principles in effect leave the field largely to considerations of well-being. We should have to decide about the value of incentives and their damage to fraternal relations.

We should have to decide what degree of private property most enhanced the quality of life. What sorts of property rights are most economically efficient? Does diffusion of economic power prevent concentration of political power? How plastic is human motivation? Would a change from private property to communal property bring the psychological changes that would make the new institutions in the end more beneficial? I shall not try to answer any of those questions, which are both difficult and familiar. It is their nature that now most concerns us, and it is clear that they raise issues that can be brought within the ambit of well-being. There would also always be a place on a social scale for a principle of equal holdings, no matter how much qualified. And the assessment of distributive rules cannot be carried on independently of their consequences for other rights, such as political liberties. So our assessment should have to balance rights against one another and especially against considerations of general well-being. On the social scale central rights such as minimum provision, autonomy, liberty, would have an entrenched, protected place. But on the deepest level of moral assessment we should have to go behind rights to the values that they protect and be prepared to trade off these values against one another and against well-being, in the way that we have already seen in the earlier discussion of rights.[41]

6. *A glance at another setting*

What principles apply to distributions between nations?[42] The people of a neighbouring nation, hit by famine, appeal to us for help. Let us make the story as simple as possible. If we help them, let us suppose, we are not just promoting worse famine later.[43] And this is not a nation we have exploited, nor have we profited from another nation's exploitation; its trouble, let us say, was that it was too poor a nation to be worth anyone's exploiting.[44] And their famine was not the result of idleness or incompetence on their part; their ancestors simply did not get as much and as good.[45] So with the failure of the Lockean Proviso, the justifications of property seem to get no grip at all. The other principles that are prominent in autarkic, exchange, and co-operative economies—fidelity to agreements, fair bargaining, fair participation, and co-operation—also lose relevance.

One principle that still applies, of course, is the right to minimum material provision.[46] And despite the failure of the Lockean Proviso, property in a way still applies. Someone like Robert Nozick, who makes the Lockean Proviso a necessary condition of property, simply has to stop talking about 'property' in the present case.[47] But our actual concept of property, which is a legal notion largely fixed by considerations of efficiency, is more complex and more flexible than that. We allow some weight to the argument 'It's our doing, so it's ours', and also to the protection of successful co-operation. We have the surplus that our neighbours are now eyeing, partly because we are successful co-operators. But you and I co-operate for our own benefit. It is too facile to argue that we have goods that we can give to others, if the distribution destroys the conditions necessary for the production of the goods. And we cannot simply absorb our neighbours into our co-operative community, if co-operation requires that there be a fair measure of values, expectations, and standards of behaviour in common between co-operators.[48]

Then there is the connected point that co-operation is greatly enhanced if the parties are likely to have repeated encounters with one another. Defection in iterated, few-person Prisoner's Dilemmas is discouraged by a healthy risk of retaliation the next time round. So obligations between persons in different communities have much less backing than obligations in small communities—less backing not only by sentiments of affection but also, perhaps even more important, by self-interest. But though this fact may go a long way towards explaining why we make obligations to those distant from us less stringent than obligations to those close, it does little to justify it. It would justify it only if moral reasons depended for their force on their reducibility to internal reasons or to self-interest. But they do not.

This brings us to another important principle: the claim of special relations. A government has obligations to its own citizens that it does not have to its neighbours. As it stands, that point, though undeniable, does not have much strength. A government is an institution consisting of rights and obligations, but it, like any institution, stands in need of moral sanction, and it may receive it only in a modified form. But the claims of special relations can be put without reference to governments. Our government is an agent for us, for co-operators. We have a claim on the benefits of our co-operation that not everyone has, a claim arising from our having been the ones who produced it. But labour supports no claim unless as much and as good is left. Our neighbours can invoke the fatal objection that they never asked us to labour, and that if they had had the opportunity they would have been just as willing to labour as we have been.

So the point about special claims is likely to change into a point about the scope of morality. It is likely to come down to the claim that it is no good demanding of the human frame what it cannot deliver. I am motivated to co-operate by the prospects of benefits for myself and those I care about. I am willing to make sacrifices for you, a fellow co-operator, to get you to co-operate. But does our motivation just run out if we are asked to make sacrifices for starving neighbours well outside the co-operative circle?

How great a sacrifice can morality ask of us? No one denies that it can ask us to help, where the help is great and the sacrifice small. But then this might be the more testing case where what is needed to save our neighbours' lives is a sacrifice that would blight our own life prospects. Can the human frame deliver so much? Many say that in general it cannot, and that therefore, though such sacrifices would be admirable, they are not morally obligatory. But there is an evasiveness about calling persons who make such large sacrifices 'saints' or 'heroes'; putting people on pedestals not only honours them but also keeps them at a morally comfortable distance. The only defensible form of the requirement that moral demands fit the human frame is the relatively weak one that it must make sense for us to work at them, to see them as relevant ideals.[49] In any case, many moral principles already incorporate concessions to human capacities. Moral theory cannot ignore the importance of extra-moral human institutions. It has to recognize their natural genesis from deep features of human nature. We can use moral grounds to amend and even to reject an institution. But if the institution serves an important purpose, connects with something deep in human nature, and has no easy substitute, then we shall probably be limited in how much we can change it. Property is one such institution. When a person considers producing something, he weighs the cost and benefit. If there is no net benefit why should he sweat to produce it? And he usually measures his benefit, for good moral reasons we shall come to in a moment, in terms of benefit to himself or to certain persons near to him. So the existence of the product depends upon his control of its destination. The natural transition, 'It's my doing, so it's mine', is natural in part because it acknowledges the place of control in the existence of the product. Another such institution is parenthood. One of the most important prudential values is deep personal attachment, and one of the most important attachments is a parent to his child. Once one has made such a commitment, it changes the whole direction of one's deliberation. One will no longer reason occasion by occasion and ask, What would maximize well-being? And institutions interlock. One cannot assess each institution in isolation from the rest. Parenthood links with property. A commitment to particular persons alters one's motivation. It gives one a reason to produce things, if one can control their destination. We probably could not successfully change these institutions in any thoroughgoing, revolutionary way. And we probably have no moral reason to do so.

7. *How are the principles structured?*

What are the deepest level principles, the principles underlying distribution in any setting?

The principles that apply in a modern industrial state are minimum provision, promotion of well-being, and equality of all-purpose means (with all of its qualifications). So, if the many-sided practical arguments about, for instance, incentives and protections of political rights come out in a certain way, then property rights are likely also to be prominent in this setting. But now take a different setting. The principles that apply between rich nations and poor are somewhat different; minimum provision and promotion of well-being carry over, but property fits less well. With the failure of the Lockean

Proviso in this international setting, a lot of the backing for property rights disappears, and control over holdings is relevant only indirectly through various considerations of incentive. What this suggests is that certain principles—for instance, property rights and equality of all-purpose means —are not ground-floor. Property loses grip in the international setting and never had much in the small-scale family setting. Furthermore, equality of all-purpose means gets its point from the largeness of the social scale. As we have seen, it loses relevance in most small-scale settings. So property and equality of all-purpose means are, I would propose, political principles, principles for the large, social scale; they are not, at any deep level, moral principles. That is no demotion for them; depth is not the same as importance.

Take the case of property. What apparently moral rationale there is for property—mixing labour, productive use—allows us to take only the smallest first step towards determinate property rights: it supports some control over some holdings in some circumstances. All the major work to make property rights determinate is left to practical considerations: the effects of property rights on well-being and on human rights.[50] So many criticisms of property rights, Marx's for instance, can be easily accommodated within that practical debate. Do the property rights of capitalism dehumanize both work and enjoyment? Well, appeals to liberty, autonomy, and human dignity can all be accommodated in a good prudential value theory. So there can be no use of property rights as if they were moral rights at some deep level, to block genuinely fundamental moral influences on distribution. This would be to misunderstand what kind of moral work goes into producing determinate property rights. The work is done by the sort of deliberation about human rights (and the values behind them) and well-being that we saw earlier in the chapter on rights.[51] Obviously if the work is done by rights and well-being, then considerations of rights and well-being will be able to modify any details of the property rights that owe their existence to them.

There are three important principles that put in an appearance in all distributive settings: minimum provision, promotion of well-being, and some form of equality. I have just argued that certain principles on the large social scale do not hold on the small interpersonal scale. But that is not to suggest that small is deep and large superficial. What we are after are the principles that hold on all scales. Of course, that search may just be misconceived. Why think that there are any? Or if there are some, why think that they are particularly deep? Clearly one is entitled to neither presumption. One has to look. One has to work out a substantive theory and then see whether there are indeed ubiquitous principles and whether the ubiquitous support the non-ubiquitous. And this requires having a substantive theory of prudential values as well. In other words, one has to see what structures the values and principles themselves display.

Think of determinate property rights once again and ask what supports them. In the last two centuries two traditions have dominated the assessment of property.[52] The British utilitarian tradition assesses it in instrumental terms; forms of property are good or bad depending upon their social effects, such as security and incentive. The Continental tradition assesses it largely in terms of the growth and flourishing of the self; Hegel thought that self-realization was enhanced by fairly traditional forms of owning and exchanging, while Marx, on the contrary, thought that capitalist ownership degraded the self, made it thing-like. But these two traditions are really only one. They both approach the assessment of property with the critical apparatus of prudential values. They look like separate traditions because classical utilitarians confined prudential values to happiness without making quite clear what the boundaries of happiness were, and most of us value things besides, even more than, what in any ordinary sense we should call our happiness.[53] In particular, we value our humanity, our dignity as self-determining agents; we greatly value our autonomy to choose and liberty to carry out our own life plans. These are all, I have already argued,[54] properly regarded as prudential values. So the terms of assessment of both these traditions should be brought within the single framework of well-being.

What more should we bring in to assess property? We might appeal to equality of holdings or to the right to minimum provision. But they both can be met by very different sets of property rights, and so give us little to go on in assessing any particular set. We might appeal to certain political rights—for instance, the right to have an equal voice in social decisions. We might find a link between certain fairly strong property rights and certain protections of political voice. If so, then we should have to weigh these political rights against the prudential values that also figure in the assessment of property. That is a sort of weighing that I discussed earlier[55] and that I shall come back to in a moment.

Think now of equality of all-purpose means, and ask the question that we just asked about property. What supports the principle? The principle is plausible only along with its array of qualifications. The qualifications are motivated by strong quantitative considerations. For instance, one qualification allows deviations from equality if they make everyone better off, or even if they make some better off at no cost to the rest. Another qualification allows deviations if they improve the general welfare, even if, for instance, the gain is in non-vital interests (say, subsidy for the arts) and the loss is in literally vital interests (say, road safety). There is the apparently non-quantitative qualification that restricts deviations from equality in the name of fraternity, but even fraternity, in this context, is best understood as a prudential value and so is to be weighed in a quantitative way against more material prudential values such as wealth—we have, as always, to decide where greater value lies. So there is a strong element of maximizing well-being in all of the qualifications. The important question is, Do considerations of well-being in effect take over? Is the principle of equality of all-purpose means allowed a place on the political level only because it too finds a justification in maximum well-being?

Well, the case that we have found for equality of *all-purpose means* works only on the social scale. However, we cannot confine deliberation, even on the social scale, to all-purpose means. We have to get behind them to a measure of the importance that they, and other things, have in our lives. The ultimately authoritative deliberation goes on in terms of prudential values.[56] And we have seen that *equality* of all-purpose means (or of well-being, for that matter) imposes no cut-off on trade-offs except for this: that persons are to be treated equally except when deviations produce greater gain than loss.[57] The most plausible model in which equality is independent of maximum well-being is the model of same-level principles—for example, a principle of equality of well-being and a principle of maximum well-being that have to be weighed against each other. On this model we should expect equality to show up on the political level justified not by maximum well-being but by the deep level principle of equality. But, as we have seen, there is no such deep level principle. The circumstances of the social scale make equality a dominant principle and its qualifications limited in power. But what determines its dominance and the scope of its qualifications is maximum well-being. So on the political level equality is indeed a consideration to be weighed against, and to qualify, the promotion of wealth and other of the more material elements of well-being. The model of same-level principles does fit there. But on the moral level, below not only the political level but also the level of an individual's practical and reflective decision procedures,[58] equality is not a consideration that competes with well-being. On this level equality is equal respect, the moral point of view. Equal respect has weight; well-being has weight; but they do not have weight on the same scale. Equal respect is not the competitor of well-being, but its regulator. Equal respect is the principle governing trade-offs between different persons' well-being. It is the principle: treat equally except when gain is greater than loss.

Think now of the last of the three principles. What supports the right to minimum material provision? As we have seen, human rights protect a certain kind of value. In the case of this right, what is protected is the value attached to our carrying out an autonomously chosen life-plan.[59] The minimum provision is defined as the necessary material provision for our being able to do so. But the value that we attach to our doing so is prudential; it gets its value from what it contributes to making a life, seen simply from the point of view of the person who lives it, a good one. This value is to be weighed, in the way we saw earlier,[60] against other prudential values attaching to rights, such as autonomy and liberty, and all remaining prudential values. And the ultimately authoritative weighing is the moral one: equality except when gain is greater than loss.

Two general points emerge from thinking about distribution. One is the multi-level structure that its principles display. Property rights, for instance, are high storey and cannot be used, as some conservative political theorists use them,[61] to restrict what is on the ground floor. If, say, a freak storm wipes out your crop and not mine, then even though you had as much and as good as I, since the point of the Lockean Proviso is to recognize your equal claim to a good life, I must help you. Property rights have to be limited by such considerations, because no rights are so powerful as to override these central values. The only way to miss this point is to have no sense of what a substantive theory of rights is like. The second point is a specific instance of the first. There is no one principle of equality; principles of equality crop up on many levels. What we need in moral and political philosophy more than anything else is to identify them and to plot their relations to one another.

NOTES

CHAPTER ONE

1. Bentham's precursors generally spoke of 'pleasure' or 'happiness'. Hume used 'utility', though more narrowly than Bentham. See the discussion in Sidgwick 1907, bk. 4, ch. III, sect. 1, n. 2. Bentham seems to have given 'utility' its wide modern sense. Mill claims the dubious credit for the term 'utilitarian'; see *Utilitarianism*, ch. II, n. to para. 1. It avoids, he says, 'tiresome circumlocution'; but that hardly justifies its own bulk, ugliness, and inaccuracy. It could have been bulkier; Bentham once thought of proposing 'eudaimonologian'; see Baumgardt 1952, p. 505.

2. J. S. Mill, *Utilitarianism*, ch. II, para. 2. See also J. Bentham, *An Introduction to the Principles of Morals and Legislation*, ch. I, sects. 2 and 3. Neither of them was aware that the words 'happiness' and 'pleasure' are too vague and slippery to be much of an explanation. And Bentham, having used 'pleasure' and 'pain' to explain 'utility', immediately turned around and undid whatever specificity the ordinary use of those terms lent in adding, 'By utility is meant that property in any object, whereby it tends to produce benefit, advantage, pleasure, good, or happiness . . .' (sect. 3).

3. Jones 1964, pp. 655–6.

4. Sidgwick 1907, esp. pp. 111–12, 127–9, 396–8. For a good discussion of Sidgwick's account see Schneewind 1977, pt.2, esp. chs. 11–12.

5. Nozick 1974, pp. 42–5.

6. I talk here in terms of 'seeming to value', which is enough to make the retention of mental states look puzzling, but I shall go on to argue that this appearance is not misleading; see ch. I sect. 6; ch. II sects. 3, 4, 6; ch. III sect. 7; ch.IV sects. 3, 5, 6.

7. Sidgwick is well aware of this line of thought, but his objection to it is uncharacteristically thin. See Sidgwick 1907, pp. 398–402.

8. But for acute criticism from economists, see Vickers 1975; Sen 1980–1, sects.3 and 6; Hahn and Hollis 1979, Introd.

9. See Morton 1980, pp. 135–8, where, following Freud, he contrasts the 'object' and the 'aim' of a desire: 'It isn't as if the desire says "I want *that*", and then to satisfy it one has to produce just that. Rather, it says, "I want something, and here's what it must do for me".' (p.139.)

10. Hobbes sees something like this as characteristic of desire generally: '. . .there is no such *finis ultimus*, utmost aim, nor *summum bonum*, greatest good, as is spoken of in the books of the old moral philosophers . . . Felicity is a continual progress of the desire, from one object to another;

the attaining of the former, being still but the way to the latter. The cause whereof is, that the object of man's desire, is not to enjoy once only ...but to assure for ever ... I put for a general inclination of all mankind, a perpetual and restless desire of power after power, that ceaseth only in death.' (Hobbes *Leviathan* ch.XI.) Tibor Scitovsky discusses this feature of consumer desire in Scitovsky 1976.

11. That is, I do not think that we can stop with faults of fact and logic. Richard Brandt disagrees. See his account, worked out with exemplary rigour, of rational desires as desires that 'survive maximal criticism by facts and logic'; Brandt 1979, p. 10, but see chs. II–VII *passim*. What he says about the criticism of desires seems to me correct as far as it goes but incomplete, and thus it puts too much stress on information, as if all that criticism of desires needs, besides logic, is facts, the more the better.

12. See e.g. Kenny 1973, p. 61.

13. I owe the example to Derek Parfit.

14. Criticizing desires is not far short of what we mean by making sense of life. There has been a long tradition of complaint against utilitarianism that it puts *happiness* where *the meaning of life* belongs. The latest is David Wiggins, in Wiggins 1976, esp. p. 332. But he takes the notion of 'utility' to be more closely tied to Hume-like accounts of action and deliberation than it need be. And he overlooks the role that global desires and plans of life play in 'utility'; they shift the concept far closer to what Wiggins means by 'meaning' than to what he means by 'happiness'.

15. See Glover 1977, pp. 63–4.

16. I prefer 'informed' to 'rational', a word sometimes used with much the same qualification in mind. 'Rational' is often used of adapting means to ends, and seems to me to fit less well both simple tastes and deliberation about ends. 'Informed' seems to me to have more scope. (But, then, 'rational' would also become a technical term, and one could stipulate a broad sense for it too.)

17. This stark view still gets attributed to utilitarianism, e.g. in Wiggins 1976, p.340.

18. This builds enough strength into the notion of 'informed' for us not to need to resort to formulas such as 'ought to desire' or 'have reason to desire'. For instance (to use an example I am about to introduce) suppose my doctor tells me that I shall die if I do not lay off drink. Well, I might listen, agree, but not even desire to lay off it. Can I not be informed but foolish? So how could well-being be fulfilment merely of *informed* desires? 'Informed' requires more than listening and believing. I should also have to realize fully what is at stake. I should have to appreciate what losing those extra years of life means; and I should have to keep in mind just how pleasant a drink is. It is only desires formed in response to that amount of appreciation that are informed. Or take a different sort of case. Suppose a recluse accepts all the information that we give him about the joys of human companionship and even decides

that he would be better off being more gregarious. Yet he might, because his desire for solitude is very stubborn, accept all the information and not change his desires. Again, informed, it seems, but foolish—or, rather, unfortunate. But we should describe the case more fully. What might make his desire so stubborn? A number of things could, so let us take one possible explanation: people frighten him and to avoid the anxiety he shuns company. Then, it is not that he does not *desire* companionship; it is just that he also desires not to be anxious. In his particular case, the two desires are incompatible and the second is greater (and might remain greater when he is fully informed) than the first. Weakness of will is yet another kind of case, which I discuss in the text. See also ch. II n. 29.

19. The stress on 'informed' desire may seem to make the desire account incurably anthropocentric, not extendible to animals, and so in that respect distinctly inferior to a mental state account. Indeed is any account of well-being acceptable in moral and political theory if it is not so extendible?

My concern is with the notion simply of *human* well-being. Still, I do not see any obstacle to an informed desire account's applying to animals too. It does not take human powers of intellect for a desire to be 'informed'. It needs only that the desire be shaped by appreciation of the nature of its object. Pains, even for animals, cover a wide spectrum, from physical (being stepped on) to psychological (being terrified). Pains get their status as pains not solely from their phenomenological feel but also from their status in a life—that they are to be avoided, to be stopped, and so on. So part of their status as pains brings in desire and action. It may seem that it brings in desire only in a very extended sense of the term. But then no informed desire account limited only to humans will be plausible without also using a similarly extended sense of desire. The relevant sort of desire does not have to be held antecedently to its fulfilment (a human can enjoy something, want to have it continue or return, that he never knew he would enjoy, or even knew existed). The relevant sort of desire does not have to be conscious (one can be made better off by something, e.g. relaxation, that one has never focused sharply enough to form a wish for). And so on.

20. I owe the example to Roslind Godlovitch.

21. If this is the best interpretation of 'strength', then many objections to utilitarianism are wide of the mark—for instance, objections to its reducing all preferences, from ideals at one end of the spectrum to tastes at the other, to a single scale of 'intensity' (see, e.g., Sen 1980, p. 211 and Sen and Williams 1982, p. 8). Utilitarianism is not committed to such reductions. And whether enough tastes can swamp ideals depends entirely upon the structure that informed desires display. There is nothing in the informed desire account either that commits one to a reduction of all prudential values to a single substantive super-value called 'utility' (see ch. II sect. 4) or even that rules out certain forms of incommensurability (see ch. V).

22. Richard Brandt thinks not, and he makes a strong case. See Brandt 1979, ch.VII, sect. 3, esp. pp. 146–8 and ch. XIII, sect. 1; also Brandt 1982, esp. sects.8–10. For discussion of Brandt's charge see Sen 1980–1, sect. 4. For a rich discussion of this and related issues see Elster 1982.

23. See ch. VII sect. 5. The trouble that Brandt has in mind arises from a person's having conflicting rankings over time with no super ranking to resolve them. But the intrapersonal case of two rankings, mine now and mine later, is formally similar to an interpersonal case of two rankings, mine and yours. There is no super ranking in the latter case either, but we need not fall back on a mental state account. Another way is to go beyond simple ordinal rankings, either, say, by appeal to the test of potential Pareto improvement or by the adoption of some sort of cardinal scale of utility, with comparability. Unless such ways are closed, which I think they are not, Brandt's worry may be met. These too are issues that I shall return to when I talk about measurement (ch. VII).

24. The first example is Derek Parfit's, the next two are L. W. Sumner's, in whose book, *Abortion and Moral Theory*, there is a very good discussion; see Sumner 1981, esp. p. 183.

25. I shall not go on listing troubles for the desire account, though there are others. For instance, it has difficulty distinguishing between selfish and selfless action. An act of self-sacrifice has to be intentional; so it will be the object of an informed desire; so it will, when fulfilled, increase the agent's welfare. Self-sacrifice is transmuted, by this philosophers' stone, into self-interest. See Overvold 1980, Overvold 1982, Brandt 1982. This is an instance of the more general trouble that I have mentioned: informed desire spreads to objects outside the bounds of well-being. An adequate solution to the general problem ought to solve this one too.

26. I model this account on one defended in Sumner, 1981 ch. 5, sect. 21; but I have also benefited from long discussions with Sumner during his leave in 1982–3, when he was a valuable addition to the Oxford philosophical community.

27. It is not that this is a utilitarian's only hope, though I think that it is the only good one. Amartya Sen has recently asked whether we really need regard these various accounts of 'utility' as exclusive alternatives (Sen 1980–1, pp. 203–4). What instead we should do, he suggests, is to regard 'utility' as a plural notion, a vector of many different considerations. Suppose someone prefers bitter truth to comforting delusion, but is palmed off with the latter. We feel sorry for him. Then later he learns that it was all a deception. We feel sorrier for him. Why not take our sympathy as an indicator of the person's utilities? Bare desire fulfilment and experienced desire fulfilment are both relevant, and to insist on a choice between them, Sen says, seems 'arbitrary and uncalled for'. Similarly for the other hard choices we have been considering, for example, the choice between actual and informed desires.

But the doubt about Sen's eclectic approach is that if one adopted it one would have to supply some weighting for these various vectors when they merge in decision, and the weighting would have to be neither arbitrary nor left to haphazard intuitions. In this respect, the non-eclectic approaches are superior. The informed-desire account, for instance, encompasses Sen's various vectors and attaches weight to them in a manner motivated by the spirit of the notion of well-being. When the person we alluded to learns that it was all deception, his experienced hurt counts too, Sen says. But so it does on a desire account, because few want to be hurt. Similarly, for the choice between actual and informed desires; a plausible desire account gives weight to both. If the lacuna in Sen's notion of 'plural utility' is properly filled, it is likely to lead in the end to one of the other accounts. It may not be that all elements that he has in mind for his 'plural utility' will be accommodated, but perhaps all that the notion of 'well-being' should be made to carry will be.

CHAPTER TWO

1. The introduction of this restriction on the desire account marks a break with decision theory. F. P. Ramsey, in his famous paper 'Truth and Probability' (in Ramsey 1931, p. 173), which laid the foundations of decision theory, cautioned: 'It must be observed that this theory is not to be identified with the psychology of the Utilitarians, in which pleasure had a dominating position. The theory I propose to adopt is that we see things that we want, which may be our own or other people's pleasure, or anything else whatever ...' The break with 'the psychology of the Utilitarians' seems to me right, but the 'anything else whatever' seems to me to go too far in the opposite direction.

2. See Feinberg 1980, esp. pp. 173–6.

3. Aristotle took the notion of posthumous harm seriously, even though his notion of *eudaimonia* is loftier and more immune to accidents of fortune than 'well-being' is. ' ... if we deny that a dead man is happy ... even this admits some dispute; for it is popularly believed that some good and evil—such as honours and dishonours, and success and disasters of his children and descendants generally—can happen to a dead man, in as much as they can happen to a live one without his being aware of them' (*Nicomachean Ethics*, 1100a15–22). For his own cautious, unclear conclusion, see bk. 1, ch. XI.

4. I borrow the example of slander as a posthumous harm from Joel Feinberg; see his excellent discussion in Feinberg 1980, ch. 3.

5. So I believe now. But I began some years ago so convinced of the opposite that I took it as a test of adequacy that an account avoid this conclusion. I cannot find any conclusion on this subject that is entirely comfortable. A radical one that is tempting, but still not comfortable, is to decide that these issues (and the issues surrounding the Experience

Requirement generally) put so much pressure on our notion of well-being that it fragments. Perhaps we need two notions of life's going well: one with and one without the Experience Requirement. This would open up new possibilities: perhaps the former notion fits prudential value theory better, and the latter fits moral theory better (I owe this suggestion to L. W. Sumner). See the illuminating discussion in Parfit 1984, ch. 8, esp. sect. 59.

But to return to my conclusion: does the general account solve the specific problem of the desire account's undermining the distinction between selfish and selfless action? (see ch. I, n. 25.) Well, there are different kinds of case. I might not for a moment want to give up my pleasure or contentment for someone else but think that, on moral grounds, I ought to. Now, the desire account does not have to be tied to any particular theory of action. It is compatible with the view that, whatever the state of one's desires, one might recognize a moral reason to act contrary to one's prudential reasons and, because moral reasons trump prudential reasons, act in accord with the stronger (moral) reason. In that case, on anyone's account of selfless action, one has acted selflessly.

Or, to move to a different kind of case, a father might take his children's welfare so much to heart that his forgoing pleasures for their sake enhances not only *their* well-being but *his* too (e.g. Père Goriot). It is not, in such cases, that he wants his children's welfare for the selfish reason that it will enhance his own; on the contrary, he wants his *children's* welfare. If he is prudentially shrewd, he might also recognize that his life will be better, in purely prudential terms, by his living for certain other persons. But even having that level of awareness is compatible with his acting not for his own benefit but for his children's. Thus, even on the desire account, he can sacrifice certain of his own personal goods—his own pleasure, peace of mind, contentment—for his children. And that is enough for us to go on calling this a selfless action. The fact that his aim of helping his children becomes so central to his life as no longer to be separable from what makes his own life successful ought not to upset this description. One can, of course, *define* a 'selfless' action so that only acts that actually make one worse off count, and then the mere fact that his own well-being happens also to be enhanced does upset this description. But one could instead define 'selfless' so that acts done (motive now entering the account) to help another, at considerable cost to oneself, can count. The second definition is better, and more in accord with how we ordinarily speak. The first would mean that we could not call 'selfless' the act of a saintly person who had so grown in moral stature that he regarded moral failures as making his life shabby, disappointing, weak, worse in purely prudential terms, and who also thought that in the present circumstances morality required that he give up much personal benefit in order to help others. He too might be wise enough to realize that his own life is better for him personally by his acting morally, but that should not be enough to make his act selfish.

Furthermore, it would be a mistake to try to explain the distinction between selfless and selfish actions by going over to an account of well-being that tied the notion to one's own states, to the exclusion of other persons'. That would make the line between one's own well-being and other persons' unrealistically sharp. A father *might* sacrifice himself for his children solely out of duty, or he *might*, like Goriot, do it with a sympathetic merger of his well-being with his children's. It is true that the fact that this sympathetic merger can occur makes the desire account messy. But the concept of well-being seems to be similarly messy.

This issue is part of a larger one, the relation of prudence and morality; see ch. II nn. 12 and 38, ch. IV sect. 4.

6. See Barry 1965, pp. 11–15, 61–6, 71–2, 295–9 and Dworkin 1977, pp. 234 ff. (also p. 277) for arguments that they should. For further discussion of some of the issues see Williams 1973.

7. See Williams 1973, pp. 105–6, for an argument that they should.

8. John Harsanyi, in Harsanyi 1977, p. 62, says they should.

9. Brandt 1967 defines 'utility' that way; see esp. pp. 29, 34. See also Brandt 1979, p. 203. J. S. Mill seems to have thought so too. 'Of two pleasures, if there be one to which all or almost all who have experience of both give a decided preference, *irrespective of any feeling of moral obligation to prefer it*, that is the more desirable pleasure.' (*Utilitarianism*, ch. II para. 5, my italics; see also ch. II para. 8.)

10. The question of restricting 'utility' to self-regarding desires is part of the question of what we should take as the argument in utility functions. Kenneth Arrow, in Arrow 1963, takes the relevant preferences to be preferences between *alternative social policies*. That leaves it open whether people rank them on a purely self-regarding basis or on a more mixed self-regarding plus other-regarding basis. For some theoretical purposes are the relevant preferences self-regarding, and for other purposes not? And when the relevant preferences are the mixed sort and preferences between social states as a whole can enter, how can an individual rank them rationally, when his ranking is supposed to be part of the rational calculation necessary to rank social states rationally? For a good discussion, see Brandt 1967.

11. I borrow the useful terms 'ethical push' and 'ethical pull' from Nozick 1981, pp. 401 ff.

12. The complications can be great. If my desire to be moral becomes part of my own well-being, it looks as if my well-being becomes my ground to be moral. But that turns morality into a self-regarding exercise, which means that things have clearly gone wrong. A person does not, in general, see his desire to be moral as a kind of desire that enters his well-being—that misunderstands the kind of (non-prudential) value one is dealing with. It could be only in a very special, limited, secondary sense that a desire to be moral could be part of one's well-being: namely, to the extent that this goal becomes, as for most of us it does to some

extent, part of the quality of one's life from one's own personal point of view—free from guilt and loss of self-respect. Of course, the guilt and loss of self-respect would have their real source in something non-prudential: the requirements of morality, the authority of moral reasons for action. But though they have their source outside prudence, they take a prudential toll.

Then there is this complication. Most of us want to be moral, but occasionally some of us want even more to do what we know is incompatible with it. For instance, there are standards of impartiality that many of us accept but do not live up to. It is not always a matter of our succumbing to temptation; sometimes it is a matter of our never having formed serious intentions in the first place. Plato may be right that if we were fully enough informed, we should not behave like this. Still, some persons are like this, perhaps from ignorance. So we must allow that it is possible for a person's desire to be moral to be only one among many and to have a less than supreme place in his preferences. That gives us one at least partially 'informed' ordering. However, it is also true that, all things considered, most of us should prefer to see justice done rather than injustice, to have impartial distributions rather than biased ones, to act morally rather than immorally. But now we have a second 'informed' ranking, incompatible with the first. Which gives us the utility of a person who holds both?

Imagine someone who prefers retaining certain of his privileges to having justice done, yet at the same time preferring acting morally to acting immorally. That seems to me an accurate description of a not uncommon situation. But there need not be inconsistency here. We can say that such a person recognizes justice as a stronger reason for action than self-interest; here we refer to a hierarchy of reasons. But a reason can be, for him, the stronger reason and still not be his stronger desire; here we refer to a hierarchy of desires. To accept this description of the case, I have said before, does not commit one to holding that not all failures in morality are failures in knowledge. That can be left an open question. What it does commit one to saying is that, although Jones may not be able to see something as a reason for action unless it connects in some way with his desires, the connection need not be an identical ordering between strength of reason and strength of desire. Jones can have both a hierarchy of reasons for action and an inconsistent hierarchy of desires. However, although the two hierarchies can be inconsistent, the inconsistency is not internal to the concept of utility. A desire can be 'informed' if the object of desire is not repudiated when its nature is understood. Utility does not require the satisfaction of a person's fully informed preference ordering, unless it is, or will in time be made, actual. Only actual desires should be satisfied. In short, there are two hierarchies, but utility uses only one.

13. Anyone who takes this line is, of course, building up a lot of problems for later. Can this wide notion of 'well-being' ever be the one appropriate to moral theory? Does not the inclusion of the whole gamut of shabby

desires (sadism, envy, spite, intolerance, etc.) just show that moral theory has to employ a narrower notion of well-being, say one centred on basic human needs, where the sordid side of human nature does not get a look-in? (see ch.III). And is not *right* prior to *good*? Do we not have to tailor our demands for our own good to fit within the bounds of what right allows? 'An individual who finds that he enjoys seeing others in positions of lesser liberty understands that he has no claim whatever to this enjoyment', John Rawls correctly remarks in Rawls 1972, p. 31 (see Pt. Three).

14. I should repeat, to avoid terribly easy confusion, that my concern is with an account of 'well-being', not an account of motivation or action, in which the opposition between reason and desire (cognition and appetite, etc.) also figures largely. Though the two accounts bear a great deal on one another, they are not the same.

15. See Aristotle, *Metaphysics* 1072a29, 'we desire the object because it seems good to us, rather than the object seems good to us because we desire it'. See also Norman 1971, ch. III; Wiggins 1976; Wiggins 1978-9; Wollheim 1979; Platts 1980; McDowell 1978; McDowell 1979; Bond 1983.

16. Thomas Nagel seems to say that one can; see Nagel 1980, esp. p. 90.

17. I owe this example to Garrett Thomson, and I have benefited generally from long discussions with him.

18. E. J. Bond, whose approach seems to me too homogeneous, speaks as if, where there is perception of value, the perception 'generates' a desire for it. The word 'generates' certainly suggests priority, but it is hard to find anything the understanding of which would require, or even suggest, priority. See Bond 1983, p. 44. In an earlier paper, Bond offered the following argument (Bond 1979, esp. p. 56). Valuing must be prior to desiring, because something's being valuable serves to *explain* and not to *justify* an informed desire. How could it, unless it were prior? For instance, I may want something simply to spite someone else; or I may just want it—I do not know why; or I may, more respectably, want something because I value it. Here we seem to have three explanations of desire, only the last of which brings in value, and which brings it in to explain desire and so cannot be identical with the desiring.

However, if I want something to spite someone else, and it will actually do the trick, then it *is* of some value to me. We should not confuse 'value' in the (prudential) sense with which we are now concerned and 'value' in an altogether loftier (possibly moral) sense, where anything as nasty as spite is doubtfully of value. My proposal is that in Freud's case seeing an option as valuable and desiring it on properly understanding what it is like come to the same. And that seems to hold in this case of spite. The second explanation—that people sometimes just want things and do not know why—is not relevant. I have an impulse to sing; I just feel like it. But that is a very dubious case of *informed desire*. Informed desires require awareness of, and are a response to, the nature of the object of the desire. An impulse does not seem to be an informed desire in the right sense.

19. 'Seeing in a favourable light' is a phrase from McDowell 1978, see esp. pp. 15–17. McDowell rightly objects to the view that desire makes things valuable by blindly fixing on them as its object. But something like that happens *sometimes*. More importantly, he makes understanding prior to desire. But, in cases like the present one, insisting on a priority either way makes desire and understanding too independent. And making them independent to that degree makes it hard to explain the special sort of understanding involved in 'seeing in a favourable light'. Certainly, that desire is not blind does not mean that it has to be subordinate to understanding.

20. See MacIntyre 1981, p. 62: 'To have understood the polymorphous character of pleasure and happiness is of course to have rendered these concepts useless for utilitarian purposes'.

21. A somewhat similar conclusion is reached, though by a different argument, in Narveson 1967, see esp. ch. III.

22. It is not that 'utility' provides a complete account of value, because 'value' is used very broadly—for instance, of the moral categories 'right' and 'duty'. But it does cover part of value's domain: what enhances a person's own well-being.

23. It is often, even usually, understood that way. See e.g. Rawls 1982, p. 175: ' ... the one rational good is satisfaction of desire or preferences, or, more generally, the satisfaction of the most rational ordering of desires and preferences'. Rawls' calling 'utility' a 'good' suggests that it is a substantive value. (Also he implausibly equates 'utility' with 'the satisfaction of the most rational ordering of desires'; 'well-being' can be plausibly represented by an account that blends actual and ideal desires.)

Discussion of the sense in which Aristotle's *eudaimonia* is an end is helpful here. See e.g. Hardie 1965, Ackrill 1980, McDowell 1980.

24. Since utility is not a substantive value at all, we have to give up the idea that our various particular ends are valuable only because they *cause, produce, bring about, are sources of,* utility. On the contrary, they are the values; utility is not. 'Utilitarianism regards them [i.e. a person's attachments, aims, plans, etc.] as worthless in themselves and valuable only to the extent of their effects on utility. They are not any more important than what happens to be caught in the impersonal metric of utility', Sen and Williams 1982, pp. 5–6.

We also have to give up the view that utilitarianism is reductionist. Talk about 'utility' places all prudential values in a structure (of informed desires). Sen and Williams also speak of 'this high degree of assimilation' in regarding 'all interests, ideals, aspirations, and desires as on the same level' (p. 8). When they speak of 'the same level', they must have in mind reduction to a common substantive value. But the structure of informed desires is not that at all. So most of the things thought to follow from this 'reduction' do not follow: e.g. 'the neat model of maximizing one homogeneous magnitude' (p. 16), the conception of 'utilitarian rationality' (pp. 16–17). See also Bernard Williams' essay, 'Conflicts of Values', in Williams 1981, p. 78: 'The most basic version of the idea that utility provides a universal currency is that all values are versions or applications in some way of utility ... Indeed, in this version, it is not clear that there is more than one value at all, or, consequently, real conflicts between values.'

25. See Scanlon, 1975 pp. 656–8, for nearly the same principle of division (he attaches 'solely' to 'depends' in the explanation of 'subjective').

26. I come back to these questions in ch. III sect. 7 and ch. IV sect. 5. The label 'objective-list theory' I take from Parfit 1984, see pp. 466, 493, 499. Parfit defines the objective-list theory so that it is committed to there being facts about value independent of, and determining, desires ('desired because valuable, not valuable because desired'); see p. 499. So, on that definition, it cannot merge with the informed-desire account; they are no longer both able to agree to the compromise position about the relation of value and desire set out in sect. 3.

27. e.g. Rawls 1972, sect. 15, but also sects. 64, 78; Scanlon 1975.

28. R. M. Hare mounts a similar attack on talk about *objective* and *subjective* moral judgments; see Hare 1976b and Hare 1981, ch. 12.

29. See, e.g., Brandt 1979, ch. VI, esp. pp. 110–15. In order to bring out how demanding a requirement the word 'informed' is meant to mark, think of a person, apparently fully informed of all relevant facts, who none the less has some (to us) crazy aim in life—say, counting the blades of grass in various lawns. We protest that no one is the least bit interested in the information, and he replies that he knows. We insist that the information is of no use to anyone, and he replies that he knows that too. We can find no logical error that he is committing, nor any matter of fact that he denies. Still, he would not, on the standard I am using, be fully informed. It is, of course, hard to fix the boundaries of the 'factual'. But, besides that, one could not say that his desire was formed by appreciation of the nature of the object (my sense of 'informed'). Prudential values are reasons for action. Reasons are not idiosyncratic; they must be generally intelligible as reasons. Suppose that we got the blade counter to admit that the time he spent pursuing his aim could be spent doing other things, that certain other things that he could do would enhance his health or give him more enjoyment, while his crawling around on his hands and knees in all weathers is ruining his chest and is very boring, and so on. Then we could see his blade counting under no description that made it intelligible as desirable. Nor could he. He could go on reporting, as a bare matter of fact about his psychology, that he wanted to count blades of grass. But he could not say that it was his aim or end in life, because those terms (at least the uses that are relevant here) imply something more than that bare psychological fact—namely, that blade counting makes his life valuable. His desire to count blades of grass would not be a desire formed by a

perception of the nature of the object of desire. The perception of what it is to count blades of grass would not be, could not intelligibly be, what formed his desire. See later discussion in ch. IV sect. 3, ch. VIII sect. 3.

30. This point is well developed in Slote 1983, ch. 2, but Slote makes it into more of a point against having life plans than I think it is.

31. Here my direction is contrary to Derek Parfit's in Parfit 1984, ch. 15. He argues that if one adopts his Reductionist account of personal identity, then 'It becomes more plausible, when thinking morally, to focus less upon the person, the subject of experiences, and instead to focus more upon the experiences themselves.' This would allow utilitarians to counter the objection that they treat the group as a super-person with the reply that a person is a mini-group. The Reductionist account points in that direction. But prudential value theory, which also enters import-antly, in the end has whole lives, or long stretches, as its subject, and if the assessment gives long-term goals such as accomplishment and deep personal relations dominant place among substantive values, then we cannot focus on experiences. Of course the fact that prudential assessment has to take whole lives as its subject does not, on its own, show that: the assessment could take that form but come up with the substantive answer that a life that strings together lots of certain sorts of experiences is best. It is just that it looks as if the substantive answer is *not* that. See also ch. XII n. 3.

32. The case is defended in Sen 1979.

33. There are also doubts about aggregation that arise from time preferences. Some periods matter to us more than others. I do not want to consider our tendency to discount the future just because it is future; there seems to me little justification for that. But a year at the prime of life does seem to matter more than a year of callow youth or of senility. So why think that the best life can be found simply by summing the value of its several periods?

But why not? The quantities that are added already allow for the lower value of callow youth or senility. The fact that many desires in childhood and senility are intense does not matter. Intensity is not the sort of strength relevant to utility. And the objects of these intense desires will often not weigh heavily as utilities. The periods that characteristically matter less are characteristically of lower utility. There is no reason here for 'greatest sum' and 'most valuable' to come apart. These matters are well discussed in Slote 1983, ch. 1.

Of course, my conclusion needs to be backed by a fuller account of the measurement of utility, especially of how one compares fulfilment of desires in one period with fulfilment in another, when the preferences may be greatly changed (see the discussion of Brandt's objection to desire accounts, ch. I sect.5; also chs. VI and VII). My view is roughly this: there is a more stable, authoritative set of values behind the desires that grip us at various times of our life. They are the ones we all use in saying that certain periods of life—childhood, senility—matter less than equally long periods of the prime of life. But the same values are available for utilitarian calculation.

There are other worries about maximization as a prudential policy besides the ones I try to meet here. See the fuller discussion in ch. VIII n. 33.

34. The *locus classicus* is the *Nicomachean Ethics*, and the best modern work has been done in interpretations of it; see this ch. n. 23.

35. See Ackrill 1980 for an account of *eudaimonia* as a substantive inclusive end. For the distinction between a 'dominant' and an 'inclusive' end, see Hardie 1965.

36. That is the excellent semantic analysis of 'good' in Ziff 1960, ch. VI, see esp. p. 218. His account seems to me substantially correct and in need of only a minor qualification. He intends his account to apply to all non-deviant uses of 'good', except for those he quite plausibly regards as special cases (such as 'a good mile off'), which probably grew out of the central use but which a semantic analysis of the central use need not cover. But there are uses of 'good' that are non-deviant and not special that Ziff's *Semantic Analysis* should cover but does not. For instance, there are many uses of 'good' where it means roughly 'has the defining characteristics to a high degree', as in the phrase 'a good Freudian slip'. Here no interests need be relevant. Although it is possible to have interests that Freudian slips satisfy (an author of a psychology textbook might), still it is also possible for a Freudian slip to be a good one simply because it is all that it should be. But the respects in which Ziff's account fails do not matter for our purposes. All the uses of 'good' that are of interest to moral theory are the sort that Ziff's account fits.

37. See, e.g., R. B. Perry, *Realms of Value*, excerpt quoted in Brandt 1961, p. 265.

38. Of course, that is not the end of doubts. I have followed the utilitarian assumption—actually it is far more widespread—that we have a notion of good or valuable life independent of our notion of what it is right or wrong to do. Indeed, utilitarians bring this notion to moral theory and define a standard of right and wrong in terms of it. But there is a tradition that holds that *good* has status only in the context of a theory of *right*, or that the concept of *right* is prior to the concept of *good*. See Kant, *Critique of Practical Reason*, pt.1, bk. 1, ch. II; Rawls 1972, esp. pp. 30–3, 395–6, 560. But the desire account qualifies the independence of *good* and *right* in certain ways. One thing that people with mature values take as an aim is acting morally. Ethical push comes to incorporate much of ethical pull. Moreover, when a person faces a conflict between his own interest and his moral obligation, the latter wins: moral reasons trump prudential reasons. But there still remains a conception of a valuable life independent of, not subordinate to, right. That immoral desires make no claim on fulfilment, that they have no authority in determining action, which seems to be the nerve of Rawls's claim, does not mean that they

cannot make one better off. And I doubt whether even an ideal person, whose values are perfectly developed, will find that ethical push and ethical pull entirely coincide. But certainly with the mass of humanity they do not. In thinking about others (say the inept sadist who can rise to no richer life), we might well decide that their welfare is greater for their acting wrongly. Similarly, in thinking about our own lives, we may decide that, though we have no sufficient reason to act immorally, it would increase our well-being to do so. See the discussion in Slote 1983, pp. 122–3. I discuss these issues more fully in ch. IV sect. 4 and ch. VIII sect. 2.

39. J. Bentham, *An Introduction to the Principles of Morals and Legislation*, ch.I, sects. 1 and 3.

40. J. S. Mill, *Utilitarianism*, ch. II, para. 5.

41. Mill's references to 'utility' in *On Liberty* are well in accord with the desire account. 'I regard utility as the ultimate appeal on all ethical questions; but it must be utility in the largest sense, grounded on the permanent interests of man as a progressive being'; see ch. I, para. 11. Note the link between *utility* and *interests*, moreover to *permanent* interests (a notion behind which there is clearly a full conception of substantive prudential values, about which people can be mistaken). Note also the stress on *progressive* beings: there is ample evidence in *On Liberty* that Mill, like Aristotle, saw activity as central to a good life, not static states of mind or possession of goals, but forms of life that change as one's values mature. For a good discussion of the importance of activity to Mill, see Gray 1983, ch. IV, sects. 1 and 2, esp. p. 72.

42. Sidgwick 1907, pp. 111–12; see generally bk. I, ch. IX; bk. III, ch. XIV; bk. IV, chs.I–III.

CHAPTER THREE

1. These points are argued in Rawls, 1972 sects. 6, 15, 28, 60, 68; Rawls 1975a; Rawls 1975b; Rawls 1982; Scanlon 1975; Scanlon 1982; Dworkin 1981; Feinberg 1973, ch. VII sect. 5; Wollheim 1975; and by many others.

2. Both Richard Wollheim and Amartya Sen hold eclectic positions; see Wollheim 1975, Sen 1980, Sen 1980–1.

3. For a good discussion of the semantic differences, see Wiggins 1985. See also Braybrooke 1968; Richards 1971, ch. 3 sect. 3; White 1971, p. 114; Feinberg 1973, ch.VII sect. 5; Wollheim 1975.

4. I owe the example to Garrett Thomson.

5. This is an analysis defended, e.g., in Barry 1965, ch. III sect. 5A; and attacked, e.g., in Miller 1976, ch. IV sect. 2 and in Wiggins 1985.

6. A distinction is often drawn, for the whole class of needs, between *instrumental* and *absolute* (those not instrumental to a further end). But 'instrumental' fits statements such as 'an element needs a free electron in order to conduct electricity' poorly; a free electron is neither an instrument for bringing conduction about (it is the instrument *of* the conduction) nor a means to that end (which 'instrument' suggests). And 'absolute', as I shall shortly argue, fits basic human needs poorly. For the distinction roughly as I draw it, see Braybrooke 1968, p. 90; Feinberg 1973, pp. 111–12.

7. Miller 1976 takes the tough line that they are not elliptical, because what is needed in these cases is part of the relevant end and so the means-end model does not fit; ch. IV, sect. 2. For instance, if we say that humans need satisfying human relations *in order to be happy*, what we give in the last clause is the whole of which the satisfying relations are a part, not the end to which they are a means. But the part-whole model does not fit all basic needs. It is true that the means-end model has to be stretched beyond simple cause-effect relations to fit all the cases to which it is usually applied, and the interpretation of the means-end model gets difficult with the relation of ends that have more final ends. Still, if the model does not fit at all, talk about 'need' is improper.

The question whether basic need statements are elliptical is connected with the question whether the sense of the word 'need' changes from instrumental to non-instrumental cases. I do not know of any successful arguments that it does (but see Wiggins 1985 for an arresting one). What is at issue is particularly obscure. The best case for saying that there is a separate non-instrumental sense of 'need' also allows that the content of the 'in order to ϕ' clause, with its mention of health or harm or functioning, gets incorporated into the explanation of the meaning of the word 'need'. The case for saying that there is no separate non-instrumental sense allows that health or harm or function are usually taken as read. Both, therefore, give health or harm or functioning central place in the explanation of the sense of the whole sentence. And that is what matters for moral theory. Nothing of importance to morality rests on there being one sense or two.

8. Is this even an account of 'well-being'? Perhaps basic needs are indeed the best index, for moral contexts, of how well a person's life goes, but perhaps they take in too little of a person's life to be called, with its all-encompassing air, 'well-being'. But well-being does not always suggest how life goes as a whole. We are happy using 'welfare' in political contexts and confining it to some conception of basic provision. However, for discussions of 'needs' and 'welfare' that point in the opposite direction, see Richards 1971, pp. 37–9.

9. See esp. Rawls 1972, sects. 15, 25, 60.

10. See Miller 1976, pp. 136–8; Benn and Peters 1959, p. 146; Feinberg 1973, p.110; Wiggins 1985.

11. See Feinberg 1973, p. 110: ' ... what is needed to live a minimally decent life by the realistic standards of a given time and place and what is only added "gravy" ... '

12. See Benn and Peters 1959, p. 146: 'Basic needs are thus fairly precisely determinate because they are related to norms set by conditions already very widely enjoyed. They are the needs for precisely those things that most other people have got.'

13. It is not that 'basic need' is essentially contestable, which all normative notions are often thought to be. Nor is it just that it is vague. Vagueness can be cured by stipulation; essential contestability may be incurable but seems not fatal. I am saying that 'basic need' is too indeterminate to do the work assigned to it, that it cannot be made determinate by pointing out its links to notions indeterminate in much the same way, and that arbitrary stipulation undermines its status as a moral notion. I am not saying that the indeterminateness of these key notions ('harm', 'health', 'proper function', 'minimum provision', 'human right', etc.) cannot be overcome. There are ways, not arbitrary ones either—one being to fit these notions inside a broadly utilitarian, desire-based moral theory and to let utilitarian considerations determine where it would be best to fix the boundaries. But that is just another way of undermining need accounts.

14. If my crippled son has a happy disposition and leads a productive life and I have another son who is an unhappy neurotic, I might have good moral reason to help the second before the first.

15. We get closer if we bring in rights. The best case for offering the cripple the wheelchair or nothing rests on the nature and extent of rights. We have a right to bodily integrity—roughly, to those basic physical capacities necessary to live a recognizably human existence. But what if all the cripple's aims in life are sedentary and he is already living a recognizably human existence? Anyway, how do we fix what is a 'recognizably human existence'? (That is the problem of the minimum acceptable level all over again.) And is freedom from depression a right? Could the cripple trade the wheelchair for psychotherapy? We are not yet very close to moral bedrock. See the discussion of rights later, ch. XI.

16. For an example of an account of well-being that gives health this sort of priority, see Schwartz 1982.

17. One reason why it is not important is that those are desires that society would want to stamp on anyway. Another is that the strategy backfires. If the society is welfare egalitarian, then anyone who develops expensive tastes to skew allocation in his favour will get more *goods* than his mates (to bring him up to their level of welfare) but not more *welfare* (either than they get or than he would otherwise have got). In fact—this is why his strategy backfires—he will be worse off for his stratagems than he would otherwise have been, because everyone's welfare level will go down, his included, as a result of his expensive tastes. See discussions in Rawls 1975b and in Dworkin 1981, Part I, to the second of which I owe the point about the strategy's backfiring.

18. John Rawls develops this line of thought in Rawls 1975b.

19. This is what is wrong with the very similar argument that stresses not the moral irrelevance of these chance factors but the moral relevance of our responsibility for the desires we end up with. It *is* appropriate to hold us responsible for many of the desires we form, and not for most of the needs that assail us. If I form expensive tastes, it is perfectly reasonable to ask me, even to give me every incentive, to give them up and choose again. Perfectly reasonable, so long as it is tastes that are in question. But then it distorts the issue to concentrate just on expensive tastes. There is a lot that falls outside the class of 'basic needs', and so in the class of 'mere desires', that are nothing like tastes. It is far from reasonable, if a person has responsibly chosen a life centred on accomplishment, understanding, and beauty—because these are what would make something worthwhile out of his life—to tell him to give up these aims because they are more demanding on society's resources than many other persons' approach to life. Once one realizes how much ends up in the class of 'mere desires' besides 'expensive tastes', the case for ignoring 'mere desires' is much less appealing.

20. Again it is John Rawls who makes this point; see Rawls 1982.

21. See Rawls 1972, p. 527; also Rawls 1982, p. 172 and Scanlon 1975.

22. Difference in scale has not received enough attention. In *A Theory of Justice* Rawls confines attention to 'social justice', but he thinks that the Original Position, constructed to generate social principles, is the device for generating most moral principles (see Rawls 1972, pp. 120, 130, 139, 255). In *The Republic* Plato makes similar disturbing shifts in scale: 'Justice can be a characteristic of a single individual or of a whole city, can it not? ... We may therefore find justice on a grander scale in the larger thing, and easier to get hold of' (368E).

23. For an important version of a flexible need account, see Scanlon 1975; for his account of 'urgency' see esp. pp. 660–1.

24. This weakens another line of thought responsible for a lot of sympathy for need accounts. We all think morality must work with a *hierarchy* of values. Trumping of some sort goes on and has to be explained. And how can it be explained except through some such device as basic needs? See e.g. Braybrooke 1968, p. 93, where he gives as a 'fundamental principle' of morals and prudence: 'Matters of need take precedence over matters of preference'; also for defence of a more qualifying version of the principle (the trumps are not just basic needs but 'bad, entrenched, non-substitutable needs'), see Wiggins 1985. Certainly values form a hierarchy. But the need account is not the only way to generate the hierarchy, nor in any obvious way the best. Basic needs do not trump mere desires. The trumps would have to come out of a more flexible need account: important needs trump mere desires. But 'important' is 'harmful if denied', which is 'damaging to prudential values if denied'. So we are back to informed desires which not only form a hierarchy but also contain resources for introducing much complexity into it. For instance, the desire

account may end up restricting the range of informed desires that have moral weight on some such grounds as: (1) life goes better if persons do not inhibit their natural attachments and commitments, if, in effect, they accept some diminution of impartiality; (2) many effects on well-being are too slight to warrant the costs of moral sanctions; (3) on the large social scale knowledge of individual conceptions of the good is so unreliable and assessment of their value so contentious they ought in large measure to be ignored, etc. Certainly the class of my informed desires is larger than the class of my interests that you have morally to take into consideration. But there are many explanations of that.

25. See ch. II sect. 4.

26. The notion of 'human nature' will have the consequences that the need account draws from it only if it already has a large normative component. Not all ages would have accepted the inferences from 'human nature' that most of us nowadays will. This creates problems for those who believe that the application of 'objective' is confined exclusively to values that are all-purpose means to any conception of the good life. Perhaps they cannot get around the difficulty. In any case, there are other ways of applying 'objective'.

27. For defence of the neutrality of moral standards, see Rawls 1972, p. 527; Dworkin 1978; Dworkin 1981; Scanlon 1975; and very many others.

28. Thomas Nagel's argument in Nagel 1980 gets very close to this; see esp. pp. 122–3. For comments on it, see above ch. II sects. 3–4.

29. See the discussion above, ch. II sects. 3–4.

30. See above ch. II sect. 4.

CHAPTER FOUR

1. The contrast that John Rawls draws between his view (justice as fairness) and perfectionism, on the one hand, and utilitarianism, on the other, is certainly implausible. He says that his own view 'shares with perfectionism the feature of setting up an ideal of the person that constrains the pursuit of existing desires. In this respect justice as fairness and perfectionism are both opposed to utilitarianism.' See Rawls 1972, p. 262. Yet they are not opposed to utilitarianism on the informed-desire account. The only versions of utilitarianism they would, in this way, be opposed to are ones that had no 'ideal of the person' and no way of criticizing 'existing desires', which would be pretty inadequate even as versions of utilitarianism.

2. This distinction might already set off alarm bells. Do not most of the historically important forms of perfectionism pass imperceptibly

from 'prudential' to 'moral' concerns? Can any account of purely 'prudential' perfectionism get far without bringing in 'moral' matters? Is there any—especially any perfectionist—notion of 'prudence' independent of the notion of what is 'morally right'? My drawing a distinction between 'prudential' and 'moral' perfectionism does not beg any of these questions. The distinction is not meant to be beyond revision, and I come to these reasonable qualms later.

3. The transition from the notion of a perfect (*teleios*) life to that of achieving an end (*telos*) was made easy for a Greek by the etymological connection of the words. In English, however, 'perfect' comes from Latin *perficere*, the roots of which are *per* plus *facere*, i.e. thoroughly made, completed. 'Perfect', in its contemporary use, is 'flawless', and there is no longer any close connection with the realization of an end. I take these points from Passmore 1971, p. 20. Later, therefore, we shall have to look at the merits of a single ideal form of life independently of Aristotle's teleological metaphysics.

4. We see here, that when Aristotle asks whether there is *one* task or end, he wants to know not whether there is a *single* one but whether there is a *unique* one. But that is puzzling. There may be rational beings other than humans somewhere in the universe, and then rationality would not be unique to humans. Also he ends up saying that our final end is pure rationality, theoretical contemplation, a life, as Aristotle remarks, in a way more divine than human. This is a curious culmination for an argument that makes so much of the notion of what is *unique* to humans: what is unique to them is something not unique to them but what they share with the gods and possess on their own only in a debased form. This is a plain contradiction, the best way of dealing with which is simply to drop all claims of what is *unique* to humans and concentrate instead on their *single* end. The claims about uniqueness are, anyway, not essential to the argument. Aristotle's concern seems really to be the search for the one peak to what he sees as the hierarchical structure of human functions, and it would not matter if some other species turned out to have a peak of the same shape.

5. See e.g. Hardie 1965 for a discussion of 'dominant end' and 'inclusive end' and also Nagel 1972 for a discussion of an 'intellectualist' and a 'comprehensive' account of *eudaimonia*.

6. *NE*, x 7 1177a, b; 1178a.

7. *NE*, x 7 1177b; x 8 1178a.

8. ch. II sects. 3, 4.

9. This, and the following forms of moral perfectionism, can come in both hard and soft versions: the hard version would let this perfectionist principle trump all other moral principles (Nietzsche); the soft would make it one among many equally weighty principles (Rashdall; see below).

10. Nietzsche 1874, sect.6.

11. Quoted in Clark 1975, p. 51. And the not-so-young Russell wrote to Gilbert Murray (27 April 1949), 'Where democracy and civilisation conflict, I am for civilisation'; also quoted in Clark, p. 631.

12. Sometimes the Superman version becomes the more generous, though also more dangerous, Super Race or Super Class version, which says that it is not a few individuals who represent the supreme form of life, but a whole group—a natural aristocracy, say, or whites. Hastings Rashdall could write ' ... the lower Well-being—it may be ultimately the very existence—of countless Chinamen or negroes must be sacrificed that a higher life may be possible for a much smaller number of white men'. Rashdall comes out with this appalling remark to illustrate a perfectly plausible principle, and the general tenor of his discussion is far more balanced and sympathetic than this unfortunate passage suggests. The principle is that, in certain circumstances, it *might* be right to purchase a high kind of life for a few with sacrifices on the part of the many. But he shows himself well aware of the intolerable conditions that present social inequalities produce. 'I for one should certainly doubt whether, if I had the power, I could doom the world to a continuance of our present social horrors, although their removal might lead to the evanescence of research and speculation, "sweetness and light", full and varied exercises of faculties, and all the rest of it.' See Rashdall 1907, vol. 1, pp. 238–9.

13. The move to the Super Class or Super Race versions would just increase the problems. The empirical ground on which they are meant to stand is missing. It is just false that all the members of one race have greater capacities for knowledge or the appreciation of beauty than the members of another. Nor is there any natural aristocracy with a greater share of these capacities than some natural proletariat. There are only smooth gradations of degree in share, and often those fortunate in their share of one are unfortunate in their share of another.

14. For a defence of the occasion-by-occasion approach, see McDowell 1979. Martha Craven Nussbaum takes seriously the need to show in some detail how the approach works; see Nussbaum 1983–4. But even her rich, subtle discussion of a particular case of human relations leaves it entirely unclear how this approach could possibly answer questions such as the ones I am shortly to list in the text.

15. This is Philippa Foot's characterization in her article 'Virtues and Vices' in Foot 1978, see esp. p. 8.

16. Leo Tolstoy, *A Confession*.

17. Russell 1953, p. 51.

18. An observation of Paul Edwards in Edwards 1967.

19. Radical argument—in contrast to the sort of definitional argument that I described earlier—is *possible*, but I think only in the sense that

people do offer radical arguments, which need assessing. I do not think that any of them is, in the end, persuasive. 'Radical' arguments, as I use the term, are sceptical in nature; they aim to show that the values that definitional deliberation establish are not really valuable at all (the nothing-is-valuable argument that I have just sketched) or that they lack the seriousness and importance in life that we ordinarily think of them as having. A further 'radical' argument (besides the nothing-is-valuable argument) might therefore be a crude anti-realist argument that all values are just a matter of taste and so give no real reason to adopt this end or that. I see my argument in this chapter (and in this book) as neutral between realism and anti-realism on values. But it is not neutral when it comes to certain crude forms of anti-realism. A form that claims that all values are a matter of taste is not adequate to the phenomenology of deliberation about values or to our ordinary notion of 'taste'; a form that claims that we have no reason to adopt one end rather than another uses 'reason' in an indefensible way. This crude anti-realism is, I think, another unsuccessful 'radical' argument. Deliberation about values that matters for practical purposes answers the questions: What values are there? and How do they figure in my life? 'Radical' arguments answer the second question: values matter much less than we ordinarily think. Since I think that they fail, in effect the only practical question that remains is, What values are there?, which the 'definitional' argument seeks to answer.

20. Thomas Nagel, in his paper 'The Absurd' in Nagel 1979, having accepted all of these doubts about backward steps, argues convincingly that there is indeed a real step back, but of a different kind (p. 15). It does not take us to a perspective from which life looks absurd. Absurdity does not enter in that direct way. It is, rather, a critical perspective on our ordinary value judgments. 'The crucial backward step', he says, shows 'that the whole system of justification and criticism, which controls our choices and supports our claims to rationality, rests on responses and habits that we never question, that we should not know how to defend without circularity ... ' (p. 15). And yet we do no disengage from life. We take our ambitions and commitments utterly seriously. That, Nagel submits, is just the absurdity. A situation is absurd when it contains a discrepancy between pretension and reality, and such a discrepancy inevitably appears in all human lives in 'the collision between the seriousness with which we take our lives and the perpetual possibility of regarding everything about which we are serious as arbitrary or open to doubt' (p. 13).

But it is not true that our values rest on responses and habits we never question. Our values are subject to all the kind of criticism that we have been talking of. And the critical perspective that we may adopt about our value judgments we may also adopt about other judgments—our scientific beliefs, our mathematics. In their case, too, criticism leads ultimately to questions that cannot be answered without circularity. Our values can be issued challenges that reduce us to silence. But what should our reaction to this be? Should we feel that it is absurd for us to go on, as we are bound to do, taking ourselves seriously? Should we feel this about the sciences and mathematics, and our carrying on, as we are bound to do, taking them seriously? Our reaction in those cases is not, and should not be, pessimism, despair, or a sense of our absurdity. It should be caution and open-mindedness. Nagel's step back is a real one, but it leads to modesty, not to absurdity.

21. This list may not be complete. But other candidates that I can think of, and items on other proposed lists, seem to me either not to belong, or to be subsumable under one of the headings already there. Is *human life* a value? (see Finnis 1980, pp. 86–7). No, unless it comes down to item (b): the features of a human existence. *Good* life is valuable, but it is not one of the substantive values; it is the sum of them, a valuable life. Is play? (see Finnis 1980, p. 87). Not, it would seem, on its own; it is part of enjoyment, and we need that broader category. Is the development and exercise of skills? (see Dworkin 1981, Part I). Well, not exactly under that description. There are rare but trivial Guinness Book of Records skills that have no value. The development and exercise of any skill is enjoyable, and of non-trivial skills a central part of accomplishment. And so on.

22. John Rawls thinks they do. He speaks of 'the conception of the person' in Sidgwick's version of classical utilitarianism as ' ... that of a container-person: persons are thought of as places where intrinsically valuable experiences occur ... Persons are, so to speak, holders for such experiences. It does not matter who has these experiences, or what is their sequential distribution among persons ... Assuming that no such experiences have a duration greater than a specified interval of time, one need not ask whether a person having a certain valuable experience in the present interval is the same person who had a certain valuable experience in a previous interval; the temporal sequence over intervals is no more relevant than distribution among persons within the same interval.' (See Rawls 1974–5, pp. 17–18.) This conception of the container-person collecting agreeable experiences which themselves are seen as temporary, discrete, and ephemeral, cannot be got out of any plausible account of prudential value. Indeed, any plausible account would undercut it. But Rawls is too quick to think that the inadequacy of one particular value theory shows something about the adequacy of utilitarianism as a moral theory.

23. The stronger line is argued in McDowell 1980.

24. Shakespeare, *Measure for Measure*, III.i, *Claudio*: Death is a fearful thing. *Isabella*: And shamed life a hateful.

25. We also rank *natures*, e.g. human nature with its capacities and the satisfactions and dissatisfactions arising from them against canine nature with its. Or human nature against New Man, a breed produced by

genetic engineering to be contented slaves (see the discussion in Haksar 1979, pp. 3–4).

26. See references in ch. III n. 27.

27. See ch. III, sect. 7.

28. See Rawls 1972, p. 327, '... they [persons in the Original Position] are assumed to be committed to different conceptions of the good ... '; also Rawls 1980, p.539, '... justice as fairness assumes that deep and pervasive differences of ethical doctrines remain'; see also pp. 540–2. But why not assume instead that persons in the Original Position would (or could inoffensively be got to once they emerge from behind the Veil of Ignorance) agree on at least *some* goods beyond all-purpose means? Suppose that persons in the Original Position thought that they *might* turn out to have conceptions of the good that agree at certain points and that the points are quite central and important. Why would they not think it? Indeed, they might also reasonably think that substantive prudential value theory *might* show some values, besides all-purpose means, to be valuable to any human life. But then would they agree to a policy of strict value-neutrality? Would they not hedge their bets—'*if* that is the way things turn out, let us have some non-neutrality'?

29. See ch. II sect. 4.

CHAPTER FIVE

1. This is argued in ch. II sect. 5.

2. e.g. Raz 1985–6, p. 117.

3. I discuss certain scales and their relative strength in ch. VI sect. 1. Since scales can be ranked from weak to strong (depending upon how much can be said about items as a result of their being measurable on the scale), we can speak loosely, as I do in the text, of weak and strong forms of incommensurability (the weaker the scale the stronger the form of incommensurability if two items cannot be measured on it).

4. This chapter bears the title of an article that I published a few years ago (Griffin 1977). Little of the article survives here; what does appears in nn. 28 and 34.

5. For an argument for incommensurability along these lines, see Thomas Nagel, 'The Fragmentation of Value', in Nagel 1979.

6. Robert Nozick expresses the hope. See Nozick 1981, ch. V sect. 3, esp. the part entitled 'Measurement of Moral Weight'.

7. As Ronald Dworkin claims. See Dworkin 1977, Introd. pp. xi–xv, chs. 6 and 7.

8. For my attempt at a substantive theory of rights, see ch. XI.

9. See chs. XII and XIII. John Searle claims, correctly I think, that it is a conceptual truth. But that promises essentially create obligations says

nothing about the moral strength, if any, the obligations have. See Searle 1978, p. 86.

10. See ch. X sect. 2.

11. For the claim that certain moral conflicts lack the sort of rational resolution that would come from one obligation's outweighing another, see Williams 1973b, p. 173; Williams 1981, p. 74; and Wiggins 1976, p. 371.

12. Then we should get incommensurability of the sort that T. S. Kuhn may think holds between scientific theories with radically different paradigms. I speak of what Kuhn *may* think, because, in talking about 'incommensurability', he sometimes speaks more strongly than he does at other times. I am here taking him at his strongest. Unfortunately, the powerful objections to the strong versions of Kuhn's claim about scientific theories cannot simply be shifted to moral theories without begging a lot of questions. See Kuhn 1970. For powerful criticism, see Newton-Smith 1981, chs. V–VII.

For a claim that moral reasons exhibit just this form of incommensurability, see MacIntyre 1981. MacIntyre suggests that 'moral incommensurability' arises from our now using concepts from incompatible moral traditions. Hence, when *rights* are matched against *utility*, and both against *justice*, '...it is not surprising that there is no rational way of deciding which type of claim is to be given priority or how one is to be weighed against another. Moral incommensurability is itself the product of a particular historical conjunction' (p. 68). MacIntyre describes an important possibility, though his particular instance (rights, justice, and utility being from incompatible traditions) is unconvincing.

13. For example, Agamemnon's choice between the expedition and his daughter. That is Bernard Williams' example in Williams 1973b, p. 173, of which he says, 'The agonies that a man will experience after acting in full consciousness of such a situation are not to be traced to a persistent doubt that he may not have chosen the better thing; but, for instance, to a clear conviction that he has not done the better thing because there is no better thing to have done'. See also Williams 1981, p. 74, and Wiggins 1976, p. 371.

14. Furthermore, the difference between the two values that we are invited to try to compare is often greatly exaggerated. John Rawls, in Rawls 1982, pp. 179–80, invites us to consider different conceptions of the good life, one affirming aesthetic values, attitudes of contemplation towards nature, gentleness (Friends of the Earth), the other valuing risk, excitement, competition. 'These conceptions of the good are incommensurable because their final ends and aspirations are so diverse, their specific content so different, that no common basis for judgement can be found.' If by a common basis Rawls means yet another substantive value to which they can be reduced, he is probably right that one cannot be found. But then it seldom can—even in the most ordinary, humdrum cases. If that is our standard, incommensurabilities crop up everywhere. But the basis of comparison could be different in kind: different amounts of prudential

value, where 'prudential value' is not itself yet another prudential value. In any case, the 'diversity' of these two conceptions is overdone. True, gentleness and the spur of competition (to simplify a bit) are both valuable (or rather what they bring to one's life is); anyone would want to have them both in his life. No doubt sometimes one can add elements of the one only at the (painful) cost of the other, but that is partial incompatibility, not incomparability. Competition is valuable because it spurs us on to better things; gentleness is valuable because it opens life to responses and relations that are valuable. They do not come from 'aspirations' that are such 'diverse' approaches to life; they come from aspirations that are, or should be, universal and to some extent combined in everyone's life. There is a scale on which we can, and do, rank them: contribution to a good life. Certainly *sometimes* we can say that the contribution that a *certain* sort of spur of competition would make to our lives will be less than the contribution that non-competitiveness in that area would make. There may well be limits to, breaks in, the rankings, but that is a different matter.

15. There are several names in currency for each ordering. By a *weak* ordering I mean one generated by a relation that is reflexive, transitive, and complete. By a *strong* ordering I mean a *weak* ordering plus anti-symmetry (i.e. no two objects can occupy the same place in an ordering); by a *partial* ordering a *weak* ordering minus completeness. For a good summary of different kinds of orderings, see Sen 1970, ch. 1, esp. pp. 8–9. I am greatly indebted to John Broome for a discussion of these matters.

16. See Kant, *Grundlegung*, in Paton 1961, p. 102.

17. Charles Taylor develops a similar contrast; he speaks of the 'incommensurably higher', e.g. 'Integrity, charity, liberation and the like stand out as worthy of pursuit in a special way, incommensurable with other goals we might have, such as the pursuit of wealth, or comfort...'; the latter we may pursue or not as we choose, while the former we must pursue or be 'open to censure'. See Taylor 1982, pp. 135–7.

18. Or is the point about the replaceable and the irreplaceable slightly different? On the face of it, commensurability implies replaceability. But clearly some objects are uniquely valuable, beyond substitution or compensation. Without such objects certain central human emotions would not even make sense. One could not grieve for a loved spouse or child, if every lost object could be replaced. This is a theme nicely developed in Nussbaum 1984. None of that, I think, can be gainsaid. We can suffer losses, and losses of the very things we value most, that cannot be replaced no matter how favourably life subsequently goes. But we must steer clear of a type-token confusion. The prudential value is *deep loving relationships to particular persons*. It can be realized, of course, only in a relationship to this or that particular person. The particular person cannot be replaced, but the prudential value can have a new instantiation. If a particular loved person dies, *he* is dead, and his life cannot be lived by

anyone else. But when a child dies, the parents might have another child whom they would not otherwise have had. Or when his wife dies, a man might remarry. And these new relationships can enrich one's life as much as the old. It does not destroy grief that one can love again, or that the new love be as a valuable as the old. Indeed, an inability to love again itself destroys grief by focusing not on what is lost but on one's own suffering. The irreplaceability of individuals is not the incommensurability of values.

19. Charles Taylor has this sort of clash of world views in mind in his discussion of incommensurability in Taylor 1982, sect. 2.

20. Ronald Dworkin uses the word 'trump' in describing the relation of rights to utility (e.g. liberty in relation to level of prosperity); see this ch. note 7. John Rawls uses the language of 'lexical ordering' in describing the relation of liberty to, e.g., prosperity; see Rawls 1972, esp. sect. 8.

21. Rawls admits this; he thinks that liberty has priority *in a certain range*, viz. after 'a certain level of wealth has been attained'. See Rawls 1972, sects. 26 and 82, esp. pp. 152, 542–3.

22. See, e.g., Popper 1966 vol. 1, pp. 284–5: '...there is, from the ethical point of view, no symmetry between suffering and happiness... Instead of the greatest happiness for the greatest number, one should demand, more modestly, the least amount of avoidable suffering for all'. Popper has in mind their moral weight, and we are now interested in their prudential weight; still, one would expect the same asymmetry there. For general discussion of these issues, see Griffin 1979. John Rawls approvingly quotes Petrarch's remark that a thousand pleasures are not worth one pain, and correctly observes that Petrarch thereby 'adopts a standard for comparing them that is more basic than either'; see Rawls 1972, p.557.

23. I go into these points more fully (and discuss negative utilitarianism generally) in Griffin 1979.

24. I argue this in ch. XI sect. 9. See also the excellent Hart 1975, where this line of argument is powerfully developed.

25. Rawls, of course, thinks that it is. He thinks that I should be reluctant to surrender the (small) liberty to gain the (great) prosperity because I should be putting at risk any capacity to pursue what most matters to me—the central part of my life plan. But it may be that I would (surrender some political liberty) because it would help me to pursue what I most value (the relationships with people I love who live in a country without those political liberties). To know this, I should have to be this side of the Veil of Ignorance, but then I am. For a more general discussion, more closely tied to the terms of Rawls' argument, see Hart 1975, which raises powerful doubts about it even in these tighter terms.

26. I shall return to this also in ch. XI; see esp. sect. 9.

27. I owe many of the thoughts expressed here to Derek Parfit's pressing me for explanations and to his offering many himself. Readers of Parfit 1984 will hear echoes in my discussion of small step-by-step changes of the

argument he presents for what he calls The Repugnant Conclusion (see his ch. XIX). My example and his are obviously very close.

In one version (sect. 148) Parfit's argument is this. Consider a world, A+, of twenty billion people, half of them at an extremely high quality of life and the other half at an even higher one. Then consider another world, New A, with many extra groups of people at a very low quality of life but just high enough so that it would not have been better in itself if they had never existed. Now, New A is better than A+ in certain respects: first, there are twenty billion people all of whom are at a higher level than anyone in A+; second, New A is, Parfit argues, better in egalitarian terms. And since there is no respect in which New A is worse than A+, New A is better than A+. Now compare New A with New B. Though here the better-off group would lose, the worse-off group would gain far more. So unless we accept Maximax or some strict form of élitism, we cannot think that this outcome is worse. New B is better on any plausible view of beneficence, and the inequality in New B is better on any plausible view of equality. Therefore New B is better than New A. But we can continue on through the alphabet, from New B to New C, until we reach New Z, where there is an enormous population at a

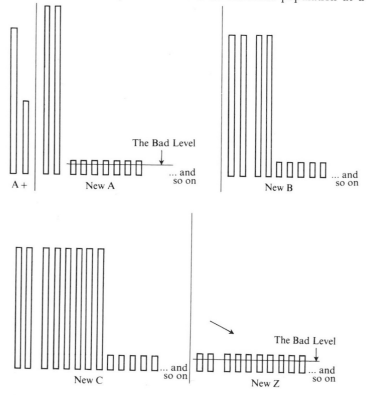

quality of life which, though just worth living, is gravely deprived, crimped, and mean—not much above the level where it would be in itself bad that lives are lived. That our reasoning carries us to New Z is The Repugnant Conclusion.

But does it? Parfit canvasses, but rejects, the possibility of stopping the slide at an early stage: namely, by refusing, on élitist grounds, to accept that New B is better than New A. I agree with him that, whatever form of élitism might be acceptable (see my ch. IV), the one needed to stop the slide from New A to New B is not. But there is another possibility, confined entirely to the reasoning about beneficence. Parfit's argument seems implicitly to employ a totting-up conception of measuring well-being; it treats well-being as measurable on a single continuous additive scale, where low numbers, if added to themselves often enough, must become larger than any initial, larger number. But this seems not true in prudential cases, and it would seem likely that this incommensurability in prudential values would get transferred to interpersonal calculation. Perhaps it is better to have a certain number of people at a certain high level than a very much larger number at a level where life is just worth living. Then we might wish to stop the slide not necessarily at the move from New A to New B, or even from New B to New C, but at that point along the line where people's capacity to appreciate beauty, to form deep loving relationships, to accomplish something with their lives beyond just staying alive ... all disappear.

(Parfit has a new discussion of this example in a forthcoming paper, 'Overpopulation and the Quality of Life', in P. Singer (ed.), *Practical Ethics*, Oxford: Oxford University Press.)

28. Look closely at this one. A person might sacrifice his eyesight, or his hearing, or his touch for enough pleasure in return, but he would not sacrifice all three for *any* amount of pleasure. (This example comes from Tribe 1972, pp. 91–2; I discuss it more fully in Griffin 1977.) Well, would he not? It would obviously take an enormous number of pleasures even to approach the value of those three senses. And then our thoughts are likely to be distracted by extraneous considerations. For one thing, pleasures crammed in such number into our lives, diminishing marginal utility is likely to apply; the values of the pleasures might form some such series as 1, $1/2$, $1/4$, etc. The sum of that series, even if the series is infinite, never exceeds a small finite number—namely, two. But it is no threat to commensurability that certain infinite series sum to a small finite number—or, more generally, that some values, because they diminish with crowding, sometimes to nothing, can never be added in a way that will make them equal certain other values. And if we take 'pleasure' broadly, to include a wide range of prudential values, thereby avoiding to some extent the effects of diminishing marginal utility, then it is doubtful that the pleasures can never outrank the value of these three senses. Would *no* amount of the satisfactions of intellectual or artistic accomplishment compensate a person for the loss of sight, hearing, and touch? Would a composer ordered to stop work on pain of those

impairments not think it worth going on if he were sure to have a good amount of time working at the level of the deaf Beethoven?

29. I have argued for a form of pluralism in ch. II sect. 4; see also ch. IV sect. 3.

30. See MacIntrye 1981, p. 62: 'For different pleasures and different happinesses are to a large degree incommensurable: there are no scales of quality and quantity on which to weigh them'. But all that this shows is that there is no commensurability of *this* kind. But this kind is not even what a utilitarian ought to be claiming.

31. John Rawls seems to think it does. 'The weakness of hedonism reflects the impossibility of defining an appropriate definite end to be maximized'; see Rawls 1972, p. 560. But we do not need a single end such as pleasure, or any single substantive value at all, to get a single scale. That will be the argument of the next chapter. The policy of maximization does not stand or fall with hedonism.

32. See ch. II sect. 4. This is one of Bernard Williams' interpretations of incommensurability in Williams 1981, p. 77: 'It is not true that for each conflict of values, there is some value, independent of any of the conflicting values, which can be appealed to in order to resolve that conflict'. Quite right. But this, too, is an extremely weak form of incommensurability (if a form at all). Utilitarians could, and should, accept it.

33. David Wiggins, in an argument that I am not sure that I follow, seems to think that we do. As I understand him, he denies that Aristotle held that there is a single substantive value (some 'universal or all-purpose predicate of favourable assessment') and *so* denies that Aristotle thought that there was a common measure of value. See Wiggins 1978–9, esp. pp. 267–8. But the two are not the same, nor is the first a necessary condition of the second.

34. Misunderstanding of just this point—of the nature of this scale and of its quantitative attribute—bedevils discussion of incommensurability. Bernard Williams complains, 'In cases of planning, conservation, welfare, and social decisions of all kinds, a set of values which are, at least notionally, quantified in terms of resources, are confronted by values which are not quantifiable in terms of resources: such as the value of preserving an ancient part of a town, or of contriving dignity as well as comfort for patients in a geriatric unit' (in Williams 1973c, pp. 102–3). Part of his worry is the way cost-benefit analysts actually arrive at their social recommendations, and who can fail to share it? What is easily measured gets prominent place; what is hard to measure either gets left out (e.g. liberty, autonomy—see the standard cost-benefit analysis procedure of leaving judgements about 'justice' to 'politicians') or gets hasty and crude treatment (e.g. human life—see virtually any cost-benefit discussion of the subject, though see also subtle treatments by E. J. Mishan, T. C. Schelling, and John Broome). But the other part of Williams' concern is to deny that these values are commensurable. But that some values lend

themselves to quantification in terms of resources and others do not shows nothing. *That* is not the scale of prudential value; it is, at best, a scale for a certain (limited) range of values. If we are able to enhance the dignity of some geriatric patients by giving them greater privacy or enhance their comfort by giving them better heating, how should we decide which to do? We could use the ranking of the patients themselves—so long as they understood the options—and provide them with whichever one they want more. If Williams' point is that these two values cannot be got on the same scale, then he is wrong. The patients, when informed, can rank them—and in the strong sense. If his point is, rather, that although they can be got on the same scale their value is not determined by their place there, then would he say that, even if the patients want the heating more, we decision-makers might determine the privacy to be more valuable and give them that instead?

Anyway, I think that Williams takes altogether too dim a view of what it is for values to be 'quantifiable in terms of resources'. It is not, he says, 'an accidental feature of the utilitarian outlook that the presumption is in favour of the monetarily quantifiable... It is not an accident, because (for one thing) utilitarianism is unsurprisingly the value system for a society in which economic values are supreme . . .' (p. 103). But to make money the common measure is not to make it the supreme value. To think so would be doubly mistaken. First, the true scale of well-being employs no supreme value, so money could not be it. And, second, whenever—in certain ranges—money functions as the common measure, it is used transparently. If I want to preserve the old stone wall and the copse (see ch. VI sect. 3) but should prefer a certain amount of money in compensation, then I should prefer what that money would give me (perhaps greater beauty) to what the old stone wall and copse give me (beauty). I discuss these points further in Griffin 1977, esp. sect. 3.

35. Isaiah Berlin sees monism and commensurability as more closely linked than they seem to me to be. But the labels 'monism' and 'commensurability' can bear so many different interpretations that it is not easy to be sure. See Berlin 1969, p. l: 'If the claims of two (or more than two) types of liberty prove incompatible in a particular case, and if this is an instance of a clash of values at once absolute and incommensurable, it is better to face this intellectually uncomfortable fact than to ignore it, or automatically attribute it to some deficiency on our part which could be eliminated by an increase in skill or knowledge; or, what is worse still, suppress one of the competing values altogether by pretending that it is identical with its rival—and so end by distorting both. Yet, it appears to me, it is exactly this that philosophical monists who demand final solutions—tidiness and harmony at any price—have done and are doing still.' Later (pp. lv–lvi) he speaks with approval of 'those who are aware of the complex texture of experience, of what is not ... capable of computation', with whom he contrasts those who think 'that we can uncover some single central principle... a principle which, once found,

so much traditional thought and action and philosophical doctrine rests, seems to me invalid, and at times to have led (and still to lead) to absurdities in theory and barbarous consequences in practice'. But this argument seems to me to overlook an important point: 'computation' on a single scale does not need a substantive 'single central principle'.

36. This is why it is puzzling that Berlin connects the defence of pluralism and incommensurability with the defence of liberalism. See his 'Introduction' to Berlin 1969; see also Bernard Williams' discussion of Berlin's views in 'Conflicts of Values' in Williams 1981, and in his introduction to Berlin 1978.

CHAPTER SIX

1. See, e.g., Tibor Scitovsky's categorical claim in Scitovsky 1976, p. 134 (see also p. 90): '...satisfaction or happiness cannot be measured, of course...' For a more cautious view, along much the same line, see Williams 1973c, pp. 101–2, which argues that although well-being, explained in some very crude hedonist way, might be measurable, the more plausible the explanation the less measurable well-being is. But then Kyburg 1984, p. 236, replies: 'It is often held that certain qualities, despite the fact that we speak of them in comparative terms, are not amenable to measurement. I have in mind such qualities as beauty, virtue, value, and the like, which are either regarded as "subjective" (and thus not fit subject matter for science), or as absolute and transcendent (and thus not fit subject matter for science). On the view of measurement that I have presented, there seems to be no reason why such qualities cannot in principle be measured.' In general, it is students of measurement who are least sceptical about the measurement of such attributes as 'utility', 'preference', 'well-being', and 'prudential value'.

2. Stevens 1959, p. 19.

3. See Suppes and Zinnes 1963, p. 14.

4. See, e.g., Siegel 1956. Despite the large number of scales that are of practical interest, Stevens' definition over-corrects our over-narrow ideas about measurement. Not *all* rules assigning numbers should be called 'measurement'. The one-to-one correlation of numbers and National Health Service patients, though a rule-governed assignment of numbers, probably should not. A patient's number functions too much like his name, and it seems better to restrict the term 'measurement' to attributes that are in some sense quantitative (on which see below, sect. 2). This point is more fully argued in Torgerson 1958, p. 17.

5. This account of the general form of a proof of measurability is developed in the following places: Scott and Suppes 1958, Suppes and Winet 1955, Suppes and Zinnes 1963.

6. What an attribute must be like in order to be 'quantitative' is partly a matter for stipulation. My requirements are relatively undemanding

—merely that $(\exists A)\ (\exists B)\ (A >_a B \lor A <_a B \lor A =_a B)$ where '$>_a$', '$<_a$' and '$=_a$' mean 'has more of the attribute than', 'less of it than', and 'same amount as'. On that definition length, weight, and hardness all count as quantities, but so do value, intelligence, funniness, and even beauty. For a more demanding requirement (the existential quantifiers of my definition become universal quantifiers) see Ellis 1968, ch. II sect. A. In contrast to both of these definitions, one of the pioneers of modern measurement theory, N. R. Campbell, has argued that proper 'quantities' appear only when we get beyond ordinal scales to cardinal ones. See Campbell 1938, pp. 141–2: 'Nobody, I think, has ever proposed to measure happiness or virtue by assigning numerals to represent its degree. But it is not uncommon to find mention of a "quantity of happiness (or virtue)"; indeed Benthamite hedonism would be meaningless unless there were such a thing as "quantity of pleasure". But the word "quantity" implies, or ought to imply, much more than a mere order . . . For all typical "quantities", mass, volume, cost and so on, are truly additive properties . . . happiness and virtue are not necessarily additive.'

7. See ch. V sect. 3.

8. I borrow this suggestion from John Broome, to whom I am indebted for discussion on many issues in this chapter.

9. That, it seems to me, is exactly what happens to 'utility' in the course of its cardinalization by appeal to levels of discrimination. This form of cardinalization goes back to Borda and Edgeworth and has been developed more recently by Goodman and Markowitz and others. See Goodman and Markowitz 1952; for a good general discussion, see Sen 1970, ch. 7. 2. It is based on three assumptions: first, that each person is able to discriminate only a finite number of levels of his utility; second, that he is indifferent between options on the same level; and third, that the difference between one level and the adjacent ones is the same at all levels. With those assumptions, we can derive a cardinal scale unique up to a linear transformation. But although it is a *cardinal* scale, is it any longer a scale of *utility*? The discriminations a person can make depend to some extent upon what his experience has been, what training has happened to come his way. Suppose a person has drunk good, middling, and poor whisky, and has made those three discriminations. Then his experience broadens and he encounters whiskies that fall between those categories, resulting, let us say, in his introducing two categories that he did not have before. It is very hard to think that, just because his discriminations have increased, his utility from the best has thereby increased.

It does not help to base the scale not on the discriminations that a person *actually* makes but on the discriminations that, with full experience, he *could* make. Some things permit finer discriminations than others. Suppose that, with my ear and my palate both at the peak of training, I make finer discriminations in my enjoyment of music than in my enjoyment of whisky. I discriminate, say, twenty levels with music, and only five with whisky. But, let us suppose, I enjoyed the best whisky as much as the best music. But then, if you improve my lot by giving me the music I find best instead of the merely passable music I now have to put up with, you increase my utility by nineteen units. If instead you give me the best whisky instead of the merely passable stuff I am now drinking, you increase my utility only four units. Yet you would increase it either way to levels that I equate. The trouble seems fundamental. This approach to the cardinal measurement of utility seems to be more a measure of a person's proneness to or capacities for discrimination, or of the extent to which the subject lends itself to discriminations, than a measure of his utility.

10. In ch. I sect. 4.

11. A theory of error is a central part of an adequate theory of measurement. How much variation in reports of quantities can there be, and in what circumstances, before one begins to wonder whether there is a scale at all? For a good discussion of these issues, see Kyburg 1984, esp. ch. IV sect. 4.

12. Well-being would seem to be a prime candidate for measurement on a ratio scale. There is a natural *zero*: a state with neither value nor disvalue, a life neither worth living nor worth not living, a condition to which one is indifferent. We should have to define 'negative value' carefully, so as to distinguish between merely the loss of benefit (where *zero* could be treated as the *status quo*) and the presence of a state that makes life worse (where we have the natural *zero* referred to above). We should also have to see whether the global preferences we formed about when life becomes worth living agree with the piecemeal judgments we make about individual features that had value and disvalue (in the second of the senses above). Could we get the result that a life that contained a net balance of individual values over disvalues was still not quite worth living? Would this show that we had got the individual values wrong, or that we ask for a certain surplus before we think life as a whole to be worth living? If the latter, then where is natural *zero*?

13. Von Neumann and Morgenstern 1953.

14. The word 'mystical' is L. J. Savage's; see Savage 1954, p. 94; he goes on to say that 'the probability-less idea of utility has been completely discredited in the eyes of almost all economists...' (p. 96). See also Morgenstern 1972, p.1181: 'All value or utility is expected value or utility, expected with certain probabilities...'

15. But not by all that much. Incommensurabilities, even of the weaker form, restrict the scope of all additive scales, probabilistic or not. Most important, the greatest restriction on the scope of the simple cardinal scale in my example comes, not from diminishing marginal utilities, but from the fact that it must measure *informed* desire. We cannot just ask people to compare packages of probabilities and pay-offs, because we should then be getting at their actual desires, the values that in fact they attach to objects, not at their informed desires, the values that the objects will prove to have to them. It is possible to apply a scale of utility taken

in conjunction with probability, such as one satisfying the von Neumann-Morgenstern axioms, to *informed* preferences. But the great increase in scope comes from applying it, as is more commonly done, to the packages of utilities and probabilities between which we observe people choosing. Then, instead of imposing the tough requirement that orderings be informed, we need merely ask that they satisfy what economists call 'consumer rationality'—for example, that 'at least as good as' be a weak ordering. (Some economists, though, recently have been jacking up the standards for 'consumer rationality'. E.g. Gravelle and Rees 1981, pp. 7–8, describes a rational decision-taker as one who (1) sets out all the feasible alternatives, (2) takes into account whatever information is readily available or worth collecting, (3) ranks the alternatives in order of preference, (4) chooses the alternative highest in this ordering. The second requirement is a big step towards what I have been calling *informed* preferences.) But this scale would not, in the interesting sense, be wider than mine, because it would not any longer be measuring the same quantity as mine. This scale would measure an empirical quantity: how valuable something seems to a certain person (see, e.g., Davidson, Suppes, and Siegel 1957). But what a person actually wants cannot be what we are after; a person can want what will be of no advantage to him, even perhaps of harm to him, and the notion that we are after must be kept close to what is in a person's interest. My scale measures a normative quantity: how valuable something is to a person's life. There are, broadly, two different conceptions of utility in play in modern discussions, each suiting a different theoretical setting. There is utility-e ('e' for 'empirical') and utility-n ('n' for 'normative'). Utility-e is the conception needed in a theory explaining how people, when subject to minimum restrictions of rationality, decide and act. It is the conception appropriate to the empirical parts of decision theory and of economics. Utility-n is the conception needed in a theory that aims to set standards for how people ought to decide and act. It is the conception appropriate to the more normative parts of decision theory, to welfare economics, to most of social choice theory, and to morality. The common, empirical von Neumann-Morgenstern scale gets its scope from its needing the presence of only subjective utility ('utility-e') and subjective probability, which can be found in very many situations of decision and action. But since moral theory needs a different conception of well-being, we have to go a different route. So, it is not that the quantity we want to measure would not allow us to cardinalize with reference to probabilities. It is, rather, that given the restrictions needed simply to get at our quantity, it is doubtful that we gain much scope by doing so.

CHAPTER SEVEN

1. ch. I sects. 1, 2 and 6.
2. ch. I sect. 3.

3. See Shapley and Shubik 1974, ch. 4 sect. 5, p. 51: 'When we move to larger groups, or a whole society, the concept of group utility takes on value overtones, becoming an expression of *social welfare* more than just a device to explain or predict the group's actions. Social welfare is (or ought to be) the optimand for planners, legislators, and other policy makers . . . ' The important move, however, is not from a small to a large scale, but from empirical theories that aim to explain decision, choice, and action to normative theories that aim to set standards for decision, choice, and action.

4. See Rawls 1972, sects. 15 and 49; and Rawls 1982.

5. ch. III sects. 4–7.

6. Parfit 1984, App. I.

7. ch. III sect. 7, ch. IV sect. 5.

8. ch. III sect. 7.

9. ch. I sect. 5.

10. Robbins 1938.

11. The proposal I have in mind is made, e.g., by John Harsanyi, Amartya Sen, Kenneth Arrow, and Donald Davidson. They all develop the proposal in different ways, but they have this common starting point. See Harsanyi 1976, ch. II; Harsanyi 1977, ch. 4; Sen 1973, pp. 14–15, 45; Arrow 1977; Arrow 1978; Davidson 1986. There is a similar proposal in Hare 1981, chs. 5 and 7. I have published a version of this chapter applied specifically to Hare's argument in a collection of essays about his recent work; see Griffin (forthcoming).

12. See Harsanyi 1976, pp. 50, 79–80; Harsanyi 1977, p. 59; Arrow 1977, p.220; Hare 1981, p. 128.

13. See esp. Harsanyi 1977, pp. 58–9.

14. Rawls 1982 develops a picture of how a well-ordered society regulated by an ordinal utilitarianism with comparability might use a deep utility function (Rawls calls it 'a shared highest-order preference') in making interpersonal comparisions (sects.6 and 7). And he goes on to suggest that the conception of a citizen who will decide by appeal to a deep utility function 'is psychologically intelligible only if one accepts, as Sidgwick did, a hedonist account of the good as a basis of an account of the rational judgment of individuals' (p. 181).

15. See ch. II sect. 4, ch. IV sects. 3 and 5.

16. Rawls thinks that resort to the deep utility function has some particularly unlikeable results. If we assume that everyone has a 'shared highest-order preference', he says, then we no longer see persons as having any particularly strong commitments to more determinate forms of the good. We think of them as ready to entertain any new convictions or aims, to abandon any past attachments and loyalties, if greater well-being can be bought that way. This results, Rawls thinks, in the loss of 'the

distinctiveness of persons': persons have no conception of how to lead a life that is peculiarly theirs; they become 'bare persons' (see Rawls 1982, esp. pp. 180–1). Rawls describes a monster (no individuality) who, not surprisingly, behaves odiously (sheds loyalties at the sight of a bigger pay-off). I doubt that the consequences are quite so horrific, but the issue is worth debating only if the most plausible form of desire account is likely to include a deep utility function, which it is not.

17. ch. IV sect. 3. I am indebted to Michael McDermott for helpful, wide-ranging discussions about comparability, especially about comparisons using objective conceptions of well-being.

18. ch. IV sect. 5.

19. The desires relevant here have to be at least minimally informed; that is, one has to know enough about what one is getting to rule out one's ending up no better off or even worse off. But it does not have to be a fully informed desire, that is, one such that if one knew more one would not want anything different. Desires that are minimally informed will at least register on the positive side of the scale of prudential value.

20. R. M. Hare rightly stresses that to form preferences one does not need antecedent values, tastes, or attitudes. Tastes and attitudes change; we often form new preferences. Many preferences—and preferences central to prudence and morality—come about because we go out and gain understanding of the nature of the options before us with the aim of giving shape to our inchoate and unenlightened desires. However, none of this helps the model of the judger's preference. Even if I form an entirely new preference, it must still be an expression of *my* values or tastes or attitudes—not, of course, necessarily antecedent ones, possibly ones that only now, for the first time, come into existence. Still, they must be mine, and not everyone need have them. Without them, I should have no preference. Of course, I have—we all have—a general vacuous preference to have a more, rather than a less, valuable life. But this general preference just takes the question of what is going on in comparisons back one stage. See Hare 1981, pp. 125–6.

21. Rawls is right, therefore, that interpersonal comparisons of well-being need some sort of identity of preferences or values (see Rawls 1982, p. 173): you and I, in making interpersonal comparisons, will have to agree in the prudential values we apply in assessing the lives of the persons we compare. But this sort of agreement on values is nothing like the agreement represented by a deep utility function. It does not 'destroy individuality' or create 'bare persons' for us to have to agree about what makes life good, any more than would our having to agree on what makes an act morally right. Nor does it involve odious behaviour (shedding loyalties, abandoning attachments): to grow in one's understanding of what is prudentially valuable involves shedding something but it is scarcely odious to do so. No doubt people will in fact have different conceptions of what makes life prudentially valuable. And given the difficulty of making such judgments, they should; it would be high-

handed to try artificially to homogenize conceptions. But the same is true of conceptions of moral right and wrong. This will mean that some disputes about interpersonal comparisons of well-being will be difficult to settle. But the informed desire account does at least give some framework, some criteria, to the dispute: judgments about prudential value have to be backed by defensible claims about what people, when informed, aim at.

22. This is Mill's view too: 'If there be one to which *all or almost all* who have experience of both give a decided preference' (my italics). See J. S. Mill, *Utilitarianism*, ch. II para. 5.

23. This conception of preference is widespread: probably dominant in economics and still strong in philosophy. See, e.g., Layard and Walters 1978, p. 124: 'Our basic theory assumes first that, for all the alternative consumption bundles he could conceivably face, the individual has a preference ordering. *This reflects his tastes.* . . . from the opportunities available to him he does the best he can, *best being defined according to his tastes*' (my italics). Also Arrow 1984, section entitled 'Choice Under Static Conditions': 'The utility theory of choice states that the choice in any given situation depends on the interaction of the externally given obstacles [i.e. income and prices] with the *tastes* of the individual . . . The utility theory asserts, more precisely, that the tastes can be represented by an ordering according to preference of all conceivable alternatives' (his italics).

24. See, e.g., Mackie 1981, p. 157: '. . . anything worth calling utilitarianism in an exact sense is committed to maximization based on calculations involving interpersonal comparisons . . . such maximizing calculations may be morally objectionable in that they neglect questions of distributive justice or the rights of individuals, and *in any case they are quite impracticable*' (my italics). Or John Rawls 1982, p. 170: '. . . given the circumstances of justice in which citizens have conflicting conceptions of the good, there cannot be any practical agreement on how to compare happiness as defined, say, by success in carrying out plans of life, nor, even less, any practical agreement on how to evaluate the intrinsic value of these plans. Workable criteria for a public understanding of what is to count as advantageous in matters of justice, and hence as rendering some better situated than others in the relevant interpersonal comparisons, must, I believe, be founded on primary goods, or some similar notion.' See also Rawls 1972, sects. 15, 49.

25. See the discussion of whether the informed-desire account is 'subjective' or 'objective' in ch. II sect. 4. See also ch. III sect. 7.

26. e.g. Rawls 1972, sects. 16, 25, 49, 60; Rawls 1975a; and Rawls 1975b; also Scanlon 1975.

27. See ch. III sect. 5, and Part III *passim*.

28. See ch. III sect. 6.

CHAPTER EIGHT

1. Not that the Requirement of Psychological Realism is easy to formulate. The rough idea that surfaces from time to time in philosophical discussion is this: moral principles must be such that our accepting them will, conjoined with normal human motivation, determine action—not necessarily unfailingly but at least often enough to give the principle a point. But what difference would it make if what we needed to get persons actually to live up to a moral principle went beyond 'normal' human motivation? If we convincingly threatened someone with roasting alive if he did not live up to a certain principle, he would be likely to do it, as self-sacrificing as it might sometimes prove to be. Hell and Purgatory show that. But what if, instead, we merely whispered into his ear each night during his childhood, 'Unless you live up to that principle, you'll roast alive'? If the whispers produced compliance, would the principle have met the Requirement? Does it matter to a moral principle that no one would follow it without fear (e.g. of ostracism) or pleasure (e.g. from praise)? The Requirement becomes too stiff if 'normal human motivation' is taken to be 'human motivation without threats or inducements from others'. But there are limits, both practical and moral, to how far fear, pleasure, and so on can be used to produce compliance. One important moral limit is autonomy: part of the dignity of life is choosing one's own path through it. Given those limits, there can be principles so demanding that compliance simply will not be forthcoming. So the Requirement must be something like this: moral principles must be such that one's believing or accepting them will, conjoined with threats and inducements that both morality and the facts of human psychology permit, determine action. One might, after all, autonomously subject oneself to threats and inducements in order to keep oneself on the straight and narrow. This formulation of the Requirement makes its application much more complicated and its use as a stick to beat certain moral theories much less easy than is usually thought. I am grateful to Philippa Foot for discussion of these issues.

2. For recent discussion of the reduction to self-interest, see Quinton 1973, pp. 5–10; Williams 1985, ch. 3; and Kavka 1985.

3. There is another problem with this way of making morality not alien. Is it enough just to place morality inside *me* (i.e. inside my self-interest)? The only plausible case for reducing morality to self-interest has to appeal to what happens in the long run. But why is it enough to get morality inside *me*? Why should I care about what happens to me much later? Is the difference between *now* and *later* in some respects like the difference between *me* and *others*? This line of thought was pursued in Sidgwick 1907, pp. 418–19, and much further and with great power in Parfit 1984, Pt. II.

4. For a good discussion, see Ullmann-Margalit 1977.

5. See ch. X sect. 2, ch. XII sect. 6, ch. XIII sects. 5–6.

6. See ch. X sect. 2, ch. XIII sect. 5.

7. This is Bernard William's objection in Williams 1985, pp. 45–6.

8. This argument is developed in Williams 1985, ch. 3.

9. ch. IV sect. 1.

10. See ch. IV sect. 3.

11. See sect. 5 below.

12. Nozick 1981, pp. 401–2; see also my discussion earlier at ch. IV sect. 2.

13. See Hobbes 1969, sect. 25; D. Hume, *A Treatise of Human Nature*, bk. III Pt. I. For contemporary examples, see references to Williams and Foot in n. 22.

14. See his article 'Internal and External Reasons' in Williams 1981.

15. Williams 1981, pp. 101–2.

16. See ch. I sect. 3.

17. See Williams 1981, pp. 103–4.

18. Williams 1981, pp. 103–5.

19. See ch. II sect. 3, ch. IV sect. 3.

20. I go into this sort of deliberation more fully in ch. IV sect.3.

21. I argue all this more fully in ch. II sect. 3.

22. Thus Bernard Williams argues that in the case of external reasons '... the new motivation [must] be in some way rationally arrived at, granted the earlier motivations. Yet at the same time, it must not bear to the earlier motivations the kind of rational relation which we considered in the earlier discussion—for in that case an internal reason statement would have to be true in the first place. I see no reason to suppose that these conditions could possibly be met.' See Williams 1981, p. 109. He contrasts the sorts of deliberation already discussed in connection with internal reasons with some form (not entirely clear) of 'rational' deliberation. But the deepest, most fateful deliberation seems to fall between his two categories—more radical than the first sort but not as totally cut off from human desires, it would seem, as the second.

There is the same sort of flaw, it seems to me, in Philippa Foot's similar argument. 'I am, therefore, putting forward quite seriously a theory that disallows the possibility of saying that a man ought (full unsubscripted "ought") to have cares other than those he does have e.g. that the uncaring, amoral man ought to care about the relief of suffering or the protection of the weak. In my view we must start from the fact that some people do care about such things, and even devote their lives to them ... These things are necessary but only subjectively and conditionally necessary, as Kant would put it.' See her 'Morality as a System of Hypothetical Imperatives', in Foot 1978, pp. 169–70. A moral person, she says, is one who *cares* 'about others, and about causes such as liberty and justice' (p. 166). But this is just what cries out for explanation, and Foot leaves it unexplained. What should I care about?

What is worth the sort of devotion and commitment that morality requires? Certainly not everything. Foot says later, a little more generously, 'I believe that a reason for acting must relate the action directly or indirectly to something that the agent wants or which is in his interest to have ... ' (p. 179). But what is that last clause, with its use of that idealized notion of interests, doing there? It opens up an enormous amount. Reasons for acting are not just a matter of a person's actual cares, concerns, aims, desires, and so on, but also of what, whether he realizes it or not, is in his interest. But then why can he not also see other considerations, not necessarily connected with his interests, as reasons? Once we ask, What *should* I care about?, and we see just how complex the relation betwen reasons and desires actually is, the distinction between 'subjective' and 'objective' gets dropped as a poor fit.

23. See ch. II sect. 4; ch. VII sect. 4.

24. Bernard Williams is a case in point; see Williams 1981, p. 109.

25. The rest of this paragraph recapitulates arguments from ch.II sect. 3; here, as there, a reader of John McDowell will hear echoes of some of his claims (see ch. II n. 19).

26. The authority problem that Bernard Willaims has with internal reasons spreads to what he says about 'character' and 'integrity' (see his 'Persons, Character and Morality' and 'Utilitarianism and Self-Indulgence' in Williams 1981 and see also Williams 1973a, sect.3, 5). We need, but he does not supply, some understanding of how we are to assess character. He often refers to 'reflection' (e.g. Williams 1985, ch. IX but see also the Index), but he says little, especially little in the way of concrete examples, about what it does.

His view is simply this. Any fully developed person has 'commitments' or 'ground projects' that he 'takes seriously at the deepest level, as what his life is about' (Williams 1973a, p. 116), projects which are 'closely related to his existence and which to a significant degree give a meaning to his life' (Williams 1981, p. 12). He cannot abandon such projects just because the reports from the utility network indicate that, as chance or the actions of others have stacked things, utility would be maximized by his doing so. That would be to ask him to commit a kind of suicide, to abandon himself. It would be to attack 'the value of integrity' (Williams 1973a, pp. 96–9).

But what does Williams mean by 'integrity' here? Whereas 'integrity' as ordinarily used, to mean something like 'honesty' or 'general uprightness', does name something valuable, 'integrity' as Williams uses it, in its more literal etymological sense of 'wholeness', does not. Persons often actually have as their 'ground project', as what their life is about, morally hideous, or merely shabby or shallow, ambitions. To ask a person whose life is centred on resentment or revenge or vanity or one-upmanship to 'abandon' himself may be exactly what he needs. Some persons most need, and all of us to no small degree would benefit from, some well chosen 'disintegration' and 'reintegration'. Even if everyone's values were perfectly respectable, there would be a more general difficulty. Williams needs to explain 'integrity' in a way that makes it, at once, valuable in some non-question-begging way and yet incompatible with acting, utilitarian fashion, as reports from the utility network demand. That is no easy job. There are, it is true, other interpretations of 'wholeness' to fall back on. We might, for instance, take it to mean a person's being all of a piece—not hypocritical, insincere, self-deceived, and so on. 'Integrity', so interpreted, would clearly be something worth protecting, but it would not be incompatible with utilitarianism. Or we might take 'wholeness' to require commitment that involves the whole of a person; 'wholeness' could then be seen as a kind of 'wholeheartedness' such that a person who takes, say, truthfulness as one of his central values must see certain features of particular situations as morally dominant and certain others —especially utilities—as morally minor. Here integrity is incompatible with utilitarianism but not valuable in a non-question-begging way; it is simply the rejection of the utilitarian approach to values.

Williams' emphasis on character and integrity connects with his preference for 'thick' ethical concepts, such as 'loyal', 'courageous', 'generous', 'grateful', over thin abstractions, such as 'good', 'right' (Williams 1985, esp. pp. 129, 140, 200). Character manifests itself in virtues and vices, and different characters, even different good ones, manifest different ones. Not only may persons properly bring different views of things to the job of sizing up a particular situation, but also the sizing up itself is best conducted not by looking for abstract good-making features but by sharpening our eye for all the detail that bears on assessment. But thick concepts have no small authority problems of their own. Which loyalties count? How much?

27. See Parfit 1984, Pt. II *passim*.

28. A good recent attempt, in the Kantian tradition, to derive substantive moral conclusions from formal features of rationality is Darwall 1983. Darwall parlays the impersonality of rationality into a modern contractualist conception of equal respect. So the success of his derivation turns partly on the acceptability of that contractualist conception. He finds in rationality a requirement that a rational principle be 'self-supporting', i.e. that it would be rational according to it to act on it (see pp. 218–20, 228–30). Then by adding certain other features of formal rationality he goes on to derive two richer requirements on a rational principle, namely, in order of increasing richness, (1) that it would be rational according to it to choose all agents to act on it when this choice is made from an impartial standpoint (a move to a form of Kantian universalization), (2) that it would be rational to choose that all act on it, were that choice made from a perspective in which one is motivated by a concern for one's ability rationally to pursue ends, but is denied any information about oneself in particular (a move to something very like Rawls' Original Position). I discuss the requirement that a principle be self-supporting at the end of ch. X sect. 2. I discuss the acceptability of the contractualist's conception of equal respect in ch. IX sects. 3 and

4 and have more to say about Kant's Categorical Imperative test in ch. X sect. 4.

29. See Hare 1952, ch. 11, Hare 1963, ch. 4.

30. Hare is well aware that his view is open to the charge of linguistic conservatism. The view in question is that from the logic of key moral terms we can derive the universality and prescriptivity of moral judgments and from universal prescriptivity we can derive a form of impartiality, broadly utilitarian, that will determine which principles and dispositions should guide action. But what if we chose to adopt different moral terms, or change our present moral terms in just the way that would prevent the derivation of universal prescriptivity? To the charge that he is making us the captive of our present conceptual scheme, Hare replies (Hare 1981, ch. 1.5) that he would be if he concentrated on 'secondarily evaluative words', but he concentrates instead on words like 'must' and 'ought', which do not encapsulate any particular moral commitment. But the real worry, I think, is different from the one he here meets, namely that even 'ought' and 'must' encapsulate particular commitments as to what morality, or moral reasoning, is. Hare's answer to this deeper worry is, I believe, that if we alter the meanings of the most basic evaluative words, we shall alter the questions we ask, and that if we want to answer *those* questions then we are stuck with *those* concepts. But the worry lingers. We might, in the course of building a moral theory, revise certain features of those key terms, so that we should no longer be asking exactly the same questions as at the start, nor entirely new ones either. Could there be, initially, any ground for saying that such partial revision will not, or should not, take place? Pressures to change concepts usually mount only in the course of theory-building. So can one do more than build one's theory always sensitive to the need for conceptual revision? This, of course, allows Hare a further response, one to which I am sympathetic. He can say that when the theory is complete one finds at the end no need to revise the universal prescriptivity of 'ought' and 'must'. But this can be claimed only at the close of theory-building, so it cannot be the source of the theory.

There is also the more familiar, much discussed problem for Hare's view: Can we derive from the logic of the key terms more than a pretty indeterminate form of universalizability and prescriptivity, nothing determinate enough to yield substantive moral principles? But I think that there is this prior problem, too.

For further discussion of Hare's views, see J. L. Mackie's objections in 'Rights, Utility and Universalization' and Hare's response in 'Reply to J. L. Mackie' both in Frey 1984.

31. See ch. II sect. 5.

32. This is a question that Derek Parfit asks in the course of his discussion of personal identity; see Parfit 1984, ch. 15. He suggests that his reductionist view of 'person' points towards saying the first. In what follows I give considerations that point towards saying the second. But it

is not clear that these views are contrary. There is an ambiguity in the expression 'the whole of one person's life'. Parts of a life, such as experiences that we value, can be contrasted to a whole life in different ways. 'A whole life' can be interpreted temporally (as Parfit does): one's life from start to finish (not a period in it). Or it can be interpreted (as I do): everything that now, or over some period, constitues one's life (not an aspect of it).

33. It is not that there are *no* reasons to hold back from a policy of maximization in the case of one person. I shall mention three that have considerable weight.

First, might it not be better to follow a policy, not of maximizing one's own well-being, but ensuring that one does not have any period that is very bad, even if the total would thereby be less? I have already given my answer in ch. II sect. 5.

A second reason to hold back is what might be called a holistic approach to evaluation, namely, the view that the value of the whole may not always be the value of the parts. (I owe this point and the following example to Paul Seabright.) For example, suppose a person who has had seventy years of very good life has an accident, and imagine each of the alternative results. In one, he is killed outright. In the other, he lives on, diminished and in some pain, for another ten years, but years which on their own would be worth having. Now if maximizing means adding, then there is no question but that the second outcome is better: seventy good years plus ten years of positive value. Yet if evaluation is sometimes holistic there is a question. Perhaps the life as a whole would be better if he is killed outright; perhaps the person would rationally prefer it.

The holistic evaluation should not really make us hold back. The example counts against maximizing in the sense of aiming at the greatest sum of the value of the parts; it is really an objection to a rather crude aggregative approach to evaluation. But it does not count against maximizing in the sense of making one's life as valuable as possible. On the contrary, it uses that conception of the maximum in favouring outright death. Even as an objection to an aggregative approach, it is unconvincing. How could outright death be the rational choice? *Ex hypothesi*, the seventy year old thinks both that the extra ten years would be worth having but that, added to the seventy very good years, they would make the life as a whole worse. One can see the value categories that might be appealed to: a person may value living, and dying, with *style*; he may treat his whole life as a kind of aesthetic object. But that we have these value categories does not mean that they can coherently be used here. Although not everyone agrees, beauty, for instance, has a value only by being appreciated and so adding to the value of persons' lives; it is implausible that in this example what is added to persons' lives justifies outright death.

A third possible reason for not maximizing is the powerful one that it is simply beyond our powers. Perhaps the most that we can reasonably hope to do is what economists call 'satisficing' (see Herbert Simon's essays collected in Simon 1982, esp. 'A Behavioral Model of Rationality'). The maximizing strategy might be stated: (1) identify all options, (2) evaluate them, (3) choose the best. But one can seldom identify all the options. Even a simple choice between keeping or breaking a promise does not, for a maximizer, consist in only two options: one can break a promise in practically innumerable ways. And one cannot decide at a certain point that further work identifying the options would cost more than it would be worth; to decide that would require investigation, which itself might cost more than it would be worth, though knowing that would itself require investigation, and so on. There is often no such thing as the 'best' outcome; in many situations that is a concept without an application. One can identify a 'best', or at least 'equal best', option if the set of options is fairly small, but real life seldom provides such sets. Perhaps in real life the rational strategy is satisficing: (1) fix an aspiration level, (2) start enumerating the options, (3) evaluate them as one goes along, (4) accept the first to be at or above the aspiration level.

Take this case. I follow the satisficing strategy and come upon option A, which meets my aspiration level. But soon it becomes clear to me that option B is better (I might have learned this without any work on my part). It would now be irrational for me not to choose B. I have a reason to choose B (it is better) and no reason not to (it costs me nothing). Satisficing is not a rational strategy in the strong sense that maximizing appears to be: it would often be plainly irrational. Anyway, how do I fix my aspiration level? For instance how do I fix an asking price for my house? My aspiration level would itself be irrational if I had a very good chance of getting something much better without much cost to me. So the only rational way to fix an aspiration level involves doing, as best one can, the complex trade-off between further costs, further benefits, and the probabilities involved. What seems to be at fault is the particular characterization of the maximizing strategy given just above. On that characterization, maximizing requires enumeration of all the options, and the impossibility of doing that undermines the whole strategy. But instead of reacting to this by going over to a satisficing strategy, one could look for a better characterization of the maximizing one. For example: (1) identify the options, stopping when one guesses that the cost of further identification will exceed the benefit (the same sort of calculation that one needs to fix the aspiration level), and then proceeding as before. For a good discussion of these issues, see Pettit 1984.

There are many further arguments for satificing, centring on the consequence that the use of a rational strategy has for an agent's character or temperament. Spontaneity is valuable; satisficing gives it some space, while maximizing gives it virtually none (see Elster 1982, ch. 2). Satisficing fosters a valuable moderation, while maximizing encourages discontent, obsessive perfectionism, sometimes even greed (see Pettit 1984). These, and several other cases, need careful consideration. Let me just state my belief that they do not make a strong case for satisficing. For instance, there are good reasons to be content with being merely fairly well off, without trying to squeeze out of life every last bit of comfort or security; that over-ambitious strategy would often involve pursuing one value at the expense of a second, greater one that relentless striving for the first excludes. These arguments for satisificing often trade on an overly narrow conception of the values that can enter a maximizing strategy. The issues that arise here connect with important issues about the self-defeating quality of certain maximizing strategies and about the difference between local and global consequentialist perspectives. What would maximizing deliberation be like in practice? Might maximization, even if it were accepted as the rational strategy, have only a limited role in our actual decision procedures? I come to these issues in ch. X sect. 2.

34. e.g. in Suppes 1967.

35. See John Rawls' illuminating account of this variety of decision theory in Rawls 1972, pp. 552 ff.; see also pp. 441 ff.

36. I have argued this earlier at ch. II sect. 4.

37. e.g. A. Sen and B. Williams in their introduction to Sen and Williams 1982, pp. 16–18.

38. J. S. Mill, *Utilitarianism*, ch. IV, esp. paras.3 and 9. The sentence I use to express Mill's conclusion comes from para. 3, where he has not yet argued that *only* happiness is a good. But when, in para. 9, he draws his final conclusion, it is stated too compactly to show what he has in mind, namely what he says in para. 3 strengthened with *only*: only general happiness is a good to the aggregate.

39. Mill 1972, p. 1414.

40. *Utilitarianism*, ch. V, n. to para. 36.

41. Also the n. to ch. V, para. 36.

42. ch. IV, paras.3 and 9.

43. Economic theory, which gets its framework from utilitarianism, may suffer from a tendency to the same conflation. The social welfare function traverses the same ground: individual good, to uncontentious forms of the common good, to contentious forms, and finally to standards for action. So it incorporates the whole of moral philosophy. The risks of conflation are even greater in economics; the term 'social welfare function' often includes voting procedures (e.g. majority rule), on the ground that they are devices for determining society's choices. But voting procedures often have purely practical justifications: we need a solution (better rather than worse, but sometimes any solution rather than continued conflict); solutions of conflicts of interest should promote social stability, etc. So the *best* voting procedure may not produce an individual's *best* or a group's *best* or the morally *best*. It is yet another standard.

44. See F. Hutcheson, *An Inquiry Concerning Moral Good and Evil* (1725), sect. III, para. 8: 'that action is best, which procures the greatest happiness for the greatest numbers'. C. Helvétius, *De l'esprit* (1758),

discours II, ch. XXIII: 'Les principles d'une bonne morale ... doivent toujours être appuyés ... sur ... l'intérêt public, c'est à dire celui du plus grand nombre.' C. Beccaria, *Dei Delitti e delle Pene* (1754, English trans. 1770): 'la massima felicità divisa nel maggior numero'. J. Priestley, *An Essay on the First Principles of Government* (1758), p. 17, Part I, of liberty: 'The good and happiness of the members, that is of the majority of the members of any state is the great standard'. For a thorough discussion of the history of the formula up to Bentham, see Baumgardt 1952, pp. 35–59.

45. See his *A Fragment on Government* (1776), Preface, sect. 2 and *passim*. On Bentham's dropping the formula in favour of simply 'the greatest happiness', see Baumgardt 1952, p. 505. See also Bentham's note of 1822 to his use of 'the principle of utility' in *An Introduction to the Principles of Morals and Legislation* (1789), ch. I, sect. 1; the gloss in the footnote also supports a simple 'the greatest happiness' reading.

46. Mill speaks of 'The Greatest Happiness Principle', which *could* mean 'the greatest happiness of the greatest number', but it need not; it could also mean simply 'the greatest total happiness' without regard to number. 'The greatest happiness of the greatest number' was used twice in Sidgwick 1907, pp. 420 and 499, as one version of the principle of utility, but this is only a lapse; it is clear (see pp. 415–16) that Sidgwick understands the principle of utility as requiring simply the greatest total utility possible.

47. e.g. Baier 1958, p. 192; Britton 1959–60; Popper 1966, vol. II p.285; Rescher 1966, esp. pp. 8 and 25 but *passim*; Narveson 1967, p. 126; Franklin 1968, p. 162; Wolff 1968, p. 7; Rawls 1972, p. 22 n.9; Williams 1973c, p. 96; Dworkin 1977 p. 23; article on 'Utilitarianism' in Flew 1979; MacIntyre 1981, p. 62.

48. This point is hardly original. The first to make it was a nineteenth-century economist (Edgeworth 1881, pp. 117–18); more recently much the same point has been made by game theorists (von Neumann and Morgenstern 1953, p. 11) and general linguists (Jespersen 1924, p. 246). But the point should not be overdone. It does not show, for instance, as Peter Geach thinks it does, how to 'shoot down' utilitarianism, because the fault is entirely removed simply by shifting to the formula 'the greatest happiness', which most utilitarians use anyway. See Geach 1977, pp. 91–4.

49. Von Neumann and Morgenstern 1953, p. 11.

50. Of course, double dependent superlatives can be coherent so long as one or both are hyperbolic. In a letter to *The Times* some years ago Mr James Raimes wrote in support of multiple forms of art (such as lithography) as against rare forms (such as Old Master paintings), and he ended with a call for 'the very best art for the most people at the lowest price possible'. But it is likely that Mr Raimes did not mean any of his three superlatives strictly; what he wants is good art at modest prices for large numbers of people to enjoy. And no doubt what he meant by 'good

art' would cover examples that might still differ a bit between themselves in degree of goodness. The trouble comes in formulae in which the dependent functions are to be strictly maximized: every degree of variation is meant to count. So these various ways of avoiding the trouble do not help such formulae as 'the greatest number of radios assembled in the shortest possible time'. *The Times*, 9 March 1968.

51. I am sure that many persons will be unconverted by this argument. They will still think that the formula is all right and that our job is just to find words to express what we have always really had in mind in using it. Perhaps one of the superlatives is eliminable, or not a strict maximum. Well, the likely candidate for elimination is 'the greatest number', but that just leaves the formula 'the greatest happiness', and if that is what one means, one should say it. Or suppose that it is not quite so simple, that the superlatives are lexicographically ordered. Well, the principle might then go: first maximize happiness but, if there are ties, maximize number. Maximization of number would have a modest role to play, although it might get some appeal from seeming to introduce considerations of justice, and I shall discuss it further from this point of view in a moment. Or suppose that both maxima are eliminable and that what we really have in mind is a rate: the act with the highest utility is, we should then say, the one which produces the greatest amount of happiness per person affected by the act. But the trouble with all these suggestions is that, although they give coherent standards, they are not plausible as interpretations of what the original formula means. And if these new standards are meant, then they should be stated, and the original formula simply scrapped.

52. Von Neumann and Morgenstern 1953, pp. 10 ff.

53. For an explanation of the Prisoner's Dilemma, see ch. X n. 1.

54. See Frankena 1963, p. 34; if we 'understand the principle of utility as enjoining us to promote *the greatest good of the greatest number*', it 'thus becomes a double principle ... it has become a combination of the principle of utility with a principle of justice'. See also Rescher 1966, p. 25: 'the principle of utility is a two-factor criterion ("greatest good", "greatest number"), and ... these two factors can in given cases work against one another'.

55. For instance, we could produce such a distribution by upsetting an equal distribution where everyone is well off, even thereby lowering the total, so long as we benefit more persons by the change than we harm. The case against finding in 'the greatest number' an adequate account of justice is well, and much more fully, argued in Rescher 1966, pp. 25–8, from which I draw my points here.

56. Rawls 1972, p. 27; see also Nozick 1974, pp. 32–3.

57. e.g. Bernard Williams and Philippa Foot; see the references in n.22.

58. ch. II sect. 5.

59. Pt. Two, esp. ch. V.

60. chs. IX and XI.

61. Sidgwick 1907, pp. 404, 506–9; the second passage cited is the close of the book, where Sidgwick unflinchingly faces the possibility of a fundamental contradiction in our apparent intuitions of what is reasonable in conduct.

62. See ch. II sect. 5 and ch. V.

CHAPTER NINE

1. Those familiar with the writings of Ronald Dworkin will recognize these expressions. He uses 'equal concern and respect' to mark a 'fundamental and axiomatic' right from which not only more particular rights but also the general authority of collective goals are to be derived (see Dworkin 1977, esp. pp. xiv–xv but also pp. 180–3, 272–8). I take his expression and split it into two parts of very different significance. I think that what he means by 'equal concern and respect', at least judging by its fundamental place in his argument, is what I mean here by 'equal respect'. One of the points that I want to argue throughout this Part is that there is no single moral 'principle of equality', that equality of different things matters at different points in moral theory, and that we have to keep them straight.

2. See ch. X sect. 3.

3. ch. VIII sect. 2, but see also the discussion of ethical pull in ch. VIII sect. 5.

4. Some utilitarians (e.g. Mill) have tried to ground obligations in our desires or ends. But the failure of this attempt is not also a failure of utilitarianism. It is a mistake to think that because utilitarianism is essentially teleological in one way (viz. in maintaining that right and wrong are determined by how possible actions promote our ends) it has to be teleological in every way (e.g. in maintaining that what makes this, or anything, an obligation is that it does promote human ends).

   It is a mistake to see utilitarianism and Kantianism as systematically opposed. It is possible to produce a powerful combination of a substantially utilitarian theory with a largely Kantian conception of obligation, as R. M. Hare's work clearly shows. My own account of obligation is less close to Kant's than Hare's is.

5. As do, e.g., G. J. Warnock in Warnock 1971 and J. L. Mackie in Mackie 1977, ch. 5. Both Warnock and Mackie limit their claims to 'narrow morality' ('a system of a particular sort of constraints on conduct—ones whose central task is to protect the interests of persons other than the agent and which present themselves to an agent as checks on his natural inclinations or spontaneous tendencies to act') in contrast to 'broad morality' ('a general all-inclusive theory of conduct: ... whatever body of principles [someone] allowed ultimately to guide or

determine his choices of action'); see Mackie 1977 pp. 106–7. My objections will also come from 'narrow morality'.

6. Warnock 1971, pp. 19–26.

7. Mackie 1977, p. 111.

8. Mackie 1977, p. 116.

9. Warnock 1971, p. 76; Mackie 1977, p. 114.

10. For Rawls' criticism of the utilitarian conception of impartiality, the Ideal Observer, as an undesirable impersonality, see Rawls 1972, pp. 188, 190; for his argument that the Ideal Contractor conception provides the superior interpretation of impartiality, see pp. 189–90.

11. e.g. in John Mackie's unpublished lectures, *Justice and Rights*; see also R. M. Hare's discussion in Hare 1975 *passim* but esp. pp. 89–95, 101–7.

12. e.g. in Diggs 1982, pp. 112–14.

13. *Utilitarianism*, ch. V, n. to para. 36.

14. See, e.g., Rawls 1972, pp. 36, 44 ('the aggregative-distributive dichotomy') and Rawls 1974–5, p.19 (utilitarianism 'puts no value on the distribution of good'; it 'gives no weight to distribution ... '). See also Sen 1973, p. 23 ('utilitarianism ... is much too hooked on the welfare *sum* to be concerned with the problem of distribution ... '). See also Williams 1973, p. 142 (an implication of utilitarianism is that 'questions of equitable and inequitable distribution do not matter').

15. For the first two remarks see Mackie 1978. For the third see Rawls 1972, pp. 27, 187, and Nozick 1974, pp. 32–3.

16. For an example of someone who takes 'separateness' as a *reason* for adopting a particular view about impartiality, see Nozick 1974, pp. 32–3.

17. See Rawls 1972, p. 255 (where the Original Position is equated with 'the point of view of noumenal selves'); Rawls 1980, pp. 549–50. For contrast of Ideal Observer and Ideal Contractor, see Rawls 1972, pp. 188–90.

18. Rawls 1972, see p. 60 for their preliminary statement and pp. 302–3 for their final and full statement.

19. Rawls 1972, p. 3.

20. Rawls 1972, p. 4.

21. 'Thousands Who Need Not Die Each Year', *Sunday Times*, 27 March 1983.

22. Rawls 1978, p. 47. On the limits in scope of the two principles of justice, see p. 49: 'The first principles of justice as fairness are plainly not suitable for a general theory'; see also his n. 4.

23. Rawls 1972, p. 88; see in general sect. 14.

24. Rawls 1972, p. 83. Rawls also limits his attention to a society composed of healthy people, on the ground that the special needs of the ill and the handicapped need special treatment and are likely to distort our

judgment about the normal. See Rawls 1975a, p. 96. But this exclusion does not help with the examples either. For further discussion of this exclusion, see ch. XI n. 23.

25. Rawls 1972, p. 4.

26. Rawls 1972, p. 218.

27. Rawls 1972, p. 248.

28. Rawls 1972, p. 277.

29. Rawls 1972, p. 178.

30. Rawls 1972, sect. 31.

31. Rawls 1972, p. 449.

32. Rawls 1978, p. 48.

33. Rawls 1972, p. 573.

34. There is another way that Rawls' contractualism is not rich enough. I have been speaking of Rawls' treatment of *justice* as fairness, but there are comparable troubles for his account of *rightness* as fairness. A good example to consider is that of promising (see Rawls 1972, pp. 344 ff.). For example, should long-term promises be binding, even if entered into in good faith, and even if the circumstances have not changed? Lady Diana Cooper reports: 'She [Lady Curzon] told me an amazingly characteristic fact about George [Lord Curzon]. On marriage he made her sign a pledge that, in case of his death, she would never remarry.' (Quoted in Ziegler 1983, p. 118.) But suppose, years later, with her husband dead, Lady Curzon wanted to remarry and deeply regretted that promise of her distant, youthful self. Is she obliged to keep it? How would appeal to contractualism settle the matter? There are at least two ways one can see the institution of promising: one where all promises (so long as they were made by a person capable of understanding their terms, not repudiated by the promisee, etc.) are binding; another where all such promises are binding so long as they are not very long-term. Both institutions are compatible with Rawls' two principles of justice. How are we to choose between them? The Original Position tells us nothing, or nothing relevant. What one must appeal to is one's conception of what would be right. And this conception is not, therefore, *rightness as fairness*, because it is detached from the whole contractarian apparatus.

35. Rawls 1972, pp. 102–3.

36. Rawls 1972, pp. 141–2.

37. Rawls 1972, pp. 119–20; see also Rawls 1980, p. 536, where 'best deal' considerations are said not to be the only ones but are thereby acknowledged to be important ones.

38. Rawls 1972, p. 103.

39. Rawls 1972, p. 176–7.

40. Rawls 1972, p. 177.

41. Rawls 1980, p. 560.

42. That formulation is derived from Scanlon 1982, p. 110. Scanlon sees contractualism not as an expression of the moral point of view but as that very closely connected thing, an account of what kind of judgment moral ones are. So I here alter his focus. Still, to give an account of the moral point of view is to give an indication of what morality is and so adopt a view about the nature of moral judgments. They are different matters, but close.

43. Scanlon 1982, p. 111.

44. Scanlon 1982, p. 112.

45. See B. J. Diggs' discussion of the compromise element in his own contractualism in Diggs 1982, pp. 103–4.

46. Gauthier 1982a; see also Gauthier 1977 and Gauthier 1982b.

47. Gauthier 1982a, pp. 160–1; see also Gauthier 1985.

48. Diggs 1981. Although Diggs' version of the 'moral judge' can be developed with the capacious conception of 'reason' that I use in the text, it seems likely that Diggs himself would keep it tighter. The conception of the moral judge is derived from what Diggs calls 'the Imperative of a moral social morality', namely, 'Join others wherever possible, (1) in acting in ways that each person together with others can reasonably and freely subscribe to as a common morality and (2) in treating each person in ways consistent with the person's developing and freely exercising his capacity as a rational being to govern himself' (p. 276). The judge acts in the spirit of the Imperative, so he seeks a decision that all parties can reasonably subscribe to (p. 281). The judge's decisions, as Diggs explains rationality (pp. 277–8), will therefore probably be like the decisions of Gauthier's arbitrator. See also Diggs 1982.

49. See Sen 1973, pp. 15–23. Sen subsequently presented a second, still weaker version of the Weak Equity Axiom in Sen 1975, p. 285. He eventually rejected the Axiom as too strong in Sen 1980.

50. I discuss this further in Griffin 1981.

51. See ch. X sect. 3.

52. See ch. V sect. 6.

53. Rawls 1972, pp. 141–2. The distortion to the moral point of view that enters with unanimity also enters with certain conceptions of equality, namely those that see equality as requiring that we include each person's point of view separately and thus that we find the assessment that is least unacceptable to the person to whom it is most unacceptable. For an example, see Thomas Nagel's paper, 'Equality', in Nagel 1979, esp. p. 123.

54. As, e.g., John Harsanyi does; see Harsanyi 1976, Part A, but esp. pp. 4 and 14.

55. This is Rawls' vision; see the subtle discussion in Rawls 1972, sect. 81.

56. See Mackie 1977, ch. 6 sect. 2.

57. Captain Oates was a member of Scott's polar expedition of 1911–12. Finding himself weakened beyond hope of survival, he walked out into the cold to die, with the words 'I am just going outside and may be some time.'

58. For a rich development of this line of thought, see Nagel 1980, esp. p. 90. I have borrowed (immediately below) the example of wanting to be an accomplished pianist from him too; see p. 122.

59. ch. VII sect. 4.

60. For discussions of the analogy with secondary qualities, sympathetic and unsympathetic respectively, see McDowell 1985 and Williams 1985, ch. VIII, esp. pp. 149–52.

61. Nagel uses the analogy with secondary qualities to bolster up this distinction, which I think it does not do. See Nagel 1980, pp. 80–4.

62. There is a good survey of the difficulty that major moral theories have in accommodating the distinction between obligation and supererogation in Heyd 1982, Pt. I.

63. Two recent attempts to find relatively short answers of both these kinds are Williams' argument about 'integrity', which he uses to support not only a strong personal moral perspective but also something approaching a deontologist's conception of responsibility (see his remarks about 'negative responsibility' in Williams 1973a, sects. 3 and 5; but see also 'Persons, Character and Morality' and 'Utilitarianism and Self-Indulgence' in Williams 1981 and my earlier discussion at ch. VIII sect. 3, esp. n. 26); and Nagel's treatment of the 'obscure topic of deontological constraints' (see Nagel 1980, pp. 126–35).

64. There are, no doubt, many ways of bringing out the force of deontological reasons. See for example Nagel's suggestive remarks about the centrality of intention in the deontological picture; Nagel 1980, pp. 131–3. He does not deny moral role to outcomes, however caused. But he thinks that sometimes, on moral grounds, we will not intentionally do (e.g. torture) what would have a better outcome, and that this shows that deontological constraints also have moral weight. He then tells us where 'the strength of the deontological view lies'. He asks, 'what is the essence of *aiming*, what differentiates it from merely producing a result knowingly'? The difference, he answers, is that action intentionally aimed at a goal is guided by that goal; hence, action aimed at evil, even that good may come, is guided by evil. But the essence of evil, he says, is that it should repel us: 'That is what evil *means*'. So to aim at evil is to swim 'head on against the normative current'. But this does nothing to *justify* deontological constraints. The metaphor of swimming head on against the normative current does not even fit; we do *evil* that *good* may come, so there is a surface current in one direction and an undertow in the opposite. But the confusing normative eddies can be explained in many different ways (for example, one does not need the deontologist's

perspective to account for the repulsion that a decent person would feel at torturing), and one would not be tempted by Nagel's explanation, unless one already believed deontological constraints to have independent weight. Indeed Nagel may well accept this; he may see his remarks more as an exposition of than as an argument for deontology.

65. See ch. X sect. 5, ch. XIII sects. 2, 6.

CHAPTER TEN

1. The story is this: each of two prisoners finds himself in a situation where he correctly reasons that if:

You

		confess	stay silent
	confess	Each gets 10 years	I go free, you get 12 years
I			
	stay silent	I get 12 years, you go free	Each gets 2 years

Self interest therefore counsels him to confess. Confessing is better for him whatever the other prisoner does. If the other confesses, it is better for him to confess; if the other stays silent, it is better for him to confess. Now the other will reason similarly. So they will both confess, thereby getting ten years each, while if they had both stayed silent they would have got only two. Despite the contrived nature of this example, dilemmas of this form are important in real life. One feature of the prisoners' situation that makes the grip of their dilemma particularly tight is that nothing affects the consequences except what they do in this situation. In real life, of course, what a person does in one case can affect his reputation or set an example, and thereby affects how things will go for him in the future. So, if we treat lack of influence on the future as essential to a Prisoner's Dilemma, then there are very few two party Prisoner's Dilemmas in real life. But if we take a less purist line and do not treat it as essential, then there are many of them. One important case is nuclear arms' control. Every time a new round of escalation is possible, the United States and the Soviet Union would each have its best result if the other did not produce the new arms while it did, its worst result if it did not while the other did, its second best if neither did, and its third best if both did. But each is better off producing the new arms whatever the other does. So each produces them, thereby getting its third best result. And once we move to many-party cases, especially situations where numbers are very large, as they are in modern societies, then the reputation one gains or the example one sets often plays no role at all, and unfortunately pure Prisoner's Dilemmas abound. There is the following depressing one. Each of us is best off himself if others help those in distress while he does not, worst off if he does while others do not, second best if all do, and third best if none do. But each is better off not helping, whatever the others do. There are good discussions of both the formal features of Prisoner's Dilemmas and their possible real-life instances in Parfit 1984, ch. II and Axelrod 1984, ch. I.

The Prisoner's Dilemma is an abstract specification of one kind of situation in which the pattern of pay-offs is determined by the joint actions of the participants. There are other kinds, many of which also have important real-life instances. The whole range of situations is studied in the Theory of Games (see e.g. von Neumann and Morgenstern 1953, Luce and Raiffa 1957, and Brams 1976), and it is a test of a moral or political theory that it can come up with good advice in all of these situations.

2. It is a contentious matter whether *any* kind of utilitarian reasoning, even the kind that I imagine here in which the agent ignores the effects of what groups do and concentrates on his own action in isolation, would lead to the conclusion that I ought to burn logs. Mancur Olson has argued, as I do here, that the conclusion 'holds true whether behaviour is selfish or unselfish, so long as it is strictly speaking "rational". Even if the member of a large group were to neglect his own interests entirely, he still would not rationally contribute towards the provision of any collective or public good, since his own contribution would not be perceptible.' (Olson 1965, p. 64) To which Brian Barry has replied, 'This is surely absurd. If each contribution is literally "imperceptible" how can all the contributions together add up to anything?' (Barry 1978, p. 32.)

The most directly pertinent discussion that I know of is in Regan 1980 (but see also the closely related discussion in Parfit 1984, sects. 28–9). Regan thinks that a person who argues as I do is committed to 'logically inconsistent assumptions. On the one hand, he is committed to the assumption that a single crossing never makes a difference to the state of the grass. From this it follows that there is no difference (as far as the state of the grass is concerned) between the consequences of no one's crossing and one person's crossing ... [or] between the consequences of one person's crossing and two persons' crossing ... and so on. Since the relation of "there being no difference between the consequences of ... " is transitive, we can conclude that there is no difference (as far as the grass is concerned) between the consequences of no one's crossing and the consequences of everyone's crossing. But this is inconsistent with another premiss of the argument, the premiss that the overall consequences of everyone's crossing are much worse than the overall consequences of everyone's walking around' (pp. 59–60).

But the relation 'there being no *perceptible* difference between the consequences of ... ' is non-transitive. And the value at stake with lawns and buildings is aesthetic; perception is necessary for change in the sort of value that here concerns a utilitarian. Besides, not every single act (crossing the lawn, burning a log fire) has to make, over time, an actual difference. It may be that four or five crossings/fires have an effect that the lawn/buildings will entirely recover from (the grass will revive in a few hours; the next rain will wash a certain amount of deposit off the buildings) and that we shall get back to the *status quo ante*. But a hundred crossings/fires, let us say, will do permanent perceptible damage—though, since the grass will revive a bit and the buildings have some of the deposit washed off by the next rain, the damage might be done by only ninety-five of the crossings/fires. And from the fact that the damage of n crossings is indistinguishable from the damage of $n + 1$, and so on, it does not follow that the damage from n crossings is indistinguishable from the damage from $n + 50$. A series of imperceptible changes can grow into a perceptible change, and so a change in value, even when any individual one is reversed in short order.

Regan is well aware that the important relation might be thought to be 'there being no *perceptible* difference ... ' But of this he says that there must be some point at which a single crossing either produces a recognizable change in the grass or at least changes the likelihood that the persons around will enjoy the grass less. 'If this were not so, then the whole string of changes together could make no difference' (p. 61). But this is just to assert that there could not be a series of minute changes each of which, singly, made no perceptible difference but enough of which, in aggregate, did. And there do seem to be cases. I might do something (a hair's-breadth turn of the screw) that produced such a minute change in your nerve endings that you noticed no change, but were there a hundred such changes you would be in noticeable pain. There is nothing in this claim to give rise to Wang's paradox: it is not a matter of saying that the addition of a lot of 'no differences' produces 'some difference'. Each succeeding state differs from the previous one in minute physiological structures, and enough such physiological changes rise to consciousness. Furthermore, the eventual rise to consciousness is possible even when the move from one physiological state to its immediate successor has no effect not only on consciousness but also on the probability of being in any particular state of consciousness. One does not have to resort to Regan's differences in probability to avoid paradox; the physiological story can do that without them. If utilitarianism can avoid the embarrassment of the problem of moral outlook, it cannot be because there will always be some minute but genuine disutility somewhere along the line. Sometimes there is, and sometimes not.

3. For an example of a contractualist's derivation of a rule against cruelty, see Richards 1971, ch. 10 sect. I; for Richards' strained discussion of cruelty to animals, which never once mentions their pain, see pp. 182–3.

4. See discussion in ch. IX n. 34.

5. An intriguing historical question is how act utilitarianism ever became the dominant interpretation. Bentham, Mill, and Sidgwick were pretty certainly not act utilitarians, on this tight interpretation. When did this interpretation edge the others out? Was it with G. E. Moore? See, e.g., Moore 1966, p. 121: '... it must always be the duty of every agent to do that one, among all actions which he can do on any given occasion, whose *total consequences* will have the greatest intrinsic value.'

For recent examples of what looks like the tight interpretation, usually (not surprisingly) by authors who do not find much to say for it, see Hodgson 1967, p. 1; Williams 1973a, p. 128; Brandt 1979, ch. XIV, sect. 2 and ch. XV sect. 3; Regan 1980, p. 12; etc.

6. For excellent discussions, see Adams 1976 and Parfit 1984, ch. I sect. 6.

7. See the discussion in Diggs 1982, pp. 103–4.

8. See Bales 1971.

9. ch. VIII sects. 2 and 4.

10. The main sources are Hare 1976a and Hare 1981, ch. 2 sect. 1 and ch. 3.

11. The chief difference between Hare's proposal and mine, besides the one I now go on to talk about, is that I suggest not only two decision procedures but also separating decision procedures from the criteria of right and wrong (I mentioned this separation earlier and return to it briefly in a moment). So I have, in a sense, three levels. And this may still not be enough. The two decision procedures that I have in mind are for individuals. Perhaps a political decision procedure (a procedure for governments) would be different again. Perhaps the practical decision procedure of an intelligent, scrupulous individual need not have restrictions quite as tough as the decision procedure that we should want for government agencies. Hare might say that a political decision procedure can be accommodated on the intuitive level without extensive rebuilding. So it can: 'acceptance utility' can be used of 'acceptance by an individual', 'acceptance by persons generally in society' (two interpretations which Hare gives it in Hare

1981), but also of 'acceptance by members of the judiciary/by the police/by all agents of the government/etc.'. But this gives scope for considerable complexity. Still, what seems to me entirely right is Hare's insistence on a multi-level structure in moral thought. For more on this see ch. XI sect. 9.

12. cf. Aristotle, *Nicomachean Ethics*, II.1, II.4; also III.5, X.9; and *Politics* Eta 13.1332a42–1332b3.

13. Parfit 1984, Pt. I.

14. Sect. 2.

15. Sect. 10.

16. p. 49.

17. Is there not strong 'local' colour to the way Parfit defines 'success-fully following a theory'? 'Say that someone *successfully follows Theory T* when he succeeds in doing the act which, of the acts that are possible for him, best achieves his T-given aims' (p. 53). This seems to assume that decisions are made occasion by occasion. And it is possible to some extent to live this way. But one important decision we make is whether indeed to live this way, a decision which itself then determines the set of 'acts that are possible'. That set is not a datum, not fixed by human (or even one individual's) psychology. It is an agent's key, strategic decisions that importantly determine the set.

18. Sects. 9, 17.

19. Bernard Williams has a similar worry about the psychological implica-tions of a multi-level view, see Williams 1985, pp. 107–8 and my discussion later at ch.XI sect. 9.

20. Related issues arise in what Amartya Sen called an Assurance Game. See Sen 1967 and Sen 1974. See also the informative exchange between Kurt Baier and Sen: Baier 1977 and Sen 1977; and the discussion in Elster 1979, ch. I sect.4, ch. III sect. 7.

21. See, e.g., Kurt Baier, in Baier 1977, who identifies three central problems of Prisoner's Dilemmas: the (1) isolation, the (2) co-ordination, and the (3) assurance problems (pp. 197–8).

22. The sort of global consequentialism I am discussing here should be distinguished from Donald Regan's rigorously worked-out proposal of 'Co-operative Utilitarianism', which says: 'What each of us ought to do is to co-operate with whoever else is willing to co-operate in producing the best possible consequences, given what the non-co-operators are doing' (see Regan 1980, p. 124; that Regan sees this formula as a complete test of moral right and wrong is clear from his various summaries of co-operative utilitarianism on pp. x, 11, 124, 135–6, and 211). This seems to me to make co-operation far too central to morality. Regan's criterion fits some of morality poorly; it lacks scope. It gives an odd and roundabout justification for a ban on baby-battering. And it gives the wrong verdict in the case where co-

operation is well under way, to the benefits of which I can add little, but where I can do more with some private enterprise of my own. And I think it misses some points about fairness. No doubt we should produce the best consequences by our all co-operating and showing up for votes unless there are votes spare, no long-term damage will be done by skiving, etc. But that tells us nothing about issues of fairness, of the sort that I discuss in the next section, that turn not on the quality of consequences but on *who* can legitimately be let off contributing.

23. This way of speaking is, of course, very loose. Before I choose what to do, all consequences are hypothetical; and after I have chosen, only one set of consequences will be actual. In that sense, I never choose between actual consequences. So by 'actual' consequences I mean what would actually happen if I were to act in a certain way (and 'hypothetical' consequences must be understood accordingly). But this looseness of speech does not matter, because it is eliminable. This looseness of speech is well pointed out in Singer 1982.

24. The problem is raised in Diamond 1967, and the example I use is adapted from his. My thoughts have been much clarified through conversation with John Broome and by reading an early version of Broome 1984.

25. Kurt Baier, in his reply to an earlier version of this argument, objected not that the sort of concern for individuals in the principle of equal chances was anything so blatant as inconsistent with impartial maximiza-tion, but rather that it was 'contrary' to its 'spirit'. That earlier discussion was carried on in terms of 'spelling out' utilitarianism, so let me use that vocabulary. Utilitarianism, Baier says, contains a conception of impartial-ity ('everybody to count for one, nobody for more than one') that implies 'only that all persons matter equally, not that every person matters.' In fact he adds, it would be easier for a utilitarian, in applying his maximizing standard, if no particular person mattered at all; otherwise 'he would be emotionally torn apart by those maximizations that require him to sacrifice one for the greater good of all'. He sums up: 'Equal regard for persons here is tantamount to equal disregard'. (Baier 1985, pp. 121–2.)

I find it difficult to pin down Baier's point. Perhaps it is this. When we tease out the spirit of the principle of utility, we find—to put it more bluntly than Baier does—that it is really pretty dreadful: no one matters very much; at least, a utilitarian will induce that attitude so that he will be able emotionally simply to get through life; a maximizer is unlikely to have even that modicum of concern for persons that the principle of equal chances represents. But this seems to me to pack far too much into the sort of 'equal disregard for persons' that a utilitarian can be saddled with. Being torn apart need not be outside the emotional repertoire of a maximizer. And even if, for a quiet life, he turns himself into a detached bureaucratic deadbeat, there is no reason why part of his bureaucratic approach could not be to equalize chances in order to break ties. Strictly speaking, 'equal disregard' means merely 'everybody to count for one'. But that familiar sort of impartiality does nothing to direct us to reject the principle of equal chances. It does not, as I admitted in my paper, do anything to force us to accept it either. I claimed only that a utilitarian can parlay his deep notion of equal regard into that principle among others. I think that he gets attractive development of that underdetermined notion of 'equal regard' if he does so.

Baier's point then, if I am right, is close to the now familiar observation that utilitarianism ignores 'the separateness of persons'. If it ignores it, why would it insist on it in a principle of equal chances? But the observation, though familiar, is distressingly obscure. 'The separateness of persons' is sometimes used as a reason why utilitarians are wrong to transfer the intrapersonal maximizing standard to interpersonal cases. But the only clear sense to attach to the observation is that utilitarians do indeed make the transfer. The observation cannot, therefore, be a *reason* why the transfer is wrong. Modern contractualists, who are chief among those pressing this observation against utilitarians, go on to impose restrictions on the operation of utilitarian trade-offs which look attractive only up against the counter-intuitive permissiveness of utilitarianism. But once seen on their own, their restrictions are discovered to suffer from equally counter-intuitive strictness. The notion of 'the separateness of persons' is far too obscure to help us decide whether the indisputable sense in which utilitarianism ignores the separateness of persons rules out its including a principle of equal chances.

I agree with Baier that one cannot extract the principle of equal chances from the principle 'everybody to count for one'. That would be to misunderstand what Bentham and Mill meant by it; they meant it is a mere spelling-out of the principle of utility. And, of course, there is a big difference between an equal right to happiness (as embodied in 'everybody to count for one') and a right to equal happiness. And, true, utilitarianism embraces only the first.

If I understand Baier correctly, then, he thinks that maximization displays a sort of moral insensitivity that rules out utilitarianism's being sensitive to equal chances. But we ought to drop the vague, rhetorical 'equal regard', 'equal disregard', and 'individuals do (do not) matter'. There are ways in which utilitarianism allows individuals to matter, and ways in which it does not. 'Everybody to count for one' means that in a way individuals *do* matter; they matter (weigh) equally in the calculus. Maximization means that in trade-offs *which* person benefits does not matter, only the sum. But that is part of the view about when trade-offs are justified. And individuals do not matter in the sense that utilitarianism offers no protections for individuals against the results of maximization. But what remains mysterious is why Baier thinks if utilitarianism excludes protection of individuals against the results of maximization (disregards persons in *that* sense) then it cannot include equal chances for individuals when there are equal maxima (regard persons in *that* sense).

26. There is, though, a special problem for my proposal that does not

bother a Ross-like pluralism. My proposal makes the maximizing principle lexically prior to the two tie-breaking principles. And there is a general problem with any lexical ordering: why should there be such sharp cut-offs in relevance? Why should equal distribution or equal chance at it matter importantly until different total utilities appear on the scene and then *not at all*? Is there a coherent notion of equal respect that does not count equality of well-being in trade-off situations but does count it outside those situations? Is it not only coherent but also plausible? Equality crops up in different places all through moral theory. There are *many* possible principles of equality, several of them plausible and no doubt many of them to be accepted. One of the hard jobs in moral theory is to sort out these easily confused, but different, principles of equality and to get one's thinking about equality straight. To decide whether the conception of equality in this padded-out utilitarianism is acceptable requires a lot of work, especially in sorting out our intuitions. It is hard to reject this conception of equality from the start as incoherent or as suffering from internal conflicts in the 'spirit' of its parts. I suspect that it even has something to recommend it. But that is contrary to what I take to be accepted opinion, so needs a lot of argument. I give some of the argument at ch. IX sect. 3 and ch. XI sects. 5, 9.

27. It is this deep notion that would also animate ranking, say, taking turns above tossing coins. Suppose the situation will recur. You as the parent might always opt for a fifty per cent chance for each child, or you might, because this sort of randomizing could just result in a freak run of benefits for one of them in particular, prefer directing it once to one child and next to the other. The second approach does seem better—better because safer, and safer precisely in more surely producing the *fairer* or *equal* distribution that seems to be at the heart of this principle. Does this not show, after all, that there is a powerful independent principle of fairness? I do not think so. Utilitarianism's basic, original equipment is a commitment to equal distribution and a standard to govern deviations. The standard governing deviations does not sanction any in this case. So there is no justification here to deviate. This is what the deep conception of equal respect at work in impartial maximization would say. I am indebted here, and elsewhere in this section, to conversations with R. M. Hargrave.

28. Broome 1984 suggests that it is.

29. There are different kinds of free-riding. Sometimes my free-riding adds a real, though often very small, extra burden on each of the others (e.g. my taking my private car on the roads at rush hour, when the rest of you use buses; I may slow things up so little for each of you that you do not even notice; but I do slow things up a *bit*). Other times my free-riding adds no extra burden (e.g. when I have a log fire, and the next rain washes the deposit away). Still, in both kinds of case there is a steady burden that all the rest of you bear, *viz.* a benefit forgone. I can get my questionable justification going for my having the benefit ('no harm done') only because the rest of you are denying it to yourselves.

30. This point has been made before; a good discussion is Sumner 1971, esp. p.109, but he holds that a fair procedure such as random selection stands outside utilitarianism as something which, though it might often be adopted on utilitarian grounds (e.g. if it were the only procedure that a group would consent to), might sometimes not be (e.g. if one could get away with loading the dice).

31. Here I just follow Derek Parfit's powerful reply to those who argue that in a nation-wide election the consequences of my act can never explain why I ought to vote; see Parfit 1984, pp. 73–5.

32. Expected benefit is actual benefit multiplied by the chance that one will produce it, i.e. the product of the average net benefit per citizen and two hundred million, divided by one hundered million.

33. Parfit 1984, ch. 3.

34. Nor does Parfit say that it is. I take it that his position is this. He considers the common claim that in Contributor's Dilemmas involving very many persons what each person does would make no difference. This, he says, is just false, and he goes on to show with great ingenuity that very often it does make a difference. But *often* is compatible with *sometimes not*. See Parfit 1984, esp. pp. 66–7.

35. It is certainly too weak to solve all problems of 'fairness'. All that I am proposing is that it solves the free-rider problem. That still leaves other, central problems; e.g. a society with a small group of rich exploiters and a large group of poor exploited has a structural unfairness that is not removed just by giving all entrants into the society (say, babies at birth) an equal chance of being among the exploiters. I discuss this sort of structural injustice later in ch. XIII.

36. For a good discussion of how consequences enter the Categorical Imperative test, see Paton 1965, ch.VII sect. 4, ch. XIV sects. 4 and 5, ch. XVII sect. 4. For a contrary view, see Singer 1963, ch. IX sect. 3.

37. This is Paton's Formula I, or 'The Formula of the Universal Law'; see Paton 1965, ch. XIV. For another good discussion of the test see Nell 1975, ch. V.

38. Since fairness is a 'perfect duty', what ought to appear is a contradiction in conception, rather than a contradiction in the will; see Paton 1965, pp. 148, 171–2. But it is hard to see how to make a convincing case for the appearance of either sort of contradiction.

39. The much-discussed problems raised by talk of 'moral relevance' I pass by. They are satisfactorily answered only by constructing a complete substantive moral theory, which then settles what has moral weight and what does not.

40. The case is elegantly stated by M. G. Singer; see Singer 1963, pp. 91, 189, 196, 209 and also Singer 1955, p. 375; Singer 1977, p. 406. I have

somewhat changed his arguments but think that what I present is still in their spirit.

41. In Paton's classification, Formula II, 'The Formula of the End in Itself'; see Paton 1965, ch. XVI.

42. There is textual support for this reading of Kant: e.g. *Grundlegung*, Paton's trans., Paton 1961, pp. 67–8 (marginal pagination); '. . . the man who has a mind to make a false promise to others will see at once that he is intending to make use of another man *merely as a means* to an end he does not share. For the man whom I seek to use for my own purposes by such a promise cannot possibly agree with my way of behaving to him, and so cannot himself share the end of the action.'

43. ch. IX sects. 3 and 4.

44. See Baier 1985, pp. 123–4.

45. Baier 1985, esp. pp. 125–9.

46. I must, however, acknowledge the difficulties of applying the broad principle of equal chances. If, when I walk up to the doctor, he takes me rather than you, his choice is in a way random; it is chance that I am injured in the arms and you in the legs. Chance distribution does not have to be man-made. When the principle of equal chances is observed, and when not, is hardly always easy to say. Clearly more needs to be said about what this principle amounts to, particularly about what is to count as having an equal chance.

47. ch. IX sects. 3 and 4.

CHAPTER ELEVEN

1. See Thomson 1971.

2. Dworkin 1977, esp. Introduction, pp. xi–xv and chs. 6 and 7.

3. Nozick 1974, pp. 28–33.

4. For useful discussions on the relation of 'rights' to 'duties' see e.g. Arnold 1978; on the relation of 'right' and 'permission' see Nozick 1974, p.92; on the relation of 'rights' and 'entitlements' see McCloskey 1965, p. 117.

5. Hohfeld 1923.

6. e.g. Melden 1977, ch. VI; McCloskey 1975, pp. 413–14.

7. They are elements supported by Mill, and more recently hinted at in Berlin 1969, Introduction, p. lx; and appealed to, at least some of them, in Hart 1979.

8. See ch. IV sect. 3.

9. I am therefore distinguishing 'autonomy' from 'liberty'. They both often get lumped together under the heading 'freedom', but I think that there are many reasons for keeping them separate. It helps to have separate names for two very different stages of agency: the early stage of

choosing one's path through life (autonomy) and the later stage of not then being stopped by others from going down it (liberty). Also what is true of the one cannot simply be transferred to the other. On this account autonomy can be (and often is) attached to criteria of very different stringency, all the way from common-or-garden choosing for oneself (say, not dominated by Mother) up to one's choices being totally outside the causal nexus (non-heteronomous, in Kant's sense).

10. This positive freedom is suspect in many eyes. 'Poverty can be evil', John Lucas writes, 'and great poverty is a great evil: but it is a different evil from lack of freedom.' See Lucas 1966, p. 147.

11. This is close to Dworkin's position; see Dworkin 1977, p. 267.

12. See Rawls 1972, p. 27; Nozick 1974, pp. 32–3, and by now many others.

13. ch. IX sects. 3 and 4.

14. See esp. ch. IX *passim*, ch. X sect. 3; I summarize my remarks about equality in ch. XIII sect. 4.

15. It is, according to the United Nations Declaration of Human Rights. It is, according to the US Supreme Court in its decision *Griswold* v. *Connecticut* (381 US 479) and *Roe* v. *Wade* (410 US 113); see discussion in Wellman 1978.

16. Someone might hope that some of this indeterminateness could be dispelled by appeal to justice, that is, by appeal to the idea that rights are, roughly speaking, the claims that a just society would grant. But justice is no more basic than rights. The issues about rights before us now form a large portion of the stuff of a theory of justice, so there is no independent notion of justice to help us with these issues.

17. This is a good place for a brief further thought about what a substantive theory is. The theory grounds rights in, among other things, personhood. But to the sceptical eye this may look like no 'grounding' at all. It may seem merely a shift from one normative notion to another. After all, the content of the notion of a 'person', at least 'person' as it figures here in this substantive theory, is not a purely semantic matter; most of us would single out autonomy and living out one's individual life plan as central to being a person, but we well know that other persons, especially in other ages, have not thought these features important. Even if it were a purely semantic matter, the semantics might just be reflecting a certain normative outlook. And if normative considerations enter in the choice of a concept of 'person', why not let them enter earlier with the choice of what is to be a human right? Why the indirection? The appearance of grounding rights in a concept like personhood may, to the sceptical eye, look illusory; a substantive 'theory' may seem to be no theory at all, because its *explanans* may seem as much in need of grounding as its *explanandum*.

But this carries scepticism too far. True, not everyone uses this concept of personhood. In that sense it is not totally outside the normative circle.

But that does not mean that the notion of rights is not explained by it. Explanation in morals does not fail to be explanation unless it employs notions either that are not normative or that everyone employs. It is enough if it grounds a vague, troublesome, criterionless *explanadum* in an *explanans* that is more definite, clearer, and in the use of which we are more sure.

Also, think of the alternative. The sceptical spirit prompts us to make normative decisions at an earlier point, directly about human rights. Well, what would we then deem to be rights? What boundaries would they have? Are we to maximize their observance? If we are honest, we shall admit that we are baffled. We need help with all these questions, and the substantive theory is meant to give it.

Of course, not everyone accepts the values in which rights are grounded (try convincing an Indian father in a culture in which arranged marriages are still standard that he is violating his child's right to autonomy). But this just shows that the debate about the existence of the right should be shifted back one stage to a debate about whether autonomy, all things considered, makes a better life. There is a lot to be said about that.

18. Mackie 1978, pp. 354–5.

19. See the useful discussion of Mill's view in Lyons 1976.

20. See e.g. Gewirth 1982, p. 160.

21. Rawls 1972, sect. 11.

22. See his 'Rights, Utility, and Universalization', in Frey 1984.

23. There may well be doubt about this approach: perhaps trade-offs, especially the sort that I shall presently consider, are not central to explaining moral status. John Rawls' approach, in contrast, is to suggest that we get straight the principles that apply to normal people, with normal capacities and health, and attend only later to the special demands of the abnormal. Otherwise, our intuitions, he fears, will be distorted by the special urgency of the ill and handicapped (see Rawls 1975a, p. 96). His approach would be possible if it were possible to work out a notion of equal respect without determining what morality requires in these hard cases. And hard cases would arise even in a society of normal people. They do not arise simply from illness and handicap, but also arise when a society makes hard choices about how to balance demands of saving life, on the one hand, and promoting the constituents of a good life such as art and education, on the other. But we do not have determinate enough notion of equal respect to give us any answers, even in the relatively easy cases, independently of answers in the hard cases.

24. ch. IX sect. 3.

25. ch. IX sect. 3.

26. See ch. V.

27. ch. X sect. 2.

28. For a good discussion of forms of 'indirect ' utilitarianism, see Williams 1973.

29. See the helpful discussion in Scanlon (forthcoming). I have benefited from seeing a Ts. of that article and from discussion with Scanlon.

30. See ch. III sect. 5, ch. IV sect. 5.

31. ch. X sect. 2 and ch. IX sect. 3.

32. ch. X sect. 2.

33. ch. IX sect. 3.

34. I have discussed this more fully at ch. X sect. 2.

35. Warnock 1971, esp. ch. 2; Mackie 1977, ch. 5; see also Williams 1973a, pp. 107, 134–5 and Williams 1973c, p. 112.

36. See esp. Williams 1973a, pp. 106–10.

37. ch. X sect. 2.

38. ch. III sect. 3.

39. See above, nn. 2 and 3.

CHAPTER TWELVE

1. 'Analysis', however, is the first step. For good examples of it, see J. Feinberg 1970, esp. chs. 4 and 8, and Kleinig 1971.

2. This point is made in Kleinig 1971, p. 74.

3. For a good discussion of the link between desert and personal identity, see Parfit 1984, Pt. III esp ch. 15. Parfit discusses two general sorts of view about personal identity: Reductionist (that the fact of a person's identity over time consists simply in the holding of certain facts about physical and psychological continuity) and Non-Reductionist (that it consists in some further fact, e.g. the existence of a separately existing entity or ego); see sect. 79. Some Non-Reductionists think that only the deep further fact carries with it desert and thus that, if Reductionism is true, no one deserves reward or punishment. My own view is that, on the very general characterizations of the two views given above, Reductionism is more plausible than Non-Reductionism, but that the most plausible version of Reductionism still leaves us with all the problems about desert that I am concerned with in this chapter (and the problems about distribution that I go on to in the next chapter). As Parfit says, reduced psychological connectedness would reduce responsibility (p. 326). Moral or religious conversion would seem to me a good example. But this particular sort of rupture in psychological connectedness has no clear bearing on personal identity. The notion of psychological continuity is extremely obscure. Suppose someone's values, beliefs, dispositions etc. change radically (Saul on the road to Damascus, a patient at a turning

point in psychoanalysis, a wrongdoer who undergoes a moral conversion). Certainly there is rupture in many key sorts of psychological connectedness. Yet it is often in such cases that one also feels most at one with one's own past; it is often only then that one lifts oneself out of the present moment and sees one's life as a single, comprehensible whole. These are complicated cases: in one sense there is especially strong unity of person, in another weak unity (at least, great change). The notion of psychological continuity is too crude to lend the Reductionist much help in explaining what personal identity is reducible to. Also, some weakenings of psychological connectedness (e.g. moral conversion) weaken continuity of desert without weakening continuity of person. See also ch. II n. 31.

4. His prima facie obligation of 'gratitude' is an example; see Ross 1930, pp. 21–3. Treating gratitude as an obligation raises problems as to whether morality allows some degree of partiality. A person usually builds up debts of gratitude to friends and family, because they have most opportunities to help. How much can these debts qualify equal respect? Where does gratitude end and favouritism begin?

5. Even if a community is disbanding, Kant says, and its members scattering to the four corners of the earth, they must execute the last murderer left in gaol, 'for otherwise they might all be regarded as participators in the murder ... ' Kant 1887, p. 198. See also Kant 1965, pp. 101–2, 104–7.

6. See John Rawls' powerful dismissal of desert as a ground for distributing 'income and wealth, and the good things in life generally'; Rawls 1972, sect. 48, esp. p. 310. See also D. A. J. Richards' contractarian theory of punishment, which, he says, has no place for desert; Richards 1971, pp. 127–32.

7. This is pointed out in Feinberg 1970, p. 82.

8. 'Gratitude is a debt, 'tis true, but it differs from all other debts; for though it is always to be paid, yet it is never to be demanded.' Anon., 'Characters and Observations', early eighteenth-century, quoted in Gross 1983, p. 199.

9. I am paraphrasing Lucas 1980, ch. 12, esp. pp. 203–4, where the case is beautifully put.

10. Ronald Dworkin distinguishes a distribution of resources that is 'ambition-sensitive' from one that is 'endowment-sensitive', and he thinks that equality allows the former but not the latter; see Dworkin 1981, p. 311. I earlier used what is in effect the same distinction in contrasting what creates no merit (endowment) from what does (doing better than *par* for one's endowments). But my suggestion now is that, though the disinction is important, it has no *moral* import: it supplies no moral reason for a distribution of resources to be ambition-sensitive. Not all that matters, even to how we ought to behave, matters morally.

11. See Feinberg 1970, p. 83.

12. Herbert Morris in his Introduction, Morris 1971, p. 1.

13. See M. Buber's distinction between 'real' and 'neurotic' guilt, in Buber 1965, ch. VI; and a good discussion of similar topics in Taylor 1985, ch. IV.

14. Dostoevsky, in a letter to Katkov, editor of the monthly *Russian Messenger*, gave this first outline of *Crime and Punishment*: 'My novel, besides, contains the hint that the punishment laid down by the law frightens the criminal much less than our legislators think, partly because he himself feels the desire to be punished.'

15. See *The Genealogy of Morals*, Second Essay, sect. 19, repr. in Nietzsche 1927, p. 706.

16. This is most brilliantly argued in *The Possessed*, in the suppressed chapter, 'At Tihon's', which contains Stavrogin's confession. Stavrogin, overcome by a sense of emptiness, becomes increasingly violent. 'I wanted to put powder under the four corners of the earth and blow it all up, but it didn't seem worth the effort.' He allows an intense but superficial attraction to lead him to rape a young girl, who out of shame kills herself. He feels a terrible need for punishment, which takes the form of violence directed against himself. 'I conceived the idea of somehow crippling my life'; so he marries a lame servant in his lodgings. In time he writes a confession, for distribution to the police, the press, and all his acquaintances. He even comes to feel pity for the girl and wonders whether it is repentance. Tihon, whom he consults, knows that it is not. What Stavrogin regrets is not her death but how it haunts him. He looks to the publication of his confession to bring relief; it is his 'last measure'. Tihon advises him against it. The confession reveals his contempt for the persons to whom it is addressed. He wants forgiveness from two or three selected persons, Stavrogin insists, 'but by all means let everyone else hate me'. Tihon knows that Stavrogin will not be able to bear the ridicule that his extravagant gesture in confessing will attract. Tihon urges him to become a novice for a few years under a wise old monk whom he recommends. As it is, Tihon fears for him; he fears a new crime solely as a way to escape publishing the confession.

17. Although I borrow the label 'atonement' from theology, I make what I call the Atonement View grimmer and less connected with spiritual growth than theologians do. The Christian doctrine of atonement is not a doctrine of pure payment of moral debts. It began as an account of a sinner's reconciliation with God: 'at-one-ment'. So it too is completed only with a spiritual growth that overcomes the estrangement caused by sin. But, then, it naturally came to include the means of achieving this reconciliation, and expiation entered there. The word 'atonement' is now used in popular speech more of the means than of the end, and I follow this use. See Dillistone 1968, esp. ch. I; for a good brief account see Dillistone 1983. See also Hodges 1955 and Moberly 1978, esp. Postscript.

18. Benjamin Whichcote, *Moral and Religious Aphorisms*, 1753. Also Aristotle,

Rhetoric II, 'We withdraw our wrath from the man who admits that he is justly punished'.

19. I find it especially hard to work out the consequences of the view I develop here for capital punishment. A lot has to be said, but there is what seems to me a striking argument against it: since I must respond to the wrongdoer as someone capable of repentance and reform, it seems that I may never, no matter what he has done, even if he has killed, respond by killing him. Execution seems hardly appropriate for someone who can reform, and even less appropriate for someone who has already reformed.

20. For the case for punishment's being a symbol, see Moberly 1968, esp. pp. 200 ff.; Feinberg 1970, ch. 5, 'The Expressive Function of Punishment'.

21. See Lord Denning, in evidence reported in the *Report of the Royal Commission on Capital Punishment*, Cmd. 8932, 1953, para. 53, who describes punishment as 'the emphatic denunciation by the community of a crime'. It is not. Denunciation is only a side-effect, and justified only if there are those who will listen, and only if it is the best form for the message to take, etc. See also Moberly 1968 and Feinberg 1970 on punishment as symbol.

22. See Axelrod 1984; see also Trivers 1971 and discussion in Elster 1979, p. 145.

23. The exception is Richards 1971; see pp. 127–32. But there the whole discussion takes roughly four pages, and although the brevity leaves it far from clear, it seems that he ends up adopting substantially the position that I argue for here. (There are differences, though: he says that punishment is justified only when it acts as a general deterrent or it ensures compensation. But this must be too strong a requirement. It would mean that a punishment that reformed but did not generally deter was not justified.)

24. I am passing over all the difficulties with the notion of proportionality. Our judgments about the size of the punishment that 'fits' the crime rest on the shakiest sorts of intuition. I say that this rough notion of proportionality has to be made less so. But can it be? Certainly the punishments that we have seen as 'fitting' the crime have varied wildly over time—not so much in their relative positions (though even there too), but certainly in their absolute positions. See, e.g., *The Boston Evening-Post*, 18 Oct. 1742:

'*Capital Punishment*'

We hear from *Hartford* in *Connecticut*, that two Men were lately convicted there of counterfeiting the Bills of Credit on the Colony, and sentenced to be branded in the Forehead with a hot Iron, to have both their Ears cut off, and to kept in Prison *during Life*. If some such *moderate* Punishment were to be inflicted upon such Offenders in this Province, instead of *Death*, 'tis tho't we would soon exceed any of our Neighbours in Convictions.

25. See Bentham 1789 for several good arguments for limiting the degree of punishment: esp. ch. XIII, the discussion of punishment that is 'unprofitable' or 'needless', and ch. XIV *passim*. But Bentham's concern is effective social engineering, and he nowhere mentions the single most important determinant: the role of desert at the core of punishment.

26. Quinton 1954; Hart 1968, ch. I esp. sect. 2a. There is more point to insisting on what is and is not punishment than Hart allows here, and to insist on the difference does not burke any substantive problems; they can still arise, but in a form that helps make them and possible solutions clearer.

27. When philosophers speak of 'retributivism', they are well aware that the name covers different views; see, e.g., Hart 1968, ch. IX, pt.2. The two most important ones, to my mind, are the Atonement View and the weaker Accountability View—both at the heart of retributivism, both moral views, both non-utilitarian, but differing between themselves in the weight they give to desert. The Accountability View is the more plausible, the chief doubt about it, which I shall come to in a moment, being whether it occupies a place different from the Repentance View.

28. I have a well-known nineteenth-century case in mind—the aftermath of the sinking of the *Mignonette*. See Simpson 1984.

29. That is the appearance; the reality is quite different. On the question of free will, Bentham was an agnostic, Mill a compatibilist.

Bentham often sounds like a hard determinist. He accepted the mechanical account of action in psychological hedonism—hence the purple passage with which the *Principles* starts; 'Nature has placed mankind under the governance of two sovereign masters, *pain* and *pleasure*. It is for them alone ... to determine what we shall do ... the chain of causes and effects ... [is] fastened to their throne ... every effort we can make to throw off our subjection, will serve but to demonstrate and confirm it' (ch.I sect. 1). (See also ch. XVII sect. 19 where Bentham remarks on the ambiguity of 'free'; and n. to ch. XIII sect. 2, where the end of punishment is said to be 'control' of action—even what Bentham calls 'reformation' seems to be a form of social control.) But the purple passage, Bentham hastens to add, is only purple: 'metaphor and declamation'. Bentham certainly accepts universal causation, but he never showed much interest in the question of free will. In a letter to George Wilson (8 July 1789), he wrote, '*Entre nous* I don't care two straws about liberty and necessity at any time. I do not expect any new truths on the subject: and were I to see any lying at my feet, I should hardly think it worthwhile to stoop to pick them up.' Baumgardt suggests that Bentham relegated the whole issue to the category of idle metaphysics, which ethics, being a descriptive study, could get along well without (Baumgardt 1952, p. 87–92, 395–9). See also the discussion of Bentham's account of motivation in D. Lyons 1973, ch. I sect. 3.

Mill too can sound pretty harshly determinist. Like Bentham, he was a psychological hedonist. And his discussions of sanctions (*Utilitarianism*, ch.

III) and of virtue (ch. IV) at times makes human behaviour seem
crudely mechanical. But Mill, who discussed the free will problem in
some detail, was a soft determinist, and he believed universal causation to
be compatible with moral responsibility. 'When we say that all human
actions will take place of necessity, we only mean that they will certainly
happen if nothing prevents ... We are exactly as capable of making our
own character, *if we will*, as others are of making it for us' (Mill 1843, bk.
6 ch. II sect. 3). The main sources are Mill 1843, bk. 6 chs. I–II; and
Mill 1865, ch. XXVI. There is a good discussion in Ryan 1970, ch. VII.

CHAPTER THIRTEEN

1. Perhaps this is not the most perspicuous way to define this particular
   dimension. It might be better to break it down further, say into three
   dimensions of size (principles centred on fine-grained interpersonal
   comparisons are possible in families, but not in modern nation-states),
   nature of motivation (families are moved by concern for each other, while
   parties to a contract are moved by self-interest), and relations to production
   (you and I can co-operate in production, but parents do not generally
   produce the family's goods jointly with their children, and you and I
   cannot produce goods jointly with persons who will be living a hundred
   years from now).

2. Hume 1751, sect. 3 pt.1; see also Hume 1738–40, bk. 3 pt.2 sect.2.

3. Hume 1751, sect. 3 pt.1.

4. Hume thought that the extremes were symmetrical, because he saw no
   ground for justice except self-interest. We accept the demands of justice,
   he thought, because in the long run it is in our interest to do so. But it is
   in our interest only so long as goods are tolerably plentiful. In dire
   scarcity the ground is removed from under all principles of justice. But
   Hume was wrong to think that self-interest is a rich enough ground for
   justice. It would give me no reason to accept any principle of justice that
   required me to defer to anyone who could not hit back: say, a subject
   people who will not make trouble in my lifetime, or a future generation
   who cannot. The question of the *grounds* of justice is different from the
   question of our psychological *capacity* always to act justly. In desperate
   straits all but the best of us are likely to get ruthlessly selfish. But rules of
   justice will still apply. David Miller discusses some anthropological
   evidence that in extremely poor societies where survival is in question
   notions of justice actually play little role; see Miller 1976, ch. VIII.

5. These are Robert Nozick's terms; see Nozick 1974, pp. 153–60. For
   similar distinctions see Matson 1983 ('top-down' and 'bottom-up' principles of distribution) and Flew 1983 ('forward-looking' or 'backward-
   looking' principles). John Rawls' discussion of 'procedural justice' is also
   relevant; see Rawls 1972, sect. 14.

6. Robert Nozick's concentration on justice in acquisition is a case in point; see Nozick 1974, esp. 150–3.

7. On 'procedural' justice see Rawls 1972, sect. 14; on 'process values' see Summers 1974–5, and Lucas 1980, ch. 4.

8. This is a central argument of Karl Marx in *Capital*.

9. This is a case argued in the justly influential Reich 1964.

10. See, e.g., Rawls 1972, p. 62: 'All social values—liberty and opportunity, income and wealth, and the bases of self-respect—*are to be distributed equally* unless an unequal distribution ... is to everyone's advantage ... For simplicity assume that the chief primary goods *at the disposition of society* are rights and liberties, powers and opportunities, income and wealth ... ' This passage is quoted by Anthony Flew (his italics) who also quotes the crass collectivist assumption made in the blurb of Michael Harrington's *The Twilight of American Capitalism*: 'A notable study which analyses reasons why sharp inequalities in sharing of *the nation's wealth* are inevitable outcomes of American capitalism'; see Flew 1983, p. 163.

11. See, e.g., Nozick 1984, p. 149: '... we are not in the position of children who have been given portions of pie by someone who now makes last minute adjustments to rectify careless cutting. There is no *central* distribution, no person or group entitled to control all the resources, jointly deciding how they are to be doled out.' Or Matson 1983, p. 107: 'On the agreement model of justice the question of *distributing* anything hardly arises. The main idea of justice from the bottom up is that people are to keep what they produce unless they voluntarily exchange it for what others have made. It is no part of the agreement model that there will be a Master Distributor at all, distinct from the producers.'

12. Robert Nozick sometimes writes as if it can be; see Nozick 1984, ch. 7 sect. I. But Nozick seems to hold a more developed view: appropriation plus productive use (pp. 174–7). There is a good discussion of Nozick's views about acquisition in Lyons 1982, see esp. p. 363.

13. I use here the formula 'as much and as good' rather than the somewhat more common 'enough and as good'. Locke uses the second formula in introducing the Proviso (Locke 1690, sect. 27). He uses the first as well (sect. 36: 'as good and as large a Possession'; sect.37: 'the same plenty'). And when he uses the second, his gloss makes it clear that he means the first (sect. 33).

   Robert Nozick tries to turn the Lockean Proviso into something much weaker than my reading of it here. 'The crucial point', he says, 'is whether appropriation of an unowned object worsens the situation of others' (Nozick 1974, p. 175). He distinguishes a weaker and a stronger sense in which another's situation might be 'worsened' (p. 176). The weaker is that an appropriator prevents another from freely using, without appropriation, what he could before; the stronger includes that condition but adds the further condition that an appropriator takes away another's opportunity to improve his situation. Nozick takes the proviso in the weaker sense: does any appropriation leave others worse off than they are at the time of the appropriation?

This seems to me implausible both as an interpretation of Locke (see Locke 1690, sect. 34, where what matters is said to be not just leaving as good but as good for the others' improvement) and as a moral principle. Take this case. There is a continent where everyone ekes out an existence by subsistence farming. One isolated tribe hits on the idea of irrigation, and their yield soars. It was just a matter of time before a member of another tribe stumbled on these innovators. By chance I am the one who does, and I rush home and appropriate the most plentiful water supplies, which were previously unvalued and unowned. I then produce vast crops on my land, and the rest of you, because of what I can afford to pay you, come to work my lands for me. Eventually I buy your lands, by offering a trifle more than the value you are able to get out of them. I trade the agricultural surplus to other tribes and become even richer. According to Nozick's version of the proviso, I am justified: you are not worse off than you would otherwise have been. So you and your heirs are condemned to live only slightly above subsistence level, while I and my heirs, through no merit of ours, live in luxury.

Nozick is aware of this sort of attack. His defence is to say that in this case you are *not* in fact as well off as you would have been but for my appropriation. If I had not stumbled on the innovating tribe, one of you would be likely to have done so eventually (p. 181). He founds upon this fact a limit on property rights—e.g. 'a time limit on patents, as a rough rule of thumb to approximate to how long it would have taken, in the absence of knowledge of the invention, for independent discovery' (p. 182). But this defence is not strong enough. It underestimates how much a surge in wealth for one person on one occasion can affect opportunities on all further occasions. Suppose that it is likely that it would have taken a generation before one of you stumbled upon the innovating tribe (I am utterly incompetent at finding my way about and when I stumbled on the innovating tribe I was far more lost than any of you ever get). In the space of a generation I can become vastly rich, and my wealth can revolutionize my future prospects. I can go off and get educated, hire advisers, and so on, while all of you toil away as subsistence farmers. So even if I have control of the water for only a generation, that is long enough to make me far more likely than any of you to come upon the next thing that advances wealth, and, in virtue of that, even more likely to come upon the next after that, and so on. A process of enhancing my welfare at the expense of yours is now entrenched. Nozick's version of the Lockean Proviso looks plausible because it looks innocent: it gives me control over the value that I alone have added (what could be more reasonable than that?) so long as I do not thereby make the rest of you worse off than you would otherwise have been (what could be fairer than that?) But at each point in time the story to be told about 'how you would otherwise have been' is determined by earlier unfavourable distributions. Once you miss out on one opportunity—even if solely because of my navigational incompetence—your future opportunities may well shrink, and go on shrinking. Then Nozick's version of the proviso looks far from innocent.

14. Locke 1690, e.g. sects.31, 32, 34. I am following the usual interpretation of Locke and taking the provisos to be necessary conditions of justified appropriation. This has been vigorously disputed in Waldron 1979. He thinks that the proviso against waste is indeed a necessary condition but that the proviso of as much and as good is only sufficient. What seems to me to count against Waldron's reading is that Locke regarded my having as much and as good as you as one of my *rights* (for a not entirely clear mention of the right see sect. 36, for a perfectly clear one see sect. 46). It is true that there are passages where Locke mentions only the proviso against waste as a necessary condition (sect. 46). But that is because Locke is speaking there of a setting, before the advent of money, when there is such abundance that everyone may take as much as he can use (i.e. no waste). It is not that the proviso against waste is the only necessary condition, but rather that it is the only one relevant to a setting of plenty.

15. Nozick 1974, p. 175.

16. By J. R. Pennock, 'Thoughts on the Right to Private Property' and by Jean Baechler, 'Liberty, Property, and Equality', both in Pennock and Chapman 1980. Baechler lists (p. 273, p. 278 n. 1):

Greek	ἴδιος	τὰ ἴδια
Latin	proprius	proprietas
German	eigen	Eigentum
English	proper	property
Italian	proprio	proprietà
French	propre	propriété

17. The empirical evidence about the growth of property is well reviewed by L. C. Becker in 'The Moral Basis of Property Rights' in Pennock and Chapman 1980. He also shows the impossibility of any quick move from this evidence to conclusions about property. Humans are, he grants, territorial, acquisitive, and egoistic; but they are also loving, co-operative, loyal, and capable of enduring bonds. And it is an important fact about humans that they are adaptable to change. Becker also points out that territoriality, as humans seem to display it, is as much a group phenomenon as an individual one; so if it has lessons for property, it may support group property rather than private property.

18. Some people think that it is. See Dunn 1984, p. 39: Dunn attributes to Locke the view that since labour is the source of ownership, 'entitlement and merit are fused together ... those who possess more will be those who deserve to do so'. See also Miller 1976, ch. VIII sect. 4: Miller observes that in, for example, pure market societies that are growing and full of opportunities, desert is in fact regarded by the society as important; some such principle as 'let each look after himself and be rewarded in

proportion to the talents he displays' naturally arises in situations in which each can cope, if he will. See also Becker in Pennock and Chapman 1980, p. 100–1: he speaks there of the 'labour-desert' justification which he characterizes, ' ... when labour produces something of value to others ... then the labourer deserves some benefit for it.'

19. See ch. XII sect. 3. Lane 1979, p. 68 makes the point that desert creates a strong claim not for material reward but for recognition, and that pay, once a certain level is passed, is valued by the 'meritorious' not for what it brings but for what it says about their achievement.

20. See ch. XI sect. 2.

21. See ch. III sect. 3.

22. So, for instance, Robert Nozick argues; see Nozick 1974, pp. 160–74. Also David Lyons suggests that we can get property rights out of, among other things, a liberty-right to do what is not harmful to others (a minimal right to land might be seen as a special case of such a right, although our actual, fuller, rights to land have to be fleshed out in other ways). But appropriations that have *no* detrimental effects on others are very rare; that test would be too strong. And if 'not harmful to others' means that they would be no worse off than I am, then the appeal is to equality, not to liberty. See Lyons 1982.

23. ch. XI sects. 2 and 6.

24. This too is argued in Nozick 1974, pp. 268–71.

25. This is not the opinion of the drafters of eighteenth-century declarations of human, or natural, rights. Virginia's 'A Declaration of Rights' of 12 June 1776 says: 'That all men are by nature equally free and independent, and have certain inherent rights ... namely the enjoyment of life and liberty, with the means of acquiring and possessing property ... ' It is well known that in the following month the drafters of the Declaration of Independence of 4 July 1776 (wisely) displayed doubts about the fundamental status of property (chiefly because Jefferson thought it a civil rather than a natural right) and for Virginia's 'life, liberty, and property' substituted 'life, liberty and the pursuit of happiness'. However, Clause II of the French Declaration of 1789 restored property to a fundamental place: 'The end of all political associations is the preservation of the natural and imprescriptible rights of man; and these rights are liberty, property, security, resistance of oppression.' Property has kept this place in the United Nations 1948 *Universal Declaration of Human Rights*, art.XVII: 'Everyone has the right to own property alone as well as in association with others.'

26. This ch. sect. 2.

27. This ch. sect. 3.

28. ch. IX sect. 1.

29. A striking example of this is the convergence of R. B. Brandt's utility-based distributive rules and Ronald Dworkin's rights-based rules.

They disagree (apparently—how much they really disagree depends on what Dworkin would eventually offer as his substantive theory of rights) over how equality figures at the deepest level, but from their different starting points arrive at astonishingly similar conclusions about the distributive rules that should be at work in society. See Brandt 1979, ch. XVI and Dworkin 1981.

30. See ch. III.

31. ch. III sect. 4.

32. ch. III sect. 4.

33. ch. III sect. 4.

34. ch. III sect. 5.

35. ch. III sect. 5; see also ch. IV sect. 5.

36. What is dubious is to ask such questions as Dworkin's, 'Which among various conceptions of equality states an attractive political ideal, if any does?' There are many conceptions of equality, most of them state a political ideal attractive in one setting, or at one level, and unattractive at another. Or Sen's question, 'Equality of what?', the only possible answer to which is, 'Very many different things'. And the large variety of places where equality is relevant raises doubts about the generality of approach in such campaigns as Lucas' 'Against Equality' and Flew's against *The Politics of Procrustes*. See Lucas 1965, Flew 1981.

37. ch. IX sect. 3.

38. ch. IX sect. 3.

39. There are those who would resist the accommodation of fraternity within prudential values. Fraternity, they say, is a different kind of good, a communal good—that is, a good the value of which is not the sum of values to the individuals involved. A communal good, in other words, has to be explained at least in part as a value not to individual members of the community but to the community itself. Other such values might be a sense of community, solidarity, *esprit de corps*, or national sense of purpose. But I do not think that there are any such things as communal goods, on this definition. The arguments that seem to support their existence confuse different theses. It is clear that one cannot explain certain values just by reference to how an isolated individual life goes. To explain fraternity requires bringing in the character of a group, relations between its members, and so on. Fraternity is clearly the sort of value that an individual cannot enjoy on his own. But one must not confuse a definitional thesis, a causal thesis, and a value thesis. The definitional thesis says that certain goods (e.g. fraternity) can only be defined in terms which make reference to groups, personal interaction, and so on. The causal thesis says that certain goods can occur only if persons interact in certain settings in certain ways. The value thesis says that certain values cannot be explained simply in terms of a sum of values in individual lives. For there to be communal values the third thesis has to succeed, but all

that seem plausible are claims that turn out to support only the first or second thesis. Admittedly, fraternity is not an easy notion to pin down. It can be understood as I propose in the text as a kind of prudential value: a valuable sort of personal relation. But, no doubt, some will think that that interpretation leaves out something vital. They might think that it is neither merely a *prudential* value nor a *communal* value as defined just above but rather a *moral* value, a view about what equal respect requires, a view that is more powerful than the one I accommodate in the text in that it rules out any deviations from equal distribution. But if fraternity has such a strong consequence, then to defend its status as a value is to defend this strong interpretation of equal respect. And how will a defender of fraternity do that? (I am grateful to Jeremy Waldron, who is more of a friend of communal values than I am, for discussion of these issues.)

40. ch. X sect. 2.

41. ch. XI sects. 7–9.

42. It has been suggested that in a sense none do—that the notion of 'distributive justice' does not apply in this setting. See Lucas 1980, p. 220: 'The concept of distributive justice is applicable within the context of limited associations, with limited and definite aims held in common. Such aims give guidance how the fruits of common activities should be distributed.' He even doubts that a modern nation-state has limited and definite enough aims to allow 'distributive justice' to be applied to it; so groups of such states clearly would not. ' ... before questions of distribution arise, there has to be an association which produces the goods to be distributed, whose values justify some suitable basis for distribution.' But this is implausible. It assumes that there are no group-independent principles of distribution, that we can have no adequate idea of what each person is due apart from the aims of the co-operative group. But there are principles independent of the aims of the group. And the aims of co-operative groups do not readily generate *any* distributive principles. Their aims are generally selfish: each co-operator seeks greater benefit from co-operating than he can get without co-operating. In any case, the moral principles that apply to distribution inside a co-operative group— e.g. the demand for equal provision expressed in the proviso of 'as much and as good'—apply outside it too, e.g. to international cases.

43. See, e.g., Hardin 1977, p. 18: 'India, for example, now has a population of 600 million, which increases by 15 million each year ... every one of the 15 million lives added to India's population puts an additional burden on the environment ... However humanitarian our interest, every Indian life saved through medical or nutritional assistance from abroad diminishes the quality of life for those who remain, and for subsequent generations. If rich countries make it possible, through foreign aid, for 600 million Indians to swell to 1.2 billion in a mere 28 years, as their current growth-rate threatens, will future generations of Indians thank us for hastening the destruction of their environment?'

44. If someone thinks that every rich nation owes restitution to every poor nation, then (to isolate issues) take some science fiction. Let us say that we wake tomorrow to be greeted by peaceful extraterrestrials, who have had to abandon their planet when it froze over.

45. There are a lot of unsettled questions about what the proviso amounts to. Suppose two nations had as much and as good land, but then, through no one's fault, the land in one of them suffered serious erosion. Or suppose that two nations started with as much and as good, but one of them struck vast amounts of oil.

46. It is not much talked about in the context of famine, although the United Nations *Universal Declaration of Human Rights*, which is so profligate in its assignment of rights that it may not be a precedent of much interest, says that everyone has 'the right to a standard of living adequate for the health and well-being of himself and his family, including food . . .' (art. XXV).

47. Nozick 1974, ch. 7 esp. pp. 178–82.

48. This is a point well made by J. R. Lucas (Lucas 1980, ch. 13) and Michael Walzer (Walzer 1983, chs. 2 and 3). But they over-make it. The United States, during its period of highest immigration, managed to assimilate vast numbers of people from very different backgrounds. They all arrived looking for a better life, and that is probably the only quality that a co-operator needs to have. Also I should not myself over-make the point about the casual link between retention of goods and incentive to produce them. No doubt most governments of rich industrial nations could substantially raise income tax in order to help poor nations and not affect incentives at all.

49. ch. IX sect. 4.

50. To get a sense of just how much work has to go into making a set of property rights determinate, consider A. M. Honoré's useful taxonomy of the rights and obligations (and also rules and liabilities) that make up our contemporary concept of property. Honoré's taxonomy (slightly expanded by L. C. Becker) goes:

    1. (claim) right to possess
    2. (liberty) right to use
    3. (power) right to manage
    4. (claim) right to income
    5. (liberty) right to consume or destroy
    6. (liberty) right to modify
    7. (power) right to alienate
    8. (power) right to transmit
    9. (claim) right to security
    10. absence of term
    11. prohibition of harmful use
    12. liability to execution (i.e. confiscation for payment of debt)
    13. residuary rules (i.e. rules governing reversion to another)

These elements may be combined in a large number of ways. A particular instance of ownership may have some of them and not others, or have them only to a certain degree; or some of these elements may be held by one person and some by another; or all the elements may be held jointly by several people, etc. See Honoré 1961 and L. C. Becker, 'The Moral Basis of Property Rights', in Pennock and Chapman 1980.

51. ch. XI esp. sects. 8 and 9.

52. Here I follow the suggestion in Ryan 1984, pp. 161–2.

53. Pt. One.

54. ch. XI.

55. ch. XI sect. 9.

56. ch. III sect. 7.

57. ch. IX sect. 3.

58. See ch. X.

59. ch. XI.

60. ch. XI sect. 9.

61. e.g. Nozick, Flew, and Matson; see their works referred to in n. 5; in Nozick 1974, see esp. p. 238.

BIBLIOGRAPHY

Ackrill, J. L. 1980, 'Aristotle on *Eudaimonia*', in A. O. Rorty (ed.), *Essays on Aristotle's Ethics*, Berkeley: University of California Press.

Adams, R. M. 1976, 'Motive Utilitarianism', *Journal of Philosophy* 73.

Aristotle, *Metaphysics*.

—— *Nicomachean Ethics*.

—— *Politics*.

—— *Rhetoric*.

Arnold, Christopher 1978, 'Analyses of Right', in E. Kamenka and A. Tay (eds.), *Human Rights*, London: Edward Arnold.

Arrow, Kenneth J. 1963, *Social Choice and Individual Values*, New Haven: Yale University Press, 2nd edn.

—— 1977, 'Extended Sympathy and the Possibility of Social Choice', *The American Economic Review, Papers and Proceedings* 67.

—— 1978, 'Extended Sympathy and the Possibility of Social Choice', *Philosophia* 7.

—— 1984, 'Utility and Expectation in Economic Behavior', in *Collected Papers of Kenneth J. Arrow*, vol. 3, Oxford: Blackwell.

Axelrod, Robert 1984, *The Evolution of Cooperation*, New York: Basic Books.

Baier, Kurt 1958, *The Moral Point of View*, Ithaca: Cornell University Press.

—— 1977, 'Rationality and Morality', *Erkenntnis* 11.

—— 1985, 'Maximization and Fairness', *Ethics* 96.

Bales, R. E. 1971, 'Act Utilitarianism: Account of Right-Making Characteristics or Decision-Making Procedure', *American Philosophical Quarterly* 8.

Barry, Brian 1965, *Political Argument*, London: Routledge and Kegan Paul.

—— 1978, *Sociologists, Economists and Democracy*, Chicago: University of Chicago Press.

Baumgardt, David 1952, *Bentham and the Ethics of Today*, Princeton: Princeton University Press.

Beccaria, C. 1754, *Dei Delitti e delle Pene*.

Benn, S. & R. Peters 1959, *Social Principles and the Democratic State*, London: Allen and Unwin.

Bentham, Jeremy 1776, *A Fragment on Government*.

—— 1789, *An Introduction to the Principles of Morals and Legislation*, 2nd edn. 1823, 3rd edn. 1838.

Berlin, Isaiah 1969, *Four Essays on Liberty*, Oxford: Oxford University Press.

—— 1978, *Concepts and Categories*, London: Hogarth.

Bond, E. J. 1979, 'Desire, Action, and the Good', *American Philosophical Quarterly* 16.

—— 1983, *Reason and Value*, Cambridge: Cambridge University Press.

Brams, S. J. 1976, *Game Theory and Politics*, New York: Free Press.

Brandt, Richard B. (ed.) 1961, *Value and Obligation*, New York: Harcourt, Brace and World.

—— 1967, 'Personal Values and the Justification of Institutions', in S. Hook (ed.), *Human Values and Economic Policy*, New York: New York University Press.

—— 1979, *A Theory of the Good and the Right*, Oxford: Clarendon Press.

—— 1982, 'Two Concepts of Utility', in H. B. Miller and W. H. Williams (eds.), *The Limits of Utilitarianism*, Minneapolis: University of Minnesota Press.

Braybrooke, David 1968, 'Let Needs Diminish that Preferences May Prosper', *American Philosophical Quarterly Monograph* No. 1.

Britton, Karl 1959–60, 'Utilitarianism: The Appeal to a First Principle', *Proceedings of the Aristotelian Society* 60.

Broome, John 1984, 'Selecting People Randomly', *Ethics* 95.

Buber, Martin 1965, *The Knowledge of Man*, London: Allen and Unwin.

Campbell, N. R. 1938, 'Measurement and its Importance for Philosophy', *Proceedings of the Aristotelian Society*, suppl. vol. 17.

Clark, R. W. 1975, *The Life of Bertrand Russell*, London: Cape.

Darwall, Stephen 1983, *Impartial Reason*, Ithaca: Cornell University Press.

Davidson, D., P. Suppes and S. Siegel 1957, *Decision-Making: An Experimental Approach*, Stanford: Stanford University Press.

Davidson, D. 1986, 'Judging Interpersonal Interests', in J. Elster and A. Hyllard, (eds.), *The Foundations of Social Choice Theory*, Cambridge: Cambridge University Press.

Diamond, P. A. 1967, 'Cardinal Welfare, Individualistic Ethics, and Interpersonal Comparison of Utility: A Comment', *Journal of Political Economy* 75.

Diggs, B. J. 1981, 'A Contractarian View of Respect for Persons', *American Philosophical Quarterly* 18.

—— 1982, 'Utilitarianism and Contractarianism', in H.B. Miller and W.H. Williams (eds.), *The Limits of Utilitarianism*, Minneapolis: University of Minnesota Press.

Dillistone, F. W. 1968, *The Christian Understanding of Atonement*, Welwyn: James Nisbet.

—— 1983, 'Atonement' in A. Richardson and J. Bowden (eds.), *A New Dictionary of Christian Theology*, London: SCM Press.

Dunn, John 1984, *John Locke*, Oxford: Oxford University Press.

Dworkin, Ronald 1977, *Taking Rights Seriously*, London: Duckworth.

—— 1978, 'Liberalism', in S. Hampshire (ed.), *Public and Private Morality*, Cambridge: Cambridge University Press.

—— 1981, 'What Is Equality?' Pts. I and II, *Philosophy and Public Affairs* 10.

Edgeworth, F. Y. 1881, *Mathematical Psychics*, London: Kegan Paul.

Edwards, Paul 1967, 'The Meaning and Value of Life', in P. Edwards (ed.), *The Encyclopedia of Philosophy*, New York: Macmillan, vol. 4.

Ellis, Brian 1968, *Basic Concepts of Measurement*, Cambridge: Cambridge University Press.

Elster, Jon 1979, *Ulysses and the Sirens*, Cambridge: Cambridge University Press.

—— 1982, 'Sour Grapes—Utilitarianism and the Genesis of Wants', in A. Sen and B. Williams (eds.), *Utilitarianism and Beyond*, Cambridge: Cambridge University Press.

Feinberg, Joel 1970, *Doing and Deserving*, Princeton: Princeton University Press.

—— 1973, *Social Philosophy*, Englewood Cliffs: Prentice-Hall.

—— 1980, *Rights, Justice, and the Bounds of Liberty*, Princeton: Princeton University Press.

Finnis, John 1980, *Natural Law and Natural Rights*, Oxford: Clarendon Press.

Flew, Antony (ed.) 1979, *A Dictionary of Philosophy*, London: Pan Books.

—— 1981, *The Politics of Procrustes*, London: Temple Smith.

—— 1983, 'Justice: Real or Social?', *Social Philosophy and Policy* 1.

Foot, Philippa 1978, *Virtues and Vices*, Oxford: Blackwell.

Frankena, W. K. 1963, *Ethics*, Englewood Cliffs: Prentice-Hall.

Franklin, R. L. 1968, *Freewill and Determinism*, London: Routledge and Kegan Paul.

Frey, R. G. (ed.) 1984, *Utility and Rights*, Minneapolis: University of Minnesota Press.

Gauthier, David 1977, 'The Social Contract as Ideology', *Philosophy and Public Affairs* 6.

—— 1982a, 'On the Refutation of Utilitarianism', in H. B. Miller and W. H. Williams (eds.), *The Limits of Utilitarianism*, Minneapolis: University of Minnesota Press.

—— 1982b, 'Justified Inequality?', *Dialogue* 21.

—— 1985, 'Justice as Social Choice', in D. Copp and D. Zimmerman (eds.), *Morality, Reason, and Truth*, Totowa, New Jersey: Rowman and Allenheld.

Geach, Peter 1977, *The Virtues*, Cambridge: Cambridge University Press.

Gewirth, Alan 1982, *Human Rights*, Chicago: University of Chicago Press.

Glover, Jonathan 1977, *Causing Death and Saving Lives*, Harmondsworth: Penguin Books.

Goodman, L. A. and H. Markowitz 1952, 'Social Welfare Functions Based on Individual Rankings', *American Journal of Sociology* 58.

Gravelle, H. and R. Rees 1981, *Microeconomics*, London: Longman.

Gray, John 1983, *Mill on Liberty: A Defence*, London: Routledge and Kegan Paul.

Griffin, James 1977, 'Are There Incommensurable Values?', *Philosophy and Public Affairs* 47.

—— 1979. 'Is Unhappiness Morally More Important than Happiness?', *Philosophical Quarterly* 29.

—— 1981, 'Equality: On Sen's Weak Equity Axiom', *Mind* 90.

—— (forthcoming), 'Well-Being and its Interpersonal Comparability', in N. Fotion and D. Seanor (eds.), *not yet titled collection of essays on the philosophy of R. M. Hare*, Oxford: Clarendon Press.

Gross, J. (ed.) 1983, *The Oxford Book of Aphorisms*, Oxford: Oxford University Press.

Hahn, F. and M. Hollis (eds.) 1979, *Philosophy and Economic Theory*, Oxford: Oxford University Press.

Haksar, V. 1979, *Equality, Liberty, and Perfectionism*, Oxford: Clarendon Press.

Hardie, W. F. R. 1965, 'The Final Good in Aristotle's Ethics', *Philosophy* 40.

Hardin, Garrett 1977, 'Lifeboat Ethics: The Case Against Helping the Poor', in W. Aiken and H. La Follette (eds.), *World Hunger and Moral Obligation*, Englewood Cliffs: Prentice-Hall.

Hare, R. M. 1952, *The Language of Morals*, Oxford: Clarendon Press.

—— 1963, *Freedom and Reason*, Oxford: Clarendon Press.

—— 1975, 'Rawls' Theory of Justice', in N. Daniels (ed.), *Reading Rawls*, Oxford: Blackwell.

—— 1976a, 'Ethical Theory and Utilitarianism', in H. D. Lewis (ed.), *Contemporary British Philosophy*, 4th ser., London: Allen and Unwin.

—— 1976b, 'Some Confusions About Subjectivity', in J. Bricke (ed.), *Freedom and Morality*, Lindley Lectures, University of Kansas.

—— 1981, *Moral Thinking*, Oxford: Clarendon Press.

Harsanyi, John 1976, *Essays on Ethics, Social Behavior, and Scientific Explanation*, Dordrecht: Reidel.

—— 1977, *Rational Behavior and Bargaining Equilibrium in Games and Social Situations*, Cambridge: Cambridge University Press.

Hart, H. L. A. 1968, *Punishment and Responsibility*, Oxford: Clarendon Press.

—— 1975, 'Rawls on Liberty and Its Priority', in N. Daniels (ed.), *Reading Rawls*, Oxford: Blackwell.

—— 1979, 'Between Utility and Rights', in A. Ryan (ed.), *The Idea of Freedom*, Oxford: Oxford University Press.

Helvétius, C.-A. 1758, *De L'esprit*.

Heyd, David 1982, *Supererogation*, Cambridge: Cambridge University Press.

Hobbes, Thomas 1651, *Leviathan*.

—— 1969, Selections, in D. D. Raphael (ed.), *British Moralists 1650–1800*, Oxford: Clarendon Press.

Hodges, H. A. 1955, *The Pattern of Atonement*, London: SCM Press.

Hodgson, D. H. 1967, *The Consequences of Utilitarianism*, Oxford: Clarendon Press.

Hohfeld, W. N. 1923, *Fundamental Legal Conceptions*, New Haven: Yale University Press.

Honoré, A. M. 1961, 'Ownership', in A. G. Guest (ed.), *Oxford Essays in Jurisprudence*, Oxford: Clarendon Press.

Hume, David 1738–40, *A Treatise of Human Nature*.

—— 1751, *An Enquiry Concerning the Principles of Morals*.

Hutcheson, F. 1725, *An Inquiry Concerning Moral Good and Evil*.

Jespersen, O. 1924, *The Philosophy of Grammar*, London: Allen and Unwin.

Jones, Ernest 1964, *The Life and Work of Sigmund Freud*, Harmondsworth: Penguin Books.

Kant, I. 1785, *Foundations of the Metaphysics of Morals*.

—— 1788, *Critique of Practical Reason*.

—— 1887, *The Philosophy of Law*, trans. W. Hastie, Edinburgh: Clark.

—— 1965, *The Metaphysical Elements of Justice*, trans. John Ladd, New York: Bobbs, Merrill.

Kavka, Gregory 1985, 'The Reconciliation Project', in D. Copp and D. Zimmerman, (eds.), *Morality, Reason, and Truth*, Totowa, New Jersey: Rowman and Allenheld.

Kenny, A. J. P. 1973, 'Aristotle on Happiness', in his *The Anatomy of the Soul*, Oxford: Blackwell.

Kleinig, J. 1971, 'The Concept of Desert', *American Philosophical Quarterly* 8.

Kuhn, T. S. 1970, *The Structure of Scientific Revolutions* 2nd edn., Chicago: University of Chicago Press.

Kyburg, Jun. H. E. 1984, *Theory of Measurement*, Cambridge: Cambridge University Press.

Lane, R. E. 1979, 'Capitalist Man, Socialist Man', in P. Laslett and J. Fishkin (eds.), *Philosophy, Politics, and Society*, 5th ser., Oxford: Blackwell.

Layard, P. R. G. and A. A. Walters 1978, *Micro-Economic Theory*, New York: McGraw-Hill.

Locke, John 1690, *The Second Treatise of Government*.

Lucas, J. R. 1965, 'Against Equality', *Philosophy* 40.

—— 1966, *Principles of Politics*, Oxford: Clarendon Press.

—— 1980, *On Justice*, Oxford: Clarendon Press.

Luce, R. D. and H. Raiffa 1957, *Games and Decisions*, New York: Wiley.

Lyons, David 1973, *In the Interest of the Governed*, Oxford: Clarendon Press.

—— 1977, 'Human Rights and the General Welfare', *Philosophy and Public Affairs* 6.

—— 1982, 'The New Indian Claims and Original Rights to Land', in J. Paul (ed.), *Reading Nozick*, Oxford: Blackwell.

McCloskey, H. J. 1965, 'Rights', *Philosophical Quarterly* 15.

—— 1975, 'The Right to Life', *Mind* 84.

McDowell, John 1978, 'Are Moral Requirements Hypothetical Imperatives?', *Proceedings of the Aristotelian Society*, suppl. vol. 52.

——1979, 'Virtue and Reason', *The Monist* 62.

——1980, 'The Role of *Eudaimonia* in Aristotle's Ethics', in A. O. Rorty (ed.), *Essays on Aristotle's Ethics*, Berkeley: University of California Press.

—— 1985, 'Values and Secondary Qualities', in T. Honderich (ed.), *Morality and Objectivity*, London: Routledge and Kegan Paul.

MacIntyre, Alasdair 1981, *After Virtue*, London: Duckworth.

Mackie, J. L. 1977, *Ethics*, Harmondsworth: Penguin.

—— 1978, 'Could There Be a Right-Based Moral Theory?', *Midwest Studies in Philosophy* 3.

—— 1981, 'Obligations to Obey the Law', *Virginia Law Review* 67.

Markowitz, H. 1952, see L. A. Goodman, and H. Markowitz, 1952.

Matson, Wallace 1983, 'Justice: A Funeral Oration', *Social Philosophy and Policy* 1.

Melden, A. I. 1977, *Rights and Persons*, Oxford: Blackwell.

Mill, J. S. 1843, *A System of Logic*.

—— 1859, *On Liberty*.

—— 1861, *Utilitarianism*.

—— 1865, *An Examination of Sir William Hamilton's Philosophy*.

—— 1972, *Collected Works of John Stuart Mill*, vol. xvi, F. E. Mineka and D. N. Lindley, (eds.), Toronto: University of Toronto Press.

Miller, David 1976, *Social Justice*, Oxford: Clarendon Press.

Moberly, E. R. 1978, *Suffering, Innocent and Guilty*, London: SPCK.

Moberly, W. H. 1968, *The Ethics of Punishment*, London: Faber and Faber.

Moore, G. E. 1966, *Ethics*, Oxford: Oxford University Press.

Morgenstern, O. 1953, see J. von Neumann and O. Morgenstern,
—— 1972, 'Thirteen Critical Points in Contemporary Economic Theory', *Journal of Economic Literature* 10.

Morris, Herbert (ed.) 1971, *Guilt and Shame*, Belmont, CA: Wadsworth.

Morton, Adam 1980, *Frames of Mind*, Oxford: Clarendon Press.

Nagel, Thomas 1972, 'Aristotle on Eudaimonia', *Phronesis* 17.

—— 1979, *Mortal Questions*, Cambridge: Cambridge University Press.

—— 1980, 'The Limits of Objectivity', in S. M. McMurrin (ed.), *The Tanner Lectures on Human Values, 1980*, Salt Lake City: University of Utah Press.

Narveson, Jan 1967, *Morality and Utility*, Baltimore: Johns Hopkins Press.

Nell, Onora 1975, *Acting on Principle: An Essay on Kantian Ethics*, New York: Columbia University Press.

Neumann, J. von and O. Morgenstern 1953, *The Theory of Games and Economic Behaviour*, 3rd edn., Princeton: Princeton University Press.

Newton-Smith, W. H. 1981, *The Rationality of Science*, London: Routledge and Kegan Paul.

Nietzsche, Friedrich 1927, *The Genealogy of Morals*, in *The Philosophy of Nietzsche*, New York: Modern Library.

—— 1874, *Untimely Meditations: 3. Schopenhauer as Educator*.

Norman, Richard 1971, *Reasons for Action*, Oxford: Blackwell.

Nozick, Robert 1974, *Anarchy, State, and Utopia*, Oxford: Blackwell.

—— 1981, *Philosophical Explanations*, Oxford: Clarendon Press.

Nussbaum, Martha Craven 1983–4, 'Flawed Crystals: James's *The Golden Bowl* and Literature as Moral Philosophy', *New Literary History* 15.

—— 1984, 'Plato on Commensurability and Desire', in *Proceedings of the Aristotelian Society*, suppl. vol. 58.

Olson, Mancur 1965, *The Logic of Collective Action*, Cambridge: Harvard University Press.

Overvold, M. C. 1980, 'Self-interest and the Concept of Self-sacrifice', *Canadian Journal of Philosophy* 10.

—— 1982, 'Self-interest and Getting What You Want', in H. B. Miller and W. H. Williams (eds.), *The Limits of Utilitarianism*, Minneapolis: University of Minnesota Press.

Parfit, Derek 1984, *Reasons and Persons*, Oxford: Clarendon Press.

Passmore, John 1971, *The Perfectibility of Man*, London: Duckworth.

Paton, H. J. 1961, *The Moral Law*, London: Hutchinson, 3rd edn.

—— 1965, *The Categorical Imperative*, London: Hutchinson, 5th edn.

Pennock, J. R. and J. W. Chapman (eds.) 1980, *Property, Nomos 22*, New York: New York University Press.

Peters, R. 1959, see S. Benn and R. Peters.

Pettit, Philip 1984, 'Satisficing Consequentialism', *Proceedings of the Aristotelian Society*, suppl. vol. 58.

Plato, *Republic*.

Platts, Mark 1980, 'Moral Reality and the End of Desire', in M. Platts (ed.), *Reference, Truth and Reality*, London: Routledge and Kegan Paul.

Popper, Karl 1966, *The Open Society and Its Enemies*, London: Routledge and Kegan Paul, 5th edn.

Priestly, J. 1758, *An Essay on the First Principles of Government*.

Quinton, A. M. 1954, 'On Punishment', *Analysis* 14.

—— 1973, *Utilitarian Ethics*, London: Macmillan.

Raiffa, H. 1957, see R. D. Luce and H. Raiffa 1957.

Ramsey, F. P. 1931, *The Foundations of Mathematics*, London: Routledge and Kegan Paul.

Rashdall, Hastings 1907, *The Theory of Good and Evil*, London: Oxford University Press.

Rawls, John 1972, *A Theory of Justice*, Oxford: Clarendon Press.

—— 1974–5, 'The Independence of Moral Theory', *Proceedings and Addresses of the American Philosophical Association* 47.

—— 1975a, 'A Kantian Conception of Equality', *Cambridge Review* 96.

—— 1975b, 'Fairness to Goodness', *Philosophical Review* 84.

—— 1978, 'The Basic Structure as Object', in A. I. Goldman and J. Kim (eds.), *Values and Morals*, Dordrecht: Reidel.

—— 1980, 'Kantian Constructivism in Moral Theory', *Journal of Philosophy* 77.

—— 1982, 'Social Unity and Primary Goods', in A. Sen and B. Williams (eds.), *Utilitarianism and Beyond*, Cambridge: Cambridge University Press.

Raz, Joseph 1985–6, 'Value Incommensurability: Some Preliminaries', *Proceedings of the Aristotelian Society* 86.

Rees, R. 1981, see H. Gravelle and R. Rees 1981.

Regan, Donald 1980, *Utilitarianism and Co-operation*, Oxford: Clarendon Press.

Reich, Charles A. 1964, 'The New Property', *Yale Law Journal* 73.

Rescher, Nicholas 1966, *Distributive Justice*, Indianapolis: Bobbs-Merrill.

Richards, D. A. J. 1971, *A Theory of Reasons for Action*, Oxford: Clarendon Press.

Robbins, L. 1938, 'Interpersonal Comparisons of Utility', *Economic Journal* 43.

Ross, W. D. 1930, *The Right and the Good*, Oxford: Clarendon Press.

Russell, B. 1953, 'A Free Man's Worship', in his *Mysticism and Logic*, Harmondsworth: Penguin.

Ryan, Alan 1970, *John Stuart Mill*, New York: Pantheon Books.

—— 1984, *Property and Political Theory*, Oxford: Blackwell.

Savage, L. J. 1954, *The Foundations of Statistics*, New York: Wiley.

Scanlon, T. M. 1975, 'Preference and Urgency', *Journal of Philosophy* 72.

—— 1982, 'Contractualism and Utilitarianism', in A. Sen and B. Williams (eds.), *Utilitarianism and Beyond*, Cambridge: Cambridge University Press.

—— (forthcoming), 'Levels of Moral Thinking', in N. Fotion and D. Seanor (eds.), *not yet titled collection of essays on the philosophy of R. M. Hare*, Oxford: Clarendon Press.

Schneewind, J. B. 1977, *Sidgwick's Ethics and Victorian Moral Philosophy*, Oxford: Clarendon Press.

Schwartz, T. 1982, 'Human Welfare: What It Is Not', in H. Miller and W. Williams (eds.), *The Limits of Utilitarianism*, Minneapolis: University of Minnesota Press.

Scitovsky, Tibor 1976, *The Joyless Economy*, New York: Oxford University Press.

Scott, D. and P. Suppes 1958, 'Foundational Aspects of Theories of Measurement', *Journal of Symbolic Logic* 23.

Searle, J. R. 1978, 'Prima Facie Obligations', in J. Raz (ed.), *Practical Reasoning*, Oxford: Oxford University Press.

Sen, A. K. 1967, 'Isolation, Assurance and the Social Rate of Discount', *Quarterly Journal of Economics* 80.

—— 1970, *Collective Choice and Social Welfare*, San Francisco: Holden-Day.

—— 1973, *On Economic Inequality*, Oxford: Clarendon Press.

—— 1974, 'Choice, Orderings and Morality', in S. Körner (ed.), *Practical Reasoning*, Oxford: Blackwell.

—— 1975, 'Rawls versus Bentham: An Axiomatic Examination of the Pure Distribution Problem', in N. Daniels (ed.), *Reading Rawls*, Oxford: Blackwell.

—— 1977, 'Rationality and Morality: A Reply', *Erkenntnis* 11.

—— 1979, 'Utilitarianism and Welfarism', *Journal of Philosophy* 76.

—— 1980, 'Equality of What?', in S. McMurrin (ed.), *Tanner Lectures in Human Values* I, Cambridge: Cambridge University Press.

—— 1980–1, 'Plural Utility', *Proceedings of the Aristotelian Society* 81.

Sen, A. K. and B. Williams (eds.) 1982, *Utilitarianism and Beyond*, Cambridge: Cambridge University Press.

Shakespeare, W., *Measure for Measure*.

Shapley, L. and M. Shubik 1974, *Game Theory in Economics*, Santa Monica: Rand (R-904/4-NSF).

Shubik, M. 1974, see L. Shapley and M. Shubik 1974.

Sidgwick, Henry 1907, *The Methods of Ethics*, 7th edn., London: Macmillan.

Siegel, S. 1956, 'A Method for Obtaining an Ordered Metric Scale', *Psychometrica* 21.

—— 1957, see D. Davidson, P. Suppes, and S. Siegel 1957.

Simon, Herbert A. 1982, *Models of Bounded Rationality*, Cambridge, MA: M.I.T. Press.

Simpson, A. W. B. 1984, *Cannibalism and the Common Law*, Chicago: University of Chicago Press.

Singer, M. G. 1955, 'Generalization in Ethics', *Mind* 64.

—— 1963, *Generalization in Ethics*, London: Eyre and Spottiswoode.

—— 1977, 'The Principle of Consequences Reconsidered', *Philosophical Studies* 31.

—— 1982, 'Incoherence, Inconsistency, and Moral Theory', *Southern Journal of Philosophy* 20.

Slote, Michael 1983, *Goods and Virtues*, Oxford: Clarendon Press.

Stevens, S. S. 1959, 'Measurement, Psychophysics, and Utility', in C. W. Churchman and P. Ratoosh (eds.), *Measurement: Definition and Theories*, New York: Wiley.

Summers, R. S. 1974–5, 'A Plea for Process Values', *Cornell Law Review* 60.

Sumner, L. W. 1971, 'Co-operation, Fairness and Utility', *Journal of Value Inquiry* 5.

—— 1981, *Abortion and Moral Theory*, Princeton: Princeton University Press.

Suppes, P. and M. Winet 1955, 'An Axiomatization of Utility Based on the Notion of Utility Differences', *Management Science* 1.

Suppes, P. and J. L. Zinnes 1963, 'Basic Measurement Theory' in R. D. Luce, R. Bush, and E. Galanter (eds.), *Handbook of Mathematical Psychology*, New York: Wiley.

Suppes, P. 1957, see D. Davidson, P. Suppes, and S. Siegel 1957.

—— 1958, see D. Scott and P. Suppes 1958.

—— 1967, 'Decision Theory', in P. Edwards (ed.), *The Encyclopedia of Philosophy*, New York: Macmillan.

Taylor, Charles 1982, 'The Diversity of Goods', in A. K. Sen and B. Williams (eds.), *Utilitarianism and Beyond*, Cambridge: Cambridge University Press.

Taylor, Gabriele 1985, *Pride, Shame, and Guilt*, Oxford: Clarendon Press.

Thomson, J. J. 1971, 'A Defence of Abortion', *Philosophy and Public Affairs* 1.

Tolstoy, Leo 1888, *A Confession*.

Torgerson, W. S. 1958, *Theory and Methods of Scaling*, New York: Wiley.

Tribe, Laurance 1972, 'Policy Science: Analysis or Ideology', *Philosophy and Public Affairs* 2.

Trivers, Robert 1971, 'The Evolution of Reciprocal Altruism', *Quarterly Review of Biology* 46.

Ullman-Margalit, Edna 1977, *The Emergence of Norms*, Oxford: Clarendon Press.

Vickers, J. M. 1975, 'Utility and its Ambiguities', *Erkenntnis* 9.

Waldron, Jeremy 1979, 'Enough and As Good Left for Others', *Philosophical Quarterly* 29.

Walters, A. A. 1978, see P. R. G. Layard and A. A. Walters 1978.

Walzer, Michael 1983, *Spheres of Justice*, Oxford: Robertson.

Warnock, G. J. 1971, *The Object of Morality*, London: Methuen.

Wellman, Carl 1978, 'A New Conception of Human Rights', in E. Kamenka and A. Tay (eds.), *Human Rights*, London: Edward Arnold.

Whichcote, B. 1753, *Moral and Religious Aphorisms*.

White, A. R. 1971, *Modal Thinking*, Oxford: Blackwell.

Wiggins, David 1976, 'Truth, Invention, and the Meaning of Life', *Proceedings of the British Academy* 62.

—— 1978–9, 'Weakness of Will, Commensurability, and the Objects of Desire and Deliberation', *Proceedings of the Aristotelian Society* 79.

—— 1985, 'Claims of Need', in T. Honderich (ed.), *Morality and Objectivity*, London: Routledge and Kegan Paul.

Williams, Bernard 1973a, 'A Critique of Utilitarianism', in J. Smart and B. Williams, *Utilitarianism: For and Against*, Cambridge: Cambridge University Press.

—— 1973b, *Problems of the Self*, Cambridge: Cambridge University Press.

—— 1973c, *Morality: An Introduction to Ethics*, Harmondsworth: Penguin Books.

—— 1981, *Moral Luck*, Cambridge: Cambridge University Press.

—— 1982, see A. K. Sen and B. Williams 1982.

—— 1985, *Ethics and the Limits of Philosophy*, London: Fontana.

Winet, M, see P. Suppes and M. Winet 1955.

Wolff, R. P. 1968, *The Poverty of Liberalism*, Boston: Beacon Press.

Wollheim, Richard 1975, 'Needs, Desires, and Moral Turpitude', in R. S. Peters (ed.), *Royal Institute of Philosophy Lectures* vol. 8, London: Macmillan.

—— 1979, 'The Sheep and the Ceremony', Cambridge: Cambridge University Press.

Ziegler, Philip 1983, *Diana Cooper*, Harmondsworth: Penguin.

Ziff, Paul 1960, *Semantic Analysis*, Ithaca: Cornell University Press.

Zinnes, J. L. 1963, see P. Suppes and J. L. Zinnes 1963.

INDEX